ZAGATSURVEY®

2007

SAN FRANCISCO BAY AREA RESTAURANTS

WILSON SONSINI GOODRICH & ROSATI
ALUMNI NETWORK
Powerful Contacts. Powerful Resource. Staying Connected.

Local Editor: Meesha Halm

Staff Editor: Randi Gollin

Published and distributed by
ZAGAT SURVEY, LLC
4 Columbus Circle
New York, New York 10019
Tel: 212 977 6000
E-mail: sanfran@zagat.com
Web site: www.zagat.com

Acknowledgments

We thank Jon, Olive and Jude Fox, Maria Gagliardi, Danielle Reed, Steven Shukow and Karen Solomon, as well as the following members of our staff: Victoria Elmacioglu (assistant editor), Jessica Grose (editorial assistant), Maryanne Bertollo, Reni Chin, Larry Cohn, Carol Diuguid, Andrew Eng, Schuyler Frazier, Jeff Freier, Natalie Lebert, Mike Liao, Dave Makulec, Becky Reimer, Thomas Sheehan, Joshua Siegel, Carla Spartos, Sharon Yates and Kyle Zolner.

Contents

About This Survey

Here are the results of our *2007 San Francisco Bay Area Restaurant Survey,* covering 1,082 establishments as tested, and tasted, by 7,476 local restaurant-goers. To help you find San Francisco's best meals and best buys, we have prepared a number of lists. See Most Popular (page 9), Noteworthy Newcomers (page 10), Top Ratings (pages 11–16), Best Buys (page 17), Prix Fixe Bargains (page 18) and 45 handy indexes (pages 213–299). Top Ratings broken down by region can be found at the beginning of each section.

This marks the 27th year that Zagat Survey has reported on the shared experiences of diners like you. What started in 1979 as a hobby involving 200 of our friends rating NYC restaurants has come a long way. Today we have over 250,000 active surveyors and now cover dining, entertaining, golf, hotels, resorts, spas, movies, music, nightlife, shopping, theater and tourist attractions. All of these guides are based on consumer surveys. They are also available by subscription at zagat.com, and for use on PDAs and cell phones.

By regularly surveying large numbers of avid customers, we hope to have achieved a uniquely current and reliable series of guides. More than a quarter-century of experience has verified this. If understood properly, these guides are the restaurant industry's report card, since each place's ratings and review are really a free market study of its own customers.

This year's participants dined out an average of 3.2 times per week, meaning this *Survey* is based on roughly 1.3 million meals. Of these 7,400-plus surveyors, 47% are women, 53% men; the breakdown by age is 9% in their 20s; 29%, 30s; 21%, 40s; 21%, 50s; and 20%, 60s or above. Our editors have synopsized our surveyors' opinions, with their comments shown in quotation marks. We sincerely thank each of these people; this book is really "theirs."

We are especially grateful to our longtime San Francisco editor, Meesha Halm, who is both a Bay Area restaurant critic and a cookbook author.

Finally, we invite you to join any of our upcoming *Surveys* – to do so, just register at zagat.com. Each participant will receive a free copy of the resulting guide when it is published. Your comments and even criticisms of this guide are also solicited. There is always room for improvement with your help. Just contact us at sanfran@zagat.com.

New York, NY
September 21, 2006

Nina and Tim Zagat

What's New

Splashy hot spots are still making waves citywide, but many of this year's newcomers manifest a markedly maverick mien. Given the diversity of choices, it's little wonder that surveyors rate the San Francisco dining scene high on creativity. And over one-third report that they eat out more than they did two years ago.

Breaking the Mold: This year's iconoclasts include the sexy minimalist Ame, offering Japanese-influenced American fare, and nine-table Coi, featuring Cal-French tasting menus, both Downtown; the Mission's signless hipster den, Bar Tartine, and industrial-chic American, Range; and architectural avatar Redd in Yountville.

Seafood Surges: Tourists assume SF is a seafood town, yet aside from Fisherman's Wharf and high-end places like Aqua, the pickings have been slim. But the tide is turning with the arrival of Sea Salt in Berkeley and Woodhouse Fish Company in the Castro, while Go Fish in St. Helena and Pescheria in Noe Valley will dock this fall.

Subcontinental Spice: Surveyors tout Italian and French fare as favorites, but Indian may be this year's 'it' cuisine, with spice-seekers savoring such stylish new spots as Dosa in the Mission and Junnoon and Mantra on the Peninsula.

Here Today, Gone Tomorrow: French Laundry legend Thomas Keller is among a handful of restaurateurs opening temporary ventures. He plans to unveil a casual Yountville eatery, ad hoc, this autumn, only to turn it into a hamburger haunt called Burgers and Half Bottles by 2007.

Sierra Supping: As the Bay Area's well-heeled continue their weekend exodus to Lake Tahoe, the culinary scene is growing more sophisticated, hence increased coverage in this *Survey.* Options include spots like Sol y Lago and Wild Goose, both run by chefs with city pedigrees.

Price to Pay: The cost of an average meal in SF rose a modest 1.2% from last year to $35.96. Still, that's 10.8% higher than the U.S. norm of $32.45. Still, the city's 20 most expensive places averaged $98.30, up 15.3% from last year's $85.27.

Future Eats: High-profile places opening this fall in the upscale shopping mecca Westfield San Francisco Centre include Bradley Ogden's Lark Creek Steak, Charles Phan's Out the Door, Straits Cafe, an offshoot of NYC's 'wichcraft, and Zazil. Another culinary cluster concept is on tap for The Presidio with small-plates entrant Pres a Vi coming to the Letterman Digital Arts Center complex this October, followed by Chez Spencer offspring La Terrace and, nearby, Shawn and Ray Tang's Presidio Social Club.

San Francisco, CA
September 21, 2006

Meesha Halm

Ratings & Symbols

Name, Address, Phone Number & Web Site

Zagat Ratings

Hours & Credit Cards

	F	D	S	C
	▽ 23	9	13	$15

Tim & Nina's ◐ ⓢ ⧷

*999 Mission St. (The Embarcadero), 415-555-7233;
www.zagat.com*

Open "more or less when they feel like it", this bit
of unembellished Embarcadero ectoplasm excels at
seafood with an Asian-Argentinean-Albanian twist; the
staff seems "fresh off the boat", and while the view of
the garbage barges is "a drag", no one balks at the
bottom-feeder prices.

Review, with surveyors' comments in quotes

Top Spots: Places with the highest overall ratings, popularity
and importance are listed in BLOCK CAPITAL LETTERS.

Hours: ◐ serves after 11 PM
    ⓢ closed on Sunday
    Ⓜ closed on Monday

Credit Cards: ⧷ no credit cards accepted

Ratings are on a scale of **0** to **30**.

F	Food	D	Decor	S	Service	C	Cost
23		9		13		$15	

0–9 poor to fair		**20–25** very good to excellent	
10–15 fair to good		**26–30** extraordinary to perfection	
16–19 good to very good		▽ low response/less reliable	

Cost (C): Shows surveyors' estimate of the price of
dinner with one drink and tip as a benchmark. Lunch is
usually 25% less.

For newcomers or survey write-ins listed without ratings,
the price range is indicated as follows:

I	$25 and below	**E**	$41 to $65
M	$26 to $40	**VE**	$66 or more

Most Popular

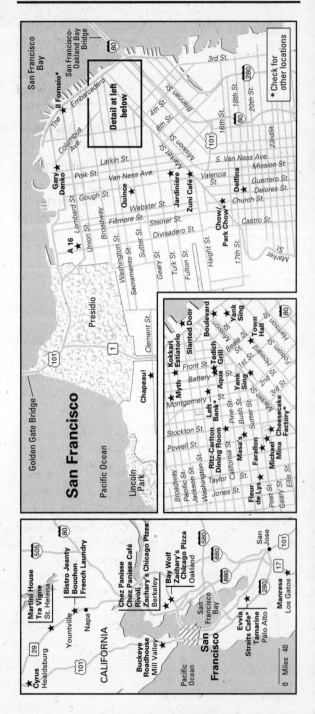

San Francisco Bay

San Francisco-Oakland Bay Bridge

80

3rd St.

The Embarcadero

Il Fornaio*

Columbus Ave.

Detail at left below

4th St.

5th St.

6th St.

Brannan St.

Mission St.

16th St.

18th St.

20th St.

280

23rd St.

* Check for other locations

101

Larkin St.

Gary Danko

Polk St.

Van Ness Ave.

Quince

Gough St.

Webster St.

Jardinière

Zuni Café

Valencia St.

S. Van Ness Ave.

Mission St.

Guerrero St.

Delfina

Delores St.

Church St.

Chow/Park Chow*

Castro St.

Lombard St.

Broadway

Fillmore St.

Steiner St.

Divisadero St.

17th St.

Market St.

A 16

Union St.

Washington St.

Sacramento St.

Sutter St.

Geary St.

Turk St.

Fulton St.

Haight St.

Presidio

1

Clement St.

Chapeau!

Golden Gate Bridge

San Francisco

Pacific Ocean

Lincoln Park

101

Kokkari Estiatorio

Slanted Door

Boulevard

Yank Sing

Myth

Tadich Grill

Town Hall

Front St.

Battery

Aqua

Yank Sing

Beale St.

Mission St.

Howard St.

Folsom St.

80

Harrison St.

1st St.

2nd St.

3rd St.

Montgomery

Left Bank*

Pine St.

Bush St.

Sutter St.

Market St.

Cheesecake Factory*

Stockton St.

Ritz-Carlton Dining Room

Masa's

Michael Mina

Powell St.

California St.

Farallon

Broadway

Pacific St.

Jackson St.

Washington St.

Taylor St.

Jones St.

Fleur de Lys

Post St.

Geary St.

Ellis St.

Martini House
Tra Vigne
St. Helena

505

80

Bistro Jeanty
Bouchon
French Laundry

Chez Panisse
Chez Panisse Café
Rivoli
Zachary's Chicago Pizza
Berkeley

Bay Wolf
Zachary's Chicago Pizza
Oakland

580

San Jose

101

Cyrus
Healdsburg

29

Yountville

Napa

CALIFORNIA

101

Buckeye Roadhouse
Mill Valley

Pacific Ocean

San Francisco

San Francisco Bay

680

880

280

Evvia
Straits Café*
Tamarine
Palo Alto

17

Manresa
Los Gatos

0   Miles   40

Most Popular

Each surveyor has been asked to name his or her five favorite places. This list reflects their choices followed in parentheses by last year's rankings. Places outside of San Francisco are marked as: E=East of SF; N=North; and S=South. When a restaurant has locations both inside and outside the city limits, we include the notation SF as well.

1. Gary Danko (1)
2. Boulevard (2)
3. Slanted Door (4)
4. French Laundry/N (3)
5. Michael Mina (13)
6. Aqua (7)
7. Delfina (8)
8. Farallon (10)
9. Kokkari Estiatorio (17)
10. Chez Panisse/E (6)
11. Chez Panisse Café/E (5)
12. Jardinière (12)
13. Chapeau! (19)
14. Quince (40)
15. Zuni Café (9)
16. A 16 (21)
17. Fleur de Lys (14)
18. Evvia/S (11)
19. Myth (–)
20. Manresa/S (–)
21. Ritz-Carlton D.R. (33)
22. Yank Sing* (35)
23. Left Bank/E/N/S (24)
24. Zachary's Pizza/E* (15)
25. Bistro Jeanty/N (16)
26. Chow/Park Chow/E/SF (36)
27. Il Fornaio/E/N/S/SF (28)
28. Tamarine/S (22)
29. Straits Café/S (18)
30. Rivoli/E (25)
31. Cyrus/N (–)
32. Masa's (20)
33. Buckeye Roadhse./N (–)
34. Tadich Grille (–)
35. Cheesecake Fac./S/SF (–)
36. Martini House/N (–)
37. Town Hall (26)
38. Bay Wolf/E (37)
39. Tra Vigne/N (31)
40. Bouchon/N (–)

It's obvious that many of the restaurants on the above list are among the San Francisco area's most expensive, but if popularity were calibrated to price, we suspect that a number of other restaurants would join the above ranks. Given the fact that both our surveyors and readers love to discover dining bargains, we have added a list of 80 Best Buys and restaurants offering prix fixe bargains on pages 17–18. These are restaurants that give real quality at extremely reasonable prices.

* Indicates a tie with restaurant above

Noteworthy Newcomers

Each year the San Francisco Bay Area welcomes a new crop of restaurants, ranging from high-end ventures from established chefs to the latest hipster hot spots. The following list represents our editors' take on some of the most notable new arrivals to debut over the past year. For a full list see the Noteworthy Newcomers index on page 264.

Ame	O'Reilly's Holy Grail
Avenue G	Ottimista Enoteca
Bar Crudo	Pappo/E
Bar Tartine	Range
Bong Su	Redd Restaurant/N
Bovolo/N	Rest. at Meadowood/N
Brick	Rogue Chefs/S
Cav Wine Bar	Scott Howard
Coi	Sea Salt/E
Dosa	Sebo
farmerbrown	Senses Rest.
(415) Asian	Sino/S
Joe DiMaggio's	Sparrow
Junnoon/S	supperclub
La Ciccia	Tamarindo Antojeria/E
Mamacita	Terzo
Mantra/S	Thea Mediterranean/S
NoPa	Tres Agaves
N.V./N	Woodhouse Fish Co.

There's just as much culinary promise on the horizon with several must-visit destinations in the works: **The Alembic** in Haight-Ashbury, an American gastropub focusing on artisanal ingredients; upscale Southern-style lounge **Blue Mirror**, BBQ bôite **Fillmo' Betta** and **Yoshi's World Class Jazz House and Japanese Restaurant**, an offshoot of Oakland's Yoshi's, all in the Fillmore Jazz Heritage Center; **Orson**, a funky Cal-Med in SoMa's former Red Dot Outlet warehouse from Citizen Cake owner (and Orson Welles fan) Elizabeth Falkner; **Prana**, a restaurant/lounge/gallery in SoMa serving modern Indian; and **Sam's Chowder House**, a cliffside New England–style seafood house in Half Moon Bay from Cetrella owner Paul Shenkman.

Top Ratings Overall

Excluding places with low voting.

Food

29 Gary Danko	Boulevard
French Laundry/N	Chez Panisse Café/E
28 Cyrus/N	L'Auberge Carmel/S
Marinus/S	Mirepoix/N
Chez Panisse/E	Tartine Bakery
Kaygetsu/S	26 Erna's Elderberry/E
27 Fleur de Lys	Tamarine/S
Manresa/S	La Forêt/S
La Folie	Cafe Gibraltar/S
Michael Mina	Fork/N
Terra/N	Aqua
Ritz-Carlton Din. Rm.	Cafe La Haye/N
Rivoli/E	Hana Japanese/N
Farmhouse Inn/N	Marché/S*
Sushi Ran/N	Kirala/E
Le Papillon/S	Woodward's Garden
Quince	Jardinière
Redd Restaurant/N	Chapeau!
Sierra Mar/S	La Toque/N
Masa's	Oswald/S

By Cuisine

American (New)
29 Gary Danko
    French Laundry/N
27 Manresa/S
    Michael Mina
    Terra/N

American (Traditional)
25 Mama's Wash. Sq.
24 Lark Creek Inn/N
    Gayle's Bakery/S
23 Buckeye Roadhse./N
    Liberty Cafe

Asian Fusion
26 House
24 Eos Rest./Wine Bar
    CAFÉ KATi
    Flying Fish Grill/S
    Silks

Bakeries
27 Tartine Bakery
25 Mama's Wash. Sq.
    Downtown Bakery/N
24 Gayle's Bakery/S
    Boulange

Barbecue
24 Bo's Barbecue/E
23 Buckeye Roadhse./N
22 Memphis Minnie's
20 Q
    Everett & Jones/E

Cajun/Creole/Southern
21 Kate's Kitchen
20 Everett & Jones/E
19 Elite Cafe
18 PJ's Oyster Bed
    House of Chicken/Waffles

Californian
28 Chez Panisse/E
27 Farmhouse Inn/N
    Sierra Mar/S
    Boulevard
26 Jardinière

Chinese
25 Koi Palace/S
    Great China/E
    Yank Sing
    Ton Kiang
    O'mei/S

Top Food

Continental
26 Fresh Cream/S
24 Chantilly/S
23 Anton & Michel/S
   Ecco/S
20 Maddalena's/S

Dim Sum
25 Koi Palace/S
   Yank Sing
   Ton Kiang
22 Fook Yuen Seafood/S
   Mayflower

Eclectic
26 Willi's Wine Bar/N
24 Firefly
   Va de Vi/E
   Picco/N
   Willow Wood Mkt./N

French
27 La Folie
26 La Forêt/S
   La Toque/N
   Cafe Jacqueline
   Fresh Cream/S

French (Bistro)
27 Mirepoix/N
26 Chapeau!
   Syrah/N
25 K&L Bistro/N
   Bistro Jeanty/N

French (New)
28 Cyrus/N
   Marinus/S
27 Fleur de Lys
   Manresa/S
   Ritz-Carlton Din. Rm.

Hamburgers
23 Joe's Cable Car
22 Mo's
   In-N-Out Burger/E/N/SF
21 Taylor's Automatic/N/SF
20 Barney's/E/N/SF

Indian
25 Amber India/S
24 Ajanta/E
   Vik's Chaat Corner/E
23 Shalimar/E/SF
   Indian Oven

Italian
27 Quince
26 Delfina
   Acquerello
   Frascati
25 Oliveto/E

Japanese
28 Kaygetsu/S
27 Sushi Ran/N
26 Hana Japanese/N
   Kirala/E
   Zushi Puzzle

Latin American
24 El Raigon
   Fonda Solana/E
   Limón
23 Fresca
   Charanga

Mediterranean
28 Chez Panisse/E
27 Rivoli/E
   Chez Panisse Café/E
26 Cafe Gibraltar/S
24 Coco 500

Mexican
24 La Taqueria/S/SF
23 Doña Tomás/E
   Mamacita
   Pancho Villa/S/SF
   Colibrí Mexican

Middle Eastern
25 Truly Mediterranean
24 Helmand
   Dish Dash/S
22 Yumma's
21 A La Turca

Pizza
25 Pizzetta 211
   Pauline's Pizza
24 Tommaso's
   Postrio
   Zachary's Pizza/E

Seafood
26 Aqua
25 Swan Oyster Depot
   Hog Island Oyster
   Passionfish/S
   Farallon

Top Food

Spanish/Basque
25 Piperade
Zuzu/N
23 César/E
Zarzuela
Bocadillos

Steakhouses
25 Cole's Chop House/N
Alexander's Steak/S
24 Harris'
El Raigon
Ruth's Chris Steak

Tapas (Latin)
25 Zuzu/N
23 César/E
Zarzuela
Bocadillos
22 Alegrias

Thai
25 Thep Phanom Thai
24 Soi Four/E
23 Manora's Thai
Marnee Thai
Royal Thai/N

Vegetarian
24 Millennium
23 Greens
20 Café Gratitude/E/SF
19 Medicine Eatstation
Udupi Palace/E

Vietnamese
26 Tamarine/S
25 Slanted Door
24 Pho 84/E
Crustacean
23 Thanh Long

By Special Feature

Breakfast
27 Tartine Bakery
26 Campton Place
25 Dottie's True Blue
Boulette's Larder
Mama's Wash. Sq.

Brunch
26 Erna's Elderberry/E
La Forêt/S
Campton Place
25 Zuni Café
Navio/S

Child-Friendly
21 Picante Cocina/E
Taylor's Automatic/N/SF
20 Barney's/E/N/SF
16 Pasta Pomodoro/E/S/SF
13 Mel's Drive-In

Hotel Dining
28 Cyrus/N
Les Mars Hotel
Marinus/S
Bernardus Lodge
27 Michael Mina
Weston St. Francis
Ritz-Carlton Din. Rm.
Ritz-Carlton Hotel
Farmhouse Inn/N
Farmhouse Inn

Late Night
27 Redd Restaurant/N
25 Bouchon/N
Zuni Café
24 Fonda Solana/E
23 Mamacita

Newcomers/Rated
27 Redd Restaurant/N
25 Ame
Range
24 Scott Howard
N.V./N
23 Bar Tartine
Mamacita
22 Bovolo/N
Thea Mediterranean/S
21 Sea Salt/E

People-Watching
27 Boulevard
26 Jardinière
25 Myth
Zuni Café
24 Town Hall

Small Plates
26 Tamarine/S
Fork/N
Willi's Wine Bar/N
25 Isa
24 Eos Rest./Wine Bar

Top Food

Tasting Menu
29 Gary Danko
   French Laundry/N
28 Cyrus/N
27 Manresa/S
   Michael Mina

Trendy
25 Myth
23 Bar Tartine
19 XYZ
   Frisson
18 Lime

Wine Bars
27 Sushi Ran/N
26 Bouchée/S
24 Eos Rest./Wine Bar
23 Bar Tartine
   A 16

Winning Wine Lists
29 Gary Danko
   French Laundry/N
28 Cyrus/N
27 Michael Mina
24 Rubicon

Worth a Trip
29 French Laundry/N
   Yountville
28 Cyrus/N
   Healdsburg
   Marinus/S
   Carmel
   Chez Panisse/E
   Berkeley
   Kaygetsu/S
   Menlo Park

Top Decor

29 Garden Court
28 Sierra Mar/S
   Ahwahnee Din. Rm./E
   Pacific's Edge/S
   Auberge du Soleil/N
27 Navio/S
   supperclub
   Farallon
   Ana Mandara
   Cyrus/N
   Shadowbrook/S
   Ritz-Carlton Din. Rm.
26 Fleur de Lys
   Teatro ZinZanni
   French Laundry/N
   Marinus/S
   Erna's Elderberry/E
   Sutro's at Cliff Hse.
   Jardinière
   Gary Danko
   Madrona Manor/N

   BIX
   Étoile/N
   Carnelian Room
   Martini House/N
   Roy's at Pebble Beach/S
   La Forêt/S
   Lark Creek Inn/N
   Manka's Inverness/N
   Kokkari Estiatorio
   Wente Vineyards/E
25 Seasons
   Myth
   Silks
   Campton Place
   Big 4
   Aqua
   Boulevard
   Farmhouse Inn/N
   Le Colonial*
   Postino/E*
   Ame

Outdoors

Angèle/N
Auberge du Soleil/N
Barndiva/N
Bay Wolf/E
B44
Bistro Aix
Brix/N
Casanova/S
Enrico's Sidewalk
Étoile/N
Foreign Cinema
Gar Woods/E
Isa

Jack Falstaff
John Ash & Co./N
La Note/E
Lark Creek Inn/N
Martini House/N
Nepenthe/S
Ritz-Carlton Terrace
River Ranch Rest./E
Sociale
Sunnyside Resort/E
Tra Vigne/N
Wente Vineyards/E
Zazie

Romance

Acquerello
Ame
Auberge du Soleil/N
Aziza
Bong Su
Cafe Jacqueline
Casanova/S
Chez Panisse/E
Chez Spencer
Cyrus/N
El Paseo/N
Erna's Elderberry/E
Fleur de Lys

Gary Danko
Jardinière
Khan Toke
La Forêt/S
L'Auberge Carmel/S
Le Papillon/S
Madrona Manor/N
Manka's/N
Marinus/S
Martini House/N
Sierra Mar/S
Venticello
Woodward's Garden

Rooms

Ahwahnee Din. Rm./E
Ana Mandara
Aqua
Asia de Cuba
BIX
Bong Su
Boulevard
Cetrella Bistro/S
Evvia/S
Farallon
Frisson
Garden Court
Grand Cafe
Jardinière
Jeanty at Jack's
Junnoon/S
Kokkari Estiatorio
Le Colonial
Mantra/S
Martini House/N
Masa's
Michael Mina
Myth
Ritz-Carlton Din. Rm.
Sino/S
St. Orres/N

Views

Ahwahnee Din. Rm./E
Albion River Inn/N
Angèle/N
Auberge du Soleil/N
Beach Chalet
Bella Vista
Caprice/N
Carnelian Room
Étoile/N
Greens
Guaymas/N
Ledford House/N
Navio/S
Nepenthe/S
Pacific's Edge/S
Rest. at Meadowood/N
Roy's Pebble Beach/S
Scoma's/E/SF
Sierra Mar/S
Slanted Door
Sol Y Lago/E
Sutro's at Cliff Hse.
Waterfront
Wente Vineyards/E
Wild Goose Rest./E
Wolfdale's/E

Top Service

28 Gary Danko
Ritz-Carlton Din. Rm.
Erna's Elderberry/E
French Laundry/N
27 Le Papillon/S
L'Auberge Carmel/S
Masa's
Seasons
Cyrus/N
Marinus/S
26 Chez Panisse/E
Michael Mina
Acquerello
La Folie
Farmhouse Inn/N
Campton Place
Terra/N
La Toque/N
Mirepoix/N
Madrona Manor/N

Manresa/S
Chapeau!
Kaygetsu/S
25 Silks
Fleur de Lys
Ritz-Carlton Terrace
Albona Rist.
Fresh Cream/S
Emile's/S
La Forêt/S*
Quince
Sierra Mar/S
Boulevard
Jardinière
Aqua
Auberge du Soleil/N
Rivoli/E
Chez TJ/S
Pacific's Edge/S
Chez Panisse Café/E

Best Buys

Top Bangs for the Buck

1. Caspers Hot Dogs/E
2. Rosamunde Grill
3. In-N-Out Burger/E/N/SF
4. Saigon Sandwiches
5. Arinell Pizza/E/SF
6. Papalote Mexican
7. Taqueria Can-Cun
8. Yumma's
9. Taqueria 3 Amigos/S
10. Truly Mediterranean
11. La Taqueria/S/SF
12. Downtown Bakery/N
13. Cactus Taqueria/E
14. Pancho Villa/S/SF
15. Pho Hoa-Hiep II/E/S/SF
16. El Balazo
17. Lanesplitter/E
18. Thai Buddhist Temple/E
19. Tartine Bakery
20. Red's Java House
21. La Cumbre Taqueria/S/SF
22. Nick's Crispy Tacos
23. Burger Joint/S/SF
24. Boulange
25. So
26. Gioia Pizzeria/E
27. Pluto's Fresh Food
28. Fenton's Creamery/E
29. Picante Cocina/E
30. Tacubaya/E
31. Joe's Cable Car
32. Vik's Chaat Corner/E
33. House of Chicken/Waffles/E
34. Kate's Kitchen
35. Dottie's True Blue
36. Pho 84/E
37. Cafe Lo Cubano
38. Asqew Grill/E/SF
39. Gayle's Bakery/S
40. Pork Store Café

Other Good Values

A La Turca
Baker St. Bistro
Blue Jay Cafe
Bocadillos
Boulette's Larder
Betty's Fish & Chips/N
Burma Super Star
Canteen
Chapeau!
Chow/Park Chow/E/SF
Citizen Thai
Da Kitchen/S
Dopo/E
farmerbrown
Firefly
Giordano Bros.
Goood Frikin' Chicken
Helmand
Hyde St. Bistro
Jay's Cheesesteak
jZcool/S
King of Thai
Le Charm
Nicky's Pizzeria Rustica
NoPa
Osha Thai Noodles
Pacific Catch/N/SF
Pakwan/E/SF
Pesce
Pizzeria Delfina
Pizzeria Picco/N
Pizzetta 211
Powell's Place
Saha
Shabu-Sen
Shalimar/E/S/SF
Taqueria Tlaquepaque/S
Taylor's Automatic/N/SF
Ti Couz
Tommaso's

Prix Fixe Bargains

Dinner
($30 & Under)

Ajanta/E	15.50	Le Charm	28.00
Alamo Square	12.50	Mandarin	29.95
Alfred's Steak	30.00	Marica/E	24.00
Axum Café	12.00	Maya	29.95
Baker St. Bistro	14.50	Mecca	29.95
Basque Cultural Ctr./S	17.95	Moosse Café/N	20.00
Bistro Liaison/E	28.00	One Market	29.00
Caffe Delle Stelle	22.95	Passage to India/S	13.95
Cetrella Bistro/Café/S	24.95	rnm	28.00
Chez Panisse Café/E	28.00	Sanraku Four Seasons	24.00
Christophe/N	23.00	Sonoma Meritage/N	24.00
Côté Sud	25.00	Stokes Restaurant/S	29.00
Della Santina's/N	30.00	SUMI	30.00
Gayle's Bakery/S	11.95	Three Seasons/E	29.95
Gaylord India/S	24.95	Town's End	17.95
girl & the fig/N	28.00	Trattoria La Siciliana/E	25.00
Globe	29.00	2223 Restaurant	22.23
Hayes St. Grill	29.00	Watercress	20.00
Lark Creek Inn/N	29.50	Zazie	19.50

Lunch
($25 & Under)

Absinthe	21.95	Juban/S	4.95
Ajanta/E	11.50	Lark Creek Inn/N	19.50
Anjou	16.00	Left Bank/S	22.95
Asia de Cuba	22.00	Market/N	14.95
Bacar	21.95	MarketBar	24.00
Bistro Liaison/E	14.95	Martini House/N	25.00
BIX	21.95	Maya	19.95
Brix/N	20.00	Moose's	16.95
Brother's Korean	6.95	Pakwan/E	10.99
Café Marcella/S	19.95	Passage to India/S	10.95
Chez Panisse Café/E	24.00	Rubicon	25.00
Destino	21.95	Sanraku Four Seasons	8.95
Espetus Churrascaria	18.95	Scoma's	21.50
Grand Café	20.00	Shanghai 1930	15.95
Helmand	9.95	Straits Café/S	20.00
Hunan Home's	5.00	231 Ellsworth/S	20.00
Hurley's	17.00	Yankee Pier/N	9.95

City of San Francisco

Top Ratings in SF Proper

Excluding places with low voting.

Food

29	Gary Danko		Acquerello
27	Fleur de Lys		Cafe Jacqueline
	La Folie		Campton Place
	Michael Mina		Frascati
	Ritz-Carlton Din. Rm.		Kokkari Estiatorio
	Quince		House
	Masa's	25	Maki
	Boulevard		Swan Oyster Depot
	Tartine Bakery		Dottie's True Blue
26	Aqua		Hog Island Oyster
	Woodward's Garden		Isa
	Jardinière		Ame
	Chapeau!		Slanted Door
	Zushi Puzzle		Boulette's Larder
	Delfina		Thep Phanom Thai

By Cuisine

American (New)
- 29 Gary Danko
- 27 Michael Mina
- 26 Campton Place
- 25 Ame
- Myth

American (Traditional)
- 25 Mama's Wash. Sq.
- 23 Liberty Cafe
- BIX
- 22 Ella's
- 21 Maverick

Asian Fusion
- 26 House
- 24 Eos Rest./Wine Bar
- CAFÉ KATi
- Silks
- 22 SUMI

Bakeries
- 27 Tartine Bakery
- 24 Boulange
- 23 Liberty Cafe
- 21 Citizen Cake
- 19 Il Fornaio

Californian
- 27 Boulevard
- 26 Jardinière
- 25 Fifth Floor
- Canteen
- 24 Scott Howard

Chinese
- 25 Yank Sing
- Ton Kiang
- 24 San Tung
- 23 R & G Lounge
- Tommy Toy's

French
- 27 La Folie
- 26 Cafe Jacqueline
- 25 Isa
- Chez Spencer
- 24 Boulange

French (Bistro)
- 26 Chapeau!
- 25 Fringale
- Chez Papa Bistrot
- Clémentine
- 23 Jeanty at Jack's

French (New)
- 27 Fleur de Lys
- Ritz-Carlton Din. Rm.
- Masa's
- 25 Seasons
- 24 Rubicon

Hamburgers
- 23 Joe's Cable Car
- 22 Mo's
- In-N-Out Burger
- 21 Taylor's Automatic
- 20 Barney's

Top Food

Indian/Pakistani
23 Shalimar
   Indian Oven
22 Pakwan
21 Dosa
19 Naan 'n Curry

Italian
27 Quince
26 Delfina
   Acquerello
   Frascati
25 Tratt. Contadina

Japanese
26 Zushi Puzzle
25 Maki
   Kabuto
24 Kyo-Ya
   Ebisu

Latin American
24 El Raigon
   Limón
23 Fresca
   Charanga
22 Espetus Churrascaria

Mediterranean/Greek
26 Kokkari Estiatorio
25 Zuni Café
   PlumpJack Café
24 Coco 500
   Cortez

Mexican
24 La Taqueria
23 Mamacita
   Pancho Villa
   Colibrí Mexican
22 Nick's Crispy Tacos

Middle Eastern
25 Truly Mediterranean
24 Helmand
22 Yumma's
21 A La Turca
20 La Méditerranée

Noodles
24 San Tung
22 Osha Thai
21 So
20 Citrus Club
   Hotei

Pizza
25 Pizzetta 211
   Pauline's Pizza
24 Tommaso's
   Postrio
   Pizzeria Delfina

Seafood
26 Aqua
25 Swan Oyster Depot
   Hog Island Oyster
   Farallon
23 Pesce

Spanish/Basque
25 Piperade
23 Zarzuela
   Bocadillos
22 Alegrias
20 B44

Steakhouses
24 Harris'
   El Raigon
   Ruth's Chris Steak
   Morton's Steak
23 House of Prime Rib

Tapas (Latin)
23 Zarzuela
   Bocadillos
22 Alegrias
20 Ramblas
   Iluna Basque

Vietnamese
25 Slanted Door
24 Crustacean
23 Thanh Long
22 Three Seasons
   Ana Mandara

By Special Feature

Breakfast
27 Tartine Bakery
25 Dottie's True Blue
   Boulette's Larder
   Mama's Wash. Sq.
24 Boulange

Brunch
26 Campton Place
25 Dottie's True Blue
   Zuni Café
24 Ritz-Carlton Terrace
22 Ella's

Top Food

Child-Friendly
25 Yank Sing
21 Taylor's Automatic
20 Barney's
16 Pasta Pomodoro
13 Mel's Drive-In

Hotel Dining
27 Michael Mina
   Westin St. Francis
   Ritz-Carlton Din. Rm.
    Ritz-Carlton Hotel
   Masa's
    Hotel Vintage Ct.
26 Campton Place
   Campton Place Hotel
25 Ame
   St. Regis Hotel

Late Night
25 Zuni Café
23 Scala's Bistro
   Brother's Korean
22 Tsunami Sushi
19 Brazen Head

Newcomers/Rated
25 Ame
   Range
24 Scott Howard
23 Bar Tartine
21 Mamcita

Newcomers/Unrated
   Bong Su
   NoPa
   Sebo
   Senses Rest.
   Terzo

Outdoor Seating
25 Isa
24 Ritz-Carlton Terrace
22 Sociale
   Foreign Cinema
21 Zazie

People-Watching
27 Boulevard
26 Jardinière
25 Myth
   Zuni Café
24 Town Hall

Power Scenes
26 Aqua
24 Rubicon
23 Jeanty at Jack's
22 One Market
21 Jack Falstaff

Romance
27 Fleur de Lys
   Ritz-Carlton Din. Rm.
26 Woodward's Garden
   Jardinière
   Cafe Jacqueline

Small Plates
25 Isa
24 Eos Rest./Wine Bar
   Cortez
23 Pesce
   Chez Nous

Tasting Menus
29 Gary Danko
27 La Folie
   Michael Mina
   Ritz-Carlton Din. Rm.
   Masa's

Trendy
25 Myth
21 Levende
19 XYZ
   Frisson
18 Lime

Winning Wine Lists
29 Gary Danko
27 Michael Mina
   Boulevard
25 Myth
   Fifth Floor

Top Food

By Location

Castro/Noe Valley
24 Firefly
    Incanto
23 Fresca
22 Rist. Bacco
    SUMI

Chinatown
23 R & G Lounge
22 Jai Yun
    Yuet Lee
    Hunan Home's
    Great Eastern

Cow Hollow/Marina
26 Zushi Puzzle
25 Isa
    PlumpJack Cafe
24 Boulange
23 A 16

Downtown
27 Michael Mina
    Masa's
26 Aqua
    Campton Place
    Kokkari Estiatorio

Embarcadero
27 Boulevard
25 Hog Island Oyster
    Slanted Door
    Boulette's Larder
24 Ozumo

Fisherman's Wharf
29 Gary Danko
23 Grandeho Kamekyo
22 Ana Mandara
    Mandarin
    Scoma's

Haight-Ashbury/Cole Valley
24 Eos Rest./Wine Bar
    Boulange
23 Grandeho Kamekyo
21 Zazie
20 Pork Store Café

Hayes Valley/Civic Center
26 Jardinière
25 Zuni Café
22 Hayes St. Grill
    Espetus Churrascaria
21 Cav Wine Bar

Lower Haight
25 Thep Phanom Thai
    Rosamunde Grill
23 Indian Oven
    rnm
22 Axum Cafe

Mission
27 Tartine Bakery
26 Woodward's Garden
    Delfina
25 Chez Spencer
    Truly Mediterranean

Nob Hill/Russian Hill
27 Fleur de Lys
    La Folie
    Ritz-Carlton Din. Rm.
26 Acquerello
    Frascati

North Beach
26 Cafe Jacqueline
    House
25 Mama's Wash. Sq.
    Tratt. Contadina
24 Tommaso's

Pacific Heights/Japantown
27 Quince
25 Maki
24 CAFÉ KATi
    Boulange
23 Vivande Porta Via

Richmond
26 Chapeau!
25 Ton Kiang
    Pizzetta 211
    Kabuto
24 Aziza

SoMa
25 Ame
    Fifth Floor
    Yank Sing
    Fringale
24 Coco 500

Sunset/West Portal
24 Ebisu
    Koo
    San Tung
23 Thanh Long
    Fresca

Top Decor

29	Garden Court		BIX
27	supperclub		Carnelian Room
	Farallon		Kokkari Estiatorio
	Ana Mandara	25	Seasons
	Ritz-Carlton Din. Rm.		Myth
26	Fleur de Lys		Silks
	Teatro ZinZanni		Campton Place
	Sutro's at Cliff Hse.		Big 4
	Jardinière		Aqua
	Gary Danko		Boulevard

Top Service

28	Gary Danko		Fleur de Lys
	Ritz-Carlton Din. Rm.		Ritz-Carlton Terrace
27	Masa's		Albona Rist.
	Seasons		Quince
26	Michael Mina		Boulevard
	Acquerello		Jardinière
	La Folie		Aqua
	Campton Place	24	Ame
	Chapeau!		Fifth Floor
25	Silks		Myth

Top Bangs for the Buck

1. Rosamunde Grill
2. In-N-Out Burger
3. Saigon Sandwiches
4. Arinell Pizza
5. Papalote Mexican
6. Taqueria Can-Cun
7. Yumma's
8. Truly Mediterranean
9. La Taqueria
10. Pancho Villa
11. Pho Hoa-Hiep II
12. El Balazo
13. Tartine Bakery
14. Red's Java House
15. La Cumbre Taqueria
16. Nick's Crispy Tacos
17. Burger Joint
18. Boulange
19. So
20. Pluto's Fresh Food

Other Good Values

Alamo Square
A 16
Baker St. Bistro
Burma Super Star
Chapeau!
Chow/Park Chow
Firefly
Helmand
Hyde St. Bistro
Le Charm Bistro

L'Osteria del Forno
Luna Park
Mixt Greens
Nicky's Pizzeria Rustica
Osha Thai Noodles
Pakwan
Pesce
Shalimar
SUMI
Ti Couz

City of San Francisco

	F	D	S	C

Abigail's Bakery and Cafe
	–	–	–	M

2120 Greenwich St. (Fillmore St.), 415-929-8889
More than just another place to get a cuppa joe in the Marina, this new 30-seat cafe in the thick of Restaurant Row fuels its patrons with all-day sustenance, from fresh-baked baguettes, brioche and breakfast items to sit-down dinner service featuring hearty, Californian-inspired bistro fare from Josh Bush (of the late Foreign Cinema); weekend brunch is also served.

Absinthe ● M
	20	22	20	$44

398 Hayes St. (Gough St.), 415-551-1590; www.absinthe.com
"Effortlessly stylish", this "movie-set version" of a French brasserie in Hayes Valley feels like "*la belle époque*" – but perhaps "imagined by Jerry Garcia" – what with its "transporting" "retro Paris" atmosphere, "satisfying" Gallic-Med fare and "cocktail menu that makes the experience really worthwhile" ("wish they served real absinthe"); *oui*, service can be "haphazard" pre-curtain time when it's a "beehive of activity", swarming with "opera patricians, hip youngsters" and an "assortment of sophisticates", but it gets "better" "after the rush"; N.B. a post-*Survey* chef change may impact the Food Score.

Ace Wasabi's
	22	15	17	$31

3339 Steiner St. (bet. Chestnut & Lombard Sts.), 415-567-4903; www.acewasabissushi.com
A Marina mecca to "eat, drink and be horny", this "ridiculously crowded" "party place" reels in "twentysomething" "busty blondes" and "collegiate meatheads" who "slam their sake" while "singing along" to "extremely loud" rock 'n' roll; the "unexpectedly good" fin fare and "adventurous rolls" are "not authentic Japanese by any means" (nor "necessarily cheap"), but "the sushi chefs are a real laugh", and bingo nights are "always fun."

Acme Chophouse M
	20	19	18	$47

AT&T Park, 24 Willie Mays Plaza (bet. King & 3rd Sts.), 415-644-0240; www.acmechophouse.com
Odds on scoring an "acme" meal paired with "amazing wines" at a "baseball stadium" might be low, but Traci Des Jardins' "upbeat" South Beach meatery "escapes the stereotype", delivering "huge portions" of "succulent" "sustainably" raised, "simply prepared" steaks and chops with "just the right accompaniments"; a "precision" staff navigates the "madhouse" of fans "rubbing shoulders with famous Bay Area coaches", but cynics scowl at the "steep prices" for "food as predictable as a Bonds' homer."

Acquerello ⑤ M
	26	23	26	$67

1722 Sacramento St. (bet. Polk St. & Van Ness Ave.), 415-567-5432; www.acquerello.com
"Bust out the wallet" (and possibly the ring) at this "formal", "stunningly elegant" Russian Hill Italian where patrons "of Bill Gates' worth" are treated to a "tour de force of decadence";

you'll be "pampered" with "butlerlike service" ("any better, and I'd worry that the waiters all had ESP"), "sublime" *alta cucina* and vino "aired out in decanters"; still, a handful of hipsters huff that it attracts an "older crowd" and feel the "funky" "Venetian decor" "needs a face-lift."

Alamo Square | 19 | 17 | 18 | $28 |

803 Fillmore St. (bet. Fulton & Grove Sts.), 415-440-2828
For "nothing fancy" fin fare with "French flair" for just a few francs, anglers rely on this "relaxed" "good for the 'hood" sea-fooder in the "edgy" Western Addition staffed with "friendly" service that helps "diners pick any combination of the offered fish, preparations and sauces"; *bien sûr*, the "intimate setting" is "easily overcrowded", but with "free parking", an "affordable" prix fixe and free corkage on Wednesdays, for many it's a reel "dream come true."

A La Turca | 21 | 8 | 17 | $19 |

869 Geary St. (Larkin St.), 415-345-1011
A pilgrimage to this outpost of Istanbul in "the seedy Tenderloin" is "like a visit to Ankara", thanks to its expatriate customer base and what may just be some of "the best Turkish food in town"; "service is on the slow side" and "the ambiance is that of a laundromat, but these folks can cook up a storm", and "cheap eats" advocates aver "at least we didn't go broke!"

Albona Ristorante Istriano ⊠ Ⓜ | 24 | 19 | 25 | $40 |

545 Francisco St. (bet. Mason & Taylor Sts.), 415-441-1040; www.albonarestaurant.com
Offering "a different take" on Venetian food, this "unusual", "intimate" North Beach outpost of Istrian cuisine is where "doting" host Bruno Viscovi "welcomes you as if you were a guest in his home", "orders your dinner" and gives you an "emotional, in-depth" "history of his native homeland" near Croatia, Slovenia and Italy that's "surpassed only by the food itself"; it's a "great change of pace", in fact, you may try "things you've never eaten before."

Alegrias, Food From Spain | 22 | 16 | 20 | $31 |

2018 Lombard St. (Webster St.), 415-929-8888
"If you're looking for an authentic, family-run Spanish restaurant" "identical" to what you'd find if you were "sitting at a table in Barcelona", *ándale* to this "reliable" Marina Iberian; sure, it may "not wow a foodie friend", but the "homey" interior almost "feels like you're sitting in your *abuela*'s dining room", plus the "traditional tapas" ("large enough to share"), a "live guitar on weekends" and a "wonderfully warm staff" help to ensure a "satisfying experience."

Alfred's Steak House ⊠ Ⓜ | 21 | 19 | 20 | $48 |

659 Merchant St. (bet. Kearny & Montgomery Sts.), 415-781-7058; www.alfredssteakhouse.com
"Take a trip down memory lane" at this "old-school steakhouse" "throwback" Downtown boasting a "dark-wood labyrinth" of "red-leather booths" and "salty service" from "tuxedoed waiters"; "start with a martini" or something from the "100-item scotch menu" followed by a "Caesar salad made at the table", then "tackle a massive, aged piece of meat that's worth every penny"; if a few beef "it's lost its luster", loyalists insist this "landmark" is "just what the doctor ordered."

Alice's   20 | 16 | 18 | $19

1599 Sanchez St. (29th St.), 415-282-8999

"Always full of locals", this Noe Valley haunt is "not your typical fluorescent-lit Chinese restaurant"; although the "darned good, economical" "slightly Californian-ized" fare (brimming with "lots of fresh vegetables" and "not loaded with oil") and the "interesting glass globe" decor are a "mirror image" of the competition "around the corner", "there's never a line and the service seems to be friendlier."

Alioto's   18 | 17 | 17 | $39

8 Fisherman's Wharf (bet. Jefferson & Taylor Sts.), 415-673-0183; www.aliotos.com

There may be "far better seafood restaurants away from the Wharf", but when the "tourist bus crowd" wants "cracked crab" or shrimp Louie "the way they were served 40 years ago", they confess this waterfront restaurant where you can "watch the boats in the harbor" is a "sentimental favorite"; however, locals who carp about the "outdated decor", "pushy waiters" and "mass-produced" "Italian-style" grub shrug it's "hard to figure out why it's famous."

Ame   25 | 25 | 24 | $67

St. Regis Hotel, 689 Mission St. (Third St.), 415-284-4040; www.amerestaurant.com

Set in the lobby of SoMa's St. Regis Hotel, this "minimalist" yet "sexy" "Japanese-influenced" New American from Hiro Sone and Lissa Doumani (St. Helena's Terra) is off to "a promising start"; the "highly imaginative", "beyond-eclectic", seafood-centric menu "kicks some serious foodie butt" with the "sublime" flavors of its "exquisite" entrees, enhanced by a "special" wine cellar and "extensive list" of sakes; service is "attentive", if "inconsistent" at times (perhaps because "it's still early" days).

Americano   20 | 23 | 19 | $47

Hotel Vitale, 8 Mission St. (The Embarcadero), 415-278-3777; www.americanorestaurant.com

"When the weather's good", the recently enlarged "scenic patio facing the Embarcadero" at the "hip" Hotel Vitale "swirls" "out of control" with "beautiful" "Gen-Xers" enjoying the "happy-hour scene"; but those who "wade through" the "packed bar" note "it's worth staying for more than martinis" because the Cal-Italian fare is "wonderfully creative" and "flavorful" and the "dining room is the chicest"; still, cynics snipe the food's "secondary" and huff that "you must be good looking to eat here."

Amici's East Coast Pizzeria   20 | 12 | 17 | $19

216 King St. (3rd St.), 415-546-6666
2033 Union St. (Buchanan St.), 415-885-4500
www.amicis.com

These "informal" pie purveyors' "lightly topped", "blistered" brick-oven offerings are the "closest" rendition "on the Left Coast", especially if "crackling", "super-thin crust is your game" insist "pizza snobs"; skeptics sniff it's "more like the work of a Californian" than a "real NY pizzeria" ("soy cheese?" "come on!"), and decry the "bland", "child-friendly" "Formica dining room", but even they laud the "free" "lightning-fast" delivery – a Bay Area "rarity."

ANA MANDARA
22 | 27 | 21 | $47

Ghirardelli Sq., 891 Beach St. (Polk St.), 415-771-6800;
www.anamandara.com
"Start the evening in the swanky" jazz lounge upstairs then
descend to the "fab faux" "colonial" Indochine "movie-set
space" on Fisherman's Wharf that "drips with the romance of
W. Somerset Maugham's Far East" for "artistically presented"
New French–Vietnamese fare "so good that you'll need to wear
elastic pants"; still, fence-sitters sigh "if only the food were as
delectable as the decor" and note that sometimes "service is so
slow one imagines the kitchen is in Saigon."

Andalu
22 | 20 | 19 | $35

3198 16th St. (Guerrero St.), 415-621-2211; www.andalusf.com
"One of the original SF" tapas "pioneers", this "loud", "lively"
"loungey" "finger-food heaven" in the Mission still "rises above
the rest", luring hordes of "young hipsters" with "delectable"
Eclectic small plates, each a "delight to the senses", plus an "extensive wine list" ("try a flight with your meal") and "interesting
cocktails"; but the less-impressed pooh-pooh it's more "style
than substance" with "snooty service" to boot.

Andrew Jaeger's
House of Seafood & Jazz ●
▽ 16 | 15 | 16 | $36

The Condor, 300 Columbus Ave. (Grant Ave.), 415-781-8222
Boasting "local color and shades of Carol Doda's past", North
Beach's former Condor Club makes a fitting home for New
Orleans restaurateur Andrew Jaeger's branch of his bawdy
Bourbon-Street-meets-Broadway boîte dishing up "a double
treat – jazz and jambalaya"; while some early visitors "wouldn't
rush back for the" "average" Cajun-Creole specialties, others
suggest listening to the live band in the bar and ordering from the
bistro menu because "the formal dining room makes you feel like
you're missing out on the party next door."

Angkor Borei
22 | 14 | 22 | $20

3471 Mission St. (Cortland Ave.), 415-550-8417;
www.cambodiankitchen.com
"Run by the kindest, almost supplicating family", this "unsung"
"hidden gem" near Bernal Heights is a "hole-in-the-wall in the
best sense of the word" – and a "great port to anchor in if you're
a vegetarian" or just craving cheap Cambodian eats; insiders
overlook the "dated" "low-budget" dining room ("feels like
Phnom Penh"), because there's "a flavor explosion inside" with
"awesome" favorites bested by "fresh, bright" ingredients –
and free delivery.

Anjou ⊠Ⓜ
23 | 19 | 22 | $42

44 Campton Pl. (bet. Post & Sutter Sts.), 415-392-5373;
www.anjou-sf.com
"Don't let this secret out!" confide *amis* of this "petite" "simple
Parisian bistro" "tucked in a nondescript alley" near Union
Square that's only "visible by its adorable yellow-and-white-
striped awning"; the "two-tiered" "brick and brass"–appointed
dining room is so "warm and toasty" it feels like a "grown-up
slice of France" while the "consistently delicious" Gallic goods
are "delivered with charm" and real accents, rendering it a
"great find" for a pre-show meal.

Annabelle's Bar & Bistro

▽ | 18 | 18 | 18 | $38 |

68 Fourth St. (bet. Market & Mission Sts.), 415-777-1200;
www.annabelles.net

It's always been "fun to eat" at the long wooden bar at this historic SoMa "sleeper" (circa 1913), and "watch convention-goers wander back to their hotels" Downtown, but until a 2006 remodel, there was "nothing exciting about the food, decor or service"; change is afoot following a spruce-up of the "old-time San Francisco–style" bistro interior and the arrival of a new chef who's ushered in a seasonal, organic Californian menu.

Antica Trattoria Ⓜ

| 23 | 19 | 21 | $38 |

2400 Polk St. (Union St.), 415-928-5797; www.anticasf.com

For a "piece of *bella Italia* without the cheesy North Beach factor", Russian Hill locals head to this "authentic", "wonderful neighborhood trattoria" "tucked away where the tourists won't find it"; "genuine Italian waiters waltz around" the "cozy" dining room serving "scrumptious", "rustic" "regional" *cucina* "cooked to perfection" "at decent prices"; however, "go early or be prepared to use sign language" because the "cramped quarters" get mighty "boisterous."

Anzu

| 23 | 19 | 21 | $51 |

Hotel Nikko, 222 Mason St. (O'Farrell St.), 415-394-1100;
www.restaurantanzu.com

"East meets West" at this Downtowner that "crosses steak, raw" fin fare and Sunday jazz brunch under one roof; the "high-priced" beef is "matched by quality", but the biggest lure is "skillful" "master sushi chef" Kazuhito Takahashi's "fish flown in from Japan" topped with "freshly grated wasabi"; if a handful feel that the atmosphere's "stuffy" and service suffers from "typical hotel restaurant" syndrome, most agree it's an "excellent choice" for Nikko guests or pre-theater dining.

Aperto

| 20 | 15 | 20 | $31 |

1434 18th St. (Connecticut St.), 415-252-1625;
www.apertosf.com

A "big fave of the Hill crowd", this "longtime" Potrero Italian trattoria with an "intimate neighborhood vibe" "draws back" "lotsa regulars" for its "good food", "friendly staff" and "relatively low prices"; while a few shrug that it's "nothing out of the ordinary", locals deem the "dependable" chow "pleasing", (there's "always a special that satisfies"), adding that no reservations means "you can always get in" no matter how "busy."

AQUA

| 26 | 25 | 25 | $68 |

252 California St. (bet. Battery & Front Sts.), 415-956-9662;
www.aqua-sf.com

For "flawless fish" worthy of Neptune, plus chef Laurent Manrique's "flavorful" "foie gras additions", "financial moguls" and "celebrities" drop anchor at this "stunning, high-ceilinged" "deep-pocket" "deep-sea" Downtowner; it's a "real dining adventure" with "exquisitely prepared" Cal-seafood with a slight French influence, "omnipresent" "white-glove service" and a "resident wine expert to help with the extensive list"; if gripers find it hard to part with "hard-earned clams" for "crammed" tables and a "punishing" "noise level", Aqua-nuts concur it "still delivers one of the most impressive experiences in town."

Arinell Pizza ⇄   24 | 5 | 12 | $7
509 Valencia St. (16th St.), 415-255-1303
See review in East of San Francisco Directory.

A. Sabella's   19 | 17 | 19 | $39
2766 Taylor St. (Jefferson St.), 415-771-6775; www.asabellas.com
"Although corny", "after spending the day browsing the Wharf", it's
a "San Francisco treat" to "have a drink and watch the Bay" at
this "always busy" waterside way-station where the "seafood is
pumped out and tourists are pumped through"; sure, the "Cal-
style", "simple" "fresh" fish is "predictable" and "pricey", and
the decor and service are like "traveling back" in time, but given
that it's been around since 1920, "something must be going right."

Asia de Cuba   21 | 25 | 20 | $55
Clift Hotel, 495 Geary St. (Taylor St.), 415-929-2300; www.clifthotel.com
The "mixed crowd" of Clift "Hotel guests and locals out on the town
makes for a good vibe" at this "super-chic" Downtown outpost
boasting "glitz and glam help", a "packed bar" with "barely dressed
women" and "truly innovative" Asian-Cuban cuisine; what "ties
everything together": the Philippe Starck decor that's almost "too
sexy for its patrons" ("love the community table"); sure, it's "dark to
the point of silly" and some say it's best left to "posers and tourists",
but most enjoy "rubbing elbows (literally) with the beautiful people."

AsiaSF   17 | 19 | 21 | $37
201 Ninth St. (Howard St.), 415-255-2742; www.asiasf.com
Although you drag "visiting relatives" to SoMa's "gay Asian-diva
dance club dive-turned-touristy straight-girl bachelorette destination" for the "outrageously fun" "only in SF" gender illusionist
floorshow, the Cal-Asian small bites and entrees are also an "entertaining experience" – and "surprisingly good" for a "partying"
place; "if the "Miss *Transamerica*" "'waitresses' weren't so busy
lip-synching and gyrating, they could be more attentive", but "it's
a hoot", so "eat, drink" "exotic" cocktails and "be merry."

A 16   23 | 19 | 20 | $40
2355 Chestnut St. (bet. Divisadero & Scott Sts.), 415-771-2216;
www.a16sf.com
As "jam-packed" with "beautiful" "yuppie" "*ragazzi*" as "the
highway running through Campagna", this Marina enoteca "raz-
zles and dazzles" with "supercharged" Southern Italian food and
a "wine list that begs you to explore the lesser-known regions of
The Boot"; at "crunch time", "service slows like the *autostrada* in
August", but that's "A-ok" with "serious foodies" who insist that
the "crackling-crust pizzas" are "in a league of their own"; N.B. a
post-*Survey* chef change may impact the Food score.

Asqew Grill   19 | 12 | 14 | $14
1607 Haight St. (Clayton St.), 415-701-9301
3583 16th St. (Market St.), 415-626-3040
3348 Steiner St. (Chestnut St.), 415-931-9201
www.asqewgrill.com
For "good, quick", "surprisingly tasty" "cheap eats", this
Californian-style "meat-on-a-stick" outfit "skewers other fast-
food places"; while "nothing fancy", the "mix-and-match menu"
"keeps it from getting boring", offering "endless" kebab variations "to fit all diets, tastes and budgets" with a choice of sides;

true, "you order at the cash register" and "there isn't much ambiance" but "when you're too lazy to cook", you can't beat it with a you-know-what; N.B. there's an East Bay branch too.

Avenue G ●⬛Ⓜ | – | – | – | M |
1000 Clement St. (11th Ave.), 415-221-7111
The Inner Richmond has long been a hotbed of ethnic eateries, so it's no surprise that this upscale yet unpretentious bistro presents an Eclectic menu encompassing the home cooking of the area's various cuisines, with dishes ranging from feijoada to Dungeness crab pot pie; the reasonably priced fare is prepared in an open kitchen and accompanied by a globe-trotting wine list, along with soju and sake cocktails; N.B. the kitchen stays open till midnight, and even later on weekends.

Axum Cafe | 22 | 9 | 17 | $15 |
698 Haight St. (Pierce St.), 415-252-7912; www.axumcafe.com
This straight-out-of-Africa Lower Haight Street spot might be "lacking in the decor department", but axum how they feel about their "friendly" fave and fans insist the "terrifically fast", "filling vegetarian and meaty Ethiopian stews" and "tasty beers" "at unbelievably cheap prices" "speaks for itself"; "who doesn't love eating with their hands?" quip patrons who also give the "prompt service" and "authentic presentation" a thumbs-up.

Azie | 20 | 22 | 18 | $46 |
826 Folsom St. (bet. 4th & 5th Sts.), 415-538-0918;
www.restaurantlulu.com
"Lots of places talk fusion", but LuLu's "sexy" SoMa scenester sibling "actually does it well" presenting "innovative" "food as architecture" downstairs in the "upbeat" "hipster bar" and upstairs in a dining room that resembles "an illuminated bento box"; the jaded jibe that the high-priced "minuscule" Asian–New French morsels have "lost some luster", but even they concede that when "the mood is right", there's nothing like "lowering the curtains to your booth" "for a romantic rendezvous"; N.B. a post-*Survey* chef change may impact the Food Score.

Aziza | 24 | 23 | 20 | $41 |
5800 Geary Blvd. (22nd Ave.), 415-752-2222; www.aziza-sf.com
Eschewing the bedouin and belly dancer "kitschy" conceit, this "dark", "dazzling" "rocking neo-Moroccan temple of couscous" in the Outer Richmond conjures up modern Marrakesch "reimagined for San Francisco"; heed the "friendly" servers and "stuff yourself silly" on the "no-brainer $39 tasting menu" bursting with "truly unusual", "superb" Californian-adapted delicacies – paired with a "spectacular herb-infused cocktail", it "really puts you in the mood to whirl like a dervish."

bacar | 22 | 23 | 21 | $51 |
448 Brannan St. (bet. 3rd & 4th Sts.), 415-904-4100;
www.bacarsf.com
Three levels of "urban-chic" dining, an "incredible" 1,000-plus-bottle wall of vino (the "list resembles *Encyclopedia Britannica*") and "classy" jazz six nights a week adds up to one "awesome" SoMa venue that's "wonderful on the eyes"; while this loftlike "'it' place" "clearly loves its wine" (check out the "scrumptious flights"), diners also divulge that the "inventive" "seasonal menus result in the freshest", "startlingly good" Cal-Med dishes,

all served by an "engaging, knowledgeable staff"; N.B. lunch only on Fridays.

Baker Street Bistro 20 | 15 | 19 | $30
2953 Baker St. (bet. Greenwich & Lombard Sts.), 415-931-1475
Marina *amis* want to keep this "enchanting" send-up of an "authentic" *petit* Parisian bistro ("down to the waiters") under their chapeau, but *oui*, the "secret" is out because the "solid" "straightforward" "French classics" "would cost three times more" across the pond (the "prix fixe is a steal"); sure, it's "jam-packed" – expect "sardine class" seating, "perfect for cuddling up" – but it's "always lovely in the evening", and it "really comes into its own for" alfresco weekend brunches.

Balboa Cafe 19 | 18 | 18 | $34
3199 Fillmore St. (Greenwich St.), 415-921-3944; www.plumpjack.com
For "Gavin sightings" and the "best Bloody Marys", you can't beat "The 'Bal'" – Cow Hollow's "quintessential watering hole" "favored by Pacific Heights' swells" and "members of City Hall", where "waiters wear white coats and serve sublime burgers"; "later in the evening", "watch out for the drunken stockbrokers", "cougars" and "aging frat boys" who "come to score more than food"; P.S. skiers can't wait to get "off the slopes" and into the "Squawllywood scene" at the Olympic Valley branch near Tahoe.

Bambuddha Lounge ⊠ Ⓜ 16 | 22 | 14 | $34
Phoenix Hotel, 601 Eddy St. (bet. Larkin & Polk Sts.), 415-885-5088; www.bambuddhalounge.com
Exuding an "exotic, über-chic tiki vibe", replete with throbbing DJ booths and "lovely poolside dining", the Tenderloin's Phoenix Hotel attracts "city hipsters", "bachelorette parties" and the occasional "music-world celebrity" who come to "nosh and dance"; the "decent" Pan-Asian small plates are "better than expected for a scene" and the "tropical drinks are great too", nevertheless, a few Zen-sters scoff that the "eye-candy" waiters seem "more concerned with partying than serving."

Baraka 21 | 19 | 19 | $41
288 Connecticut St. (18th St.), 415-255-0387; www.barakasf.net
It may be "out of the way" on Potrero Hill, but this "different, delightful" bistro "brims with the 'in' crowd" lured by the "eclectic mix of scrumptious" Southern Mediterranean tapas and more large plates than before, "lovingly delivered by gracious French-speaking servers"; the "sexy" "candlelit" dining room awash with "red walls" and "velvet banquettes" makes it a "great date place", but "claustrophobics" carp it's kinda "cramped"; N.B. a recent chef change may impact the Food score.

Bar Crudo ⊠ ▽ 25 | 18 | 19 | $35
603 Bush St. (Stockton St.), 415-956-0396; www.barcrudo.com
This "spanking fresh" Downtown oyster bar shells out "innovative crudo" and other globally inspired "raw-fish dishes in a tiny spot you could easily miss" decked out with barstools downstairs and an upstairs nook; the "sparkling seafood" is "definitely the star" – next to the "heaven-in-a-bowl" "chowder that may be ruled illegal by the Supreme Court (it's that good!)"; add in a "great selection of Belgian beers" and you've got a "cozy" "date place" – just expect escargot-paced service.

Barney's Gourmet Hamburgers

23 | 12 | 14 | $15

3344 Steiner St. (bet. Chestnut & Lombard Sts.), 415-563-0307
4138 24th St. (Castro St.), 415-282-7770
www.barneyshamburgers.com

What some consider the "best burgers in the Bay Area" come in an "infinite variety" (including veggie) at this "consistent", "family-friendly" chain that's also known for "creative" toppings, "incredible" curly fries" and "mean milkshakes" that will "leave you happily overstuffed"; a few rue the "variable service" and "greasy-spoon" decor, but the "hulking" portions and "good" prices make it a perennial "favorite."

Bar Tartine Ⓜ

23 | 20 | 20 | $38

561 Valencia St. (17th St.), 415-487-1600

Despite "no sign" ("look for a giant antler light chandelier"), it's "a mob scene" at this "friendly", "foodie-hipster" haunt that may be the "best thing to hit the Mission" since their "hugely popular" Tartine Bakery sibling opened; natch, "it's worth it for the bread alone" and "desserts are ethereal", but don't miss the "wonderful" small and large plates of "country-style" Cal-Med cuisine and the "price-conscious" pours; still, a tart-tongued few feel "service suffers due to their popularity."

Basil Thai Restaurant & Bar

22 | 17 | 18 | $25

1175 Folsom St. (bet. 7th & 8th Sts.), 415-552-8999; www.basilthai.com

Supporters of this "consistently great" Thai "treat" in SoMa tout it as a "top pick" thanks to "well-presented", "delicious" dishes, "fun drinks" and "modern, serene" digs with a "bright, airy feel" (including "cool bathrooms"); "friendly" service contributes to the "relaxed atmosphere", and best of all, it's "easy on the pocketbook."

Beach Chalet Brewery

13 | 20 | 13 | $27

1000 Great Hwy. (bet. Fulton St. & Lincoln Way), 415-386-8439;
www.beachchalet.com

Expect mostly "tourists" at this "jammed" historic "oceanfront oasis" in the Outer Sunset where the "spectacular" coastal views are like "heaven on earth" and the "interesting" WPA murals "can't be beat"; vets advise "stick to the burgers" and "tasty homemade microbrews" because the New American vittles, much like the service, are "not the worst but not the best."

Belden Taverna Ⓩ

∇ 23 | 21 | 22 | $40

28 Belden Pl. (bet. Bush & Pine Sts.), 415-986-8887

Nestled among the Italian- and Parisian-style cafes on Downtown's European alley, this "rocking" Moroccan-Med newcomer serves moderately priced, "unique", "excellent" dishes, "unusual" wines and "fab" desserts ferried by a "warm" staff; "everyone looks great in the coppery glow" of the bi-level interior, and the outdoor seating's "good for people-watching" in the "always wonderful" "Belden Place scene."

Bella Trattoria

20 | 17 | 18 | $32

3854 Geary Blvd. (3rd Ave.), 415-221-0305; www.bellatrattoria.com

"Worth a drive to the Inner Richmond", this "all-around enjoyable neighborhood" "hideaway" offers "great homestyle" Southern Italian chow including "wonderful" pastas and gnocchi at "reasonable prices" in a "cozy", "candlelit" setting; though a few bella-ache about "long waits" and "slow service", the "cute waiters with cute accents" may help compensate; N.B. no lunch served on weekends.

Betelnut Pejiu Wu

| 23 | 22 | 18 | $35 |

2030 Union St. (Buchanan St.), 415-929-8855;
www.betelnutrestaurant.com
"Still sizzling after more than a decade", this "exotic" "blast from the colonial Shanghai past" supplies a "vibrant" Pan-Asian "smorgasbord" of small plates including "amazing" signature green beans as well as "superb" cocktails to a Cow Hollow crowd of "babes" and "businessmen" ("eating is not the only sport taking place"); a few are wu-ful over "outlandish waits" and "inconsistent" service, but the "transporting" experience at "surprisingly reasonable prices" makes it "worth repeat visits."

B44

| 20 | 17 | 18 | $37 |

44 Belden Pl. (bet. Bush & Pine Sts.), 415-986-6287; www.b44sf.com
Past "the gauntlet of restaurant hawkers" and "European smoking crowds" lies this hidden "Barcelona" by way of Belden alley boîte, where the resident "Catalonia magician" whips up "wonderful, rich tapas", Spanish seafood and a broader "choice of individual paellas" than you knew was imaginable; "it's definitely not fine dining" in the contemporary "crammed", sometimes "cacophonous dining room" where service varies, but in "pleasant weather", "eating alfresco" "is always on the mark."

Big 4 ❶

| 21 | 25 | 23 | $52 |

Huntington Hotel, 1075 California St. (Taylor St.), 415-771-1140;
www.big4restaurant.com
Nob Hill's "venerable" "gem" in the Huntington Hotel evokes an "English gentlemen's club" replete with "wonderful" wood paneling, "lots of green leather" and a brace of "blue bloods" perched in the "classic" piano lounge; the "respectful", "delightful" staff makes everyone feel like the "railroad barons" referenced in the name, and the New American fare is "solidly delicious", featuring all manner of "wonderful wild game"; it may be "over-the-top expensive", but it's "worth it" to experience that old "San Francisco mystique."

Bistro Aix

| 22 | 17 | 20 | $37 |

3340 Steiner St. (bet. Chestnut & Lombard Sts.), 415-202-0100;
www.bistroaix.com
"An underrated gem in the Marina", this "always-satisfying" Cal-French offers "classic bistro fare done right" using "quality" ingredients complemented by "unique" wines at tabs tantamount to a "steal" (try the "excellent" early *oiseau*, Sunday–Thursday); service is "fast" and "friendly", and if the "cozy", "adorable" digs get a tad too "lively", there's a "charming" heated patio that makes you "feel like you've stepped into an Impressionist painting."

Bistro Boudin ✄

| 19 | 15 | 16 | $21 |

160 Jefferson St. (near Pier 43½), 415-928-1849;
www.boudinbakery.com
"Raising the bar in Fisherman's Wharf", this bakery-cum-American bistro showcases SF's legendary sourdough including "tasty" clam chowder in a bread bowl, "wholesome" sandwiches and brick-oven pizza, all at "decent" prices for an "area full of tourist traps"; "glorious views" across the Bay along with the "great" attached museum and demonstration facility help com-

pensate for sometimes "slow" service, though a few a crusty sorts say "just buy a loaf and leave."

Bistro Clovis Ⓜ   21 | 16 | 19 | $38 |
1596 Market St. (Franklin St.), 415-864-0231
Although it's "conveniently located" for a pre-performance meal before the San Francisco symphony and opera at the Civic Center, this "wonderful bistro" "makes you feel like the Eiffel Tower is just outside" thanks to the "straightforward", "delightful" French classics ("the tarte tatin is a must") and the "true accents" of the staff that "expertly" helps patrons navigate the *carte du vin* that includes "good wine samplers"; best of all, tabs are "reasonable", and it's "amazingly accessible for reservations."

Bistro 1689 Ⓢ Ⓜ   – | – | – | M |
1689 Church St. (29th St.), 415-550-8298
On what's shaping up to be Noe Valley's newest Restaurant Row, this snug Victorian storefront bistro offers an ever-changing menu of reasonably priced Cal-French fare crafted by a former Anzu chef; the attractive, golden yellow dining room, punctuated by two-toned brown banquettes and eye-catching paintings, is far more upscale than the Chinese restaurant it replaced; N.B. a $30 three-course "First-Seating Special" is offered nightly from 5:30–6:30 PM.

BIX   23 | 26 | 22 | $53 |
56 Gold St. (bet. Montgomery & Sansome Sts.), 415-433-6300;
www.bixrestaurant.com
"You can't help but feel glamorous" at this "art deco supper club" "tucked away on a century-old alley" Downtown where "SF socialites and celebrity politicians" hobnob and "impeccable" servers in "white jackets and black bow ties" "shake a mean martini tableside"; swan by the "thirtysomething" "after-work crowd" that crams the bar "at six for chicks" and settle down for "fabulous" French-American fare in the "swanky", "breathtaking two-level dining room" "punctuated by a sweeping balcony" while being serenaded by "cool jazz."

Blowfish Sushi To Die For   21 | 20 | 16 | $38 |
2170 Bryant St. (20th St.), 415-285-3848;
www.blowfishsushi.com
Like the namesake "pufferfish" it "doesn't serve", "the heart-pounding house music" and "pervy" "anime playing" on plasma screens at this Mission "rock concert hall masquerading" as a Japanese restaurant certainly "won't kill you", but whether it's "distracting or fun depends on your mood" and birth date; "senior" surveyors "wish you could get a normal roll for single digits"; nevertheless "cell-phone fingering" singles gladly shell out big clams for "experimental sushi" and "hypnotic sake cocktails"; P.S. there's a "slick sister in San Jose."

Blue Jay Cafe   18 | 13 | 12 | $19 |
919 Divisadero St. (McAllister St.), 415-447-6066
Dishing out "good" "rib-sticking Southern cuisine" and "cheap beers" in "way-cool" "diner" digs with a "fine neighborhood feel", this Western Addition "nouveau" "soul food joint has the right idea", making it a popular "hipster/hip-hop hangout" for brunch and for live jazz on Wednesday nights; while some sing the blues about "slow" "surly service that puts a damper on the experience", for most it's "worth the wait" to get in.

Blue Plate, The [symbol]   23 | 19 | 21 | $34
3218 Mission St. (29th St.), 415-282-6777; www.blueplatesf.com
"Don't let the name fool you", this "funky" Bernal boîte "is no greasy spoon" and the "fantastically executed", "great urban" "comfort-style" New "Americana food" "definitely" doesn't go for "diner prices"; "a hipster vibe prevails", and an "equally" "edgy staff complements" the "ever-changing", "quirky" cuisine that's really been "stepped up lately" according to the Blue-clued who also adore the "cute", "charming" heated garden that lets you "escape the dining din."

Bocadillos [symbol]   23 | 18 | 18 | $33
710 Montgomery St. (Washington St.), 415-982-2622; www.bocasf.com
Piperade's younger sibling, a tiny, "tantalizing tapas" joint "in the shadow of the Transamerica" draws "crowds" of Downtown types, all lured by "salty satisfaction" of the "namesake bocadillos" along with a "delicious assortment" of "intensely flavored" small dishes from chef-owner George Hirigoyen's Basque homeland; "they don't take reservations" so "tables are hard to come by", nevertheless many "love the communal feel", the "attentive staff" – and the "great selection" of "affordable", "Spain-centric and food-friendly wines."

Bodega Bistro   ∇ 22 | 10 | 17 | $21
607 Larkin St. (Eddy St.), 415-921-1218
"A cut above the typical" "bare-bones" Tenderloin joint, this "true delight" offers "bargain-bite" hunters and "yuppies" alike a choice of "real-deal" "Hanoi street food" "for a steal" (try the "phantastic pho") along with "more elegant, expensive French-influenced" Vietnamese fare; few mind the "garish" "Barney-colored walls", "heinous convention center chairs" and oft "lackadaisical service", because it's "great" to "let chef-owner Jimmy cook for you."

Bong Su Restaurant and Lounge   – | – | – | E
311 Third St. (Folsom St.), 415-536-5800; www.bongsu.com
The sweet aroma of plumeria (aka bong su) wafts through this serene SoMa upstart from Anne Le and Tammy Huynh (also of Tamarine), an upscale showcase for regional Northern, Central and Southern Vietnamese cuisine; the hostesses' sexy backless uniforms add a contemporary twist, nevertheless the atmosphere is long on ceremony, with a gong signaling the start of dinner service and shared small plates and a communal table for walk-ins fostering the Southeast Asian tradition of family-style meals; there's also a stylish 50-seat lounge.

Boulange de Cole [symbol]   24 | 16 | 15 | $15
1000 Cole St. (Parnassus St.), 415-242-2442
Boulange de Filmore
2043 Fillmore St. (bet. California & Pine Sts.), 415-928-1300
Boulange de Polk [symbol]
2310 Polk St. (Green St.), 415-345-1107
La Boulange at Columbus [symbol]
543 Columbus Ave. (Union St.), 415-399-0714
La Boulange at Union [symbol]
1909 Union St. (Laguna St.), 415-440-4450
"Francophiles" "feel as if they're at a curbside patisserie in Paris", "buttery crumbs and all", at these "always-packed",

"quaint" self-serve cafe/bakeries from the "Bay Breads empire"; providing you can "maneuver through the strollers" and "lingering hipsters", there's "nothing like latte in a bowl" and "warm, moist, buttery" almond croissants "to start your day" or the "delightful" lunchtime "treat" of a "killer" tartine; P.S. "if you're looking for a hearty meal" – or dinner – "look elsewhere."

Boulette's Larder   25 17 18 $31
The Embarcadero, 1 Ferry Bldg. (Market St.), 415-399-1155;
www.bouletteslarder.com
An "exciting" concept "for the *Barefoot Contessa*s among us", this Embarcadero emporium is both a "take-out treasure" selling "ambitious cooks'" meal kits and a "funky" cafe serving lunch and a "fantastic Sunday brunch"; "snag" a seat out on the picnic tables or at the communal table with a "terrific view" of the Bay Bridge near the open kitchen and watch the staff cook up "delicious" New American "market-fare" using the "freshest" organic ingredients; P.S. the "intimate space" can be rented for "special dinner parties."

BOULEVARD   27 25 25 $62
Audiffred Bldg., 1 Mission St. (Steuart St.), 415-543-6084;
www.boulevardrestaurant.com
"After all these years", this "boisterous", "beautiful" "belle epoque landmark" with a "classy atmosphere" set in an "enviable" Embarcadero location with "wonderful Bay views" still "mesmerizes" "visiting VIPs", "learned tourists" and "big-blowout" celebrants, delivering "all the trimmings" that more than "live up to the hype"; the "exquisite experience" of Nancy Oakes' "sublime" "down-to-earth while out-of-this-world" Cal-French "food artistry" accompanied by "unparalleled wines" "thrills" "each time", while the staff "bends over backwards" "to make you feel rich for a day", regardless of whether you're in "jeans or furs."

Brandy Ho's   21 11 17 $22
217 Columbus Ave. (bet. Broadway St. & Pacific Ave.), 415-788-7527;
www.brandyhos.com
"Incendiary" insiders insist this "excellent" Chinatown Hunan resource is "numero uno" for "fairly priced", "flavor-intensive" chow from a "menu designed for both the adventurous and the staid" (though you might want to specify mild or medium unless you have an "asbestos mouth"); the decor's "relatively void of tacky ornamentation", but regulars prefer to "sit at the bar and watch the wok folks at work."

Brazen Head, The ●∅⊟   19 19 20 $34
3166 Buchanan St. (Greenwich St.), 415-921-7600;
www.brazenheadsf.com
Even after more than 25 years, this "little piece of heaven" is still a bit of an "insider's" secret "nestled on a residential corner" in Cow Hollow with "no sign" to alert the hoi polloi; a "fantastic" staff serves "good, solid, unfashionable" American fare at "affordable" prices along with "unbelievable martinis", and the "loyal" regulars, "rendezvous"-ers and "local celebs" who "keep it busy late into the night" know it's dinner- and cash-only at this "cozy" tavern.

Brick ●   – – – M
1085 Sutter St. (Larkin St.), 415-441-4232
Exposed century-old brick walls flank this edgy new hangout on the edge of the Tenderloin that's equal parts restaurant, cocktail

lounge and art gallery; the focal point of the dining room is an exhibition kitchen that churns out a rotating roster of New American small plates, which can also be enjoyed at a copper-topped bar where bartenders pour creative cocktails.

Brindisi Cucina di Mare ⊠

| 17 | 17 | 17 | $39 |

88 Belden Pl. (Pine St.), 415-593-8000; www.brindisicucina.com

Surveyors are of two minds about this Belden Place sophomore Downtown, with some insisting the seafood-focused Italian fare is "wonderful" and others opining it's merely "ok", while service can be "genuine" and "attentive" or "spotty" and "uncaring"; all agree, however, that the "lovely" atmosphere, "delightful" outdoor dining and "decent", "well-priced" wines make it a "good place for groups."

Brother's Korean Restaurant

| 23 | 6 | 14 | $24 |

4014 Geary Blvd. (bet. 4th & 5th Aves.), 415-668-2028
4128 Geary Blvd. (bet. 5th & 6th Aves.), 415-387-7991 ●

Hawking "the best Korean in town" – just "ask anyone in line" – these twin "smoke-filled", late-night tabletop BBQ joints in the Richmond are "always packed" with expats "sitting around the hot coals stuffing themselves silly" on "excellent" Seoul food; sure, the decor's "the pits" and the staff borders on "surly", but the "spicy", "cheap" eats are "highly addictive" and worth every "dry cleaning" bill.

Buca di Beppo

| 14 | 16 | 16 | $25 |

855 Howard St. (bet. 4th & 5th Sts.), 415-543-7673;
www.bucadibeppo.com
See review in South of San Francisco Directory.

Burger Joint

| 19 | 13 | 14 | $12 |

700 Haight St. (Pierce St.), 415-864-3833
807 Valencia St. (19th St.), 415-824-3494 ⊟

Offering "top-notch" burgers made with "quality" beef from Niman Ranch, "huge" hot dogs and "awesome" milkshakes, these joints in the Lower Haight and the Mission are an "easy" choice for a "quick" meal (or a "pre-flight" patty at the SFO branch); though a few naysayers knock the "no-decor" decor and opine the noshes are "overrated" and "underwhelming", more maintain the "great prices" and "health-conscious" ingredients make it a "satisfying" alternative.

Burma Super Star

| 24 | 13 | 18 | $23 |

309 Clement St. (4th Ave.), 415-387-2147; www.burmasuperstar.com
"The waits are insane" and the quarters "cramped" at this "mom-and-pop" "hole-in-the-wall" in the Inner Richmond, but "if judged solely" on the "fantastic" "Calcutta-meets-Kowloon" by way of Bangkok eats, this Burmese "lives up" to its name; standouts on the "varied" menu include "killer" tea-leaf salad and "delicious" samosa soup, and the "pleasant" staff and "unbeatable prices" make it shine all the brighter; P.S. "pros" know to hit the "bar across street" – "they'll call your cell when your table's ready."

Butler & The Chef Cafe, The

| ∇ 18 | 17 | 15 | $19 |

155A South Park St. (bet. 2nd & 3rd Sts.), 415-896-2075;
www.oralpleasureinc.com
Considered "cute as can be" by SoMa Francophiles, this "neighborhood" bistro offers a "variety" of market-driven Parisian sta-

ples such as "yummy croissants", "rich" soups and quiches at "reasonable" prices (breakfast and lunch only); service is surprisingly "friendly", and if the "microscopic" outdoor seating area's unavailable, you can get takeout and dine in nearby South Park for a midday "escape."

butterfly embarcadero   18 | 20 | 18 | $39
Pier 33 (Bay St.), 415-864-8999; www.butterflysf.com
With its "great" location "right on the water" featuring "amazing" views and "lovely" decor, it's no wonder "locals and tourists alike" flock to this "trendy" Cal-Asian eatery and "nightclub" on the Embarcadero; however, while apt pupae praise the "upbeat atmosphere" (thanks to a "jamming DJ") and "terrific" food with "Mission ambitions", foes frown over service that's more "Fisherman's Wharf", "unbearable noise levels" and "pricey" fare, counseling "come for the cool" cocktails and then wing it "elsewhere for dinner."

Cafe Bastille   17 | 17 | 16 | $31
22 Belden Pl. (bet. Bush & Pine Sts.), 415-986-5673; www.cafebastille.com
"Another Belden Place favorite for alfresco dining", this Downtowner offers the definitive "authentic" Parisian cafe experience from the "great people-watching" and "realistic" decor to the "attitude" of the French-accented staff; while a few storm the "casual" bistro cuisine is "mediocre", more noblesse oblige sorts say if you downgrade your "high expectations" and order the "delicious" mussels and other "classics", you'll savor an "ooh-la-la" meal at a *très* "reasonable" price.

Café Claude   19 | 18 | 17 | $33
7 Claude Ln. (bet. Grant Ave. & Kearny St.), 415-392-3515;
www.cafeclaude.com
"Like you fell asleep and woke up in France", this "petite", "atmospheric", "charming bistro-in-an-alley" Downtown is a "fresh-air delight on a sunny day", offering a "soothing, intimate escape" from the "throngs of Union Square" shoppers; live weekend jazz, "unique decor", including a "zinc-topped bar, flown in from Paris", and a "simple, unpretentious" Gallic menu (from a new chef) heighten the "authentic" experience – as does the staff's "snooty airs" according to a put-off few.

Café de la Presse   16 | 18 | 14 | $33
352 Grant Ave. (bet. Bush & Sutter Sts.), 415-249-0900;
www.cafedelapresse.com
A "much-needed" 2005 "overhaul by the owners of Aqua, et al." has "turned" this popular corner "foreign-newsstand-cum-bistro" into a Downtown "destination"; "Francophiles" and "visiting Europeans" "linger over "*Le Monde*" and "just pressed" coffee and dive into "simply and generously prepared" dishes while soaking up the "French joie de vivre"; if a few feel "service seems to be flown in from abroad", the more forgiving shrug "it's new" and still "coming along."

Cafe Divine   ▽ 18 | 18 | 18 | $22
1600 Stockton St. (Union St.), 415-986-3414
For a "nice inexpensive place to snack" and "hang out" in "high-priced" North Beach, head to this "heavenly" counter-service cafe with a "beautiful" "high-ceilinged" room and "huge plate-glass windows" "overlooking Washington Square Park" ("that's

paradise"); the panini, pastas and salads are "satisfying", service is "attentive" and the live "Django Reinhardt"–inspired music (Thursdays–Sundays) adds to the "cool", "relaxing atmosphere."

Café Gratitude   20 | 16 | 18 | $21
2400 Harrison St. (20th St.), 415-824-4652
1336 Ninth Ave. (bet. Irving & Judah Sts.), 415-824-4652
www.cafegratitude.com
The "Dr. Bronner's-meets-Birkenstocks" posse "feels the love" and gives "gratitude" to this "delightfully quirky" "New Agey" trio in the Mission, Inner Sunset and Berkeley, where "tasty" nut-laden vegan and "mostly raw" dishes are "labeled" with "positive" affirmations like 'I am Happy' and served by "blissed-out" staffers; it's "worth trying even if you're not looking for a lifestyle change", still, cynics counter "despite the good karma", "I am Annoyed" by the "communal dining" and "heavy feeling of self-satisfaction in the air."

Cafe Grillades   ▽ 18 | 11 | 18 | $13
501 Hayes St. (Octavia St.), 415-553-8500; www.cafegrillades.com
See review in South of San Francisco Directory.

Cafe Jacqueline Ⓜ   26 | 19 | 20 | $47
1454 Grant Ave. (bet. Green & Union Sts.), 415-981-5565
Chef "Jacqueline herself continues to make scrumptious" "savory and sweet soufflés" at this "quaint" North Beach spot, the "ultimate" French "hideaway" for dining with an "important date"; "as the lights dim, its romantic character emerges" and you "feel like you're in France"; *oui*, "you have to wait for" the "star of the show" so "share a salad if you're impatient", but "when it finally arrives, all puffy and golden, you just want to devour it in one bite."

CAFÉ KATi Ⓜ   24 | 17 | 22 | $46
1963 Sutter St. (bet. Fillmore & Webster Sts.), 415-775-7313;
www.cafekati.com
"A surefire way to convince a visitor you know all the best little hideaways" is with a "surprisingly high-end experience" at chef/owner/pioneer Kirk Webber's "crowded", "diminutive" "neighborhood" joint near Japantown; "old favorites remain, but there's always something" "divine, architectural and inventive" on the Asian fusion menu ("at times it feels utterly wrong to destroy such works of art"), plus the "lovely staff is adept at making "great wine pairings" "without breaking the bank."

Cafe Lo Cubano   15 | 16 | 14 | $14
3401 California St. (Laurel St.), 415-831-4672; www.cafelocubano.com
"Fun" for "lunch, an informal dinner" of "not-to-be-missed pressed sandwiches" or a cuppa "real cafe con leche", this "casual" Cuban cafe has quickly become a "neighborhood favorite" in Presidio Heights; the "relaxed", "'70s living room"–like digs are conducive to "chatting with friends" or just "hanging out" and listening to Cubano music; if a handful huff about "slow service", others shrug "most patrons don't seem to be on a schedule" anyway.

Café Tiramisu Ⓢ   21 | 17 | 19 | $38
28 Belden Pl. (bet. Bush & Pine Sts.), 415-421-7044;
www.cafetiramisu.com
"Of all the cafes lining" Downtown's "charming" Belden Place, this "busy, bustling" Italian is at the "top of the food chain" proffering "melt-in-your-mouth pasta" and "superb seafood" to a

"festive crowd"; while the "hot-blooded servers" work "miracles" inside the "cramped setting" where "everyone's sitting on each other's laps", it's still preferable to "eat outside and feel like you are in Europe"; P.S. "corny name" aside, the "tiramisu is actually good!"

Caffe Delle Stelle | 16 | 14 | 17 | $30 |
395 Hayes St. (Gough St.), 415-252-1110
This Hayes Valley haunt may "not be the best Italian in the city", but its "workmanlike" chow "works well for a quick, tasty" "pre-theater" "bite" "without losing lotsa lira", which is why "there's always a line out the door" before curtain time; inside, the "kitschy" "white Christmas lights" and pitchers of "sparkling water" served "gratis" set a "festive" stage for the true "stars" of the show: the "flirtatious", "handsome European waiters."

Caffe Macaroni ⊠⊅ | 21 | 14 | 20 | $27 |
59 Columbus Ave. (Jackson St.), 415-956-9737;
www.caffemacaroni.com
By far the "friendliest place in over-touristy North Beach", this "zany" trattoria – complete with "singing waiters" and "dried macaroni glued to the ceiling" – is "pasta-and-vino central" for noodlers craving "slightly irreverent and flirty overtures" with their fettuccine; while the doll-size dining room is "hideously cramped", the "earthy", "old-school" Neapolitan chow is "always better than I remember", and "when the owner is around, dinner is a riot."

Caffè Museo | 18 | 14 | 11 | $20 |
San Francisco Museum of Modern Art, 151 Third St. (bet. Howard & Mission Sts.), 415-357-4500; www.caffemuseo.com
"If only the art were this tasty" quip culture-vultures who "add fuel to the body to view more exhibits in this multilevel museum" at SFMOMA's "cheery" cafe serving "surprisingly good" Italian-Med paninis, pizzas and pastries; true, it's "more of a cafeteria", but you'll find a "variety of items to please everyone", plus sidewalk seating that offers prime Yerba Buena "people-watching"; N.B. open past 6 PM on Thursdays only.

California Street Delicatessen & Café | ∇ 18 | 11 | 15 | $22 |
Jewish Community Ctr., 3200 California St. (Presidio Ave.), 415-922-3354
"Oy!" – "finally a great NY deli in SF" kvell the "chosen people" and "goyim" alike and "what better place than the Presidio's Jewish Community Center" (the "casual" half since "splitting [shuttered] Sydney's into two restaurants"); "it's a mitzvah" to nosh on bubbe-inspired "comfort food" kicked up a notch by consulting chef Joyce Goldstein; if early reports suggest service is a "bit all over the place", the faithful feel it "has promise."

Campton Place | 26 | 25 | 26 | $75 |
Campton Place Hotel, 340 Stockton St. (bet. Post & Sutter Sts.), 415-955-5555; www.camptonplace.com
"Through all its iterations" (including a recent change of ownership and the early 2006 debut of ex-Navio chef Peter Rudolph's and a New American–Med menu), this "posh", "low-decibel" Downtowner remains a "perennial favorite" thanks to a "serene" yet "swish" room and "royal service"; you can't help but feel "pampered" while "nibbling on all the little extras" and musing over the "marvelous wine list" – this is "truly the place to camp" for "special occasions" or "between Neiman's and Saks stops – but that's where you have to shop to afford the place."

Canteen   25 | 14 | 20 | $42
Commodore Hotel, 817 Sutter St. (Jones St.), 415-928-8870
Chef-owner Dennis Leary's 20-seat "sleeper sensation" in the Commodore Hotel is "a silk purse if I ever saw one" marvel those lucky to gain entry to the "quirky", retrofitted "1950s diner" where he prepares a "short, always changing" roster of "clever" Californian cuisine that "matches many multi-stars" "without the pretension"; "there's "minimal" decor and "no lingering over dinner", but acolytes love that "the whole operation takes on the aspect of a magic show."

CARNELIAN ROOM   15 | 26 | 19 | $57
Bank of America Ctr., 555 California St., 52nd fl. (bet. Kearny & Montgomery Sts.), 415-433-7500; www.carnelianroom.com
"Out-of-town guests are thrilled" with the "million-dollar" "panoramic views" of Downtown and the Bay at this "formal", "jaw-dropping" aerie perched on top of the Bank of America building; "bring your camera" because "you can't beat the view", but alas, "you can't eat the view", and despite a recent remodeling and "menu retooling", the Traditional American fare and "old-school waiters" still don't warrant the sky-high prices – little wonder insiders suggest "drinks at sunset" instead.

Catch   17 | 19 | 17 | $35
2362 Market St. (bet. Castro & 16th Sts.), 415-431-5000; www.catchsf.com
A "neighborhood favorite with a boy tickling the keys, boys 'bout the fire pit enclave and pretty boys tending to the tables" with "just enough 'tude", this Castro seafooder "provides amazing people-watching" on the front patio at "arguably one of the most colorful" SF intersections along with "tasty vittles"; but disappointed anglers carp "sometimes it's better to 'release' than to 'catch'", citing "uninspired" fare and a staff that "can't be bothered."

Cav Wine Bar ⬧   21 | 21 | 22 | $34
1666 Market St. (bet. Franklin & Gough Sts.), 415-437-1770; www.cavwinebar.com
Whether you "know nothin' 'bout drinking wine" or consider yourself an "oenophile", this newly uncorked, "trendy", "industrial-chic" Hayes Valley "nook" makes vino "approachable" thanks to the "knowledgeable", "unpretentious" staff that helps you navigate the "unbelievably" "vast list" of some 300 "well-priced" selections, including 40 by the pour; "pair your marvelous" choice with an "excellent cheese plate", "delightful" Mediterranean small and large plates and "equally beguiling desserts" just right for "nibbles pre-symphony" or a late-night dinner.

Cha Am Thai   20 | 14 | 16 | $19
Museum Parc, 701 Folsom St. (3rd St.), 415-546-9711; www.chaamthaisf.com
"When you want to reminisce about your last trip to Koh Samui" or simply need a place to "kill the craving for some pad Thai", these "long-standing" Siamese brothers in SoMa near the Yerba Buena and Berkeley offer "reliably good", "cheap and plentiful" plates in a "bustling atmosphere"; however, the less-cha-rmed are "underwhelmed" by the "dated, uninspired" decor and cuisine, concurring "there are better offerings in town."

Cha Cha Cha
20 | 17 | 15 | $24

1801 Haight St. (Shrader St.), 415-386-5758
2327 Mission St. (bet. 19th & 20th Sts.), 415-648-0504
www.cha3.com

"Perhaps it's just the sangria talking", but cheerleaders for this SRO "raucous" Pan-Latin "kitsch" couple that's been "serving tapas since before it became 'in'" chorus "rah-rah-rah" over the "party" atmosphere at the "hippie-ish", "voodoo-y feeling" Haight original and the more "yuppie" "Caribbean Zone–meets-*Cheers*" Mission outpost; the not-so-small plates are "cheap", in fact, they're "good enuf" to make the "absurdly long waits" and "spotty service" "tolerable."

CHAPEAU! Ⓜ
26 | 18 | 26 | $46

1408 Clement St. (15th Ave.), 415-750-9787

"Tip your hat and say 'wow'" advise amis disarmed by this "over-crowded little slice of Paris" in the Inner Richmond serving "superb" French bistro classics "at a fraction" of what you'd expect (the "prix fixe is a screaming deal") with "flair and joie de vivre"; "consummate host" "Philippe Gardelle is everywhere" – "seating diners", "carving tableside", "pouring wine", "doing the cooking", even "kissing the ladies" "adieu" "upon leaving" and in general, "making each meal memorable."

Charanga Ⓢ Ⓜ
23 | 18 | 21 | $26

2351 Mission St. (bet. 19th & 20th Sts.), 415-282-1813;
www.charangasf.com

"Skip the long lines" of "noisy and crowded neighbors" in "The Mish" and head to this "unsung hero of tapas joints in the city", a modest yet "lively room" that doesn't require "dressing up" with a "truly friendly" staff; "go with a group and try everything" on the "flavorful, inventive" Pan-Latin–Caribbean menu, including "small plate favorites" like "memorable seviche" and "exquisite yuca", with "fantisimo" sangria to boot.

Chaya Brasserie
21 | 22 | 20 | $49

132 The Embarcadero (bet. Howard & Mission Sts.), 415-777-8688;
www.thechaya.com

Like its LA siblings, this "busy looker on the Embarcadero" with a "crisp, friendly" staff "pulls off serving" "pristine sushi" and New French fare "on the same menu", bested by a "dazzling setting" overlooking the Bay Bridge; "take a group and you'll still be able to please everyone" attests the business lunch bunch who also head here for "luscious drinks" during happy hour; still, a few chide the chow's "not transcendent" and a "bit overpriced."

CHEESECAKE FACTORY, THE
16 | 16 | 15 | $26

Macy's, 251 Geary Blvd., 8th fl. (bet. Powell & Stockton Sts.),
415-391-4444; www.thecheesecakefactory.com

"Hordes" of "tourists" and "hungry shoppers" "wait an eternity" to sit, then "spend hours poring over the menu the size of a Dickens novel" at this "noisy", "gawdy" chainster where you can get "predictable" American renditions of "anything your heart desires" in portions so "enormous" that "you can't fit in the famous" namesake "indulgence"; sure, "if you've seen one, you've seen them all", but even cynics suggest the "view can't be beat" at the Macy's outpost Downtown; N.B. there are branches in Santa Clara and San Jose.

Chenery Park   23 | 19 | 22 | $38

683 Chenery St. (Diamond St.), 415-337-8537; www.chenerypark.com

"Trying to put Glen Park (where?) on the map", this "charming" "neighborhood gathering place" delivers "delicious down-home" New American eats "with an elegant flair" and Cal-leaning wines in "simple", art-filled "multistoried" digs with "free, easy dining"; "Tuesday is family night", drawing parents "desperate for something more than a burger with their kids", but "every night is family-friendly" thanks to a "cheerful" staff that makes everyone feel "cordially welcomed."

Chez Maman   20 | 15 | 17 | $25

803 Cortland Ave. (Ellsworth St.), 415-824-2674
1453 18th St. (bet. Connecticut & Missouri Sts.), 415-824-7166
2223 Union St. (bet. Filmore & Steiner Sts.), 415-771-7171
www.chezmamansf.com

"Test your high school French" at these "teeny, tiny cafes" prof-fering Chez Papa "bistro fare without the fuss" and "one of the finest burgers to be had" – "if you can get a seat", because at the "petite" Potrero perch and slightly bigger Bernal and Cow Hollow sibs, there's just a "counter with a coupla tables" and "one ex-tremely harried French" server; still, "you have to love a place that's open from" late-morning "coffee through nightcaps."

Chez Nous   23 | 16 | 19 | $34

1911 Fillmore St. (bet. Bush & Pine Sts.), 415-441-8044;
www.baybread.com

"Nothing touches" Pacific Heights' "cozy", "convivial" Med "treat" that "never fails to impress out-of-towners with its San Francisco simplicity and perfectly done neighborhood feel", despite its "luncheonette atmosphere"; the "delectable small plates" offer a "wonderland" of "exciting" tastes – even for such a "tapas-crazed city" – while the "hip" staff is "fast, friendly" and "knowledgeable regarding wine"; if tables are a tad "close for comfort", it's "worth all the elbow bumping when those little" morsels "hit your table!"

Chez Papa Bistrot   24 | 17 | 20 | $41

1401 18th St. (Missouri St.), 415-255-0387; www.chezpapasf.com

"The one that started it all", leading to the Hill's "explosion as a foodie destination", this "convivial" Potrero bistro, much "like its wife", Chez Maman, "transports you" to France "on a foggy San Franciscan night"; the "upscale" classics and "exceptionally well-selected wines" are *très* "authentic", while the "chic staff" chatting in its "native tongue", "cozy (tight) quarters" and "funny outdoor tables on the slanting sidewalk" complete the "homey" Gallic picture; N.B. a recent chef change may impact the Food score – and steer the menu toward Provence.

Chez Spencer ⊠   25 | 22 | 22 | $50

82 14th St. (bet. Folsom & Harrison Sts.), 415-864-2191

"Hidden behind a gate" on a "desolate block", this "wonderful" Mission "find" makes you feel like you've "walked through the closet into *Narnia*", and landed "in a different, inviting world" concur chroniclers; descend into the "delightful garden" patio or the "hip-as-hell" former garage interior "crawling with charac-ters" and "splurge without puting on a tux" on "remarkable", "rustic" wood-fired French dishes delivered by an "attentive" staff; N.B. a sibling called La Terrace is slated to open fall 2006.

Chloe's Cafe ⊟

22 | 12 | 16 | $15

1399 Church St. (26th St.), 415-648-4116

"Lines out the door" "so long it hurts" at this "sunny corner cafe" are a "testament to the lengths Noe Valley-ites will go to avoid cooking breakfast at home"; if "by divine intervention you score" a seat, "you won't be disappointed" by the "scrumptious", "down-home" Traditional American morning fare including French toast and egg scrambles; as for service, "you'd be in a bad mood too if hordes of people were demanding a table" in a room "the size of my bedroom."

Chou Chou Patisserie
Artisanale & French Bistro

21 | 17 | 22 | $33

400 Dewey St. (Woodside Ave.), 415-242-0960; www.chouchousf.com

Forest Hills foodies flock to this "cozy, intimate" "Francophonic gem" (pronounced shoo shoo) with "gracious" accented waiters and a "genuine" Gallic vibe "evocative of a 1960s Parisienne diner", for a "lovely" weekend brunch or "authentic" country-style stews and "divine" savory pot pies that "take your mind off the lack of space"; *bien sûr,* the "sinful" signature fruit tarts are "the stars here and worth the trip" to this "sleepy neighborhood."

CHOW/PARK CHOW

20 | 15 | 18 | $22

215 Church St. (bet. 15th & Market Sts.), 415-552-2469
1240 Ninth Ave. (bet. Irving & Lincoln Sts.), 415-665-9912

"When you don't feel like cooking" or "paying big bucks", follow the lead of everyone from "picky eight-year-olds to vegetarians" and head to this "very San Francisco–funky" New American outfit in the Castro and Inner Sunset with a "lively neighborhood feel" and "spot-on service"; the "diverse menu pleases all palates", making it the "go-to" "chow house" for "satisfying" comfort food, while the terrace makes for "delicious people-watching"; N.B. there's a branch in Lafayette too.

Circolo Ⓢ

18 | 22 | 16 | $39

500 Florida St. (Mariposa St.), 415-553-8560; www.circolosf.com

"Am I in the '80s in LA?" wonder surveyors who head round to this "modern, hip", "hard-to-find Mission supper club"; it's copasetic in the lounge, where twentysomethings down "good cocktails" and "surprisingly tasty" Nuevo-Latino–Asian "snacks"; but the social circle is divided about the "museumlike" dining room, with a handful "blown away" by the "creative food offerings" and others put off by "fusion-confusion" fare and "rushed" servers eager to clear for "the nightclub hours to follow."

Citizen Cake/Cupcake

21 | 17 | 17 | $31

399 Grove St. (Gough St.), 415-861-2228;
www.citizencake.com Ⓜ
Virgin Megastore, 2 Stockton St., 3rd fl. (Market St.), 415-399-1565;
www.citizencupcake.com

"Cake-queen" Elizabeth Falkner offers more than "killer desserts near the Civic Center" – culture vultures also head to her "hip", "hectic" Hayes Valley haven for "terrific cocktails" and "modern", "fresh-from-the-market" Californian fare; "sweets"-seekers insist that's just the "icing" – "save room" for the "baked goods bliss" and "architectural dessert masterpieces" – or just "buy from the bakery" 'cause service can be "slow"; P.S. the Union Square "cupcake outpost" also offers "satisfying panini" and salads.

Citizen Thai and The Monkey

20 | 20 | 18 | $31

1268 Grant Ave. (Vallejo St.), 415-364-0008; www.citizenthai.com
This North Beach Monkey business is actually two restaurants under one "fun" thatched roof; upstanding Citizens are treated to a "cool environment" and "finely presented", "high-end" Thai small plates in the downstairs white-tablecloth venue, while "the happy bar crowd" "use their outside voices for conversation" in the "exotic-looking" Monkey noodle bar, which ladles up street food cafeteria-style, till 1 AM on Fridays and Saturdays.

Citrus Club

20 | 13 | 15 | $16

1790 Haight St. (Shrader St.), 415-387-6366
"If you don't mind the wait, the flickering lights" and the blaring "techno", join the club at this Pan-Asian noodle bar on Haight dishing up "soup to cure whatever ails you" "served in a bowl larger than my head" and "oodles of noodle dishes" "for almost nothing"; it "may not be the best in the city", but it's one of the "best for the price" with "great date atmosphere" to boot.

Clémentine ☒

24 | 21 | 22 | $41

126 Clement St. (bet. 2nd & 3rd Aves.), 415-387-0408
"A real find" hidden in the primarily Asian *arrondissement* of the Inner Richmond, this bang for your franc debunks the "cliché" that a Gallic bistro must be "too close for comfort" or full of "attitude" to be "authentic"; *mais oui*, the "French-speaking staff is surprisingly friendly", the "satisfying" "old classics" (like "heavenly escargot") offer "great value", plus "you can actually "carry on a conversation in the dark, romantic" candlelit dining room.

Cliff House Bistro

16 | 23 | 17 | $37

1090 Point Lobos Ave. (Geary St.), 415-386-3330; www.cliffhouse.com
This Cliff hanger at the Outer Richmond's Point Lobos is "loved" by locals "for its historical significance" and tourists for its "amazing panoramic" Pacific seascape, offering "a rare opportunity" to "get your eggs" and "popovers and watch the seals" and "crashing surf" in the bistro or take in "wonderful sunsets" from Sutro's "gorgeous", glassed-in, two-story dining room; still, even after the "beautiful" $18 million renovation, most agree the "view is more delicious" than the "mediocre" Californian fare.

Coco 500 ☒

24 | 20 | 21 | $43

500 Brannan St. (4th St.), 415-543-2222; www.coco500.com
"Queen of comfort food" "Loretta Keller outdoes herself" at her "edgier" Inner Richmond "reincarnation of Bizou", where a "darling" staff serves a Cal-Med menu of "tempting" mix-and-match small and large plates in a "chic" room rollicking with a "happening" cocktail-swilling crowd; "come get your greens" – fried green beans, that is, and other "old-time faves" like "not-be-missed beef cheeks", plus newfangled "delights", all best "shared with friends"; still, some sound off that "500 is for the decibel" reading.

Coi Ⓜ

27 | 25 | 25 | $108

373 Broadway (Montgomery St.), 415-393-9000; www.coirestaurant.com
"Daniel Patterson has done it again" – his "elegant", "intimate" nine-table newcomer Downtown is a "wonderful successor to fabulous Elisabeth Daniel" declare loyalists who laud the "wonderful" wine choices, "pampering service" and "sensational" four- ($75) and nine-course ($105) Californian-French tasting

menus; the "extremely fresh", organic ingredients deliver an "intense" "rush of flavors around every turn" – little wonder why it's a "big hit", even with "jaded San Franciscan foodies"; P.S. the adjoining "little lounge" serves a more rustic, affordable à la carte menu until midnight.

Colibrí Mexican Bistro   23 | 20 | 20 | $34

438 Geary St. (bet. Mason & Taylor Sts.), 415-440-2737;
www.colibrimexicanbistro.com
"Holy guacamole!" – it's "excellent and made tableside" marvel munchers who descend on this "chichi" "Mexico City"–style small plateria and late-night bar in a deserted stretch of Downtown for "upscale Mexican" food served in a "festive, grown-up atmosphere"; sample "interesting", "great mole" dishes, "get tipsy" on "top-shelf margaritas" (the bartenders "really know their south-of-the-border spirits"), "then sit back, watch the magic unfold" and congratulate yourself on a "smash pre-theater" choice.

Cortez   24 | 22 | 21 | $49

Adagio Hotel, 550 Geary St. (Taylor St.), 415-292-6360;
www.cortezrestaurant.com
The "founding chefs" departed, still this "swanky" Downtowner decked out like a "Miró in 3-D" with a "buzzing" bar is "hitting its groove"; "start with soup shooters" in shot glasses, then "awaken your taste buds" with "excellent" Med small plates – "each morsel has a personality of its own", all served by an "informed" staff; while it's easy to run "the check into the stratosphere", few mind since it's "one of the best options" in the theater district.

Cosmopolitan, The ⑤   22 | 21 | 20 | $44

Rincon Ctr., 121 Spear St. (bet. Howard & Mission Sts.), 415-543-4001;
www.thecosmopolitancafe.com
"A happening place, with lots of life" and a "smart" "New York feel", this SoMa spot "can't be beat" for "after-work appies", "must-have martinis" and, natch, "pretty good Cosmos too"; the finance group concurs it's also a "great place to entertain a client Downtown" – the New American offerings are "surprisingly good for a happy-hour place" – plus, service is "professional" and wine bottles are 50 percent off with an entree on Thursdays.

Côté Sud ⑤   22 | 18 | 19 | $36

4238 18th St. (Diamond St.), 415-255-6565; www.cotesudsf.com
For a "bit of Provence" in the Castro, Francophiles set sail for this "funky walk-up" Victorian house that "satisfies" bistro "cravings" with "sumptuous" country classics (like "brilliant cassoulet") and an "interesting wine list" offering choices from the "Languedoc region"; sure, the "unbeatable $25 prix fixe is the draw", but the "pleasant covered deck and gracious host" also make it a "favorite" place to "return to again and again for a cozy evening."

Couleur Café   ▽ 15 | 16 | 20 | $26

300 DeHaro St. (16th St.), 415-255-1021; www.couleurcafesf.com
From the folks behind Gallic stalwarts Chez Papa and La Suite comes this colorful cafe set in a Quonset hut–like building at the bottom of Potrero Hill; unlike its more formal sibs, this "unpretentious" outpost offers "reasonably priced" French fare, plus soccer and cinema screenings to keep Francophiles entertained; but despite an "exceedingly accommodating" staff, "erratic execution" suggests the kitchen is "still getting the kinks out."

Crave
| – | – | – | I |

2367 Market St. (17th St.), 415-865-0192

Tasty bites before or after a night in the Castro is the conceit behind this new restaurant and lounge serving clever yet affordable New American small plates till 2 AM Friday–Sunday; however, the bi-level boîte, with low-slung tables, a DJ booth and a downstairs bar tricked out with an LED light system that transforms the room's colors, is a destination in its own right.

Crustacean
| 24 | 18 | 20 | $49 |

1475 Polk St. (California St.), 415-776-2722; www.anfamily.com

"Don't wait for crustacean season to enjoy the delicious" Vietnamese "crab feasts" and "addictive" "garlic noodles from this secret kitchen" at lower Nob Hill's "mini-mall" offshoot of Thanh Long; the decor that once "sent you into a Hong Kong–1970s time warp" has been "brightened up", but the "perky" servers, "dress code" and "hilarious plastic bibs" remain so "roll up your sleeves" because those "succulent critters" are "messy as hell."

Deep Sushi Ⓢ
| 22 | 18 | 13 | $36 |

1740 Church St. (bet. 29th & 30th Sts.), 415-970-3337; www.deepsushi-sf.com

With its "too cool for school" vibe, "hippest sushi chefs around", a "stylish", "innovative" Japanese menu, a sake list that "requires multiple trips" to "explore" and no visible sign outside, this "trendy" techno-blaring, Tobiko-sized dining room helped put Noe Valley on the MUNI map; but while the thirtysomething local crowd might be "drunk enough" to "not notice the ditzy service", others feel flat out "ignored" and fume this "spendy" spot is "too damn loud."

Delancey Street Ⓜ
| 17 | 15 | 21 | $28 |

600 The Embarcadero (Brannan St.), 415-512-5179

For "comfort food and the comfort of knowing that you are supporting a life-changing" nonprofit substance abuse recovery organization, diners do right "by society and their stomach" at this "commendable" Embarcadero commissary, with "wonderful" waterside views and proximity to AT&T Park; however, while the "street"-smart staff "tries very hard", the "bargain" Eclectic fare, with nightly ethnic specials, isn't as "inspired as the cause."

DELFINA
| 26 | 19 | 22 | $44 |

3621 18th St. (bet. Dolores & Guerrero Sts.), 415-552-4055; www.delfinasf.com

There's "good-reason" why "celebs" and "San Franciscans fight to get into this tiny", "filled-to-the-rafters", "buzzing" Mission trattoria – namely "incredibly flavorful", "superb", "rustic" Tuscan fare that "surpasses expectations" "served by hot hipster chicks" "with just the right touch of anarchy" and "polish"; "you're pretty much stuck with a 6:30 PM reservation or walk-in luck unless you plan weeks in advance", but there's always the bar, plus the "new pizza cafe attached to the restaurant is also amazing!"

Destino
| 20 | 19 | 19 | $32 |

1815 Market St. (bet. Guerrero & Valencia Sts.), 415-552-4451; www.destinosf.com

A "plain facade" belies the "festive fun" that awaits at this "vibrant" bistro on the Castro's edge; the "unique blend of South and Central American flavors" with an emphasis on Peruvian dishes and the "unusual" pisco sours are "always an adventure for the palate" while the "*alfajores* cookies are worth making a pact with the devil" for; but while canoodlers commend the "cozy, seductive" quarters, quibblers kvetch it's too "cramped."

de Young Cafe Ⓜ   15 | 17 | 10 | $19

Golden Gate Park, de Young Museum, 50 Hagiwara Tea Garden Dr. (bet. John F. Kennedy & Martin Luther King Jr. Drs.), 415-750-2614; www.deyoungmuseum.org

A "surprising" addition to Golden Gate Park declare culture-seekers who "de-light in the new de Young" museum cafe, a "welcome respite" from the "trendy architectural masterpiece" with "lovely" tables overlooking the sculpture garden and "fresh" Californian fare made with "local" artisanal ingredients; still, detractors declare that the "criss-cross pattern to place orders" "must have been designed by a Surrealist" – it feels "like being in a Jackson Pollack"; N.B. open till 8:45 PM Fridays only.

Dosa Ⓜ   21 | 18 | 18 | $25

995 Valencia St. (21st St.), 415-642-3672; www.dosasf.com

"It's about time we got South Indian in the Mission" agree admirers of this "super-friendly" yet "hip" newcomer; the saffron-colored room is dominated by a large bar where you can latch onto a "great lychee" cocktail – and, of course, you'll "need a fix" of "delicate dosas", "delicious uttapam", "excellent vegetarian" options and "curries that taste just like home" to "trendy" expats; P.S. expect "lines out the door" "since they don't accept reservations."

Dottie's True Blue Cafe   25 | 12 | 18 | $17

522 Jones St. (bet. Geary & O'Farrell Sts.), 415-885-2767

Even if this "tiny" "down-home cafe" in the Tenderloin "doubled the size", the "long queues" past the "panhandlers" would still bend "round the corner" as "early-risers", biz travelers and other "devoted customers" are just dotty over the "terrific" American breakfast, brunch and home-baked goods served till 3 PM closing; "once inside", expect "sit-as-long-as-you-like service" and "huge portions" that require "a day of walking to work off."

Dragon Well   21 | 15 | 18 | $23

2142 Chestnut St. (bet. Pierce & Steiner Sts.), 415-474-6888; www.dragonwell.com

For "slightly Californianized Chinese on Chestnut", this "feel-good" Marina Sino "gets the job done", luring "families early evening and dates later on" with "fresh, light" "spins" on the "classics" that "won't bog you down" at "can't-be-beat" prices; the "decor is basic, but the warm lighting" and "quick service" make the "bustling atmosphere feel cozy" – no wonder Dragon ladies and gents deem it a "dependable neighborhood stop."

E&O Trading Company   19 | 21 | 17 | $34

314 Sutter St. (bet. Grant Ave. & Stockton St.), 415-693-0303; www.eotrading.com

"Trader Vic's for the office set", this "noisy", "kitschy" "faux exotic" Downtown "watering hole" with San Jose and Larkspur branches delivers "all the sensory treats of Southeast Asia" from "an all-over"-the-map collection of "innovative" small plates "exploding with flavor" – "the only thing missing is the humidity"; "don't miss the corn fritters", and now that it's no longer a microbrewery, "don't forget to indulge in tropical drinks" that "make happy hour happy."

E'Angelo M ⌿

20 | 11 | 19 | $27

2234 Chestnut St. (bet. Pierce & Scott Sts.), 415-567-6164

Although this "no-frills" Marina "time warp" resembles "an Italian from the Sputnik era" ("paper menus and checkered tablecloths"), "cheapo" dates and "quick meal"–seekers insist it's "what a neighborhood" joint "ought to be"; "Soup Nazi–style" waiters shuttle plates of "tasty" homemade pasta, "old-school" veal dishes and "house wine in drinking glasses" – "they know what's good for you, so don't plan on leaving until your plate is clean."

Ebisu

24 | 14 | 18 | $32

1283 Ninth Ave. (Irving St.), 415-566-1770; www.ebisusushi.com

"Only sushi snobs who need to keep finding new places pass" on this "popular" Inner Sunset Japanese where finatics endure "super-long lines" "by buying a Sapporo and chatting" with others in the "cold fog" before joining the "madhouse inside"; for a "satisfying" experience, "you gotta sit at the bar", indulge in "imaginative rolls" and "top-flight" sashimi "as fresh as a fishing ship's" and tell your "boisterous" "chef to keep going."

Eguna Basque ⌿

∇ 12 | 17 | 18 | $30

1657 Powell St. (bet. Green & Union Sts.), 415-362-2141;
www.ilunabasque.com

Twentysomething hipsters who haven't stayed up too late at chef Mattin Noblia's late-night joint, Iluna Basque, next door can be found milling at his petite companion North Beach cafe fiddling with WiFi and filling up on French bistro breakfast and lunch fare including croissants, crocque monsieurs, salads and café au laits; an artistic setting with orange-and-pink-painted walls and chalkboard menus completes the Euro picture; N.B. no dinner served.

El Balazo

19 | 14 | 13 | $12

1654 Haight St. (Clayton St.), 415-864-2140

When you can't get to the Mission, bound over to this Haight-Ashbury Mexican taqueria promising "get-it-your-way" "gut-buster" burritos in "inventive combos" ("shrimp, seafood, nopales, carnitas, it's all on the menu") with "appropriate for the nabe" '60s-inspired names; sure, the kaleidoscope "paint job is looking a bit tired" and it's "slightly pricey", but few mind when faced with such "tasty" "treats", aqua frescas and a "nice selection of salsa."

Elite Cafe

19 | 19 | 19 | $42

2049 Fillmore St. (bet. California & Pine Sts.), 415-346-8668;
www.theelitecafe.com

"Welcome to the neighborhood" declare denizens who wheel their wagons round to this "beautifully remodeled" Upper Filmore standby reborn with a "delightful" Cajun-Creole menu under new owners (ex The Meetinghouse); sure, the "comfortable" booths and "happening bar" are "packed tighter than an andouille sausage", but the "boffo" buttermilk "biscuits better than most places south of the Mason-Dixon line" make it "real easy to stay" a spell; P.S. the "spicy brunch" remains the panacea for "hangovers."

Eliza's

22 | 16 | 15 | $23

2877 California St. (bet. Broderick & Divisadero Sts.), 415-621-4819
1457 18th St. (bet. Connecticut & Missouri Sts.), 415-648-9999

A decade-plus after "inventing the craze for tasty Asian food that's good for you", this "upscale", "arty" duo in Pac Heights and on

Potrero Hill is "still going strong"; the "cheap" eats, "beautifully presented" amid a "modern" "blown-glass decor", are "the antithesis of Chinatown", while "in contrast, the harried staff" that "literally rushes your plates away" as you're eating "your last forkful" "gives new meaning to fast food" – and motivation for takeout.

Ella's   22 | 14 | 18 | $21

500 Presidio Ave. (California St.), 415-441-5669;
www.ellassanfrancisco.com

"Yuppies", "stroller" moms and "churchgoers" "still line up around the block" for the "heavenly breakfast" and "fantastic brunch" at this "super-friendly" Traditional American "favorite" in Presidio Heights, now under new ownership; admirers "rave" that the "mile-high biscuits" and "stupendous pancakes" "can't be beat" – it's "worth the wait on the weekends"; still, a handful huff it can be "expensive" – are the "eggs made of gold"?

El Metate   ▽ 23 | 13 | 18 | $8

2406 Bryant St. (22nd St.), 415-641-7209

Although this "charmingly cramped", "middle-of-nowhere" Mission Mexican is a "hole-in-the-wall", it's still "littered with hipsters" – and the owner "treats it like a five-star restaurant", serving "delicious", "fresh-grilled vegetable burritos" and fish tacos that "blow the competition out of the water"; "even during a big rush", the staff is "super-friendly", but a dearth of seats inside and out prompts patrons to "take it to go."

El Raigon ⊠   24 | 20 | 20 | $44

510 Union St. (Grant Ave.), 415-291-0927; www.elraigon.com

"As close to Buenos Aires as most gringos will ever get" in North Beach, this "inviting" Argentinean "red-meat temple" "covered in hides and gaucho memorabilia" "breaks the stuffy steakhouse mold"; gallop over for "massive" Montana beef "prepared to perfection" estancia-style over charcoal and wood with "exceptional" South American sides and a "winner" of a wine list; still, a few carp about "topsy-turvy service" – "let's hope it improves."

Emmy's Spaghetti Shack   19 | 15 | 16 | $24

18 Virginia Ave. (Mission St.), 415-206-2086

Bernal's "sceney" "down-home" Italian house of carbs, replete with an "intimate insider feel", "resident weekend DJs" and "kitschy aprons hanging from the ceiling", "attracts a young punk-indie" "late-night" crowd "willing to shout" over "cheap, addictive spaghetti" and meatballs while knocking back "40 ouncers alongside fine wines"; however, no reservations can mean "long waits" while service from the "tattooed" "ranges from pleasant to 'does she know we're sitting here?'"; N.B. now takes credit cards.

Emporio Rulli   21 | 22 | 14 | $20

2300 Chestnut St. (Scott St.), 415-923-6464
Stockton Street Pavilion, 225 Stockton St. (Post St.), 415-433-1122
www.rulli.com
See review in North of San Francisco Directory.

Enrico's Sidewalk Café   19 | 20 | 17 | $36

504 Broadway (Kearny St.), 415-982-6223;
www.enricossidewalkcafe.com

The Beat goes on at this "historic", "lively" sidewalk cafe that remains "the best scene in North Beach for star-spotting", "great live jazz" nightly and "bangin' mojitos"; "if you can tear your eyes away" from "all that's happening" on Broadway, you'll notice that the "alfresco patio" with heat lamps and "lovely main room" have "enough charm to fill a small European country", plus the Cal-Med morsels are "better than you'd expect."

Eos Restaurant & Wine Bar | 24 | 19 | 20 | $41 |

901 Cole St. (Carl St.), 415-566-3063; www.eossf.com

It may "not be the revelation" it was "during its dot-com heyday", but this "hip", "unassuming" Cole Valley "find" remains the "standard-bearer of superb" Cal-Asian fusion fare, delivering "delectable small plates" brimming with "flavors that resonate" and "unusually interesting" flights of vino; "relax" in the "urban-chic" dining room or "excellent" bar and let the "well-educated" staff help you wine and dine "your way through the evening"; P.S. "parking is tough" so "take a taxi."

Eric's | 21 | 13 | 17 | $20 |

1500 Church St. (27th St.), 415-282-0919

"Don't be fooled by the Caucasian name" – this "popular Noe Valley" Victorian storefront is home to "fresh", "extremely flavorful" Chinese; while purists pout the chow is "not as good as a trip to Chinatown" or "Clement Street", most "can't live without" the "interesting" combos – but they can live without the "get-them-in-and-out" service; P.S. "boo-hoo, no delivery – but to-go is great."

Esperpento | 20 | 15 | 15 | $26 |

3295 22nd St. (Valencia St.), 415-282-8867

A "pioneer" of the tapas craze, this "loud, terrific Spanish" "favorite" remains a "madhouse on weekends" overrun by "mariachis" and "large parties" of Missionites who come for the "great, garlicky" shared plates and "flowing sangria"; it's truly a "hot" spot, "especially upstairs", which can be "a bit of a sweat-box", but all is "forgiven" – even when the staff "disappears into thin air" – "because it's a very cheap", "very fun" "night out."

Espetus Churrascaria | 22 | 15 | 21 | $43 |

1686 Market St. (Gough St.), 415-552-8792; www.espetus.com

Carnivores happily submit to "death by meat" at Hayes Valley's Rio-diculous all-you-can-eat Brazilian churrascaria where "cute waiters in gaucho attire parade around" "nonstop" "with skewers of every kind of grilled" protein "for your approval and ingestion"; it's "pricey", but it's a "pig-out par excellence", so eat till "your button pops off your pants" – but leave room for the "interesting drinks", "perfect desserts" and the *madre* of "delicious salad bars" – the only bone offered to vegetarians.

FARALLON | 25 | 27 | 24 | $60 |

450 Post St. (bet. Mason & Powell Sts.), 415-956-6969;
www.farallonrestaurant.com

"They should hand out snorkels at the door" quip *agua*-nuts who get in the swim of this "underwater grotto", an "over-the-top" Downtown "wonderland" that feels like a "surreal" "aquarium"; the "jaw-dropping decor", replete with "fantastic lights shaped like deep sea creatures and floors with ocean mosaics" – "exquisite" seafood so "fresh" it would impress "Captain Nemo" and "pampering" service make it a "feast for the palate and the eyes", and especially "cool for clients and out-of-towners" who'll "brag about the experience for months."

farmerbrown

– | – | – | M

25 Mason St. (Turk St.), 415-409-3276; www.farmerbrownsf.com
Soul food gets a Californian spin at this Tenderloin rookie sourcing local, organic produce from Bay Area African-American farmers; the rough-hewn room is dominated by a long bar where hipsters can find Southern comfort with mint juleps and down-home classics like fried chicken and pulled pork; N.B. it's now open for dinner only, though breakfast, lunch and Sunday jazz brunch are in the works.

1550 Hyde Café & Wine Bar Ⓜ

23 | 17 | 22 | $42

1550 Hyde St. (Pacific Ave.), 415-775-1550; www.1550hyde.com
"Sit elbow to elbow with the locals as the cable cars clang by outside" this "unpretentious" Russian Hill bistro that uncorks "lovingly prepared", seasonal organic Cal-Med cuisine and an "outstanding wine list" ("not a bad one in the bunch"), navigated by "attentive" servers; gripers grouch that the industrial modern decor is "somewhat austere" (feels "colder than a SF summer") and find quarters "cramped", but supporters adore the "intimate dining" experience.

Fifth Floor Ⓩ

25 | 25 | 24 | $83

Hotel Palomar, 12 Fourth St. (Market St.), 415-348-1555;
www.fifthfloorrestaurant.com
"Dazzled" diners "would climb to the 50th floor" of SoMa's Hotel Palomar for the "heavenly" Cal–New French gastronomy, now created by chef Melissa Perello, at this "impressive, innovative, expensive" experience; "relax" in a "tiger-striped" "interior that makes you feel sexier", and "spoil" yourself with a "mind-bending wine list" and "impeccable", "seamless service"; sure, prices seem "weighted toward millionaires", but "if it was good enough for Julia Child's 90th birthday", "it's good enough for me"; N.B. renovation plans underway for late 2006.

Fior d'Italia

18 | 19 | 20 | $41

San Remo Hotel, 2237 Mason St. (Chestnut St.), 415-986-1886;
www.fior.com
"Is it my imagination or is the food even better since they moved after the fire?" ponder patrons of "America's oldest Italian restaurant", who maintain that the new "romantic setting" in North Beach's San Remo Hotel has "injected" more life into this "reliable" standby; the "stepped-up staff" "falls over themselves to be helpful" while the "solid fare" "withstands time" – it's a "classic" "worth rediscovering"; still, the less-impressed tut it's for "tourists" – and "overpriced" to boot.

Firecracker Ⓜ

22 | 18 | 19 | $26

1007½ Valencia St. (21st St.), 415-642-3470
"Pow!" – this "inventive", "healthy bent" Cal-Chinese boîte in the "heart of the funky Mission" crackles as a "fantastic date restaurant" thanks to a kitchen that "kicks it up a notch" with "just the right amount of spice and flavor" and "moody", "fiery red decor" that's "warm and hip"; sure, the "Westernized" chow isn't the "most authentic", but it's "solid enough and open late enough to be helpful" to famished fans.

Firefly

24 | 20 | 22 | $40

4288 24th St. (Douglass St.), 415-821-7652; www.fireflyrestaurant.com
A "prototype of what a neighborhood restaurant should be", Noe Valley's long-running culinary light is the "perfect place to feel

comfortable and impress a date" exclaim loyalists lured by the "fantastically friendly staff", "super-romantic", "relaxed vibe"and "playful, tantilizing" "Eclectic down-home fare" and "fine wine list"; "cooked with love and sophistication", the seasonally changing offerings "please vegetarians and carnivores alike", while the "dumplings better than the dimples on Shirley Temple" are "worth crossing town for."

FLEUR DE LYS ⌀

27 | 26 | 25 | $88

777 Sutter St. (bet. Jones & Taylor Sts.), 415-673-7779;
www.fleurdelyssf.com
For a "fairy-tale" evening, don "party clothes, sashay into this dreamy" Nob Hill "shrine" to "nouvelle cuisine" and "cocoon yourself" in the "opulent", *Arabian Nights*–like" setting with "ambiance out the wazoo"; "eat like a queen" on Hubert Keller's "beyond artistic", "rich" Cal-French prix fixe menus (including a "great vegetarian" option) – "every course, every bite, is truly divine" – as are the "phenomenal wines".– all "flawlessly presented" by a "fantastic" staff that adds to the "exquisite experience"; P.S. "crack open that extra piggy bank – this one will cost you"; N.B. jacket required.

Florio

20 | 19 | 20 | $39

1915 Fillmore St. (bet. Bush & Pine Sts.), 415-775-4300; www.floriosf.com
"Paris or Milan – take your pick" from the "Fra-talian" offerings at Pac Heights' "cramped", "cozy neighborhood bistro", the "perfect" perch on a "foggy night" for a "fun" date or dinner with friends; service is "remarkably speedy yet gracious" while the "reasonably priced" fare "never tries to push the envelope" – in fact, "forget looking at the menu, just order the steak frites" – it will have you "raving in French."

Fog City Diner

19 | 19 | 19 | $33

1300 Battery St. (The Embarcadero), 415-982-2000; www.fogcitydiner.com
"Click your heels because you're not in Dorothy country" at this "famous", "posh" "retro" roadhouse on the Embarcadero that's definitely a "diner, but oh, what a diner"; diehards declare "blow your horn" for the "consistently tasty" New American "favorites" as well as the "froufrou" small plates, but cynics shrug little has changed since its "heyday" in the "old VISA commercials", scoffing it's "more for the tourists."

Foreign Cinema

22 | 24 | 20 | $44

2534 Mission St. (bet. 21st & 22nd Sts.), 415-648-7600;
www.foreigncinema.com
"After all these years", this "funky" "dot-com refugee" in the Mission "still deserves an Oscar" for its "magic combo" of dinner and a movie, with "personable service" presenting "refined" Cal-Med meals "amongst the stars"; the "stunning outdoor courtyard replete with heat lamps and a foreign film playing on a huge wall" – as well as the "somewhat industrial", "cool Fellini-esque interior" – set the "scene" for a "perfect date" or a "fab" brunch with "mom"; but critics snipe that the "decor surpasses" the "snooty" staff.

(415) Asian Restaurant and Lounge

∇ 21 | 23 | 17 | $42

Jewish Community Ctr., 415 Presidio Ave. (Sacramento St.),
415-409-0400; www.restaurant415.com
"Finally, some sophistication in Patagonia Heights" quip customers of this "slinky" Pan-Asian newcomer in the Jewish Community

Center that's "thriving" in the hands of the Garibaldis and California Street Delicatessen owners; exec chef John Beardsley of "previous incarnation Sydney's" and sushi chef Akira Yoshizuma "draw the beautiful crowd" with "surprisingly good" kosher rolls and "unique" dishes best "shared"; if a few find "service enthusiastic but sparse", the more sanguine say it's still "finding its way."

Fournou's Ovens
20 | 21 | 21 | $56

Renaissance Stanford Ct., 905 California St. (Powell St.), 415-989-1910; www.fournousovens.com

Tucked away in the Renaissance Stanford Court, this "old-world" Nob Hill venue remains a "sentimental favorite" for loyalists "who can't resist the warmth of those ovens", the "solid" Cal-Med fare, "pleasant classical piano in the background" and "cozy" charm of dining directly in the exhaustive "wine cellar"; but skeptics are luke-warm about the "predictable, unremarkable" fare, "crusty" service and "tired" vibe, sighing it "feels like what it is: a hotel dining room."

Frascati
26 | 20 | 24 | $44

1901 Hyde St. (Green St.), 415-928-1406; www.frascatisf.com

This "unpretentious" and "well-kept secret" "tucked away in Russian Hill" is a "cute little locals' eatery" where it's advised to "come hungry" for the "always changing menu" of "hearty and full-flavored" Cal-Italian dishes and the "inventive dolci" like the famous bread pudding; fans say the "charm factor is high", due in part to the "gracious" and "personal service" and the fact you can (and should) "grab the cable car line to the front door"; N.B. a post-*Survey* owner change may outdate the overall score.

Fresca
23 | 18 | 18 | $32

2114 Fillmore St. (California St.), 415-447-2668
3945 24th St. (bet. Noe & Sanchez Sts.), 415-695-0549
24 W. Portal Ave. (Ulloa St.), 415-759-8087
www.frescasf.com

"Word of mouth has been getting louder and louder" – much like the "lively" crowds after downing pisco sours at this "festive" Nuevo Peruvian trio also known for "seriously good", "generations-old recipe for roast chicken" and "divine" "open-air seviche bars"; but while the "warm" rooms "cast in the glow of golden deities" are "inviting", even the Incan-inclined reveal that the "long waits" and "inconsistent service" need "improvement" to justify "high" prices.

Fringale
25 | 17 | 22 | $46

570 Fourth St. (bet. Brannan & Bryant Sts.), 415-543-0573; www.fringalerestaurant.com

With chef Thierry Clement and a new owner at the reins, "SF's best non-luxe" Gallic bistro "charmer" has "achieved a comfort-able groove", "bringing a bit of France" with a "gourmet Basque" accent to SoMa, complete with "elbow-to-elbow" seating in "tight quarters"; the "authentic, satisfying" fare is "not showy or chic or even inventive, but earthily delightful" and "done to per-fection", while the "wine list is focused yet solid" – *mais oui,* um, *sí,* it's "definitely a keeper."

Frisson
19 | 25 | 19 | $52

244 Jackson St. (bet. Battery & Front Sts.), 415-956-3004; www.frissonsf.com

Downtown's "swanky" "celeb hangout" looks like "*Sex and the City* dining at first glance", with "twentysomethings" in their "best threads" mingling in the "happening bar" and lingering over "imaginative" New American morsels in the "circular dining room" that feels like the "coolest conversation pit ever"; but while the "disco" vibe moves "foodie-dance types", a baffled bunch "left hungry" blurt "holy small food for a lot of money, Batman" – "skip" it and "stay for drinks."

Frjtz Fries   18 | 14 | 12 | $14
579 Hayes St. (Laguna St.), 415-864-7654; www.frjtzfries.com
"Funky" and "cool", "just like the Hayes Valley", this "cramped" "DJ/arthouse/teahouse" pumps out "cheap" Belgian eats and "hip" beats – best "enjoyed in a window seat" or the "secret back garden"; the "shtick" is "frjckkin good fries frjed to perfectjon" with "unusual" sauces "washed down with great ales", but there are also "creative crêpes" and "salads to balance out" the menu; the only downer is that "the staff pretty much are dips too."

GARDEN COURT   19 | 29 | 20 | $53
Palace Hotel, 2 New Montgomery St. (Market St.), 415-546-5010; www.gardencourt-restaurant.com
"Step back in time" and "dine in Eden" on "elegant" Cal fare in the "grand style of yesteryear" at this "fancy" ballroom, ranked No. 1 for Decor in this *Survey*, a "must-see" former carriage entrance to the historic Palace Hotel boasting a "lovely stained-glass" dome and chandeliers so "spectacular", you'll "look up the whole time"; it's a "splurge treat" for "ladies who lunch", weekend brunch or a "mother/daughter tea" – the "guiltiest pleasure ever", with a "polished staff and silver cake stands" – though a less-courtly few feel the food's "overshadowed" by the "luxe surroundings."

Garibaldis   23 | 21 | 20 | $42
347 Presidio Ave. (bet. Clay & Sacramento Sts.), 415-563-8841
"Mingle with locals", a "hip, older crowd" and "nouveau comfort-seekers" over "impressive" Cal-Med fare and "outstanding drinks" at this "elegant, non-trendy" "Presidio Heights pacesetter" – or head to the "livelier" "Rockridge favorite" for a "merry old time"; "it's the kind of place" you go to feel "special for a birthday" – or to "perk up your spirits with a midweek meal" (if they ever eliminate "lamb from the menu, we'll go into serious withdrawal").

GARY DANKO   29 | 26 | 28 | $100
800 N. Point St. (Hyde St.), 415-749-2060; www.garydanko.com
Gary Danko is "still the king of this town" swoon "blissful" "gastronomes and oenophiles" who once again crown this "elegant" "super-nova" No. 1 in this *Survey* for Food, Service and Popularity; "catch a cable car" to Fisherman's Wharf for a "hedonistic evening of pleasure" that begins with "delightful, delicious, delovely", "flexible" New American prix fixe menus and culminates with a "cheese cart that's an event in itself"; the "smooth, unpretentious", "telepathic staff" is never "more that an arm's length away" (ditto your "dressed-to-kill" neighbors at "surrounding tables") offering "insightful wine suggestions" – wow, "it's as good as it gets."

Gaylord India   18 | 16 | 16 | $33
The Embarcadero, 1 Ferry Bldg. (Market St.), 415-397-7775; www.gaylords1.com
This trio of separately owned "white-linen-tablecloth Indian" "favorites" in SF's Embarcadero, Menlo Park and overlooking the

Bay in Sausalito continues to attract "business suits", serving a traditional lunch buffet that "shines" in "slightly showier" surroundings than "your average" curry shack; but disenchanted diners decry the "big stage, tiny performance", citing dishes that "lack fire" and "tired" digs, though a planned renovation at the South of SF branch may rev things up.

Giordano Bros.

▽ 23 | 16 | 21 | $14

303 Columbus Ave. (Broadway St.), 415-397-2767
"If you like the Steelers" or you're just "having a hometown craving", this "cool" "neighborhood stop" in North Beach "will fix you" up with "affordable", "Pittsburgh-style" "all-in-one sandwiches" like the cheese steak with coleslaw and "fries between the bun"; "ultrafriendly owners" and "great music" make it a "perfect hangout", so "kick back", "swill some beer" and "grab a very tasty" "cheap meal or a late-night snack."

Giorgio's Pizzeria

21 | 10 | 17 | $17

151 Clement St. (3rd Ave.), 415-668-1266; www.giorgiospizza.com
Inner Richmond's "charming" "old-school pizza parlor" is "one of the few truly family-friendly restaurants" around where "East Coast transplants, students" and "three-year-olds" "live in harmony" "bonding over" "tasty" Italian dishes and "thin-crust" pies under a trellis of "plastic grapes"; "go for a sit-down" dinner with "lots of kids" in tow and the "cute young waitresses" will ply them with "play dough"; P.S. "Wednesday is 'make your own' night" – every tot "in the city is there!"

Globe ◑

21 | 17 | 19 | $42

290 Pacific Ave. (bet. Battery & Front Sts.), 415-391-4132;
www.globesf.com
"Back in the swing – and swinging" until the "wee hours", this "posh" Downtowner with "unpretentious" service roundly "hits its stride" as a "sexy" "late-night and local chef hangout"; but "young professionals" confide that the "hearty" Cal-Ital eats "stand on their own any time of day", be it for a "great business lunch" ("as long as it isn't sooo loud") or for the affordable "farmer's market–inspired" prix fixe on Sunday nights; N.B. a post-*Survey* renovation may impact the Decor score.

Goat Hill Pizza

18 | 9 | 15 | $16

300 Connecticut St. (18th St.), 415-641-1440
715 Harrison St. (3rd St.), 415-974-1303
www.goathillpizza.com
More than a "local joint" to pie-people, this "legend" with "old-school red-checkered tablecloths" on Potrero Hill, beloved for its "beautiful views of Downtown" (and its takeout-only SoMa sidekick), is almost a "neighborhood tradition", turning out pizzas with a "memorable sourdough crust that frustrates the will of no-carb dieters"; fanatics flock "to shove" "endless variations and endless slices" "in their face" for the "all-you-can-eat Monday nights" but advise "stay away if you hate crowds."

Godzila Sushi

21 | 10 | 14 | $24

1800 Divisadero St. (Bush St.), 415-931-1773
Although this "cafeteria-style" Japanese joint in Pac Heights has "the atmosphere of a corner deli", the "friendly chefs" whip up plenty of "cheap" "delicious sushi"; it's "our dining table away from home" roar hordes of "hungry college kids" who "line up" for

"monstrously good" spicy tuna rolls "hotter than the breath" of its "namesake" creature; still, a few feel "you can find better."

Goood Frikin' Chicken　　　20 | 9 | 14 | $15
10 29th St. (Mission St.), 415-970-2428; www.gfcsf.com
"Watch out, Colonel Sanders" "cluck" birdwatchers of this "friendly" "barnyard find" in the Outer Mission hawking "rotisserie chickens brimming with herbs" that are "even more FLG", along with "pretty frikin'" "delicious" Middle Eastern schwarma and side dishes; the "festive, new dining room" "with murals of the Mediterranean" is a "comfortable" roost to enjoy the "avian delights", nevertheless, these "garlicky" goodies are "great" for takeout too; N.B. the Decor score may not reflect the recent refurb.

Grand Cafe　　　20 | 25 | 20 | $44
Hotel Monaco, 501 Geary St. (Taylor St.), 415-292-0101;
www.grandcafe-sf.com
"Step back into *la belle époque*" at this "dramatic dining room" with 30-ft. ceilings and "whimsical sculptures" that feels like a "grand re-creation" of a "festive" Parisian bistro tucked next door to Downtown's "glorious" Hotel Monaco; the "lively bar scene", "lovely" Cal-French fare and "well-informed staff" "make it perfect for pre-theater" dining – but it's "charming on its own"; still, a handful wish the "food and service could soar as high as the decor."

Grandeho's Kamekyo　　　23 | 14 | 21 | $32
943 Cole St. (bet. Carl St. & Parnassus Ave.), 415-759-8428
2721 Hyde St. (bet. Beach & North Point Sts.), 415-673-6828
"You can't go wrong" at this "friendly" Japanese duo offering a "surprising amount of choice" agree afishionadoes; the "sweet staff" "makes you feel like you're in your own living room", serving up the "fattest cuts" of fish and "creative rolls" with "unique" touches; the Cole Valley location is "a neighborhood safe haven" while the second "satisfies the sushi desire on the Wharf."

Great Eastern ◗　　　22 | 13 | 15 | $26
649 Jackson St. (bet. Grant Ave. & Kearny St.), 415-986-2500
A "top pick in Chinatown", this "reliable find" lures loyalists "over and over again" with a "variety of consistently good", "authentic" dim sum and some of "the finest Chinese seafood around"; while the waiters can be "a bit grumpy" and the "simple surroundings" seem "overdue for a face-lift", this Sino standby has "been there forever, so it must be doing something right."

Green Chile Kitchen & Market Ⓜ　　　▽ 20 | 19 | 22 | $15
601 Baker St. (Fulton St.), 415-614-9411; www.greenchilekitchen.com
Fast food meets the Slow Food movement at this "friendly" "welcome addition" to the Western Addition serving up "tasty turns" on the namesake "New Mexican green chile" like burritos and stews with "just enough spice" and "very good" rotisserie chickens; savor the regional American flavors with wine, Mexican beer and premium sodas in the "bustling" dining room or phone in for a take-out order and have it delivered curbside.

Greens　　　23 | 22 | 21 | $40
Bldg. A, Fort Mason Ctr. (Buchanan St.), 415-771-6222;
www.greensrestaurant.com
"The grandmother of organic vegetarian restaurants" is "still going strong" – where else can vegans and "confirmed carnivores"

"graze" "off each others' plates" while "gazing" at "fabulous bridge" and Marina views?; although the "enchanted forest" "warehouse" decor ("complete with tree in the middle") "shrieks 1978", the "knockout veggies" and "stunning wines" reveal what "heights" "alfalfa sprouts" served by "attentive" "hippies" "can rise to", particularly on "amazing prix fixe Saturday nights"; P.S. "you can't beat" the Greens to Go counter for lunch.

Hamano Sushi   21 | 12 | 16 | $31

1332 Castro St. (24th St.), 415-826-0825; www.hamanosushi.com

Judging from the "yuppies elbowing you to get to the hostess first", this "popular" Noe Valley Japanese is "still a big fish in the sushi pond"; never mind the "dated decor" – the "plump" slabs of sashimi and "delectable cooked food" are "incredibly fresh", plus there are plenty of "interesting combinations for the adventurous"; but the less fin-atic feel that following a "change of ownership" it's "not what it used to be."

Hard Rock Cafe   12 | 20 | 14 | $26

Pier 39, Bldg. Q1 (Beach St.), 415-956-2013; www.hardrock.com

"Let's face it" – you don't come to this "fun", "noisy" Fisherman's Wharf chainster for "an intimate, candlelit dinner" – you "go with the kids" to "check out the mementos of your favorite band and enjoy the music" and who knows, you may even "groove to" the American food too; but disbelievers paint it as a strictly "mediocre" "tourist attraction", scoffing "buy a T-shirt, eat somewhere else."

Harris'   24 | 21 | 22 | $55

2100 Van Ness Ave. (Pacific Ave.), 415-673-1888;
www.harrisrestaurant.com

With its "old boys' club" vibe, "rich leather seats", "tight jazz ensembles" on weekends and "well-executed menu" of "top-notch" dry-aged beef ("no froufrou dishes here"), Russian Hill's "carnivore haven" transports "you back in time" to the 1960s"; the "exceptional" steak and "surprisingly good accompaniments" "satisfy a craving, at a pretty penny" while the "super service" means your "water glass will never run dry" – though most prefer to drink "wonderful cocktails" like "martinis in little buckets."

Hawthorne Lane   24 | 24 | 22 | $57

22 Hawthorne St. (bet. Folsom & Howard Sts.), 415-777-9779;
www.hawthornelane.com

"Remains a keeper" confide lovers of the Lane who "curl up with their flames" at this "hidden SoMa gem" set in former San Francisco Newspaper Company headquarters; the "creative, original" Californian "culinary delights" made with the "freshest local produce" boast "Asian touches that enhance the palate's experience" while the "cozy" yet "cosmopolitan" environs and "staff that's just the right balance of laid-back, competent and devil-may-care" makes you "feel like you've stepped into a more elegant world."

Hayes Street Grill   22 | 17 | 22 | $44

320 Hayes St. (bet. Franklin & Gough Sts.), 415-863-5545;
www.hayesstreetgrill.com

"Paradise for pescatarians", food writer Patricia Unterman's "bustling", "retro clubby"–feeling Hayes Valley seafood grill still retains its "commanding lead among symphony- and opera-goers" thanks to a "swift", "professional staff" that "has pre-performance dining down to art"; "out of the ocean and onto the plate", the daily "catch are served up simply and beautifully" with some of the "best crunchy friends in town" and a "wine list that'll have you singing because of your supper, not for it."

Helmand, The

| 24 | 15 | 20 | $31 |

430 Broadway (bet. Kearny & Montgomery Sts.), 415-362-0641
A "friendly" "oasis" of "shabby genteel" "elegance" among North Beach's "gauntlet of strip clubs", this "reasonably priced" "white-tablecloth" Kabul eatery (owned by President of Afghanistan Hamid Karzai's brother) "leads you through a path of culinary discovery", offering up the "exotic delights" of the Helmand region; it's "pumpkin paradise" for vegetarians – and a "tasty" "change of pace" for all – and if you finish with "Turkish coffee you'll be ready to party all night."

Henry's Hunan ⊠

| 21 | 7 | 14 | $17 |

1016 Bryant St. (bet. 8th & 9th Sts.), 415-861-5808
110 Natoma St. (2nd St.), 415-546-4999
674 Sacramento St. (bet. Kearny & Montgomery Sts.), 415-788-2234
Hunan
924 Sansome St. (Broadway St.), 415-956-7727
"Simply the standard for Hunan cuisine", this 30-year-old chainlet of "divey", "bare-bones" "Chinese greasy spoons" keeps the "wok spirit" alive, "churning out" "voluminous portions" of "stick-to-your-ribs" "fiery fare" at such "lightning speed" they seem to "serve you before you order"; but it's not only a "Downtown lunch tradition" for "Financial District foodies" – heat-seekers insist it's also "perfect" for a "quick" "spicy" "dinner before a show."

Herbivore

| 16 | 13 | 15 | $18 |

531 Divisadero St. (bet. Fell & Hayes Sts.), 415-885-7133
983 Valencia St. (21st St.), 415-826-5657
www.herbivore-restaurant.com
Though "paradise for the veg" folk, this vegan duo in the Western Addition and the Mission "holds its own" as a "reliable stop" for "mixed company" of "carnivores and herbivores", delivering an "eclectic variety" of "comfort food" in a "laid-back atmosphere"; but cynics balk that the "menu is more impressive" than the "uninspiring" eats "on the plate" – "you might like it if you were a cow."

Hog Island Oyster Co. & Bar

| 25 | 17 | 19 | $31 |

The Embarcadero, 1 Ferry Bldg. (Market St.), 415-391-7117;
www.hogislandoysters.com
"So slurping good" – and "so fresh they snap back at you" – "nothing beats" the "dizzying array" of "delectable morsels" at this "lively" "lunchtime favorite" at the Ferry Building Marketplace, an Embarcadero "must-do" that's especially "great if you snag an outdoor seat"; "belly up to the counter" to experience the "casual fishmongers" vibe and "watch the oysters get shucked", order a "wine that actually matches" the "slippery delights" and enter bivalve "heaven."

Home

| 19 | 15 | 19 | $27 |

2100 Market St. (Church St.), 415-503-0333
2032 Union St. (bet. Buchanan & Webster Sts.), 415-931-5006
www.home-sf.com
"Satisfying", "hearty" Traditional American "grub" made with "mom's cooking in mind" – if "mom was a self-styled gourmet" –

lures nostalgists to these "super-friendly", "funky all-purpose feeding stations" "snazzed up with lots of eye candy"; loyalists insist it's "like eating at home" with "lots of locals nesting" at the slightly "cruisy" "Castro institution" with a "cozy back patio" and its "cheery" Union Street sibling, nevertheless, housebreakers huff it's "much ado about a very ordinary scene."

Hotei
20 | 15 | 18 | $19

1290 Ninth Ave. (Irving St.), 415-753-6045; www.hoteisf.com
"When the fog is swirling around the Sunset district", make a pilgrimage to "Ebisu's more chill twin" and hunker down over "Japanese comfort food" and "delightful soups" brimming with "fat, filling" "noodles so big, you could have a tug-of-war with them" – "without the lines of its sister restaurant"; "sweet servers" oversee the "teeny, little restaurant" that also serves up specialties like "big bad tempura" that "helps prevent a budget blowout."

House
26 | 16 | 21 | $38

1230 Grant Ave. (bet. Columbus Ave. & Vallejo St.), 415-986-8612;
www.thehse.com
"Still rocks my palate" – "wish I could live at this House" sigh nesters who make this "funky and original" North Beach boîte their "go-to" place for "uniformly creative, beautifully presented" American-Asian fusion fare not "found elsewhere"; "every bite is worth savoring" – the "melt-in-your-mouth" "exquisite fish dishes", particularly the "sea bass, beckons me back" "for many a homecoming" – while the "friendly, unobtrusive service" helps "make up for the cramped, nondescript quarters"; P.S. "make sure you have a reservation!"

House of Nanking
21 | 5 | 12 | $19

919 Kearny St. (bet. Columbus Ave. & Jackson St.), 415-421-1429
"Always a line, always worth the wait!" chants the "cult following" that queues up at this "bare-bones Chinatown" Chinese "favorite"; never mind the "cramped", "spartan digs" and the "somber" waiters who "treat everyone like a tourist" – just go along with the "eat-what-I-think-you-should-eat" "attitude" and "let them order for you" – in the end, "it'll take more time to park than to be served"; still, disbelievers wonder "what's the fuss about?"

House of Prime Rib
23 | 18 | 21 | $43

1906 Van Ness Ave. (Washington St.), 415-885-4605
"Bikers, businessmen and grandmas in Chanel" all satisfy "hankerings for a hunk o' beef" and "big martinis at a great price" at this "blast from the past" Russian Hill "stronghold"; "you have to like prime rib because there's little else" on the "pricelessly minimalist menu", but luckily, the slabs, sliced on "lovely carving carts", are "outlandishly good", and it comes with "one of the best salads and Yorkshire pudding this side of the pond"; if a few sigh "ho-hum" for most, this "one-trick-pony really prances."

Hukilau
18 | 13 | 15 | $18

5 Masonic Ave. (bet. Anza St. & Geary Blvd.), 415-921-6242;
www.dahukilau.com
"Bring your flowered shirt" and "rub elbows" with the "UCSF student crowd" that sucks down "memorable" "Mai Tais and pretends to be in the islands" at this "laid-back", "tiki"-inspired Hawaiian serving "ono standards" in the Inner Richmond, including a "dirt-cheap" "traditional plate lunch"; while "slow service" and long

waits on weekends may "make you lose your Aloha spirit", the live music and "Spam musubi will get you hanging loose in no time."

Hunan Home's Restaurant 22 | 10 | 17 | $22
622 Jackson St. (bet. Grant Ave. & Kearny St.), 415-982-2844
The decor may be "tired", even "cheesy", but Hu cares – "no Chinese restaurant worth its soy sauce would bother with such frivolities" anyway agree admirers of this "bustling" "Chinatown star"; with "fast service" and "delicious" dishes including "hot, hot, hot" "Hunan/Northern specialties" and "Taiwanese dim sum on weekends", "I'd eat outside standing up" quip patrons; P.S. the more upscale outpost in Los Altos is a "wonderful departure from the surrounding area."

Hyde Street Bistro 21 | 17 | 20 | $40
1521 Hyde St. (bet. Jackson St. & Pacific Ave.), 415-292-4415
"Charming and reliable", this "petite" "Hyden" "gem" on Russian Hill "packs a lot of punch", offering "neighborhood" regulars a "truly satisfying bistro experience", complete with a "Frenchy atmosphere and staff"; get "ready to rub elbows (literally) with the person next to you" – the "cramped" quarters make you feel like you're eating "dinner in your aunt's living room" – as does the "homey" fare; nevertheless it's "worth the walk – don't even attempt to park."

IL FORNAIO 19 | 20 | 18 | $36
Levi's Plaza, 1265 Battery St. (bet. Greenwich & Union Sts.),
415-986-0100; www.ilfornaio.com
Like "the Maytag of Italian restaurants", "you can always count on" this "reliable" bakery chain for "surprisingly tasty" "power breakfasts" and "family-friendly" meals served in an "open, airy", "festive atmosphere" that "transports you" to Tuscany, even if you're "in a mall" locale; the "homemade bread alone is worth the dough" while "enticing" "regional, monthly specialties" "keep me coming back"; but detractors toss it off as "basic" "cookie-cutter" fare with "no surprises."

Iluna Basque 20 | 19 | 17 | $35
701 Union St. (Powell St.), 415-402-0011;
www.ilunabasque.com
"Hang out, drink and munch" on Basque tapas at this "chic", "colorful spot" advise aficionados who leave the North Beach "chaos" behind at this "haven"; "we never get tired" of the "hot chef's" "refreshingly different take on the small plates craze" and "wonderful Spanish wines" – it's a "fun place to go" "time and time again"; still, a few deem it the "Antonio Banderas" of nibbles, offering "more style than substance."

Imperial Tea Court   – | – | – | I
The Embarcadero, 1 Ferry Bldg. (Market St.), 415-544-9830;
www.imperialtea.com
Shoppers seeking a serene daytime escape from the Ferry Building hustle-bustle duck into this small salon, an offshoot of Chinatown's famed tea importer, done up Asian-style with red lanterns, bird cages and straight-backed chairs; sip a world-class cuppa with traditional cookies and seeds or savor organic Northern Chinese lunch fare including soup dumplings, dim sum platters and noodles; N.B. Berkeley Teahouse, the Epicurious Gardens' branch, usually stays open until 9 PM.

Incanto
24 | 21 | 22 | $43

1550 Church St. (Duncan St.), 415-641-4500; www.incanto.biz
"Don't let the simple", "cozy decor" or remote Noe Valley address "fool you", this "offal-ly delicious", "upscale" Northern Italian with "personable service" rises "heads and shoulders over more highly touted" "Downtown destinations" declare "adventurous" eaters and "co-revelers" who steer over for "one of the most stimulating menus" around; "foodies" go hog wild, declaring the "robust, rustic, regional" specialties "sublime", the "diaphanous" pastas and "charcouterie a must" and the "Boot-oriented vino" selection "unbeatable"; still, a few feel it's a "bit over the top."

Indian Oven
23 | 16 | 18 | $27

233 Fillmore St. (bet. Haight & Waller Sts.), 415-626-1628
"Parking is a nightmare" and the "long lines" "can be daunting", nevertheless, this "warm, welcoming" Indian "favorite" "continues to be the bright spot in the Lower Haight"; "your mouth waters as you wait for sizzling dishes to land on your table" confide insiders who crow that the "tasty", "delicious" offerings are a "step above", if not the "best" around; but it fails to catch fire for a few disappointed by the "dialed-down spiciness factor."

Indigo Ⓜ
21 | 19 | 22 | $43

687 McAllister St. (Gough St.), 415-673-9353; www.indigorestaurant.com
Choose the "pre-arts dinner" at this "calm" blue boîte and you'll be "in and out for the opera, ballet or symphony" at the Civic Center – but join the "regular Joes" post-curtain for the "even better" "wine tasting paired menu" boasting all the "impressively well-selected" vinos "you can drink" and you're inked in for a "leisurely", "wonderful" New American meal; still, aficionados insist it's the "delightful" staff that "keeps pace with every demand" that makes this crowd-pleaser "worth a stop."

In-N-Out Burger ◑
22 | 9 | 17 | $8

333 Jefferson St. (bet. Jones & Leavenworth Sts.), 800-786-1000; www.in-n-out.com
Additional locations throughout SF area
For the "crème de la crème of burgers" that "Wimpy would die for" served up "fresh, fast and even wrapped 'specially for eating in the car" head to the "impossibly friendly" "joint that puts other chains to shame"; follow "regulars who know all about the secret menu" and customize your "double-double animal style" into a "3x3" with a "sack of fries to go"; yep, it's "busier than a one-armed wallpaper hanger", but it's an "addictive" "pleasure reserved for us Left Coasters."

Isa ⌧
25 | 19 | 20 | $43

3324 Steiner St. (bet. Chestnut & Lombard Sts.), 415-567-9588; www.isarestaurant.com
"Outrageously flavorful", "scrumptious French-inspired tapas" and a "friendly", "partylike atmosphere" make this "lively spot" in the Marina a "large success among small-plate salons"; "take friends willing to share" and "sample lots" of "marvelous" morsels on the "more romantic" "enchanting patio" with "twinkly" "white lights" and heat lamps – it's a "culinary adventure" with "each visit surpassing the last"; but while foodies rejoice in this "caliber" of cuisine, bean-counters carp Isa "mammoth prices for midget portions."

Isobune
17 | 13 | 15 | $25

Kintetsu Mall, 1737 Post St. (bet. Laguna & Webster Sts.), 415-563-1030
"If your kids enjoy sushi", "your ship has arrived" assert admirers who set sail for this "fun, friendly", "festive" "conveyer belt sushi" Japantown joint offering "quick and affordable" fin fare; "don't expect much in decor" as all eyes are on "those little wooden boats floating past" in the "circular water trough" allowing you to "grab" "what looks inviting"; but not everyone's onboard – a handful huff it's only for the "unadventurous or inexperienced."

Izzy's Steaks & Chops
19 | 16 | 17 | $38

3345 Steiner St. (bet. Chestnut & Lombard Sts.), 415-563-0487;
www.izzyssteaksandchops.com
"When you're craving" beef, "slink into a cozy booth" at this "clubby" "San Francisco landmark" in the Marina steeped in "old-school East Coast steakhouse atmosphere" or one of the branches North and South of SF; we "would eat there every night it if wasn't for cholesterol and tight jeans" claim carnivores who tuck into "tried-and-true" sides, particularly the "wickedly rich" "creamed spinach that'll turn anyone into Popeye"; still, gripers grumble about "mediocre meat" and "amateurish service."

Jack Falstaff
21 | 22 | 20 | $52

598 Second St. (Brannan St.), 415-836-9239; www.plumpjack.com
It may be "close to the ballpark", but this "SoMa warehouse" decked out with "buttery soft suede banquettes" definitely doesn't hawk "ballpark food" confirm fans who join "hipsters, city politicos and elites" "hoping to catching a glimpse of the hunky Mayor" at this Californian "winner"; but while many go to bat for the "imaginative" "gourmet" fare and "impressive" "market-rate wine" list, a "disappointed" few feel the chow doesn't "always hit the mark" since the founding chef left.

Jackson Fillmore Ⓜ
22 | 13 | 17 | $33

2506 Fillmore St. (Jackson St.), 415-346-5288
"Cramped and loud like an authentic Italian trattoria in the Bel Paese", this Upper Fillmore "local institution" is the best "go-to place" "for the money" for "hearty", "old-fashioned" "nothing-fancy" *cucina e vino* – and there's a "line to prove it"; they don't take reservations but the "gratis slices of bruschetta" alone are "worth the wait", plus the "curt staff" "turns tables quickly" – and "grows friendlier as you become a regular."

Jai Yun ⌀
22 | 8 | 14 | $45

923 Pacific Ave. (Mason St.), 415-981-7438
"Just making a reservation is a trip" at this "cult-followed" cash-only BYOB Chinatown "hole-in-the-wall" where English is barely spoken; still, "it's worth the hassle" for the "master chef's" "elegant, almost unbelievable versions of Shanghainese and other regional standards" served "banquet-style", "dish after mysterious" dish, based on your budget and his whim; but while groupies "spring for the higher priced menu" and dub it the "Chinese Laundry", the dubious declare it's a "better story than meal."

JARDINIÈRE
26 | 26 | 25 | $65

300 Grove St. (Franklin St.), 415-861-5555; www.jardiniere.com
"*Iron Chef* winner" Traci Des Jardins' "gorgeous circular speak-easy" is the still the "sexiest" dining destination in Hayes Valley for

both the "well-heeled" "pre- and post-opera crowd" and the "regular guy splurging"; the "sparkling atmosphere", "exquisite" service and "imaginative, locally grown PC" Cal-French fare, "from raw oysters to the cheese plate", make for a "sumptuous" "experience for all the senses" – especially if you "sit by the art deco"–inspired balcony railing "near the jazz combo" and peer down at the "swells at the bar" below.

Jay's Cheesesteak
19 | 8 | 13 | $13

553 Divisadero St. (bet. Fell & Hayes Sts.), 415-771-5104
3285 21st St. (bet. Mission & Valencia Sts.), 415-285-5200 ⊅
"Hallelujah!" cry Philly expats when they experience Brotherly Love in the form of "gigantic", "gooey" cheese steaks at these Western Addition and Mission siblings offering philling meals at "affordable prices"; "you know you're in SF" when you espy the vegetarian version and Niman Ranch ingredients on the menu, but the "greasy" goods are still the "best" "close substitute" in town.

Jeanty at Jack's
23 | 21 | 21 | $49

615 Sacramento St. (bet. Kearny & Montgomery Sts.), 415-693-0941;
www.jeantyatjacks.com
Phillipe Jeanty's "citified" "cousin" of his flagship bistro remains the ultimate power-lunch spot for Downtown "bankers" who count on "excellent", "true-blue" "trencherman's" fare that's "faithful to the Yountville menu" served by an "amiable" staff; the "pretty", "historic" multilevel interior "pays homage to the venerable Jack's" mixing in "Parisian brasserie" accents, and even if it's "not cheap", the "tomato soup alone" makes for a "wonderful" meal.

Joe DiMaggio's Italian Chophouse ⊠ Ⓜ
– | – | – | E

601 Union St. (Stockton St.), 415-421-5633;
www.joedimaggiosrestaurant.com
From the owners of Bing Crosby's in Walnut Creek, this retro North Beach chophouse pays tribute to the San Francisco–raised slugger in a sophisticated Rat Pack–inspired setting; nostalgists can slip into tufted leather booths, sip martinis and tuck into pricey steakhouse staples, wood-fired pizzas or updated Italian dishes to the strains of piped-in Dean Martin or, after 7 PM, live piano music; P.S. there's a smattering of memorabilia for Marilyn fans too.

Joe's Cable Car
23 | 14 | 17 | $16

4320 Mission St. (Silver Ave.), 415-334-6699; www.joescablecar.com
You "happily take your life into your hands" when you order a "delicious", "quality", "ground-on-the-spot" burger, "good" onion rings and "excellent" milkshake at this circa-1965 "institution" in Excelsior's "boondocks"; it's "worth the trip alone" for the "kitschy" cable-car setting and owner who's "always ready with a joke", and even if it's "ridiculously" pricey, you won't mind when "you finally bite into" the "heavenly" signature specialties.

Juban
18 | 15 | 16 | $31

Japan Ctr., 1581 Webster St. (bet. Geary Blvd. & Post St.), 415-776-5822;
www.jubanrestaurant.com
See review in South of San Francisco Directory.

Kabuto Ⓜ
25 | 12 | 17 | $38

5121 Geary Blvd. (15th Ave.), 415-752-5652; www.kabutosushi.com
Founder Sachio-San and his "sensei have moved on", but "dedicated" crowds still line up at the gong of 5 PM or "go late" to this

"tiny", "renowned" Outer Richmond "hole-in-the-wall" for the "best cuts" of "superbly fresh" sashimi and "unique sushi" so "wonderful" "words cannot do it justice"; while the "new owner gets points for enthusiasm", some loyalists are not yet sure if he "can measure up" – he has "big shoes to fill."

Kan Zaman | 17 | 21 | 17 | $23 |
1793 Haight St. (Shrader St.), 415-751-9656
For an evening of "belly-dancing and hookahs galore" make like Shakira and "wiggle" those hips over to this "funky, fun Haight eatery" that's "perfect for groups"; "sit on a pillow" at a low table, order "tasty", "unbelievably cheap" Middle Eastern meze and entrees from the "family-style menu" and indulge in a "glass of spiced wine" and the "smoke offerings"; sure, it gets "chaotic", but most dig the "other-worldly scene."

Kate's Kitchen ⊘ | 21 | 12 | 15 | $14 |
471 Haight St. (bet. Fillmore & Webster Sts.), 415-626-3984
"Still cranking out" "the perfect cure" "for the common hangover", this "great greasy spoon" with "long waits" in the "funky Lower Haight" is where "disaffected hipsters" "roll in" for "ginormous" Southern breakfasts and "roll out stuffed with a smile on the face"; if the "taste explosion" ("three words: French toast orgy") and "surly" servers don't "wake you up", the "death metal music" will.

Katia's Russian Tea Room Ⓜ | ▽ 22 | 15 | 20 | $29 |
600 Fifth Ave. (Balboa St.), 415-668-9292; www.katias.com
"Down-home – if home is Moscow" jest Ruskie-lovers who fall for the "stick-to-your-ribs" offerings at this "cozy" cafe in the Inner Richmond that's reminiscent of your Eastern European "grandma's dining room"; for "fun with a Russian accent", order plates of "authentic" blini, peroshki and borscht then chat up the "wonderful", "gregarious" proprietress – "she may even sit with you (she treated our young son like he was the Czar)."

Khan Toke Thai House | 21 | 23 | 21 | $25 |
5937 Geary Blvd. (bet. 23rd & 24th Aves.), 415-668-6654
Guaranteed "fun for out-of-towners", this Outer Richmond "staple" "whisks you away" to "Bangkok" with its "great combination" of "classic decor", "sunken tables" and "tasty" Thai dishes; it's an "authentic", "transporting" "experience" and it's only "discovered with your shoes off" (consider "a pedicure before you go" – or "wear socks without holes"); still, the un-Khanvinced "don't know what the hype is all about."

Kingfish Ⓩ | 17 | 19 | 16 | $36 |
128 King St. (bet. 2nd & 3rd Sts.), 415-348-0648; www.kingfish.net
See review in South of San Francisco Directory.

King of Thai ⊘ | 19 | 6 | 14 | $13 |
346 Clement St. (bet. 4th & 5th Aves.), 415-831-9953 ☽
639 Clement St. (bet. 7th & 8th Aves.), 415-752-5198 ☽
3199 Clement St. (33rd Ave.), 415-831-1301
420 Geary St. (bet. Mason & Taylor Sts.), 415-346-3121 ☽
184 O'Farrell St. (Powell St.), 415-677-9991 ☽
1507 Sloat Blvd. (Everglade Dr.), 415-566-9921
1541 Taraval St. (26th Ave.), 415-682-9958 ☽
For the "best noodles this side of a side alley in Bangkok", dive-savvy diners descend on this "low-cost, high-flavor Thai mini-

chain" where "unflinchingly authentic", "chopstick-lickin' good" "street-style food" provides "instant gratification"; while the "no-frills" decor won't "win any interior decorating awards", the late hours prove "handy for post-drinking snacking", plus service is so "fast" and furious "the staff moves like it's in a Nascar pit stop."

Koh Samui & The Monkey   21 | 19 | 18 | $26

415 Brannan St. (bet. 3rd & 4th Sts.), 415-369-0007; www.kohsamuiandthemonkey.com

There's "no monkeying around for a table", and what's more, you'll "go bananas" for the "perfectly spiced dishes" at this "high-style SoMa Thai" that also curries favor with its "reasonable prices" and "nifty", "unusually snazzy decor"; it's a "great place to get away from sports fans nearby, but close enough to grab a bite before or after a game" – and don't forget to swing over for a "fun" date or with a group.

KOKKARI ESTIATORIO Ⓢ   26 | 26 | 24 | $50

200 Jackson St. (Front St.), 415-981-0983; www.kokkari.com

Ascend to "Hellenic heaven" at this "chic" yet "rustic" Greek favorite Downtown that "feels like a Grecian villa" where you can rely on the "friendly staff to ease you into paradise"; "one taste of the moussaka you'll be throwing plates in celebration" quip patrons who, much like the crowd of "VIPs", "local celebs" and the "beautiful people", delight in the "delicious and delectable", "cleverly updated" dishes as well as the "convivial atmosphere."

Koo Ⓜ   24 | 18 | 21 | $32

408 Irving St. (bet. 5th & 6th Aves.), 415-731-7077; www.sushikoo.com

"Coo like a very happy foodie baby" after devouring the "wonderful, offbeat" Asian fusion small plates and "imaginative" sushi at this "pretty" yet "non-glam" "modern Japanese", a stealth, "friendly" "alternative" to trendier Inner Sunset spots; whether you opt for a table or join the "in' folks at the bar", you'll savor the "good sake" and signature dish "Spoonful of Happiness that should be Bowls of Bliss" – just "leave room to scale the Mt. Fuji dessert."

Kookez Café Ⓜ   ▽ 14 | 13 | 13 | $23

4123 24th St. (Castro St.), 415-641-7773; www.kookez.com

Located slightly uphill from Noe Valley's main drag is this American "newcomer with promise" that's "no Miss Millie's" (its predecessor) "but a good replacement nevertheless", with an "eager-to-please staff" and the same familiar Americana interior and bucolic back patio; but while some tout the "tasty brekkie" and weekend brunch and "interesting regional" dinner (served Wednesday–Sunday), critics contend some combos are "kooky" – seems they're "still getting their sea legs."

Kuleto's   20 | 18 | 20 | $41

Villa Florence Hotel, 221 Powell St. (bet. Geary & O'Farrell Sts.), 415-397-7720

A "happy, noisy" "Union Square standby", this "handsome" Downtown trattoria/wine bar is a "welcome port for tourists", theatergoers and "tired shoppers alike" who delight in the "dependable" "al forno" Italian eats; the "exhibition-style" kitchen is "great to watch", especially if your perch is at the "excellent bar" among the "buzzy crowd"; P.S. Los Gatos closed while the Burlingame branch is handy for the "airport"-bound.

Kwanjai Thai
　　　　　　　　　　　　　　　　　–　–　–　I

3242 Scott St. (bet. Chestnut & Lombard Sts.), 415-563-1285;
www.Kwanjai-Thai.com

"Über-modern styling" – think futuristic space lounge with square red plates landing on curvaceous white tables – and "uniquely modern Thai food" make this Siam spot in the Marina a "good" addition to the "'hood"; the name translates to 'favorite' and indeed, you'll find lots of crowd-pleasers like tom yum gai and satay on the menu, but remember, this isn't your ordinary curry corner; N.B. food served till midnight on weekends.

Kyo-Ya ⊠
　　　　　　　　　　　　24　22　22　$57

Palace Hotel, 2 New Montgomery St. (Market St.), 415-546-5090;
www.kyo-ya-restaurant.com

Feels like "Kyoto West" agree the awed who join "Japanese businessmen" and descend on this "elegant" Downtowner in the Palace Hotel for sushi so "impeccable" it "makes you want to say *sayonara*" to the competition; it's a "must for any purist", but such "excellence" comes at a "steep", "ouch"-inducing price, which explains why it's also dubbed "expense-account central"; while a few find service "gracious", a handful huff it's "haughty."

La Ciccia
　　　　　　　　　　　　　　　　　–　–　–　M

291 30th St. (Church St.), 415-550-8114; www.laciccia.com

Several regional Italians have recently set up shop in outer Noe Valley, and this newcomer, billed as the only Sardinian restaurant west of Dallas, extends the trend; while the menu offers several robust, slow-cooked meats ('la ciccia' is slang for 'the belly'), seafood abounds and the decor has a subtle aquamarine tone and accents that conjure up seaside life; an all-Italian wine list complements the fare.

La Cumbre Taqueria ⊘
　　　　　　　　20　8　14　$11

515 Valencia St. (bet. 16th & 17th Sts.), 415-863-8205

"*Que bueno!*" applaud admirers of this Mission "standby", a "legend on the SF taqueria scene" turning out "burritos that brim with flavor" and soft tortilla tacos that are "worth a trip", all "expertly put together" by a counter "staff that never fails to be cheerful"; San Mateoites also give the "big, juicy, quality ingredients" a hand and on a "sunny day", tote their "great fast-food" treats to the patio.

LA FOLIE ⊠
　　　　　　　　　　27　24　26　$86

2316 Polk St. (bet. Green & Union Sts.), 415-776-5577; www.lafolie.com

"Splurgers are rewarded by the generous spirit" of "genius" chef Roland Passot's "family-run" French on Russian Hill; fans are folie smitten by the "extraordinary", "artistically presented" dishes and "terrific wines", "understated" yet "outstanding" service and "beautiful" space (most prefer the "vibrant front room"); though a handful huff about ever-"ratcheting-up" prices, others boast it's "worth every penny" for "exquisite" cuisine that rivals "the best in the Bay Area."

La Méditerranée
　　　　　　　　　　20　15　18　$20

2210 Fillmore St. (Sacramento St.), 415-921-2956
288 Noe St. (Market St.), 415-431-7210
www.cafelamed.com

While "not exactly the French Riviera", these "Bay Area staples" "have stood the test of time" remaining "excellent" for "everyday"

Middle Eastern–Med fare including "heavenly hummus" and other "fresh, flavorful" meze "served up at lightning speed"; all three (Castro, Fillmore and Berkeley) are "a good bet for a casual", "inexpensive" lunch, brunch or dinner.

L'Amour Dans le Four
▽ 20 | 20 | 22 | $33

1602 Lombard St. (Gough St.), 415-775-2134; www.amoursf.biz

A "wonderful", "witty French 'ménage à trois'" of owners "put their lovin' in their oven" at this "romantic", "funky little French joint" that "charms out-of-towners"; though "tucked into a crevice" on Cow Hollow's "busy" Lombard Street, the "cozy" confines (so "intimate" you may "rub elbows with neighboring tables") feel "very much like Paris", while the "real-deal" fare, including the 'Lucky $13' early-bird prix fixe "surprises with its sophistication."

La Provence Restaurant
▽ 19 | 20 | 20 | $38

1001 Guerrero St. (22nd St.), 415-643-4333;
www.laprovencerestaurant.net

With its "warm", mustard-hued interior and French posters on the walls, this Mission newcomer Aix-emplifies a "classic Provençal" cafe; the "welcoming" staff is equally sunny, but while most find the Gallic fare to be "excellent", "refined" and "inexpensive" for this genre, a small band of resisters maintains it "misses the mark.

La Scene Café & Bar
20 | 20 | 21 | $39

Warwick Regis, 490 Geary St. (Taylor St.), 415-292-6430;
www.warwicksf.com

Though little-known this "gem in the theater district" Downtown is a "stopping place" "en route" or "after a performance" – and the ticket for a "tasty" "bargain prix fixe" Cal-Med menu accompanied by a "fine half-bottle list for those who don't want to fall asleep after intermission", all delivered by "paced" service that "knows food and time constraints"; still, it's not everyone's scene – a "disappointed" few deem the decor "bland" and the fare a bit "blah."

Last Supper Club, The
19 | 18 | 19 | $32

1199 Valencia St. (23rd St.), 415-695-1199; www.lastsupperclubsf.com

"Twentysomethings" seeking "fairly priced" Italian in the Mission applaud the "m-m-m good", "unpretentious" Southern-style *cucina* including "killer meatballs" and "excellent" cocktails delivered by an "attentive" staff at this "festive" locale; dissenters deem it "hit-or-miss" under new ownership ("it won't be your last supper of choice"), but concede it may be "best for brunch."

La Taqueria ⊉
24 | 7 | 13 | $10

2889 Mission St. (25th St.), 415-285-7117

"A necessary stop after a night out in the Mission" for more than 30 years, this "ultimate taqueria" (with a San Jose outpost) "rules" with its "superb" rice-free burritos filled with "juicy" meat and other "fresh ingredients" as well as the "best tacos" "rinsed down" by "excellent" agua frescas; *sí*, "lines are long" and the seating's "as minimalist as the name", but the counter service is "fast", tabs are "cheap" enough and if you're "jonesing for Mexican", "this is it."

Le Central Bistro 🗷
21 | 18 | 20 | $39

453 Bush St. (bet. Grant Ave. & Kearny St.), 415-391-2233;
www.lecentralbistro.com

The "central biz location" and "old-school service" keep this "paradigm of a Paris bistro" "crowded, noisy" and *très* "comfortable"; come for a "cozy martini lunch" on Friday when it's thrumming with "local notables" "playing Liar's Dice" and "you're likely to run into the mayor, current or past"; *oui*, the "white lace curtains" may be as "old" as "Herb Caen's ghost", but the "classics" made with "flair" (including "cassoulet from before I was born") remain "some of the best."

Le Charm French Bistro
22 | 16 | 20 | $36

315 Fifth St. (bet. Folsom & Shipley Sts.), 415-546-6128;
www.lecharm.com

"Sweet, romantic" and *oui*, "extremely charming", "despite its sketchy" SoMa location, this "little hideaway" with an "unpretentious staff" is most "definitely a date restaurant", "transporting you to Paris" via a "bistro-y feel" and "meticulously prepared", "diverse" "classics" with "none of the nouvelle" trappings; *amis* agree that the "delightful" $28 "prix fixe rules", especially when savored on the "adorable back patio"; N.B. a post-*Survey* refurb may impact the Decor score.

Le Colonial
22 | 25 | 20 | $49

20 Cosmo Pl. (bet. Post & Taylor Sts.), 415-931-3600;
www.lecolonialsf.com

"Walking up the tile staircase and along the elevated breezeway commences your journey" from Downtown SF to "Saigon in the '20s"; the "amazing" decor "truly brings you back to the colonial days in Asia" while the "metrosexual crowd", "inviting", "flavorful" French-Vietnamese cuisine and "expensive" tabs jet you back to reality; "later in the evening when the liquid courage" takes hold, the upstairs pho bar "gets lively" and settlers "kick up their heels."

Le Petit Robert
19 | 17 | 18 | $33

2300 Polk St. (Green St.), 415-922-8100;
www.lepetitrobert.com

Soak up the "warmth of a real French bistro" while indulging in "hearty", "deliciously rich" fare that "lives up to the pig mascot motif" and enough "red wine to keep your arteries open" at this "charming" Russian Hill spot; the "cavernous space" offers "plenty of room to read the paper" but most prefer "people-watching" on the front patio "on a sunny, lazy afternoon"; still, cynics shrug "nothing to write home about."

Les Amis
▽ 23 | 19 | 22 | $49

568 Sacramento St. (Montgomery St.), 415-291-9145

A "welcome addition" from the Plouf team, this "quaint" spot with "professional service" set in a converted "old firehouse" plies Downtown denizens with "classy, inventive" New French fare that reflects the "freshest of California's seasons"; "bring your expense account — the wine list is worth it" – and canoodle against a backdrop of "racy red doors, velvet drapes and upholstered burgundy banquettes", a backdrop befitting a "romantic dinner."

Le Soleil
20 | 14 | 17 | $24

133 Clement St. (bet. 2nd & 3rd Aves.), 415-668-4848

The "recent refurb has ratcheted up the experience" exclaim enthusiasts who long considered this Inner Richmond Vietnamese a "favorite for takeout but now want to eat" here too; the staff is "pleasant" while the "surprisingly inventive" vittles "rise to the top of the heap by virtue of fresh ingredients" and "eye-catching presentation", bringing boosters "back again and again."

Lettus: Cafe Organic 18 | 16 | 11 | $18
3352 Steiner St. (bet. Chestnut & Lombard Sts.), 415-931-2777
"Go in gym clothes and you'll fit in" at this "bright, modern" Marina newcomer offering "zesty, vibrant", "globally inspired" "organic fast food" from morning till night including salads, smoothies and other "good-for-you food" on environmentally sound paper goods with biodegradable utensils; kids' menu notwithstanding, some say the "slow" counter service is still "taking baby steps" – hopefully, they'll "iron out the kinks" soon.

Levende Ⓜ 21 | 23 | 18 | $35
1710 Mission St. (Duboce Ave.), 415-864-5585; www.levendesf.com
Whether you "grab a late-night bite" "before it turns into a nightclub" or to "build your own Bloody Mary" at the "surprisingly delicious" Sunday 'Boogie Brunch', you'll feed "all your senses" at this "seductive" Mission destination; devotees who devour "generously sized" Eclectic small plates vow this "hip" "heaven" "rocks", nevertheless, the put-off pronounce this "singles" "sceneville" a "better bar than restaurant" – "you can't even taste the food" because of the "loud" DJ music.

Le Zinc 18 | 18 | 16 | $35
4063 24th St. (bet. Castro & Noe Sts.), 415-647-9400; www.lezinc.com
"You definitely feel like you're in France" at this "charming" Noe Valley bistro where you can spend "an afternoon" on the sunny pooch-friendly patio over "small plates and a gorgeous bottle of wine" or "weekend brunch when you have forever for your meal"; "your table is your table", which translates to an "unhurried" outing for some and "long waits" and "pokey service" to cynics who also zinc it's "overpriced"

Liberty Cafe & Bakery Ⓜ 23 | 17 | 20 | $29
410 Cortland Ave. (Bennington St.), 415-695-8777
"No one can touch" the "semi-legendary, homemade chicken" and vegetarian pot pies at this "hideaway in Bernal Heights" that "oozes homey charm" coo acolytes who also order other "cozy" Traditional American "favorites" from the "smiley" staff; "save room for the miraculous desserts" from the bakery though, particularly the "decadent banana cream pie" – and "hope that it's crowded so you can sit" in the wine bar out back drinking and eating fresh "bread while waiting."

Lime ❶ 18 | 22 | 16 | $31
2247 Market St. (bet. Noe & Sanchez Sts.), 415-621-5256; www.lime-sf.com
"Indulge in an unending flow of drinks, techno music and good times" at the Castro's "glossy", "noisy" "experience" that's "more of a nightclub with food"; "super-young" "hipsters" and "pretty gay people" agree it's worth "squeezing into" for the decor that's "reminiscent of an iMac" and the Eclectic "retro" "little plates" like "tiny burgers with big taste"; but the tart-tongued taunt that the "trendy atmosphere might be wearing thin", adding "lose the 'tude."

Limón 24 | 20 | 20 | $38
524 Valencia St. (16th St.), 415-252-0918; www.limon-sf.com
Martin Castillo brings South American "*sabor*" down from the "foothills of the Andes" to his "festive if a bit frenzied" loftlike

digs in the Mission's Valencia corridor, offering "innovative" "seviche in more ways than you can count in Español", plus other "impressively tasty" Asian-inflected Peruvian dishes, all toted to table by a "hot", "helpful" staff; "bring a megaphone or an assisted hearing device" though, as "noise"-wise, "Bill Graham Presents had nothing on this place."

Little Nepal ⓜ
| 22 | 18 | 19 | $24 |

925 Cortland Ave. (Folsom St.), 415-643-3881; www.littlenepalsf.com
Instead of "climbing Everest to find authentic Nepalese cuisine", turn up at Bernal Heights' "special little place" with the "atmosphere of a cozy East Asian tearoom" and "gracious", "attentive" service, and experience the "delicately spiced" dishes of the Himalayas; while it's "somewhat like Indian" food, it's still a "nice departure", plus it's "nourishing to the body and soul" – and well "worth the trek."

Little Star Pizza ⓜ⤵
| ▽ 27 | 19 | 18 | $22 |

846 Divisadero St. (bet. Fulton & McAllistar Sts.), 415-441-1118; www.littlestarpizza.com
"Deep dish" devotees no longer have to "cross the Bay Bridge" to Zachary's for "excellent Chicago-style pizza" since citing this rising little star in the Western Addition; "the hippest, darkest pizza joint in the city" doesn't take reservations and the cornmeal-crust creations (both thick and thin) are "made to order", so kick back with a brew ("three cheers for one dollar PBRs" at happy hour) and groove to the "fantastic jukebox" while you wait.

L'Osteria del Forno ⤵
| 23 | 14 | 18 | $28 |

519 Columbus Ave. (bet. Green & Union Sts.), 415-982-1124; www.losteriadelforno.com
"There's a reason you'll see more people in line than seated" – this "humble" North Beach kitchen "turns out dishes to delight", from "so light" gnocchi to "pizza that blows away your senses" – and it's a cash-only "experience worth waiting for"; "count yourself lucky if you can squeeze" into the "intimate" space – it's "too small, but you don't want it any bigger" because "you feel like you've been invited to a [Northern] Italian home."

Lovejoy's Tea Room ⓜ
| 20 | 21 | 22 | $21 |

1351 Church St. (Clipper St.), 415-648-5895; www.lovejoystearoom.com
"Your cute detector goes off as soon as you enter" Noe Valley's "cozy" "English country tea shop", a "sweet refuge from the rush of real life" where you can savor a "civilized afternoon" with "your mom, your sister, your pals" – or even a "hetero man" – eating "finger sandwiches" and "clotted cream on everything"; it's "pricier than you'd think", but "every aspect" of the "old-school", "frilly environment", including the "mismatched china", is "delightful."

Luella
| 21 | 20 | 20 | $40 |

1896 Hyde St. (Green St.), 415-674-4343; www.luellasf.com
"Hip but relaxed", this "darling" "neighborhood hideaway" on Russian Hill "hits all the right notes" attest admirers who sing the praises of an "imaginative, diverse" Mediterranean menu, a "long, tasty wine list", "reasonable prices" and a "friendly staff with no airs"; while it can "get a bit noisy, it's worth the decibels" as you're sure to have a "great conversation over delicious dishes" like the "Coca-Cola braised pork that falls off the bone."

Luna Park
20 | 18 | 18 | $32

694 Valencia St. (18th St.), 415-553-8584; www.lunaparksf.com
It's "noisy" and "high energy", but this Mission "neighborhood anchor" with a "lively bar" and a "convivial" staff is a "perfect" "party"-"trendy" "place to catch up with friends" over "seriously good", "fairly priced" French–New American fare, "top-notch cocktails" and "not-be-missed s'mores" ("leave the campfire at home"); still, a few shout "not much comfort in the 'comfort food' when it's louder than an aircraft carrier deck."

MacArthur Park
16 | 18 | 17 | $37

607 Front St. (bet. Jackson St. & Pacific Ave.), 415-398-5700;
www.spectrumfoods.com
"Still cuts the mustard" for "hearty" ribs, or "any beef entree", insist loyalists who "treat themselves" at this Traditional American "staple" located in a "gorgeous old" Downtown landmark and in Palo Alto ("if you can snag a spot by a fireplace, life is good"); but most muse "someone left the cake out in the rain" – "happy-hour snacks" aside, lately this "old soldier" seems to be "phoning it in."

Maki Ⓜ
25 | 17 | 19 | $34

Japan Ctr., 1825 Post St., 2nd fl. (bet. Fillmore & Webster Sts.),
415-921-5215
Like "pearls in an oyster" opine patrons who fall for the "home-cooked", "delicate" Japanese "morsels" at this "tiny jewel box" Japantown "sleeper at the end of the corridor"; the "subtly distinct and wonderful" dishes, including "excellent wappa meshi and pristine sashimi", are "perfectly prepared" and "dispensed with a restrained hand" and manage to "triumph over" "tight seating" and long waits.

Mamacita ◗
23 | 19 | 17 | $32

2317 Chestnut St. (Scott St.), 415-346-8494; www.mamacitasf.com
The "*muy bueno*" "high-end Mexican" cooked in a "modern fashion" is the "real superstar" at this "always packed" Marina "hot spot" swarming with "pretty people" – nevertheless, "plan on having a pitcher of sangria" or a "potent margarita" at the bar because you'll endure a "*loco* amount of waiting time"; yes, it's also "blow-the-doors-off loud", but insiders insist the "delicious" dishes with a "subtle kick" "will keep you coming back for more."

Mama's on Washington Square Ⓜ⇗
25 | 14 | 17 | $19

1701 Stockton St. (Filbert St.), 415-362-6421
"Mama mia!" – the "way-too-long" lines can be "outrageous", nonetheless, the "wholesome American breakfasts" and "fabulous brunch", "freshly baked breads" and "dense, moist pastries" at this North Beach "haunt" give you a "reason to wake up early"; "bring the newspaper and enjoy the crowd" of "locals and tourists" – if you like brekkie, "you've found heaven"; once seated, the "friendly" "staff definitely lets you know when your time is up."

Mandalay
22 | 14 | 20 | $22

4348 California St. (6th Ave.), 415-386-3895
The "mélange of tastes" "send your taste buds into a spin" marvel Myanmar munchers who wonder "why hipsters line up" at that "more famous" Inner Richmond Burmese dive when this "homey" spot with a updated Polynesian decor is so "pleasing to the eye";

"don't miss" the "refreshing tea leaf salad" – the "thoughtful" staff does a "nice job tossing it in front of you."

Mandarin, The   22 | 24 | 20 | $41
Ghirardelli Sq., 900 N. Point St. (bet. Larkin & Polk Sts.), 415-673-8812; www.themandarin.com
Although the "novelty of upscale Chinese has worn off", diners are "impressed" by the "beautiful" palacelike surroundings and "lovely view of the Bay" from the "great window tables" of this Wharf aerie overlooking Ghirardelli Square that's "still kickin' after 35 years"; the "better-than-expected" banquet-style Sino samplings may be "fairly expensive" to Chinatown regulars, but loyalists insist it's an "uncrowded" respite from the "tacky tourist traps."

Mangarosa Ⓜ   21 | 20 | 20 | $42
1548 Stockton St. (bet. Green & Union Sts.), 415-956-3211; www.mangarosasf.com
"Where the beautiful people go" to "start the night out", this "lively" Rio-by-way-of-Rome "hip" fusion North Beach spot is exactly what you'd "imagine a Brazilian restaurant to be: it doesn't get packed till 9 PM, service is relaxed", "drinks are awesome" and the "innovative" menu is a "meat lover's" night dream; if a few beef it "fails to hang together" foodwise, most declare "it delivers" (the steak rechaud served *a tavola* over a flame "rocks").

Mangosteen ⌿   ▽ 17 | 14 | 14 | $18
601 Larkin St. (Eddy St.), 415-776-3999
"An oasis of cute in the gritty Tenderloin", this "inexpensive", cash-only Little Saigon upstart graced with a "bright" tropical decor and paintings of the namesake Southeast Asian fruit serves "tasty" "Vietnamese standards with a twist" to a "packed house"; while the "service could use help", you "get more than what you pay for" – the "crisp flavors" "always leave you smiling."

Manora's Thai Cuisine   23 | 14 | 19 | $23
1600 Folsom St. (12th St.), 415-861-6224
Still an old "reliable", this Siamese SoMa staple lures locals with a "full bar", "Thai-inspired ambiance" and "delicious fare" that's a "bit fancier" and "more creative than your average" joint ("home to the hottest green peppers I've ever eaten – and I have an asbestos palate!"); by day it attracts suits galore for lunch that's a "screaming deal", while later on "leather-clad Folsom regulars" and clubgoers come round "before a wild night" out.

Mario's Bohemian Cigar Store Cafe   21 | 15 | 15 | $17
566 Columbus Ave. (Union St.), 415-362-0536; www.mariosbohemiancigarstore.com
The cigar shop may be a memory "like SF's bohemian past", but this 35-year-old spot "overlooking Washington Square Park" still smokes assert regulars who adore the "addictive" focaccia sandwiches and Italian-style "soul food"; pair your panini with a "simple red by the carafe" or "go in the afternoon to drink coffee, rendezvous with friends" and "watch North Beach walk by."

MarketBar   17 | 18 | 16 | $38
The Embarcadero, 1 Ferry Bldg. (Market St.), 415-434-1100; www.marketbar.com
"Bring your pooch" and sit outside at this "charming" Embarcadero "pit stop" on a "farmer's market day" – the "people-watching

can't be beat", plus you can catch the "vintage trolley cars ringing by" as you enjoy a " mid-summer's lunch, or a "lazy supper" that's a "bit pricey" but takes advantage of the local larder; unless you're into a "bustling bar scene" and an "acoustically challenged" setting, stick to the alfresco dining.

Marnee Thai
23 | 15 | 17 | $22

2225 Irving St. (bet. 23rd & 24th Aves.), 415-665-9500
1243 Ninth Ave. (bet. Irving St. & Lincoln Way), 415-731-9999
www.marneethaisf.com

"It's a kick to eat" at this "unassuming" Outer Sunset original – the "owner has lots of character and advice" so let her "take care of you" and you'll dine on "awesomely delicious" Thai fare that'll leave your "taste buds in a happy state"; the Inner Sunset spinoff "might not be as much fun" without her "eccentric" presence, but you can still treat yourself to the "standards with the occasional adventuresome special" – and those "superb angel wings."

MASA'S ☒ Ⓜ
27 | 24 | 27 | $96

Hotel Vintage Ct., 648 Bush St. (bet. Powell & Stockton Sts.),
415-989-7154; www.masasrestaurant.com

Who woulda thunk the "legacy could have lasted this long" but "even with the round robin" of chefs, this "sophisticated" Downtowner remains the "king of the power dinner" – and with Gregory Short "at the helm", the "divine" New French tasting menus are "nothing short of ecstasy"; what a "rare, fantastic experience" – "every course is first rate" ("loved the little post-meal candy tray"), the "decor is soothing and romantic" and service is "impeccable" – if only "you had a better job to pay for it"; N.B. jacket required.

Massawa
▽ 22 | 8 | 18 | $18

1538 Haight St. (bet. Ashbury & Clayton Sts.), 415-621-4129

"Wash your hands before you go . . . 'cause you're going to eat with them" at this Haight Street dive that may look like a "high school cafeteria" but actually serves "delicious Ethiopian stews"; it's "fun for groups" to "soak up" the "excellent Eritrean" fare with "spongy injera bread" and wash it down with African beers and honey wine – just make sure you're "not in a real hurry."

Matterhorn Swiss Restaurant Ⓜ
19 | 17 | 19 | $38

2323 Van Ness Ave. (bet. Green & Vallejo Sts.), 415-885-6116

"Wear lederhosen (like the staff)" and head to the Alps by way of this "kitschy Swiss" "chalet-style dining room" on Russian Hill serving "authentic regional cuisine" (think schnitzel), sweet and savory fondues "cooked to your liking, by you" and a "phenomenal" vino list (the "owner is a walking wine dictionary"); pot-people declare it's "just plain fun" but party-poopers pout "not big on community dipping" or smelling like "bubbling hot cheese."

Maverick
21 | 19 | 21 | $38

3316 17th St. (bet. Mission & Valencia Sts.), 415-863-3061;
www.sfmaverick.com

True to its name, this "quirky", "genuinely friendly", "retro wood-paneled" Mission maverick presents "regional" "comfort food" "from across America", "raising it" to an "unconventional" "new level" albeit at "foodie prices"; it's "smaller than I thought a restaurant was allowed to be" and "crowded" and "loud" on weekends (you can't "hear yourself read" the "affordable, eclectic" vino list) so "go for the wine deal on Monday nights – half off all bottles!"

Max's   17 | 13 | 16 | $24

Bank of America Ctr., 555 California St., concourse level (bet. Kearny & Montgomery Sts.), 415-788-6297 ⑤
1 California St. (Market St.), 415-781-6297 ⑤
398 Geary St. (Mason St.), 415-646-8600
Opera Plaza, 601 Van Ness Ave. (Golden Gate Ave.), 415-771-7301
www.maxsworld.com
This Bay Area chain offers a "bit of New York with SF flair", piling "too much food on the plate" with "unlimited pickles" and dishing out "calorie-laden desserts" that guarantee "you'll never leave hungry"; "oy! it's good to be sung to by the aspiring opera singer" servers at some sites – the "upbeat" shtick along with the "huge menu" makes it "fun for groups of friends and family" – plus it's "worth a stop for breakfast."

Maya   21 | 20 | 19 | $40

303 Second St. (bet. Folsom & Harrison Sts.), 415-543-2928;
www.mayasf.com
"Cutting-edge", "nuevo" Mexican "food that you never get tired of" maya be the reason why amigos find this "lovely", "just plain fun" SoMa hacienda a "welcome respite from the taquerias" around town; the beautifully presented "elite eats" (try the "awesome guacamole") and the "amazing tequila selection" are "so good nobody goes just once" – just bear in mind that the "mojitos go down too easy", potentially clouding the kitchen's "memorable results."

Mayflower   22 | 10 | 14 | $24

6255 Geary Blvd. (27th Ave.), 415-387-8338
"The decor is lacking", but "they do wonders with crustaceans" at this "crowded", "family-style" Outer Richmond "favorite for dim sum" and Hong Kong seafood catering to "hard-core eaters"; it "helps if you speak Cantonese", but it's not a necessity to feast upon tank-fresh prawns, crabs and lobsters; psst: "the best dishes aren't on the menu" – "tell the manager how much you want to spend and he'll fix you a special meal."

Maykadeh   ▽ 23 | 16 | 21 | $35

470 Green St. (bet. Grant Ave. & Kearny St.), 415-362-8286;
www.maykadehrestaurant.com
At this modern-day *maykadeh* (or meeting place), the "attentive owner treats everyone like family" while the "excellent" staff delivers "tasty, authentic", "reasonably priced" "classic Persian cooking" ("with a strong emphasis on skewer meats") that's "nice for a civilized respite in North Beach" purr patrons; if a few nabobs nix the "stuffy" setting, most "muse you will feel at home" here.

McCormick & Kuleto's   20 | 23 | 19 | $43

900 N. Point St. (Larkin St.), 415-929-1730; www.msmg.com
An "extensive menu" of "reliable" seafood pulls this "rare find in Fisherman's Wharf" "out of the tourist-trap mire" that also distinguishes itself via "location, location, location"; but vistameisters say the "magnificent" "view's the dish" at this chainster – "it far outweighs the merit" of the food – so "take your out-of-town relatives", but "be sure to get a window table" – and stick to the "basics", like crab cakes and fish 'n' chips."

Mecca Ⓜ   19 22 17 $45

2029 Market St. (bet. Church & Dolores Sts.), 415-621-7000;
www.sfmecca.com

Join the "glitterati crowd" for a "Castro experience" at this "hot",
"leather-and-chrome" "champ" charged with "enticing beats"; the
"chic" bar is the "place to show off your Dolce & Gabbana duds",
though it's "too cruisey for mom", while the "swanky" setting is
suitable for sampling "solid", seasonal, globally inspired New
American fare; still, some say "service is snooty"; N.B. a post-
Survey change of chef and new ownership may impact the scores.

Medicine Eatstation Ⓢ   19 20 17 $30

Crocker Galleria, 161 Sutter St. (bet. Kearny & Montgomery Sts.),
415-677-4405; www.medicinerestaurant.com

"Take a yoga teacher or the Dalai Lama" recommend admirers who
rejoice in the "restorative", "minimalist Zen Buddhist atmosphere",
"communal tables" and "food-equals-medicine" formula at this
Downtown "haute" Japanese-vegan venue; you "feel virtuous"
eating the "real Shojin" temple cuisine – it's a "refreshing change
from Crocker Galleria's fast-food choices" – though it may not
"satisfy committed carnivores"; still, kvetchers quip "slow service"
"can make a trip to the doctor seem like fun" in comparison.

Medjool   19 21 15 $33

2522 Mission St. (bet. 21st & 22nd Sts.), 415-550-9055;
www.medjoolsf.com

"Tasty" Mediterranean-influenced Moroccan small plates boasting "exotic flavors" are just one of the "draws at this ultrachic"
multifloor mecca that "puts the Marina in the Mission"; it's "clear
the chefs here are having fun" – and so will you, whether you
sprawl on the "comfy couches" in the "cavernous" lounge or join
the "trendy" crowd for "celebratory drinks" on the "awesome
roof patio" offering "skyline views" – it almost makes you "toler-
ant" of the "snooty-patooty" service.

Mel's Drive-In ◑   13 14 15 $17

3355 Geary Blvd. (bet. Beaumont & Parker Aves.), 415-387-2255
2165 Lombard St. (Steiner St.), 415-921-2867
801 Mission St. (4th St.), 415-227-0793
1050 Van Ness Ave. (Geary St.), 415-292-6358
www.melsdrive-in.com

"If you pine for reruns of *Happy Days*", jet over to this "blast-from-
the-past" outfit and dig into "diner classics" from "big hearty
breakfasts" to "burger and milkshake" fare when the "late-night
munchies" strike; yup, it's "predictable" and ditto for the "no-frills
decor and service", "but that's not always a bad thing", especially
if you have the "kids in tow" in the station wagon.

Memphis Minnie's BBQ Joint Ⓜ   22 11 16 $17

576 Haight St. (bet. Fillmore & Steiner Sts.), 415-864-7675;
www.memphisminnies.com

Have a "swine" time at Haight Street's "funky, pig-themed" BBQ
joint serving some of the "best 'cue in the city", "Memphis-style
pulled pork that can make a grown man cry" and "melt-in-your-
mouth brisket" with greens that make you "forget you're eating
vegetables"; purists pout about the "sauces served separately",
but most insist the "tangy" stuff "hits just the right note";
P.S. there's a "terrific weekend brunch to boot."

Mescolanza
20 | 15 | 19 | $30

2221 Clement St. (bet. 23rd & 24th Aves.), 415-668-2221;
www.mescolanza.net

Like "our second kitchen" quip customers of this "cozy", "charming Italian" "neighborhood secret" that brings a "bit of North Beach to the Richmond"; the "hearty" fare boasts the "freshest of ingredients" and it's served by an "attentive staff" that "makes you feel like you're in some posh" place, making it *perfetto* "for friends, family and out-of-town guests" or just a "midweek meal."

MICHAEL MINA
27 | 24 | 26 | $105

Westin St. Francis, 335 Powell St. (bet. Geary & Post Sts.),
415-397-9222; www.michaelmina.net

"Mama Mina!", the "Aqua alum's" New American "temple of gastronomy" Downtown is "wickedly expensive" but it "holds its end of the bargain", delivering an "eating extravaganza" that pushes your "wow meter off the scales"; the tasting menu "emphasizing a common ingredient prepared" "three ways" scores an "incredible" trifecta while the "wine tomb" is an "oenophile's paradise" and the service "flawless"; however, the "much-ballyhooed interior is lost on" celebrants who don't want to "shout at their companions" over the din of "tourists squealing in the Westin St. Francis lobby."

Mifune
18 | 11 | 14 | $17

Kintetsu Mall, 1737 Post St. (bet. Laguna & Webster Sts.), 415-922-0337

Slurpers satisfy "cravings" for "oodles of noodles" at this Japantown "standby", burrowing into bowlfuls of "delicious comforting udon" and "sassy soba dishes", plus "favorites" like tempura and donburi; "fast" service and "reasonable" prices make it a "good bet for a quickie before the movies", though a few fume that they "need to put the 'fun' back into Mi-fun-e" and believe the "bare-bones" space needs a "face-lift."

Mijita
19 | 12 | 13 | $16

The Embarcadero, 1 Ferry Bldg. (Market St.), 415-399-0814;
www.mijitasf.com

"Treat yourself" to Jardinière chef Traci Des Jardins' "out-of-the-ordinary" organic "Mexican fast food" at the "Chez Panisse of taquerias" in the Embarcadero where "farmer's market" shoppers and commuters "mob" the counter to watch cooks "make the fresh tortillas", "awesome fish tacos" ("utter perfection") and "excellent carnitas", then "eat at picnic tables outside" and "watch the ferries dock"; but while amigos admit the "chow's good", some sputter it's "spendy, spendy, spendy – should takeout "cost this much"?

Millennium
24 | 22 | 23 | $42

Savoy Hotel, 580 Geary St. (Jones St.), 415-345-3900;
www.millenniumrestaurant.com

Even "carnivores won't miss the meat" at this "lovely", "high-concept" "vegan's delight" Downtown that ushers in a new era in "gourmet" eating; from the "down-to-earth staff" and "romantic" setting to the "inventive" international fare featuring "exquisite", "unusual flavor combinations" and the "spot-on organic wines", there's "nothing rabbit food about this place" – in fact, you almost "forget you're eating healthy vegetarian"; still, a few faultfinders feel it's a "little pricey."

Mixt Greens 🗷　　_ _ _ I
114 Sansome St. suit 120 (Bush & Pine Sts.), 415-433-6498;
www.mixtgreens.com
This new 'eco-gourmet' storefront cafe (run by talent with ties to
Gramercy Tavern and Gary Danko) offers Downtown workers
healthy fast-food options, including organic, seasonal specialty and
design-your-own salads, sandwiches and other guilt-free grub; the
affordable fare can be taken away (in corn-based compostable
boxes) or scarfed down in minimalist digs fashioned from recy-
cled woods and zero-VOC paints; N.B. open weekdays till 3 PM.

Mochica　　21 18 18 $33
937 Harrison St. (bet. 5th & 6th Sts.), 415-278-0480; www.mochicasf.com
"Am I in Peru?" ponder wanderers who happen upon this "unpretentious" Lima-inspired SoMa eatery that's a "true discovery" for
a "wonderful date"; "I'd return just for the sangria and the
seviche" – but you also "can't go wrong" with the "delicious fish
dishes" that "really shine" and the slate of South American
wines, all served by a "charming" staff; N.B. a branch is set to
open this fall in Bernal Heights.

Modern Tea Ⓜ　　_ _ _ I
602 Hayes St. (Laguna St.), 415-626-5406; www.moderntea.com
It's always time for tea at this contemporary Hayes Valley salon, a
hybrid retail store and all-day full-service restaurant with a newly
opened wine lounge, surrounded by an abstract glass sculpture
suggesting flowing water; like the brews (including owner Alice
Cravens' line, also sold by the ounce), the affordable Californian
menu (no red meat or pork) aims to promote organic fare made
with Fair Trade ingredients.

Moishe's Pippic 🗷⇗　　▽ 18 9 16 $13
425-A Hayes St. (bet. Gough & Octavia Sts.), 415-431-2440
You'll "scarf down" "enough to turn from an 'innie' to an 'outtie'"
quip Pippic-people who belly up to the counter at this Hayes
Valley deli "festooned with Chicago paraphernalia" for "killer
dogs" reminiscent of the Windy City, pastrami sandwiches and
"Friday beef brisket specials"; but while it's "satisfying, it's not
sublime" pout purists who "kvetch" it "makes me long for Katz's
on the Lower East Side"; N.B. closes at 4 PM.

Moki's Sushi & Pacific Grill　　24 16 18 $30
615 Cortland Ave. (bet. Anderson & Moultrie Sts.), 415-970-9336;
www.mokisushi.com
This "unfussy" recently relocated "Polynesian-influenced"
Bernal Heights joint is "the pick of the neighborhood" touting
"Hawaiian-influenced sushi" and "extensive cooked menu"
that's "light on the Spam" and "heavy on generous pieces of im-
peccably fresh fish and playful rolls" like the "very appropriately
named Ecstasy Roll"; now that the "*Gilligan's Island*" digs moved
down the street to the larger "old Geranium spot", locals are
"hopeful that waits will be shorter."

MoMo's　　17 18 16 $36
760 Second St. (King St.), 415-227-8660; www.sfmomos.com
"Considering the location just across" from AT&T Park, you'd expect this South Beach "pre-game yuppie spot" to be a "traditional sports bar" but "surprised" "orange-and-black" fans

reveal the "friendly" folk "bring out real" American food in a "posh setting" that's even suitable for a "high-powered business lunch"; still, a miffed few say "no Mo'" to the "eats" and "hit the pitchers", adding "service goes to hell when the Giants are in town."

Moose's 21 20 20 $46
1652 Stockton St. (bet. Filbert & Union Sts.), 415-989-7800; www.mooses.com

"Ed Moose will be a hard act to follow", but his "classy North Beach" "icon" is "moving forward under new ownership" and still-game loyalists say the "feel-good" vibe and "well-crafted" New American fare remain "very enjoyable"; droves commend a staff that "doesn't attempt to sell you" food "as art" and the "comfortable jazz-infused ambiance", concurring it's a "delightful", "no-rush" "place to run into politicos, sports celebs" or "SF society"; P.S. you "can't beat" the "wonderful views" of Washington Square.

Morton's, The Steakhouse 24 20 23 $67
400 Post St. (bet. Mason & Powell Sts.), 415-986-5830; www.mortons.com

"Bring a hearty appetite and a wad of cash" to this Downtown branch of Chicago's "posh chop-shop" with a "clublike atmosphere" and "old-school service" that make you "feel like a member"; once "you get past the wiggling lobster" and "shrink-wrapped" "spiel", "meat-eating men" can't think of a "more pleasant way to go than to be super-sized" by "steaks bigger than your head" with baked potatoes that could "feed four"; P.S. the "fabulous wine list" will "make expense accounts scream."

Mo's 22 12 16 $17
1322 Grant Ave. (bet. Green & Vallejo Sts.), 415-788-3779
Yerba Buena Gardens, 772 Folsom St. (bet. 3rd & 4th Sts.), 415-957-3779
www.mosgrill.com

It's "tough to one-up" this duo for "top-quality" patties – if you're looking for your beef "fix, here it is", on "artisan-crafted buns" served amid the "North Beach hustle-bustle" and on top of the Moscone Convention Center; they "grind their own meat and cut their own fries" – it's "fascinating" to watch the "huge, juicy burgers cooked on a rotating grill" – "only wish there were" mo' sites.

MYTH ☒ Ⓜ 25 25 24 $55
470 Pacific Ave. (bet. Montgomery & Sansome Sts.), 415-677-8986; www.mythsf.com

"The apple doesn't fall far from the tree" laud acolytes who go out on a limb to praise "Danko protégée" Sean O'Brien who "branched out" to this "sleek NYC"-style Downtowner, offering a "happy mixture of good design, fabulous" New American food, a "buzzy" bar, an "inspired wine list" and servers that "have their act down"; if a few are "mythtified" about this "hot reservation", the "sexy sleek" purr "can't wait to find a sugar daddy to take me again" 'cause the "only bigger show in town is Barry Bonds."

Naan 'n Curry 19 7 10 $13
398 Eddy St. (bet. Jones & Leavenworth Sts.), 415-775-1349
642 Irving St. (bet. 7th & 8th Aves.), 415-664-7225 ◗
533 Jackson St. (Columbus Ave.), 415-693-0499 ◗
336 O'Farrell St. (bet. Mason & Taylor Sts.), 415-346-1443 ◗

For "addictive curry" in "a hurry" beat a path to these "barebones", "serve yourself" BYO Paki-Indians (with a "no-frills" "high-taste" branch in Berkeley); the "deafening" "Bollywood music", "free chai", "hearty naan" and "cheap" dishes make it a "student-budget dream", plus as "every cab driver" knows, you can get a "solid meal at a late hour" (and 24/7 at the new O'Farrell branch).

Nectar Wine Lounge　　18 | 22 | 21 | $30

3330 Steiner St. (bet. Chestnut & Lombard Sts.), 415-345-1377; www.nectarwinelounge.com

"Epitomizing the Marina", this "sexy-cool" "enoteca" with an "informed staff" delivers a "bodacious" bounty of over "50 choices by the glass" with "cleverly worded" "descriptions for each one" paired with Californian small plates to "take the edge off"; it's "tough to get a seat" with all the "sophisticates clamoring to get" in, "but once you do, it's cozy"; still, whiners wail the "food's not in the same league"; N.B. a Burlingame branch is slated to open this fall.

Nick's Crispy Tacos ⊄　　22 | 10 | 13 | $12

2101 Polk St. (Broadway), 415-409-8226

Fish "tacos never tasted this good outside of Mexico" insist Russian Hill regulars who pack this makeshift Baja "bordello" to "sip agua frescas" or "margaritas from a jug" and consume "cheap, fresh" "first-rate Mexican" in an "eclectic setting" that "doubles as a nightclub" "underneath glitter balls and piñatas"; remember "Nick's way is the only way" to get the "habit-forming" creations "crispy" – just go before the "take-out counter" "turns into the Rouge."

Nicky's Pizzeria Rustica Ⓜ⊄　　– | – | – | I

2109 Polk St. (bet. Broadway & Vallejo Sts.), 415-771-4222

Taco-titan Nick Fasanella sets out to master that other quickie meal at his new "casual" pizzeria with a Venetian-style stand-up counter and a smattering of stools next door to his Russian Hill taqueria; "even a New Yorker" will qvell over the "quality slices" and "creative" rectangular brick-oven-baked pies made from "flavorful" focaccia-style dough with homemade toppings as well as the seasonal salads and modest wine selection; N.B. open till 2 AM on Friday and Saturday.

Nihon ❶Ⓢ　　▽ 22 | 25 | 20 | $43

1779 Folsom St. (14th St.), 415-552-4400; www.dajanigroup.net

If only you could "bottle the spirit" of this "loungey" izakaya-style "spirits bar" in the Mission, where snackers "shell out" for "hopped-up rolls" ("sushi burgers to die for"), "cleverly done" "Japanese tapas" and more than 160 "exorbitantly priced whiskeys"; a dimly lit, bi-level lounge with an "illuminated stone-faced bar" is "where the cool kids hang out", while upstairs, diners "chill" on the balcony or tipple in the "private VIP room."

Nob Hill Café　　20 | 14 | 19 | $29

1152 Taylor St. (bet. Clay & Sacramento Sts.), 415-776-6500; www.nobhillcafe.com

There are "no reservations, no room and no bad meals" at this "non-glam" "locals'" trattoria "hidden among high-end hotels"; it's "worth waiting outside" for a "quieter" seat "away from the open kitchen" – you may even catch the Nob Hill "elite" out for a "casual", "affordable" Northern Italian meal and the "famous 'San Francisco twins'" who, paired with the "cable car a few blocks away", give this "pleasant" "favorite" a "classic" Frisco vibe.

NoPa ⏰　　　　　　　　　　　–｜–｜–｜M

560 Divisadero St. (bet. Fell & Hayes Sts.), 415-864-8643; www.nopasf.com

A triumvirate of Chow alumni has opened this affordable North of the Panhandle eatery in the Western Addition, where chef Laurence Jossel (ex Chow and Chez Nous) prepares 'urban rustic' Cal cuisine – local, seasonal, organic fare made in the wood-fired grill, rotisserie and pizza ovens and served until 1 AM nightly; there's mezzanine seating by the open kitchen, a communal table and a concrete-topped bar mixing juiced-to-order cocktails.

North Beach Pizza　　　　　　18｜9｜14｜$17

1310 Grant Ave. (Vallejo St.), 415-433-2444
1499 Grant Ave. (Union St.), 415-433-2444 ⏰
4787 Mission St. (bet. Persia & Russia Aves.), 415-586-1400 ⏰
Pier 39 (bet. Grant & Stockton Sts., off The Embarcadero), 415-433-0400
800 Stanyan St. (Haight St.), 415-751-2300 ⏰
3054 Taraval St. (41st Ave.), 415-242-9100 ⏰
www.northbeachpizza.com

Plying "big, chewy" "pizza with tons of cheese" "for decades", these "solid", family-friendly "San Francisco institutions" throughout the Bay Area are led by "the original in North Beach", though "late-night" branches and delivery service are key "when other sidewalks have rolled up"; still, skeptics say "fast service" can be "sloppy" and pan the pies as "greasy", "doughy" disks; N.B. locations with seating pour beer and wine only.

North Beach Restaurant ⏰　　23｜18｜22｜$44

1512 Stockton St. (bet. Green & Union Sts.), 415-392-1700;
www.northbeachrestaurant.com

Devotees declare "don't bother with the other" "typical tourist traps in North Beach" when this "old-skool" "staple" awaits with "waiters in tuxes" serving "local power players" and "politicos" "great" "traditional upscale" Tuscan eats, a "huge" vino selection and "TLC" in a "classic", "romantic" setting with "house-cured" "prosciutto hanging in the basement"; opposing factions, however, find the food "tired" and "disappointing" considering "the price tag" and "attitude."

One Market ⊠　　　　　　　22｜21｜21｜$50

1 Market St. (Steuart St.), 415-777-5577; www.onemarket.com

"Bradley Ogden's" city-central "eat and be seen" power-broker" "expense-account" "hot spot" serves "fresh and creative" New American food that's not "over-the-top trendy" with an "excellent" "domestic wine list" in a "bright", "bustling" "open dining room" providing great views of the Embarcadero (and "who's planning the next merger"); "service can vary", though, depending on your "luck"; P.S. "food temple-y" types should "reserve the chef's table in the kitchen."

Oola Restaurant & Bar ⏰　　20｜21｜19｜$40

860 Folsom St. (bet. 4th & 5th Sts.), 415-995-2061; www.oola-sf.com

Troo, it's a "late-night special for the club crowd", but "that's just the least of the virtues" of this "sleek and stylish" "two-story" "former elevator repair shop" with a "cool vibe" "fitting for SoMa"; the "whimsical" self-billed 'San Francisco bistro' fare (a blend of New American and French bistro) is "extravagant and comfort food at the same time" (at "reasonable prices"), and "talented bartenders" pouring "interesting cocktails" add to the "big buzz."

O'Reilly's Holy Grail
▽ 20 | 24 | 20 | $37

1233 Polk St. (Bush St.), 415-928-1233; www.oreillysholygrail.com
"Unusual" medieval decor of "antiques", "beautiful stained glass" and "bricolage thrift" "keeps you studying the walls" at Russian Hill's "upscale pub" in an 1865 building; the "reasonably priced", "rib-sticking" Continental classics and seafood range from colcannon to seviche, and live music and Sunday Irish dancing make it a "fun destination" – even if some posit it's "still figuring itself out" and suggest "service is a bit less than professional."

Original Joe's
18 | 13 | 19 | $28

144 Taylor St. (bet. Eddy & Turk Sts.), 415-775-4877
"Hipsters" appreciate the "irony" of ordering "huge helpings" of "working man's food" from "gruff" "tuxedo-clad waiters" "who maybe served your grandfather" at this Italian-American Tenderloin "landmark" with a "1940s film noir feel"; it's "fun" to "sit at the counter, watch the show" and "time travel" – though the "comfort food" is hardly "original"; the separately owned Peninsula branch – "where Sinatra would go if he came to San Jose" – gets props for "late-night" hours; N.B. other independent Joe's abound.

Osha Thai Noodles
22 | 18 | 16 | $20

149 Second St. (bet. Howard & Mission Sts.), 415-278-9991
696 Geary St. (Leavenworth St.), 415-673-2368 ◑
819 Valencia St. (19th St.), 415-826-7738 ◑
Fraternal Siamese trio each represent "a destination and a deal" to fans of "fresh" Thai above and beyond "the ubiquitous neighborhood place"; the SoMa newcomer is "popular" with Financial folks for lunch, while hungover habitués prefer "the grime" and extended hours (3 AM on Fridays and Saturdays) of the 'loin and "hipsters" swarm the "swish" Mission venue – though service "suffers" when these "cheap" noodle houses "get busy."

Ottimista Enoteca-Café Ⓜ
20 | 21 | 20 | $28

1838 Union St. (Octavia St.), 415-674-8400; www.ottimistasf.com
"Union Street grows up" with this "rustic" Cow Hollow enoteca where an "aim-to-please staff" waits on a "date" and "girls' night out" crowd at "wine barrel" tables or on the patio; "tasty" small and bigger Italian-Med bites "seem matched to the" "interesting" vino selection (250 bottles, 30 glass pours at a "range of prices") "rather than the other way around" – it almost "feels like you've stumbled on a European bistro."

Ozumo
24 | 24 | 19 | $49

161 Steuart St. (bet. Howard & Mission Sts.), 415-882-1333;
www.ozumo.com
"Sit at the bar for the hippest view of who's who" at this "sushi and meat market rolled into one" just off the Embarcadero, where dotcom "survivors in black" and an "after-work crowd" munch on "orgasmically good" "modern and traditional" Japanese tidbits while drinking in "amazing views of the waterfront" and top-shelf sakes amid "Zen" "disco" digs; "just don't calculate how much your nigiri costs per bite"– and "good luck snagging your server."

Pacific Café
21 | 15 | 22 | $29

7000 Geary Blvd. (34th Ave.), 415-387-7091
"Skip the Wharf and pricey Downtown fisheries" for this "affordable", "old reliable" Outer Richmond "neighborhood" haunt near

the ocean "with the charm of old San Francisco"; little "has changed since opening day – certainly not" the retro '70s decor, the menu of "simple, well-prepared fresh fish", the "friendly" "staff or patrons" who get "happy" on "free jug wine" while they "wait, and wait, and wait" for a seat.

Pacific Catch

21 | 12 | 16 | $20

2027 Chestnut St. (bet. Fillmore & Steiner Sts.), 415-440-1950; www.pacificcatch.com

"Great for fish fiends", this "sardine-can"-sized Marina madhouse lures crowds with "guilt-free" "Pacific Rim–inspired" "fast food", "from Baja tacos" and "wasabi bowls brimming with rice and vegetables" to a grilled "fresh catch" of the day (with "addictive sweet potato fries"), all at "reasonable prices"; in stark contrast, the "kid-friendly" Corte Madera branch has four times the seating, plus a patio; N.B. a new branch is slated to open in Palo Alto.

Pakwan

22 | 5 | 10 | $13

501 O'Farrell St. (Jones St.), 415-776-0160 ◗
3182 16th St. (bet. Guerrero & Valencia Sts.), 415-255-2440 ⊟

"Authentic" curries with enough "spice to make your scalp sweat" and "tasty" tandooris whose "smoke" will "open your nasal passages" please Pak-addicts at these self-serve Tenderloin and (cash-only) Mission Pakistani-Indian outposts; you "can't beat the prices or portions", but you "wouldn't want to eat off the floor or with the staff" of these "bare-bones and divey" "BYOs"; N.B. there's a branch in Hayward too.

Palio d'Asti ⊠

20 | 18 | 20 | $43

640 Sacramento St. (bet. Kearny & Montgomery Sts.), 415-395-9800; www.paliodasti.com

"Genuine" "refined" *cucina* that "changes with the seasons" (Northern in the winter and fall, Southern in the spring and summer) is complemented by "superlative" Italian vinos and a "service-oriented staff" (that no longer includes founder Gianni Fassio) at this "pretty" Palio-inspired "businessperson's dream" "lunch place" and stealth choice for a "quiet" weekday dinner "sans reservations"; P.S there's still "no better deal Downtown than the pizza happy hour."

Pancho Villa Taqueria

23 | 9 | 13 | $11

3071 16th St. (bet. Mission & Valencia Sts.), 415-864-8840 ◗
Pier 1, The Embarcadero (Washington St.), 415-982-2182

Amigos of this "crowd-pleasing" taqueria trio in the Mission, Embarcadero and San Mateo "find nirvana in the warm embrace" of "monster" "bursting burritos", "piled-high" tacos and other "fresh" Mexican "munchies" and also belly up to the "salsa bar from heaven" (with "f-ing hot hot sauce"); sound effects in the "clean" "cafeteria-style" confines might include "roving musicians" and the "ear-splitting chop of the meat cleaver"; P.S. hours vary by location, but "if there's a line, wait!"

Pane e Vino

22 | 17 | 19 | $33

1715 Union St. (Gough St.), 415-346-2111; www.paneevinotrattoria.com

"Cow Hollow's tasty shrine" remains a "quintessential", "noisy" "neighborhood trattoria" where "locals bring parents and strollers as well as dates" for "simple, straightforward" and "reasonably priced" Northern Italian in a "low-key" setting staffed by servers "eager to show diners a good time"; some feel the "formerly hip" haunt has "lost a bit of its magic since the move to a bigger place", but *amici* assert it's "mellowed with age."

Papalote Mexican Grill   22 | 13 | 16 | $10 |
1777 Fulton St. (Masonic Ave.), 415-776-0106
3409 24th St. (Valencia St.), (415) 970 8815
www.papalote-sf.com

USF students and "Mission hipsters" form "lines out the door" for the "off-the-meter carne asada" and "veg-friendly" options ("soyrizo!") at these "cheap", "bustling" burrito "joints" vibrant with *papalotes* (kites), rocking music and a feel-good vibe; what "differentiates" them from the pack is "unique" "secret salsa" that elevates the "fresh", "no lard", "made-to-order Mexican eats" – though partialists pout "they are parsimonious with it."

Park Chalet   14 | 22 | 15 | $26 |
1000 Great Hwy. (bet. Fulton St. & Lincoln Way), 415-386-8439;
www.beachchalet.com

Perched where Golden Gate Park "meets the ocean" in the Outer Sunset, this glassed-in back extension of the Beach Chalet lures with "secret garden" outdoor seating "when the weather's nice" and live music by the "roaring fireplace" "when the weather's bad"; "you are paying for the view", though, not the "uninspired", "pricey" New American small plates or the "slow service."

Park Grill   19 | 20 | 22 | $47 |
Park Hyatt Hotel, 333 Battery St. (Clay St.), 415-296-2933; www.hyatt.com

"Hearty", "reliable" New American eats and a "good wine list" are proffered by an "attentive" staff at this "understated but re-fined" dining room in the Park Hyatt Hotel, a "pleasant" Downtown destination for "power breakfasts", a "low-key" busi-ness lunch or a "quiet weekday dinner" "without a wait" – espe-cially "if someone else is paying"; N.B. no dinner on weekends.

Pasta Pomodoro   16 | 13 | 16 | $19 |
3611 California St. (Spruce St.), 415-831-0900
816 Irving St. (9th Ave.), 415-566-0900
2304 Market St. (16th St.), 415-558-8123
1865 Post St. (Fillmore St.), 415-674-1826
4000 24th St. (Noe St.), 415-920-9904
655 Union St. (Columbus Ave.), 415-399-0300
1875 Union St. (Laguna St.), 415-771-7900
www.pastapomodoro.com

"Yeah, it's a chain, but" "for families" or anyone seeking "fast", "filling" and "cheap" Italian standards with "a decent glass of wine", these "neighborhood" trattorias are like the "Starbucks of pasta" – "reliable", "customer-focused" and "clean"; still, pur-ists pan the "pedestrian" provender and "iffy service", preferring to cook macaroni "at home"; P.S. the "plain"-Jane settings are enhanced by sidewalk seating at most branches.

Patxi's Chicago Pizza ⓜ   21 | 14 | 17 | $18 |
511 Hayes St. (Octavia St.), 415-558-9991; www.patxispizza.com
See review in South of San Francisco Directory.

Pauline's Pizza ⓢⓜ   25 | 15 | 18 | $21 |
260 Valencia St. (bet. Duboce Ave. & 14th St.), 415-552-2050
Despite the proliferation of Mission pizzerias, this "New Age California" concept may be "the best" considering its "fresh",

"innovative" pies with "thin, thin bubbly crusts" and "organic vegetables from their Berkeley garden" (kudos for "incredible pesto" pie), "killer salads" and "cheap carafes" from the house winery; still, some suggest "takeout is easy" since "getting a seat [or finding parking] isn't", and service can be "scattered" amid the "bright", "simple" setting.

paul k Ⓜ 21 | 17 | 21 | $42
199 Gough St. (Oak St.), 415-552-7132; www.paulkrestaurant.com
Hayes Valley's "SoHo"-style Mediterranean feels like a "welcome respite" reveal admirers who peg it as a "perfect" pre- or "post-concert" place and a "romantic" "first-date" spot "without the big white-linen expectations"; "love the energy" and the "inventive" entrees and meze laced with "uncommon flavors", plus the "staff sparkles"; still, a handful lament "if only the tables weren't so squished" and quibble that service is "consistently inconsistent."

Pazzia Ⓢ 22 | 14 | 21 | $30
337 Third St. (bet. Folsom & Harrison Sts.), 415-512-1693
"Real Italian comfort food" sustains this "small", "jam-packed" SoMa "neighborhood" "secret" serving "great carpaccio", fresh pastas, "paper-thin pizzas" and other wood-fired Tuscan fare that "won't break the bank"; "everyone speaks" the native language including the "welcoming" "imported staff" ("it has a sister restaurant in Florence"), and "the clientele is mostly Italian" ("a good sign"), so don't be deterred if "it looks ordinary when walking by" the "carry-out type" "storefront."

Pesce 23 | 18 | 21 | $36
2227 Polk St. (bet. Green & Vallejo Sts.), 415-928-8025
"The fish is still wiggling" at this "packed", "convivial" Russian Hill "neighborhood"-er whose "creative" "Venetian" (Northern Italian) vittles made with organic ingredients and "scrumptious seafood" are served on "small plates" (that "aren't small on flavor") "in a small package" (meaning the "tiny" location); "affordable prices" add to the appeal, as do the "real fun cocktails"; P.S. "bits and bites" are also available at weekend brunch and lunch.

Pho Hoa-Hiep II 21 | 6 | 13 | $10
1833 Irving St. (bet. 19th & 20th Aves.), 415-664-0469
See review in East of San Francisco Directory.

Picaro 19 | 15 | 15 | $24
3120 16th St. (bet. Guerrero & Valencia Sts.), 415-431-4089
San Francisco's first tapas bar may "not be the best", but it's "one of the cheaper, easier choices in the Mission", serving the same menu as its "more popular" sibling, Esperpento, alongside "affordable pitchers" of "killer sangria"; in the "cavernous" dining room, you'll have to "shout to be heard" (a hazard when you've got "garlic breath"), but it's "a rocking good time" – "isn't that what a Spanish restaurant is supposed to be about!?"

Piperade Ⓢ 25 | 21 | 22 | $47
1015 Battery St. (Green St.), 415-391-2555; www.piperade.com
Gerald Hirigoyen's "rustic" Downtown hideaway "still Basques in the culinary heavens where they're not afraid to cook real food" – namely "zesty", "imaginative" "regional" Spanish fare – or serve "wines you have never heard of"; the "cozy" "old-world interior", featuring a "large communal table" and overseen by a "charm-

ing" staff, likewise makes for a "nice change from the ordinary"; N.B. Piperade To-Go, located around the corner, serves breakfast and lunch fare until 3 PM.

Pizzeria Delfina

24 | 15 | 18 | $22

3611 18th St. (Guerrero St.), 415-437-6800; www.delfinasf.com
"Hallelujah! authentic Italian pizza has come to the Mission", but "spectacular thin-crust, blistered-edge" "gourmet pies" aren't all at this "great Delfina spin-off" – "tempting appetizers", "impossibly fresh salads" and select wines receive "the same attention to detail" as they get next door for a "fraction of the cost"; seating is "limited" so it's "hard to get a table" inside or "outside under the heat lamps", but for most, it's "worth the long waits."

Pizzetta 211 ♥

25 | 14 | 14 | $23

211 23rd Ave. (California St.), 415-379-9880
"Discerning, hip pizza lovers" insist that the, ahem, notoriously "difficult" "attitude" of "rustic artisan" Ria Ramsey – chef-owner of "the most unexpected little" "storefront" pizzeria "tucked away" in the Outer Richmond – is "worth enduring" for the sake of "honest", "tantalizing", "unique" pies that "turn out perfectly every time" ("try the fried-egg pizza", a signature); just "come early" and "bring a coat", because the "first come, first served" policy can lead to "chilly" waits outside.

PJ's Oyster Bed

18 | 15 | 16 | $31

737 Irving St. (9th Ave.), 415-566-7775; www.pjsoysterbed.com
Though this Creole joint in the Inner Sunset, its "colorful" "ambiance brings you to New Orleans" – where, fans promise, "charmingly eccentric" "seafood experts" earn their beads by "laying on the hot sauce" (which "tasty" cocktails quench); skeptics, however, beg to differ, citing "bland" eats ("overpriced for what you get") and "forgetful service" as evidence that this "institution" is "well past its prime."

Platanos Cafe y Cocina Rustica

21 | 19 | 19 | $31

598 Guerrero St. (18th St.), 415-252-9281; www.platanos-sf.com
"It's worth bypassing the $5 taco places and splurging on" the "gourmet" goodies at this Nuevo Latino bastion of "tropical" "chic", "one of the Mission's hidden treasures" – at least until word gets out about new partner Pascal Rigo, who has upped the ante with a small-plates menu boasting "plantains galore" (not reflected in the Food score); check it out during happy hour (3:30–6:30 PM), when the "killer sangria" is half-price.

Plouf ☒

22 | 16 | 18 | $36

40 Belden Pl. (bet. Bush & Pine Sts.), 415-986-6491; www.ploufsf.com
This "hopping" Belden Place bistro has bivalve lovers coming out of their shells "on warm nights" to "people-watch outdoors" while "hot French waiters" bear "bowls full" of "truly unforgettable" "mussels, mussels, mussels!" (*avec frites*, *naturellement*); but the "little slice of Europe" vibe isn't as evident inside where patrons feel more like "sardines" stuck in an "urban jungle."

PlumpJack Cafe

25 | 22 | 23 | $52

3127 Fillmore St. (bet. Filbert & Greenwich Sts.), 415-563-4755; www.plumpjack.com
"Don't even think of ordering a bottle you know" at this "chic", "intimate" "wine lover's dream" in Cow Hollow that's "still com-

ing on strong", luring an "A-list crowd" with "well-balanced" "gourmet" Cal-Med cuisine and "excellent service"; the "dim" lighting makes "people look prettier", but what really sets this dining "delight" "apart" is the "high-class" vino list (it's "no longer a stellar bargain" but it's still "absolutely incredible"); P.S. the "cozy après-ski" sibling in Olympic Valley is a "real gift from SF."

Pluto's Fresh Food for a Hungry Universe　　21　12　14　$13
627 Irving St. (bet. 7th & 8th Aves.), 415-753-8867
3258 Scott St. (bet. Chestnut & Lombard Sts.), 415-775-8867
www.plutosfreshfood.com
For "fantastically fresh", "reasonably healthy" "cafeteria-style" "fast food" "at working persons' prices", "you can't beat" this Inner Sunset/Marina duo; the "customized salads" and "meaty grilled sandwiches" in particular are "no-brainers" for "grab-and-go" lunches and on weeknights – even if the "Byzantine ordering system" itself can lead to "chaos during peak hours."

Poleng Lounge Ⓜ　　–　–　–　I
1751 Fulton St. (bet. Central & Masonic Ave.), 415-441-1751;
www.polenglounge.com
The Western Addition's new Balinese-inspired lounge, whose name translates to 'duality', is part Zen-inspired Pan-Asian teahouse/restaurant and part nightclub; by day, the Indonesian-style fireside front room caters to UCSF students with rice bowls, sandwiches and traditional snacks; after dark, hipsters zero in on 25-cent crispy adobe chicken wings (during happy hour) and street food prepared by a former Fifth Floor chef – with sake and sochu to wash it down – then move into the Temple Room for DJs and dancing after 10 PM.

Pomelo　　22　13　19　$21
1793 Church St. (30th St.), 415-285-2257
92 Judah St. (6th Ave.), 415-731-6175
www.pomelosf.com
For a global "culinary adventure" involving "consistently excellent" noodles and grains, this "creative" Eclectic "fast fusion" "find" is the first stop for many Noe Valley and Inner Sunset locals; the "distinctive dishes" are "subject to ups and downs", but usually there's "something for everyone" – including "many options for veggieheads" and a brunch that's "tops"; if you feel "'pommeled' by the close quarters", turn to takeout.

Ponzu　　20　20　19　$41
Serrano Hotel, 401 Taylor St. (bet. Geary & O'Farrell Sts.), 415-775-7979
In the "dark, enchanting environs" of this "funky" Downtown "pre-theater" "scene" set next door to the Serrano Hotel, groups of "friends who like to share" "skip the entrees and just sample" the "shareable" Pan-Asian small plates, pronouncing some "creative", others "overcreated"; the dishes may be "served in sort of a haphazard way", but after a "yuzu martini or two you hardly notice the muddle."

Pork Store Café　　20　12　16　$15
1451 Haight St. (bet. Ashbury St. & Masonic Ave.), 415-864-6981
3122 16th St. (bet. Guerrero & Valencia Sts.), 415-626-5523
No mere "havens of unhealthy breakfast foods", these "old-style" Traditional American diners in Haight-Ashbury and the Mission are

"piggy paradises": "crammed on weekends" with "tattooed hipsters" gorging on "hangover helpers", they can be "raucous", but if you "come on a weekday and miss the lines", you'll find it "friendly and homey" (if your home includes" "grease caked on the walls").

Postrio   24 | 24 | 23 | $60 |
Prescott Hotel, 545 Post St. (bet. Mason & Taylor Sts.), 415-776-7825; www.postrio.com

"Yeah, yeah, it's dated" aficionados of Wolfgang Puck's Downtown "SF Spago" admit, but "it still thrills to make the Dolly Levi entrance" down the "dramatic staircase" and "be bowled over" by the whole "showy" experience, starring "haute" New American cuisine (including pizza) and "knowledgeable" service – both "still going strong" despite "occasional missteps"; nevertheless, snip stylehounds, "in a market where six months is old, not updating the decor for 20 years seems criminal" – good thing a renovation is scheduled for 2007.

Powell's Place   ∇ 19 | 12 | 13 | $21 |
Fillmore Jazz Preservation Ctr., 1521 Eddy St. (Fillmore St.), 415-409-1388

Known for dishing up "real" Southern "food for the soul", gospel radio personality Emmit Powell's "SF treasure" is reclaiming its groove following a move to "cleaner", more spacious digs in the Fillmore Jazz District; although "they lack the patina that was part of the charm" of the original, everything else is "pretty much the same" – "the fried chicken is still famous" and the "friendly staff" still "inevitably" gets "the orders wrong."

Public, The ⊠ Ⓜ   19 | 21 | 18 | $37 |
1489 Folsom St. (11th St.), 415-552-3065; www.thepublicsf.com

Set in a historical "exposed-brick building" in SoMa, this "cool joint" is an "awesome" place to "chill with friends" and "watch the clubbers go by" – or just gape at the "industrial decor", perhaps "a bit tooo hip for normal people" (in striking contrast to the "friendly service"); meanwhile, "groups who want to eat reasonably" repair to the mezzanine level for "down-to-earth" Cal-Med "home cooking" that ranges from "impressive" to "fair."

Puerto Alegre   18 | 11 | 15 | $17 |
546 Valencia St. (bet. 16th & 17th Sts.), 415-255-8201

Hordes of "bar-hopping" "Mission hipsters" start here with "margaritas to make [their] lips go numb", accompanied by "the ultimate in Mexican comfort food" – as well as "roving mariachis"; even gastronomes who deem the "cheap" grub "greasy" and "mediocre" "keep returning" for the "happy", "lively atmosphere" enhanced by "warm and welcoming" service.

Q   20 | 16 | 18 | $22 |
225 Clement St. (bet. 3rd & 4th Aves.), 415-752-2298

"Want your teenagers to think you're still cool? take them" to this "vibrant" "neighborhood joint" in the Inner Richmond whose "kitschy", "quirky" decor includes "alphabet magnets to play with" and a menu of "solid" "modern" American "comfort food" "scrawled on the wall in chalk"; "from meatloaf to a vegan plate, there's something for everyone" – though "oversized" portions especially suit the "twentysomething" "crowd", emitting the same "upbeat" "energy" as the "unpretentious" staff.

QUINCE   27 23 25 $63
1701 Octavia St. (bet. Bush & Pine Sts.), 415-775-8500;
www.quincerestaurant.com
"Food is now the drug of choice" at this "tranquil" former "apoth-
ecary" in Pac Heights, whose chef-owner "crafts" daily changing
New French and "Italian-influenced" dishes "so fresh you feel
virtuous eating them" ("don't skip" the "heavenly" homemade
pastas) and a "veteran staff" of "pros" "guides you through" the
"fantastic wine list"; "good luck getting a reservation" – the 15
"tables are hard to come by" (ditto the "wonderful chef's table") –
but the experience rivals the city's "best" "with much less hype."

Ramblas   20 18 19 $28
557 Valencia St. (bet. 16th & 17th Sts.), 415-565-0207;
www.ramblastapas.com
"The hardest part is parking" nearby – otherwise, enjoying a "fun
and festive" meal at this Mission tapas bar is easy: just "ramble
in" for "decently sized small plates" whose "quality-to-cost ratio
is above average", paired with "sangria strong enough to induce
hallucinations of Barcelona"; though "nothing fancy", it's a
great place for a group" "to get cozy and stay for a while."

R & G Lounge   23 12 15 $26
631 Kearny St. (bet. Clay & Sacramento Sts.), 415-982-7877;
www.rnglounge.com
"Hugely popular with the Downtown business crowd", this
"Chinatown cheapie" is "famous for its seafood", especially
"finger-lickin' good" "salt-and-pepper crab at its best"; but
check all other expectations for fine dining at the door – "the
service is just ok", and while "fancy tablecloths" await upstairs,
"the action is downstairs" (where it's a "pity about the decor").

Range   25 21 22 $44
842 Valencia St. (20th St.), 415-282-8283
Even city folk "feel at home on the Range", calling this Mission "hot
spot", run by a husband-and-wife team, one of "the best restaurants to open in many moons"; the "exceptional" New American
menu "incorporates local organic products" in "exciting flavor"
combos, while "inspired" cocktails make it "almost as fun to stop
just for a drink" and soak up the "industrial-chic" vibe at the "cool
bar" where crowds gather "cheek to jowl" "any night of the week."

Red's Java House   15 11 14 $10
Pier 30 (Bryant St., off The Embarcadero), 415-777-5626
Return to "a bygone era" at this "venerable" ex-longshoreman's
shack on the Embarcadero, now a "blue-collar" "dive" whose
"messy" double cheeseburger on sourdough is "a nostalgic
treat"; paired with "a long-neck Bud" and a Bay view, it still costs
"less than parking valet" elsewhere; no wonder even gourmets
come to "kick back" "on the dock" "before Giants games."

Restaurant LuLu   21 19 18 $41
816 Folsom St. (bet. 4th & 5th Sts.), 415-495-5775
LuLu Petite
The Embarcadero, 1 Ferry Bldg. (Market St.), 415-362-7019
www.restaurantlulu.com
It's "no longer the hot new place", but SoMa's "barnlike temple to
slow-roasted meats" and French-Med "peasant fare" still draws

"electric crowds" "for a full-on dot-com flashback", "conventioneer" confab or just "a good time" sharing the family-style plates and "extensive wine menu"; still, crotchety folk carp the "cavernous" space evokes a "noisy" "school cafeteria", while its "open hearths" mean "you'll smell like a campfire girl" afterwards; N.B. an offshoot, LuLu Petite, is in the Ferry Plaza.

Richmond Restaurant and Wine Bar, The ⑤
▽ | 23 | 17 | 23 | $39 |

615 Balboa Ave. (bet. 7th & 8th Aves.), 415-379-8988;
www.therichmondsf.com
"Pretty swanky for" the Inner Richmond, this "relaxed" "little neighborhood hideaway" is worthy of "special occasions", thanks to a "charming" chef-owner who "stops by your table to chat" when he isn't crafting "exciting", "organic" Californian suppers with "surprising little touches" like "scrumptious homemade butter"; what's more, it's an "excellent value" – so while "locals" "hesitate" to share their "secret", they have to admit it's "worth the trek."

Rigolo ⑤
| 19 | 13 | 13 | $19 |

3465 California St. (Laurel St.), 415-876-7777; www.rigolocafe.com
"Wonderful baked goods" make Pascal Rigo's "casual" Presidio Heights "favorite" "especially good for breakfast"; the New French "bistro-lite" fare served at lunch is "decent" but "mostly just convenient" – provided, that is, you "make it through the jam of Bugaboos to get in", then withstand the "chaotic" "cafeteria-style service" amid "kids' howls" (which the "play area" may or may not allay); it's "more calm at dinner time", but "horrid" uncomfortable chairs nevertheless cry for "takeout."

Ristorante Bacco
| 22 | 19 | 21 | $36 |

737 Diamond St. (bet. Elizabeth & 24th Sts.), 415-282-4969;
www.baccosf.com
When you want a Big Night Out without "making a production out of" it, "search out" this "reasonably priced" Noe Valley "treasure" with "caring service" and a "welcoming" atmosphere that makes you feel like you're "back in Tuscany" "dining at an Italian family's home"; the "hearty", "outstanding" fare, particularly "amazing homemade pasta", "comforting risotto" and all-Boot bottlings "rarely disappoint" confide Bacco believers" who "look forward" to each "wonderful" visit.

Ristorante Ideale ⓜ
▽ | 22 | 18 | 21 | $36 |

1309 Grant Ave. (Vallejo St.), 415-391-4129
"Close your eyes" and you'll "think you're in Rome" instead of North Beach vow visitors "wowed" by the "flirty" accented staff and "*molto Italiano*" vinos along with the "crispy pizza and killer housemade pastas" that this "mellow" "hidden gem" "spins out"; don't expect "huge portions that cater to an American palate" – instead, dig into "inventive fare" that's "more about quality than quantity" – and "still great after all these years."

Ristorante Milano
| 24 | 14 | 22 | $36 |

1448 Pacific Ave. (bet. Hyde & Larkin Sts.), 415-673-2961;
www.milanosf.com
Beyond a "plain storefront" in Russian Hill lies this "sleeping giant", a "cozy", "cramped" Northern Italian trattoria locals herald as a "lovely little neighborhood joint" – "once you sit down" you

discover it's "not just your average red-sauce joint", with a staff that "treats you like an old friend"; but "if you're looking for ambiance", head elsewhere, as the feel is more "Midwestern living room" than Milano.

Ristorante Parma ☒ | 21 | 16 | 21 | $30 |

3314 Steiner St. (bet. Chestnut & Lombard Sts.), 415-567-0500
"No matter your age, expect a few kisses or at least some hand-holding from the affectionate staff" at this "old-school Italian" "garlic lover's" "paradiso on the Marina's Restaurant Row", where "consistent", "affordable" eats dished up for over 25 years and "kitschy" erstwhile Roman-ruins confines have helped build a "neighborhood" reputation as a "family" and "first-date" fave; P.S. "they don't take reservations, so be prepared to wait."

Ristorante Umbria ☒ | 18 | 16 | 17 | $34 |

198 Second St. (Howard St.), 415-546-6985; www.ristoranteumbria.com
"Generous portions" and "tasty", "traditional" straight-outta-Umbria dishes make it "worth the fight to get in" to this "homey" SoMa Italian during the "crowded lunch" hour (especially if you "score" a "curbside table") or if you're attending a "performance at Yerba Buena Center"; note that "dinner excursions" can be "more satisfying", but either way, you'll receive "charming service" from owner Giulio who's so omnipresent he "should be a politician."

RITZ-CARLTON DINING ROOM ☒ Ⓜ | 27 | 27 | 28 | $93 |

Ritz-Carlton Hotel, 600 Stockton St. (bet. California & Pine Sts.), 415-773-6198; www.ritzcarlton.com
Not just TV fans "cheer" on *Iron Chef* Ron Siegel at Nob Hill's "most adult dining room" – "class"-act patrons "dressed for a black-tie event" jest he should "be knighted" for his "dazzling", "sublime" prix fixe menus – it's a "superb showcase of Modern French cuisine" "with Japanese influences"; expect a "sense of luxury not found" elsewhere, from the "fabulous" carts of cheese, champagne, candy and cordials rolled through the "formal" room to the "synchronized" staff – just "prepare to pay" the "price for perfection."

Ritz-Carlton Terrace | 24 | 24 | 25 | $56 |

Ritz-Carlton Hotel, 600 Stockton St. (bet. California & Pine Sts.), 415-773-6198; www.ritzcarlton.com
"Even the water tastes better" at this "lovely oasis", the more "casual" cousin of the Dining Room on Nob Hill "mother ship" where patrons pony up fewer bucks for "excellent" Mediterranean lunchtime "favorites" served in a "posh" setting; the "spectacular Sunday jazz brunch" "on the terrace is the ultimate in pampering" – it's not only a "caviar lovers' heaven" but a near-"religious experience" that'll "knock out out-of-town friends"; N.B. dinner Sunday and Monday only.

rnm ☒ Ⓜ | 23 | 22 | 20 | $42 |

598 Haight St. (Steiner St.), 415-551-7900; www.rnmrestaurant.com
Hipsters seeking a "nice respite from the grittiness of the Lower Haight" salute the "friendly host" and pass through chain-mail curtains into this "hidden gem", a "trendy" "discovery" with a "NYC feel" that delivers a one-two punch of a "cool, glamorous" setting coupled with "excellent" New American–French small plates; it's the "kind of food you think about months later" and what's more, the "wine list is lovely."

RoHan Lounge Ⓜ　　▽ 18 | 21 | 16 | $25

3809 Geary Blvd. (bet. 2nd & 3rd Aves.), 415-221-5095; www.rohanlounge.com

"Savory" "not-so-Korean"–Asian fusion small plates mixed with "fruity refreshing soju drinks" and a "sexy" "unique" feel keep Seoul sisters and hipsters "coming back for more" at this "narrow", "off-the-beaten-path" Inner Richmond lounge, which changed hands about a year ago; "the live DJs are a nice accompaniment to the appetizers and cocktails" – or is it the other way around wonder the "noise"-sensitive who find "the din unbearable."

Roosevelt Tamale Parlor Ⓜ∌　　– | – | – | I

2817 24th St. (bet. Bryant & York Sts.), 415-824-2600

Renowned for its round wraps and Teddy Roosevelt memorabilia, this briefly shuttered vintage Mission tamales mecca (circa 1922) is up and running again under new ownership (also responsible for Andalu and Bar Tartine); the recently renovated digs are small and cozy while the Mexican menu features updated traditional favorites; N.B. cash only.

Rosamunde Sausage Grill ∌　　25 | 8 | 18 | $8

545 Haight St. (bet. Fillmore & Steiner Sts.), 415-437-6851

They "do one thing and they do it well" at this "spectacular" Lower Haight American sausage "haunt", a stainless-steel "stand-up space sans sit-down space" specializing in "the best wurst in the city" ("fowl, cow, pig, any animal" really) with "grilled onions, peppers and chili" on top, "all for just a few bucks"; the "friendly fräulein" even let you "take 'em next door" to the Toronado Pub to "wash down with a beer."

Rose Pistola　　22 | 19 | 19 | $41

532 Columbus Ave. (bet. Green & Union Sts.), 415-399-0499; www.rosepistola.com

"Energy charged" with a "pleasant brasserie" feel and a "lively bar", this "spirited" "classic" Italian "still has it going on after" 10 years, rising "above most touristy North Beach" establishments; the "cavernous space hums with crowds devouring" Ligurian specialties, including "housemade pastas, fresh fish and chops" and "wonderful small plates" delivered by a "cheerful" staff; still, a few thorny types tut it's "lost a little luster."

Rose's Cafe　　20 | 17 | 18 | $29

2298 Union St. (Steiner St.), 415-775-2200

"Locals go here" by the blooming "thousand", but it's still "worth fighting the crowds" to tuck into the "fresh, simple and innovative" Northern Italian fare at this "homey" Cow Hollow haunt; "outdoor service with a European feel" seals its rep as a "great ladies-who-lunch spot" while brunchers boast that "breakfast pizzas are the ultimate treat", while pooch parents yap it's "incredibly dog-friendly (they even bake their own dog biscuits)."

Rotee　　▽ 18 | 15 | 18 | $15

400 Haight St. (Webster St.), 415-552-8309; www.roteesf.com

"Kicks curry butt" believe boosters who roll up to the counter of this "friendly" Indian-Pakistani in the Lower Haight for "distinctive", "addictive" dishes served to the beat of "hip, happening Bollywood sounds"; the "zany menu descriptions" and orange-and-yellow decor add to the "fun" feel, plus "everything is ultrafresh" with enough spice to "satisfy" cravings; still, a handful shrug it's "cheap, fast and good, not great."

Rotunda 21 | 24 | 20 | $38
Neiman Marcus, 150 Stockton St. (bet. Geary & O'Farrell Sts.), 415-362-4777
Perched above Union Square away from the "hustle-bustle" on the top floor of Neiman Marcus, you feel like you're "at the heartbeat of the city" as you take in the "amazing views"; "come for the pop-overs, stay for the lobster club" – "if you're doing serious shopping" the recently remodeled, "gorgeous room filled with light" is an "absolute must" – "you feel classy among the ladies who lunch" on New American fare and the gals who "gossip" over high tea.

Roy's 23 | 22 | 22 | $47
575 Mission St. (bet. 1st & 2nd Sts.), 415-777-0277; www.roysrestaurant.com
If you "can't get over to the islands this year", let SoMa's Hawaiian-"fusion paradise" "sweep you away on gossamer" wings to a state of "tropical bliss" – Roy Yamaguchi's chain "rarely disappoints, where e'er in the world" you go; the "hospi-table" staff helps you get into the aloha spirit while the "to-die-for butterfish" and the "best lava cake in the galaxy" "beat the office blues away"; still, the Roy-ally annoyed scoff at "overly large portions and a franchise feel."

Rubicon ⑤ 24 | 21 | 23 | $63
558 Sacramento St. (bet. Montgomery & Sansome Sts.), 415-434-4100; www.sfrubicon.com
"If Dionysus appeared in SF, he'd" cross Downtown and head to this oenophile's Olympus with a "men's club" feel owned by Drew Nieporent; the "witty" Cal-French menu is "meant to complement" the "phone-book-sized" vino list – and chef Stuart Brioza "excels" at getting the "mission accomplished", delivering "equally de-licious" dishes; it's almost a "guarantee you'll see someone famous" – and that you'll be impressed by the "promising somme-liers" who took over after "wine guy extraordinaire Larry Stone" flew north to run Francis Ford Coppola's Rubicon Estate winery.

Rue Saint Jacques Ⓜ 20 | 18 | 20 | $39
1098 Jackson St. (Taylor St.), 415-776-2002; www.ruesaintjacques.com
"Bring your Gitanes" – you can't light up, but they sure match the "lovely, lively" "Parisian bistro" feel of this "Nob Hill neighbor-hood" restaurant, a "delightful" spot "for a casual glass of wine" as well as "homey", "easy-on-the-wallet" Cal-French fare "with little pretension and lots of flavor"; but a few beret-ate the "rude service" and find the fare "doesn't measure up" to expectations – and "arrives haphazardly."

Ruth's Chris Steak House 24 | 19 | 21 | $60
1601 Van Ness Ave. (California St.), 415-673-0557; www.ruthschris.com
Nob Hill's "dependable" meatery with an "old-school" feel is "packed with AMEX-wielding business diners" who blissfully "ig-nore the fact that it's part of a chain", priming themselves for "big steaks, big sides – and the big bill at the end"; "so much buttery goodness" – "yep, that's the ticket" to the "tasty sizzling" beef – from "petite to cowboy"-sized portions "you're sure to find a cut to please", plus the "attentive staff" makes sure "you don't get a bum steer."

Saha Arabic Fusion Ⓜ   ▽ 24 | 22 | 23 | $39

Carlton Hotel, 1075 Sutter St. (bet. Hyde & Larkin Sts.), 415-345-9547;
www.sahasf.com

"Who knew Yemeni" and Californian could partner "so perfectly"
declares a "dazzled" demimonde, deeming this Middle Eastern
fusioner in the Tenderloin's Carlton Hotel a "hidden treasure"; the
"attentive service" and "darkened red room" with Moroccan
metalwork and "tapestries make it feel expensive", but prices are
"reasonable" (the prix fixe "is a steal"), plus the "chef knows how
to use spice", whipping up "amazing" small plates and entrees
including vegetarian choices.

Saigon Sandwiches ⊅   23 | 3 | 9 | $6

560 Larkin St. (Turk St.), 415-474-5698

"Bang, bang, bang" goes your buck at this "postage-stamp"-size
Tenderloin Vietnamese take-out joint, a "one-trick pony" where the
pennywise "grab change" and line up for "cheap banh mi" –
"crusty baguettes" "stuffed with tangy pickled carrots, jalapeños"
and meats; the staff "cranks out" sandwiches as "fast as they
can" – good thing since you don't want time to "dwell" on the "mar-
velously awful" interior and lack of seating; N.B. closes at 5:30 PM.

Sam's Grill & Seafood Restaurant ⓢ   20 | 16 | 20 | $39

374 Bush St. (bet. Kearny & Montgomery Sts.), 415-421-0594

"As dependable as a sunrise", this seafood stalwart is where
"movers and shakers" and dialed-in tourists head for "fish the way
the old-timers remember it" served in an "old-school to the core"
"San Francisco atmosphere" that's so "authentic" you half "expect
Sam Spade to drop by"; "glad to see the new owners are not tink-
ering" with the "pleasant booths" or staff – the same "snarky",
"seasoned" waiters that probably "knew Jonah" "await you."

Sanraku Four Seasons   22 | 13 | 18 | $31

Sony Metreon Ctr., 101 Fourth St. (Mission St.), 415-369-6166
704 Sutter St. (Taylor St.), 415-771-0803
www.sanraku.com

A "haven for value-conscious" sushi-seekers, this "friendly"
Japanese duo delivers a "satisfying experience", serving up "delightfully fresh" fin fare as well as "delicious" entrees; the Sony
Metreon Center locale has a "kind of shopping mall-ish atmosphere" while Sutter Street seems sort of "unassuming", but
they're both "crowded and hectic" for "good" reason: "you can't
beat" the "heaven-sent fish" for a "fast bite."

San Tung   24 | 8 | 13 | $16

1031 Irving St. (bet. 11th & 12th Aves.), 415-242-0828

"If you're ready to Wang Chung at San Tung", remember "there's
a reason for the consistent lines": the Chinese-Korean triple
threat of "excellent handmade noodles", "great potstickers" and
"wickedly addictive" dry fried chicken – so "get there early" because the "secret jewel of the Sunset is no longer a secret"; but
while it's a "great find for the money", a disdainful few "don't love
the communal tables" and "inconsistent service."

Sauce ◗   19 | 17 | 20 | $36

131 Gough St. (Oak St.), 415-252-1369; www.saucesf.com

"On the fringes of the opera-eating zone" in Hayes Valley lies the
"perfect place to catch up with friends over something filling";

the American "comfort food" with a "creative twist" gives your "bored palate" a "wonderful change" of pace – every "dish at the table was better than the next" contend saucy-seekers; if some sigh it's too "heavy", even they find it a "cozy, friendly" place to "drop in late" for a drink in the "beautiful" redwood bar.

Savor
18 | 15 | 18 | $20

3913 24th St. (bet. Noe & Sanchez Sts.), 415-282-0344

Mediterranean "crêpes overflowing with ingredients" and "ginormous salads" make this Noe Valley "favorite" with "responsive" service a "very popular brunch and lunch spot" – and the "default" solution on "those nights when you can't face cooking and don't want fancy" food either; still, the "best part about this place is the patio", particularly "on a nice day" – but bear in mind it can be a "stroller parking lot on weekends."

Scala's Bistro ◐
23 | 21 | 21 | $43

Sir Francis Drake Hotel, 432 Powell St. (bet. Post & Sutter Sts.), 415-395-8555; www.scalasbistro.com

"You can feel" the "vibrant" "energy walking in the door" of this "welcoming" "quintessential SF" "experience" in Union Square's "gorgeous Sir Francis Drake Hotel"; the "charming old-world atmosphere" and "low-key service make you want to linger" over the "delicious, delectable" bistro dishes that "evoke" Northern Italy and France, which explains why it's "perpetually packed with tourists, shoppers and the pre-theater crowd" – and sometimes "crazy loud" to boot; N.B. a post-*Survey* refurb and chef change may impact the scores.

Scoma's
22 | 18 | 19 | $41

Pier 47, 1 Al Scoma Way (bet. Jefferson & Jones Sts.), 415-771-4383; www.scomas.com

It's "worth elbowing past the tourists" to sit by the "big picture window" providing "spectacular San Francisco Bay" views vow vaunters who "crowd" into this "old-school Italian" seafooder in Fisherman's Wharf where "time has stood still"; "come hungry" and "enjoy the 'lazyman's cioppino' as the sea lions roar" or the "huge crab salads" and "enormous" servings of "fresh, nononsense" fish; still, some say the Sausalito branch, set in a Victorian waterfront building, is much "better."

Scott Howard
24 | 23 | 22 | $60

500 Jackson St. (Montgomery St.), 415-956-7040; www.scotthowardsf.com

A "new star in the gourmet ghetto" Downtown gush gastronomes who applaud this "stylish" Cal-French newcomer; chef/co-owner Scott Howard "puts his heart and soul" into the "out-of-this-world" fare featuring "wild flavors that blend together so subtly and perfectly" – "true foodies shouldn't let another day go without experiencing" the "tantalizing" dishes, or the "imaginative cocktails"; P.S. those who take the "tiny" tidbits to task may want to revisit as the menu changed post-*Survey,* with larger portions and a simpler approach.

Sears Fine Food
17 | 12 | 16 | $21

439 Powell St. (Sutter St.), 415-986-0700

"Stockholm meets Omaha" at this "restored" coffeeshop "icon" Downtown where service is "friendly" and "breakfast is the most important meal of the day" – and they "do Swedish pancakes right" ("don't forget the lingonberries"); if a flip few frown "it's lost its charm", defenders declare a "quirky", "vintage vibe" prevails – but "stick" with the "wonderfully comforting", "tasty" stack of "mini"-flapjacks or a lunchtime meal – "dinner is far less successful."

SEASONS ⎹ 25 ⎹ 25 ⎹ 27 ⎹ $59 ⎹

Four Seasons Hotel, 757 Market St. (bet. 3rd & 4th Sts.), 415-633-3838; www.fourseasons.com

"Serene", with "nice views onto Market Street", this "beautifully paneled room" in the Four Seasons has a "genteel elegance", making it a "favorite place to be pampered"; the Cal–New French fare is "fit for all seasons" – and meals – so duck in for a "delightful breakfast", "fancy lunch" or "carefully constructed" dinner, and whether you're there for a "business confab" or a "festive reunion", the "polished staff" will "treat you as if you're wealthy."

Sebo ⓈⓂ ⎹ – ⎹ – ⎹ – ⎹ E ⎹

517 Hayes St. (Octavia St.), 415-864-2122

Despite its American chef-owners, this petite, dimly lit minimalist Japanese Hayes Valley "newcomer" exudes an "authentic feel" eschewing fusion rolls for a limited selection that favors "fine" sushi and sashimi, spiked with fresh wasabi and house-brewed soy sauce; insiders counsel "don't be a fool: do the omakase" menu at the mahogany sushi bar and turn to the "young, hip encyclopedic waitresses" for help with the "eclectic, quality" sake list, crafted by the owner of the nearby True Sake store.

Senses Restaurant ⎹ – ⎹ – ⎹ – ⎹ M ⎹

1152 Valencia St. (bet. 22nd & 23rd Sts.), 415-648-6000

This culinary chameleon (formerly Watercress, and before that Watergate) on the Valencia corridor has morphed into a fancy-pants destination offering French-Californian cuisine and an international wine list in a chic wood-paneled dining room; while it's a tough sell in the ultracasual Mission, the owners have tapped up-and-coming chef Sophiane Benouda, who mentored under Paul Bocuse, to oversee the à la carte and prix fixe menus.

Shabu-Sen ⎹ ▽ 20 ⎹ 16 ⎹ 19 ⎹ $23 ⎹

1726 Buchanan St. (bet. Post & Sutter Sts.), 415-440-0466

"Atkins" advocates, "vegans", "non–sushi eater friends" and carnivores alike all satisfy "hankerings" for "tasty shabu-shabu" and sukiyaki (and nothing else) at this "homestyle" Japantown one-"pot cooking extraordinaire" where you stir a "wonderfully fortifying" cauldron of "stewed meats and/or vegetables" yourself; it's a "fun thing to do with friends", especially "on a cold San Francisco night" – just remember you "can't blame someone else" for the outcome.

Shalimar ⊝ ⎹ 23 ⎹ 3 ⎹ 9 ⎹ $14 ⎹

532 Jones St. (Geary St.), 415-928-0333
1409 Polk St. (Pine St.), 415-776-4642
www.shalimarsf.com

"It's all about the food" at these "no-frills" Bay-area "bazaars" serving "fresh, zesty" Indian-Pakistani "comfort food" that "ignites the taste buds"; loyalists laud the "simmering sauces", "lovely", "spicy" flavors and "super-cheap" prices, though a few advise "bring booze", "cash and lots of patience" to deal with a "chaotic" setup, "rude service" and "cafeteria-style" ambiance; N.B. a Santa Clara branch opened post-*Survey*.

Shanghai 1930 Ⓩ   20 | 22 | 19 | $40
133 Steuart St. (bet. Howard & Mission Sts.), 415-896-5600;
www.shanghai1930.com
The "1930s never looked (or tasted) so good" agree admirers who
swoon over the "speakeasylike decor", "exotic" Chinese chow
that runs the "gamut of regional cuisines" and "extensive wine
list" at this underground Embarcadero experience; still, a handful
feel the "upscale" fare has "no vavoom" adding "let's face it,
you're here for the bar" lounge – it's such a "swank place to sip
martinis and watch live jazz"; P.S. "lunch specials are a bargain."

SILKS   24 | 25 | 25 | $64
Mandarin Oriental Hotel, 222 Sansome St. (bet. California & Pine Sts.),
415-986-2020; www.mandarinoriental.com
"Simply heaven!" sigh impressed guests who take the "silk route" –
and "get treated like royalty" – at this "sophisticated" "charming
venue" in the Mandarin Oriental Hotel that smoothes the sting of
"expense-account" prices with "sensational" Cal-Asian fusion
fare; you feel "hidden from the world outside", and what's more, the
"tables are actually far enough apart to carry on a private conversation", making it a "first-class" choice for "conducting business."

SLANTED DOOR, THE   25 | 22 | 20 | $45
The Embarcadero, 1 Ferry Bldg. (Market St.), 415-861-8032;
www.slanteddoor.com
"There's magic happening inside the glass walls" of Charles Phan's
"urbane Vietnamese standard setter" at the Embarcadero's Ferry
Building where fans fawn over "stellar Bay views" while "feasting family-style" on "sublime" Saigon "sensations" as "metrosexual" "waiters swish by" to make "perfect wine pairings"; a
few phos fear "throngs of tourists" make even the "shaking
beef" "vibrate differently" than in Mission days past, but it's still
worth "pushing" through the portals, providing you "can get in" –
if not, "graze" in the bar or head "Out the Door for carryout."

Slow Club   22 | 19 | 19 | $32
2501 Mariposa St. (Hampshire St.), 415-241-9390; www.slowclub.com
Settle into this "laid-back", "metal-and-wood" "industrial" "hipster
joint" in the Mission and sip a "stunning" cocktail – it'll "keep you
busy while you wait" for the "fine-tuned", mostly organic New
American "upscale grub" boasting the "freshest produce" and
"flair-aplenty"; this "dot-com survivor" "doesn't disappoint" –
"you feel like a regular from day one" – plus the "comfort grub"
menu has "something for everyone"; P.S. "brunch is great" too.

So Ⓜ   21 | 13 | 16 | $13
2240 Irving St. (bet. 23rd & 24th Sts.), 415-731-3143
Starchy types say "hello to carbs" at "San Tung junior", a hipper,
stripped-down Outer Sunset Chinese offspring of the original where
you can "fill your stomach" on the same "great" dry-fried chicken
"that has KFC beat", "amazing potstickers" and noodles "without
blowing your wallet"; "service is inconsistent", but that's probably because this "funky hole-in-the-wall" is always "too busy."

Sociale Ⓩ   22 | 21 | 20 | $43
3665 Sacramento St. (bet. Locust & Spruce Sts.), 415-921-3200
"Service is casual – in a good way" at this Presidio Heights
"charming alley" "hideout", a "neighborhood secret" with a

"European feel" that's "worth a detour" declare diners who get in the social swing over "delightful" dishes made from "updated old Italian family recipes" accompanied by "blockbusters" from a "small, eclectic wine list"; for a touch of "romance", "sit on the patio under the heatlamps and stare into your partner's eyes."

South Park Cafe Ⓢ
21 | 18 | 21 | $35

108 South Park St. (bet. 2nd & 3rd Sts.), 415-495-7275

The "tables are a bit too cozy" at this "charming SoMa square" bistro tucked into a "tree-lined" street that rivals "being in Paris", but that's part of the allure agree "sophisticated" Francophiles who fall for the Gallic "comfort food", "great prix fixe" menu and "easygoing" staff; forget "gussied-up" fare – instead, you'll find a "perfectly prepared" "predictably enjoyable" "set of French standards" – and you'll be "assured of a gratifying experience."

Sparrow
– | – | – | M

1177 California St. (bet. Jones & Taylor Sts.), 415-474-2000;
www.sparrowrestaurant.com

Although this sleek Nob Hill newcomer set in the former Watergate space is tucked away in a tony residential condominium with views of Grace Cathedral, the real drama takes place nightly in the large exhibition kitchen; from swanky, circular booths, guests watch chef Terry Lynch (ex Mustards Grill in Napa and Coach House in Martha's Vineyard) prepare daringly different French-Asian small and large plates such as a seared foie gras sandwich with banana and Thai chile jam.

St. Francis Fountain
▽ 18 | 19 | 18 | $15

2801 24th St. (York St.), 415-826-4200

You expect "Archie and Veronica" to stroll into this "old-timey" "soda fountain throwback" that's "been here since dirt" (actually 1918) where "you'll feel like a kid again" – make that a "hip" kid, since it's morphed, under new ownership, into a "Mission coolster hangout", with a "pierced, tattooed staff" delivering "down-home" breakfasts and "diner-style lunches" with "surprisingly little 'tude"; but sweet tooths "go right" for the "old-fashioned sundaes" – while hungover habitués flip for "Guinness floats."

Street Restaurant Ⓜ
22 | 19 | 20 | $32

2141 Polk St. (bet. Broadway & Vallejo Sts.), 415-775-1055;
www.streetrestaurant.com

It's just "what a neighborhood restaurant should be" reveal Russian Hill residents who hold the "lively" "cool vibe", "tasty cocktails", "fun bar", "impressively eclectic" New American "comfort food" (don't miss "fried chicken Sundays") and "friendly" staff in high regard; sure you "sometimes feel like you're yelling at your honey from across the street instead of from across the table", but most insist it's "worth the strain on your vocal chords."

SUMI
22 | 19 | 21 | $38

(fka Ma Tante Sumi)

4243 18th St. (bet. Castro & Diamond Sts.), 415-626-7864;
www.suminthecastro.com

"Call it whatever you want" shrug Castro connoisseurs but this renamed "romantic" "oasis of calm and genteel grazing" "in the heart of gay party-central" "continues to be the best" New French–Asian spot in the 'hood – and the only "place you can take mom"; but while fans are aflutter over the "smooth service" and chef

"Sumi and her helper's" "sublime flavors", a few wrestle with the cuisine – "in a city of never-ending fusion, the dishes feel done."

Suppenküche　　　21 │ 15 │ 17 │ $27

601 Hayes St. (Laguna St.), 415-252-9289; www.suppenkuche.com
"Wear your lederhosen" and "belly up to the long, communal tables" – that is, if you can get a seat at this "sparse", "humble" Hayes Valley "German dining experience" that feels like a "monastery" with a "hip", "modern-day" "European feel"; spaetzle-eaters Oktoberfest year-round, feasting upon "hearty", "rib-sticking" Bavarian fare straight outta Deutschland served in "heaping portions" that guarantee you won't "leave hungry" and hoisting mugs of "excellent beer"; N.B. valet parking is available.

SUPPERCLUB Ⓜ　　　20 │ 27 │ 23 │ $77

657 Harrison St. (3rd St.), 415-348-0900; www.supperclub.com
"Go with your freak flag flying" and "spend all night" "chilling" at this "sensory overload" SoMa offshoot of the Dutch supperclub, a "spectacle" that feels like *Eyes Wide Shut* – inside *The Matrix*"; "vegetarian or non-veg" Eclectic fare is "the only choice to make" after settling into "a plush bed with oversized pillows" – just kick back and watch the "gender-bending staff" "cater to your every whim" and "perform acrobatic tricks"; still, "conservatives" kvetch about "steep prices" for a "gimmick"; N.B. a post-*Survey* chef change may impact the Food score.

Suriya Thai Ⓜ　　　▽ 25 │ 17 │ 20 │ $23

1432 Valencia St. (bet. 25th & 26th Sts.), 415-824-6655
"Charming" chef-proprietor Suriya's "pleasant" "neighborhood secret" is "not your run-of-the-mill" Siamese stop muse Mission minions who trumpet the "innovative" yet "inexpensive" selections – "especially the pumpkin curries" – boasting "unique flavors, preparations, textures" and "fun names"; this is "Thai I can count on" – plus the "generally huge portions" are served "without pretenses" by a "very friendly" staff.

Sushi Groove　　　23 │ 19 │ 18 │ $37

1516 Folsom St. (bet. 11th & 12th Sts.), 415-503-1950 ⊠
1916 Hyde St. (bet. Green & Union Sts.), 415-440-1905
"Can sushi get any hipper" muse "cool"-hunters who get their groove on at this "date-night" duo in SoMa and Russian Hill, "rocking out on" the "urban SoHo vibe" and platefuls of "slapping fresh fish"; it's a "joy to have in the 'hood", especially if you're "young, good-looking" and dig your "inventive rolls" with a side of "fashion and tunes"; still, if you're not into "thumping house music", keep on moving; N.B. there's also a Walnut Creek offshoot.

SUTRO'S AT THE CLIFF HOUSE　　　19 │ 26 │ 18 │ $47

1090 Point Lobos Ave. (Great Hwy.), 415-386-3330;
www.cliffhouse.com
The "gorgeous ocean view from every seat" is "the thing" at this "airy glass atrium suspended" over the Pacific concur acolytes who "swoop down" for tables; it "feels celebratory just being here", especially since the "historic Cliff House" in the Outer Richmond was "newly remodeled" – it's as if the "beautiful", "glass-and-steel" "dining room with jazzy open architecture" underwent a "renaissance"; still, the "fab setting is better in the day" – and towers above the Californian fare that's "surprisingly innovative", but for most, "nothing spectacular."

Swan Oyster Depot ⊠⇥   25 | 10 | 21 | $26
1517 Polk St. (bet. California & Sacramento Sts.), 415-673-1101
A "quirky classic" since 1912, this 20-seat Nob Hill bivalve "haven" is easy to spot: it's the one with "blue-collar hospitality, highbrow seafood" – and the "world lined up on the sidewalk" from early morning till 5:30 PM closing; "forget" the "cramped" quarters and "hard stools" – "this is not a social occasion, you're here" for the "terrific oysters" and clam chowder, served by "crusty old-school men with a smile and a wink."

Tablespoon   22 | 19 | 22 | $42
2209 Polk St. (Vallejo St.), 415-268-0140; www.tablespoonsf.com
Given the co-owners' "Gary Danko and Erna's Elderberry House" pedigrees, it's little wonder why this Russian Hill "neighborhood standby" serving "high-class" New American "comfort food in a small but welcoming setting" measures up as more than "just another" "sophisticated", "intimate" bistro with an "attentive staff"; the "bold", "inventive menu" keeps "tastebuds happy", but it's the cheese – both the "pungent" sampler plate and the "to-die-for" mac 'n' cheddar – that really satisfies "your soul."

TADICH GRILL ⊠   21 | 19 | 20 | $40
240 California St. (bet. Battery & Front Sts.), 415-391-1849
"Time travel into culinary history" at Downtown's "classic" seafooder where "tradition reigns" supreme, from the "perfect cocktails" to the "massive old-fashioned menu" and "straightforward preparations of pristinely fresh" sand dabs and petrale sole delivered by "gruff waiters" "who don't care if you're a pawn or a king"; it was "good enough for grandpa" and "jostling" "suits still crowd around" the "comfortable bar", while even "gray hairs" endure the "long, long lines" just to be a part of the "controlled chaos."

Takara Ⓜ   22 | 14 | 18 | $28
22 Peace Plaza (bet. Laguna & Webster Sts.), 415-921-2000
If you're "fishing for something imaginative" around Peace Plaza, swim upstream to this "bare-bones" izakaya "at the end of Japantown" confide insiders who dive into lots of "good stuff" including "homestyle", "savory custards, tea broths, porridge and shabu-shabu" "rarely found" elsewhere as well as "creative" rolls from the "veteran sushi barmen", a crew of "capable, quietly friendly pros"; P.S. the "price is right."

Tao Cafe   ∇ 20 | 19 | 19 | $23
1000 Guerrero St. (22nd St.), 415-641-9955; www.taocafe.com
Come chow time, make tracks to "peaceful" Tao, a "diamond in the rough" Mission cafe that traffics in "good-value", "comforting" Vietnamese cuisine with a Gallic flair in a storefront with a French colonial decor evocative of 1930s Saigon; the "wonderful" owner who "cooks and runs the whole joint" hails from the East and "lived in Paris for many years" so the fare is "as authentic as it gets."

Taqueria Can-Cun ◗⇥   21 | 8 | 13 | $9
1003 Market St. (6th St.), 415-864-6773
2288 Mission St. (19th St.), 415-252-9560
3211 Mission St. (Valencia St.), 415-550-1414
They're "not much to look at", but everyone from "judges to hookers" to the "after-club crowd stuffing face" will tell ya this late-night trio is "the first and last name" in this taqueria-"filled land";

"pan-warmed tortillas and fresh avocado slices" are the key to the "great veggie burritos", but there's plenty for "meat eaters", plus "salsa verde that'll wake you up for sure" – if the "loudest" Mexican jukebox doesn't do the trick.

TARTINE BAKERY
| 27 | 15 | 14 | $14 |

600 Guerrero St. (18th St.), 415-487-2600; www.tartinebakery.com
"Bring on the butter" should be the mantra at this "crazy busy" Mission patisserie with a "line snaking out the door" quip carb-cravers who queue up for "terrific baked goods" like "stellar croissants" and "amazing pastries" as well as "heavenly panini" on "real artisinal bread"; never mind the "spartan" setting – it allows you to "focus" on your "delicious bite" and "rich hot chocolate" – and forget about the "despondent service."

Taylor's Automatic Refresher
| 21 | 12 | 15 | $16 |

The Embarcadero, 1 Ferry Bldg. (Market St.), 866-328-3663; www.taylorsrefresher.com
See review in North of San Francisco Directory.

TEATRO ZINZANNI ⧄ Ⓜ
| 15 | 26 | 21 | $100 |

Pier 29, The Embarcadero (Battery St.), 415-438-2668; www.zinzanni.org
Granted, this "oh-so-touristy" waterfront "attraction" promising 'Love, Chaos and Dinner' is "not really a restaurant", but rather "a carnival" of "crazy fun" "dinner theater" "under the big top" "where the meal is part of the show" – "and you might be too"; it's "hard to carp about "banquet"-quality Eclectic eats when the "cabaret" waiters "keep you entertained" for hours; still, "once is enough" for such an "expensive night out", but tickled ticket-holders say "it's also a night to remember."

Ten-Ichi
| 19 | 13 | 18 | $28 |

2235 Fillmore St. (bet. Clay & Sacramento Sts.), 415-346-3477; www.tenichisf.com
For "steady-eddy Japanese fare" and a "quick fix" of sushi "right in the hood", Upper Fillmore denizens head to this "welcoming" family-run standby; "no roaring fusion fare here" or decor, either – "just good eating" that's "perfect" for a "low-key weeknight dinner" or a bite "before the movies"; P.S. "you can't beat" "hot dishes like sukiyaki and tempura on a chilly San Francisco evening."

Terzo
| – | – | – | E |

3011 Steiner St. (Union St.), 415-441-3200; www.terzosf.com
"Just what Cow Hollow" needed, this "exciting" new wine bar and Med tapas spot – the 'third' (or 'terzo') venue from the Rose Pistola/Rose's Cafe folks – is "perfect" for the twenty- to fortysomething crowd that "appreciates good food" and the chance to sip affordable wines; kick back in the "modern" room with an "upscale atmosphere" made cozy by a live fire, a giant community table and lots of dining nooks and just keep ordering "more and more."

Thai House Express
| 22 | 13 | 17 | $18 |

599 Castro St. (bet. 18th & 19th Sts.), 415-864-5000
901 Larkin St. (Geary St.), 415-441-2248 ●
Nostalgists may "miss the old Victorian house" original, but thankfully the "fresh, unfailingly tasty", "wonderfully spiced" Thai fare and "friendly service" have followed to the two 'Express' shops; "fill up" at the "unassuming" "late-night" "mecca" in the Tenderloin's Little Saigon area or join the swankier clubbers at the Castro stop.

Thanh Long Ⓜ   23 | 16 | 17 | $42

4101 Judah St. (46th Ave.), 415-665-1146; www.anfamily.com

"Forget the menu – roast crab" and "secret recipe garlic noodles – that's all you have to know" about Crustacean's "less pretentious" sibling that's worth the "long waits" and the "schlep" to the Outer Sunset; "fellow finger lickers" warn "have your cardiologist on call" ("lots of butter") and "don't take a date" as "you'll be too busy slurping instead of conversing" in the "expensive" SRO French colonial–Vietnamese dining room that "passes for elegance in the Avenues."

Thep Phanom Thai Cuisine   25 | 15 | 19 | $27

400 Waller St. (Fillmore St.), 415-431-2526; www.thepphanom.com

Yes, the "Victorian drawing room" setting, replete with "cute lace curtains", feels like a "hippie time warp", but this "little joint" in the "rugged" Lower Haight is definitely "not your father's Thai restaurant"; "after all these years, it hasn't lost its touch", from the "attentive staff" to the "gorgeous seafood dishes layered with a multiplicity of flavors" and "original" combos that "will make your tongue dance" to the "bastion of traditional" "favorites."

Three Seasons   22 | 20 | 19 | $34

3317 Steiner St. (bet. Chestnut & Lombard Sts.), 415-567-9989; www.threeseasonsrestaurant.com

"Start off your night with warm sake and who knows what will happen" at this "friendly", "chic Marina Vietnamese" vow vaunters who share "delicious small plates" packed with "powerful flavors"; the "happy buns send me to my happy place" sigh the sated who also commend the "spring rolls galore" and "savory with sweet notes" claypot dishes; P.S. the "tropical colonial" decor, capped with a "stained-glass dome" is an additional "treat" at the Downtown Palo Alto offshoot; N.B. the Walnut Creek branch closed.

Ti Couz   22 | 16 | 16 | $21

3108 16th St. (bet. Guerrero & Valencia St.), 415-252-7373

"From finicky sisters to full-on hipsters, no one is ever disappointed" by the "enormous, filling", "truly authentic Breton crêpes" made with buckwheat flour, "stuffed with ingredients of your choice" and served "piping hot" at this "funky" French bistro in the Mission; "sit outside and watch the world go by" as you "satisfy your sweet and savory" cravings – and don't forget to wash the "delicate" delights "down with their trademark ciders."

Tokyo Go Go   23 | 20 | 18 | $33

3174 16th St. (bet. Guerrero & Valencia Sts.), 415-864-2288; www.tokyogogo.com

"Gorgeous twentysomethings" may have replaced the "1999 crowds" at this Mission Japanese, a progenitor of hipster izakaya, but it's still "aces" agree admirers who go-go to knock back "creative sake cocktails", nibble on "very fresh" "inventive sushi" and "inspired appetizers" in a "cool *Austin Powers*-esque" room with "thumping music"; but the less-inclined run-run elsewhere, sniping "it's not really about the food – it's more about the scene."

Tommaso's Ⓜ   24 | 16 | 20 | $27

1042 Kearny St. (bet. Broadway St. & Pacific Ave.), 415-398-9696; www.tommasosnorthbeach.com

It's "old-school and I wouldn't have it any other way" agree disciples who still "delight" in the "awesome wood-fired pizzas" and "wonderful" Southern Italian cooking ("meatballs the size of my fists!") at this North Beach "treasure" where the staff's probably "been there long enough to tell you stories about the earthquake (no, the first one)"; the neighborhood is definitely "not family-friendly", but it's worth "navigating the strip clubs" – as well as the "cramped tables" – to reach pie "heaven."

Tommy Toy's Cuisine Chinoise | 23 | 24 | 24 | $58 |
655 Montgomery St. (bet. Clay & Washington Sts.), 415-397-4888; www.tommytoys.com
What a "transporting evening – feels like you've been returned to old Shanghai" instead of Downtown attest time-travelers who "dine like royalty in ornate Asian surroundings" at this "SF landmark"; the "attentive servers" and "excellent" French-influenced, "gourmet" Chinese cuisine (featuring a "to-die-for prix fixe") "match the setting", making for a "special evening out"; if a few tut that this Toy's a "time warp", even they admit you "must try it at least once"; N.B jacket required.

Tonga Room | 12 | 25 | 16 | $38 |
Fairmont Hotel, 950 Mason St. (bet. California & Sacremento Sts.), 415-772-5278; www.fairmont.com
"Bring on the cheese and slice it thick" quip day-trippers because this "kitschy", "tiki-style" "guilty pleasure" set high atop Nob Hill in the Fairmont Hotel is like stepping into a "Dorothy Lamour movie" complete with "fake" "storm effects"; hoist a "fruity tropical" cocktail , nibble Pan-Asian–Pacific Rim pupu platters and "ogle" the "faux Polynesian" scenery, including the "band on a floating island"; but the less *Gilligan's Island*–inclined imbibe "umbrella drinks" and Skipper the "ho-hum exotic" fare.

Ton Kiang | 25 | 13 | 16 | $27 |
5821 Geary Blvd. (bet. 22nd & 23rd Aves.), 415-387-8273; www.tonkiang.net
It may be located at the "end of the earth", but it's "worth the effort" to get to this Outer Richmond Chinese that's "always mobbed" with "crazy long" lines because the reward is "Hakkan cuisine at its best", delivered by an "English-speaking staff"; the "awesome", "ultrafresh" small dishes go way "beyond the ubiquitous dumplings" – they "made a dim sum believer out of me" confide the converted who indulge "all day" and in the evening too.

Tortilla Heights ●Ⓜ | ▽ 21 | 20 | 23 | $23 |
1750 Divisadero St. (bet. Bush & Sutter Sts.), 415-346-4531; www.tortillaheights.com
The humble tortilla is put on a pedestal at Lower Pacific Heights' "happening" new Mexican hacienda; "the flavors are great, the tequila plentiful and the staff cheerful" – it's just what "the neighborhood needed!" declare denizens who enjoy their "delicious" eats in an atmospheric dining room with twinkling star-shaped lights and palm trees; N.B. food is served till 1 AM and drinks till 1:45.

TOWN HALL | 24 | 20 | 21 | $48 |
342 Howard St. (Fremont St.), 415-908-3900; www.townhallsf.com
"Every single thing clicked" attest Townies who give SoMa's former "gold-rush-era" shipping warehouse "two thumbs-up", hailing the "bustling" "cowboy-yet-city vibe", "cheerful staff" and "fun communal table"; the "lovingly crafted" fare, boasting an "appetizing collage" of New American and New Orleans flavors,

is "hearty without being heavy", plus the "hot chocolate is straight out of Willy Wonka's chocolate river"; the "only con": it's so "noisy" "you need a cell phone to talk to dinner companions"; N.B. a SoMa sib called Salt House is slated to open this fall.

Town's End Restaurant & Bakery | 22 | 16 | 19 | $28 |
South Beach Marina Apts., 2 Townsend St. (The Embarcadero), 415-512-0749

"Breakfast heaven" sigh the sated who also end up at this "friendly", "reliable neighborhood" New American "hangout" on the Embarcadero for a "hearty wholesome" weekend brunch; whether you "sit outside on a nice day or find a nook inside", it's a "great" morning stop "before the Giants game", and it kicks off with a complimentary "basket of baked goodies"; P.S. it's also "nice" for an "excellent, quiet dinner" or lunch.

Trader Vic's | 17 | 21 | 18 | $44 |
555 Golden Gate Ave. (Van Ness Ave.), 415-775-6300; www.tradervics.com

See review in East of San Francisco Directory.

Trattoria Contadina | 25 | 16 | 21 | $35 |
1800 Mason St. (Union St.), 415-982-5728

"One of the few good" North Beach "joints not catering to tourists", this "old-school" "mom-and-pop" "corner Italian" may be "off the beaten path" but it's "packed every night" with loyalists clamoring for "rich, flavorful" food made with organic ingredients; it's a "real SF treat", complete with a staff that "welcomes you as one of the family", and like most homecomings, it can get as "loud as the inside of a kettle drum."

Tres Agaves ● | 18 | 20 | 16 | $34 |
130 Townsend St. (bet. 2nd & 3rd Sts.), 415-227-0500; www.tresagaves.com

"Yuppies" and the "ballpark"-bound "no longer have to choose between a nice place and Mexican" with the arrival of this "chic, appealing" South Beach cantina owned by rocker Sammy Hagar and amigos; down an "additive margarita" to cushion the "deafening noise", no doubt "intensified by the industrial-chic design" – just "tear yourself away from the vast tequila selection" ("meant for sipping not shooting") long enough to try Globe chef Joseph Manzare's "delicious Jaliscan specialties."

Truly Mediterranean | 25 | 4 | 16 | $10 |
3109 16th St. (Valencia St.), 415-252-7482; www.trulymed.com

"Truly a great stop when in the middle of a Mission crawl" concur acolytes who alight at this "closetlike" falafel and schwarma shack for Middle Eastern–Mediterranean "handfuls of goodness" "wrapped and grilled in giant tortillas" at "unheard of" prices; "dig the soundtrack playing" – "now if only they would get some tables" – still you "can't beat it" for takeout believe "budget eaters on the run."

Tsar Nicoulai Caviar Café Ⓜ | – | – | – | E |
The Embarcadero, 1 Ferry Bldg. (Market St.), 415-288-8630; www.tsarnicoulai.com

At this caviar cafe/retail shop in the Embarcadero's Ferry Building, roe-lovers spoon up imported caviar by the ounce or order up Russian seafood delights at a 15-seat U-shaped counter crowned by a silver champagne bucket; made-to-order blini are a given, but the creative menu also features unexpected treasures like sturgeon-draped potato waffles, truffled scrambled eggs and ahi sashimi with ginger and wasabi-infused whitefish caviar served atop a fishbowl; N.B. closes at 6 PM Tuesday–Saturday.

Tsunami Sushi & Sake Bar ●⊠ | 22 | 22 | 19 | $36 |
1306 Fulton St. (Divisadero St.), 415-567-7664; www.tsunami-sf.com
Forget "run-of-the-mill rolls" – this "very trendy" Japanese outpost hidden in the Western Addition offers "intricate presentations" of "creative" sushi "found no where else" served in an "exotic, contemporary" setting; what a "brilliant sake selection" too – that's where this "late-night" "hipster" haunt "really shines" – you'll find "more choices than you've ever seen", plus the "friendly bartender is eager to share his knowledge"; the "only con": it's "kinda pricey."

Tu Lan ⊠⇗ | 21 | 2 | 9 | $12 |
8 Sixth St. (Market St.), 415-626-0927
"Get over your trepidations" and "brave" SoMa's "scary area" strewn with "crackheads" to "eat like you never imagined" on "Vietnamese food for a king/queen" at "peasant prices"; but while fans trumpet the "fast, hot, tasty" "true street food", "disappointed" cynics scoff that its "cachet" comes from "yuppies bragging they ate here and made it back to the office alive" – perhaps it's "been riding on a notice from Julia Child" for tu long.

2223 Restaurant | 21 | 19 | 20 | $36 |
2223 Market St. (bet. Noe & Sanchez Sts.), 415-431-0692
"With a loyal following" of the "terminally fabulous" "gay crowd" (along with an "eclectic" mix of "straight metrosexuals"), this "lively" "no-name restaurant" decorated with "rotating art" exhibits is "a cut above" the other Castro contenders; supporters, who swear by the "great cocktails", "huge portions of hearty" Californian–New American fare and "outstanding Sunday brunch", also laud the "fantastic service and hot guys" (which are frequently one in the same).

Universal Cafe Ⓜ | 24 | 17 | 19 | $32 |
2814 19th St. (bet. Bryant & Florida Sts.), 415-821-4608; www.universalcafe.net
"Seek out this little gem in Multimedia Gulch" suggest locals – it's the "ultimate" Mission restaurant serving an "unpretentious, creative, organically based" New American menu that "changes radically" with the seasons; the "simplicity of the flavors" shine – in fact, "home-cooked" dishes are downright "succulent" – it's the "perfect place" to go "if you're tired of eating out", plus "brunch is not to be missed"; P.S. it "fills up easily so make reservations."

Velvet Cantina Ⓜ   ▽ | 21 | 19 | 21 | $19 |
3349 23rd St. (Bartlett St.), 415-648-4142
This "favorite new Mission hipster" hangout with a "kitschy" bordello-esque lounge decked out with gilded frames, wild murals and cowhide-upholstered banquettes lacks a soft touch decor-wise, but amigos "love the casual vibe", vowing it's "great for gawking at the super-cute staff"; the "creative" menu "rises above the standard" Mexican–Nuevo Latino "formula" too, with "off-the-beaten-path entrees"; P.S. the "potent margaritas" are served till 2 AM on weekends.

Venticello
| 22 | 21 | 22 | $43 |

1257 Taylor St. (Washington St.), 415-922-2545; www.venticello.com
"Warm" and "charming" with "cable cars clanking outside", the
wood-burning oven "all fired up" and an "authentic Tuscan feel",
this "romantic, old-guard Italian" "out of the way" in Nob Hill is a
"lovely" place to "take your date to meet her parents", but it also
"caters to neighbors" with "rustic" dishes and "imaginative pizzas
and pastas"; be prepared to sit "cheek by jowl" though – it's so
"cozy" "you might think you're at one big dinner party."

Vivande Porta Via
| 23 | 16 | 19 | $36 |

*2125 Fillmore St. (bet. California & Sacramento Sts.), 415-346-4430;
www.vivande.com*
"Try and find better pasta" challenge boosters of cookbook author
Carlo Middione's Pac Heights' "home-base" "gourmet market", an
"inviting" but "austere room" reminiscent of a "butcher shop" with
"paper on the tables to occupy the kids" and "delectable" Sicilian
"delicacies" and a "wonderful wine list" to "keep the adults
happy"; still, insiders insist the "best place to sit is at the counter
where you can watch the cooks" prepare Italian specialties.

Walzwerk �®Ⓜ
| ▽ 21 | 16 | 17 | $26 |

*381 S. Van Ness Ave. (bet. 14th & 15th Sts.), 415-551-7181;
www.walzwerk.com*
"The old GDR is still alive" at this "Communist" "flashback" Mission
gastrohaus packed with "European students" and "expatriates"
who congregate to consume "copious" amounts of "hearty East
German" fare washed down with "Hefeweizen"; you can almost
feel "Lenin watch while you eat" the "cozy comfort food" in
"kitschy" "Berliner-industrial-chic" digs and chat up the "charming
proprietors" who "kindly scold you for not finishing off your plate."

Washington Square Bar & Grill
| 18 | 18 | 19 | $39 |

1707 Powell St. (bet. Columbus & Union Sts.), 415-982-8123
The "Washbag lives again" proclaim patrons who champion this
"longtime North Beach contender" with a "SF feel" that "continues to crank" out "reliable" New American–Italian chow; the
"fun, funky" "saloon" with nightly jazz is sometimes "anchored by
the inimitable Mike McCourt" while the "bistro-style" dining
room is manned by a "friendly staff" – what an "enjoyable" "return to yesteryear"; still, some shrug it's "living off its reputation."

Waterfront Restaurant & Cafe
| 17 | 21 | 18 | $45 |

*Pier 7, The Embarcadero (Broadway St.), 415-391-2696;
www.waterfrontsf.com*
"Enjoy fresh" seafood and "reliably good" Cal cuisine while taking
in the "fabulous Bay" view from the glass-enclosed patio suggest
maritimers who rely on this "sea-level" Embarcadero standby; but a
mutinous minority mutters "go for a drink" – the "bar is lovely" and
the waterfront "never disappoints" tourists but skip the "lackluster"
fare – it "doesn't live up to the rich splendor" of the nautical setting.

Woodhouse Fish Company
| – | – | – | I |

2073 Market St. (14 St.), 415-437-2722; www.woodhousefish.com
New England–style seafood shacks are spawning everywhere, and
that includes this Castro storefront serving everything from clam
chowder and lobsters to West Coast delicacies like Tomales Bay
oysters – plus draught beers, value wines and lemonade.

WOODWARD'S GARDEN ⌧ Ⓜ 26 | 17 | 21 | $45
1700 Mission St. (Duboce St.), 415-621-7122;
www.woodwardsgarden.com

Only a Mission "dot-com" survivor could manage to be "one of the most romantic spots in town with warm glowing lighting and a historic ambiance" while remaining "hidden" "under an on-ramp"; it's a "charming, yet funky" "neighborhood find" laud "loyal" locals – "can't wait to return" for the "big portions" of "intensely flavorful", seasonal New American fare and the "perfect little wine list"; still a few aesthetes chirp it feels like you're eating in a "garage."

XYZ 19 | 21 | 18 | $47
W Hotel, 181 Third St. (Howard St.), 415-817-7836; www.xyz-sf.com

"After a long day at the Moscone Convention Center", alpha-types leave the "throngs" and duck into the "chic" W Hotel's "sleek, classy" *"Sex and the City"*-ish dining room where a "professional staff" delivers "inventive", "well-prepared" New American cuisine and a "top-notch wine list"; still, a few feel the fare "seems more suited for a fashion show runway than your plate", while others confide that the "bar has a better scene."

Yabbies Coastal Kitchen 22 | 18 | 20 | $40
2237 Polk St. (bet. Green & Vallejo Sts.), 415-474-4088;
www.yabbiesrestaurant.com

"Still a hidden gem outside the reach of most tourists", this "convivial" Russian Hill seafooder is "always hopping with good energy and happy people"; "don't miss the tuna poke" and other "delicious" "fish concoctions" paired with a "wonderful" vino list, all toted to table by a "staff that loves to talk about their food and wine"; N.B. it changed ownership post-*Survey,* but the chef remains the same.

YANK SING 25 | 16 | 18 | $34
Rincon Ctr., 101 Spear St. (bet. Howard & Mission Sts.), 415-957-9300
49 Stevenson St. (bet. 1st & 2nd Sts.), 415-541-4949
www.yanksing.com

For a bit of "Hong Kong hustle-bustle without the Trans-Pacific airfare", the "Downtown set" descends on this "Cadillac of dim sum" dining and "slakes their hunger" with a "stunning array of" carted "treats", including the "dreamiest dumplings", dispensed by "trolley dollies"; it's a "must for leisurely Sunday in SF" – and the "perfect excuse for having a beer for breakfast"; still, some sing another tune, countering the "cost now exceeds the pleasure."

YaYa Ⓜ ▽ 23 | 20 | 24 | $24
2424 Van Ness Ave. (bet. Green & Union Sts.), 415-440-0455;
www.yayacuisine.com

Turn back the hands of time, say, "3,000 years", with a meal at "gracious" chef-around-town Yahya Salih's Mesopotamian "marvel" in Cow Hollow, an "intimate" dining room decked out with murals of Babylonia and an "exotic feel"; you can't "find this cuisine anywhere else" agree adventurers who dig into the "interesting selection", including "amazing Iraqi" and Middle Eastern dishes – and perhaps the "best dolmas in the cosmos."

Yuet Lee ◑ ⇥ 22 | 4 | 14 | $20
1300 Stockton St. (Broadway St.), 415-982-6020

"Don't be put off by the cloudy fish tanks in the window" or the "lighting that makes everyone look like Frankenstein" because the "fresh seafood" and Cantonese chow "at dirt-cheap prices" will make you "wonder how you've gotten by without" trying this "longtime", "old-school" "late-night dive" in Chinatown before; there's "food magic" within these "green walls" so dig into the "terrific" dishes – you may get "addicted."

Yumma's
22 | 8 | 17 | $11

721 Irving St. (bet. 8th & 9th Aves.), 415-682-0762
"The Inner Sunset has falafel covered" at this "friendly", family-run Middle Eastern haunt that also draws swarms of schwarma-seekers who praise the organic meat that "comes right off the spit and onto your plate"; although decorwise "Yumma's bum-mas", "falling somewhere between a fast-food" joint and a "high-school cafeteria", peace-keepers point out you can eat your "tasty" "quick bites" on the "nice garden patio out back."

Yuzu Ⓜ
▽ 23 | 21 | 17 | $39

3347 Fillmore St. (bet. Chestnut & Lombard Sts.), 415-775-1873
At this "sleek" Marina newcomer with an "intimate, relaxing feel", an "attentive sushi chef from Japan serves top-grade sushi" spiked with freshly grated wasabi and a "sense of humor"; kick back in the "Zen setting" and dig into the better than yuzual, "fresh" fish that "never fails to please", then dive into sake flights for a "fun twist"; still, the sound-sensitive snap it's "gotten rather noisy since being discovered."

Zagora Ⓜ
– | – | – | M

1007 Guerrero St. (bet. 22nd & 23rd Sts.), 415-282-6444
There's a "new Moroccan in town" with "warm, welcoming" service exclaim Missionites who heed the clarion call of this darkly lit, jewel-toned storefront; the "cozy" quarters and "beautiful presentation" of "delicious" dishes showcasing "interesting" – even "progressive" – "combinations of flavors" make it "good for a date", plus there's now a "tasty" Sunday brunch too, complete with Marrakech-inspired omelets and baked eggs.

Zante Pizza & Indian Cuisine
17 | 6 | 11 | $16

3489 Mission St. (Cortland St.), 415-821-3949; www.zantespizza.com
"Holy cow" – "curry and cheese" seem like strange bedfellows but "somehow the two combine to make" "one of the greatest food concoctions ever": a "wild", "unbelievably good" Indian pizza, that's worth sikhing out at this "cheap" Bernal Heights "dive"; "make sure you take out" though, because the "decor is mid-'70s bowling alley" – and "stick" to the pies since the other dishes are "mediocre at best."

Zao Noodle Bar
14 | 11 | 13 | $16

2406 California St. (Fillmore St.), 415-345-8088; www.zao.com
"Perfect for a quick bite to warm you up on a cold day" or a "casual meal with friends" concur carboloaders who fork over a few yen for a "nice variety" of "satisfying" Pan-Asian–noodle dishes at this "lively" Bay Area outfit; but while vaunters aver you get "real value and flavor for the money", the jaded jibe it's "cheap but oh-so-boring"; N.B. branches in Palo Alto and Emeryville too.

Zarzuela Ⓢ Ⓜ
23 | 16 | 21 | $33

2000 Hyde St. (Union St.), 415-346-0800
Party-ready patrons are "willing to circle the streets one million times looking for a parking spot" to "wait patiently on the sidewalk

for the good cheer" found at this "perennial favorite" in Russian Hill serving "real-deal" Iberian tapas, paella and sangria; the "charismatic" staff makes you "feel at home" while the "authentic", "constantly changing small plates" make you feel "like you're in Spain"; "prepare to shout" because it gets "crazy packed."

Zazie | 21 | 18 | 19 | $25 |
941 Cole St. (bet. Carl St. & Parnassus Ave.), 415-564-5332; www.zaziesf.com

For a "bit of France on Cole", "set your alarm early to beat the weekend brunch crowd or bring your stroller to line up" at this "quaint" bistro named after the "classic Louis Malle movie" *Zazie dans le Metro*; "never met a dish I didn't like here" – "gimme some gingerbread pancakes" on that "adorable", "toasty" garden patio "any day" – or "satisfying" dinner fare at "easy weeknight prices."

Zeitgeist ●⊅ | 14 | 15 | 9 | $13 |
199 Valencia St. (Duboce Ave.), 415-255-7505

Yup, it's more bar with "real personality" than restaurant, but if the "sun's shining, there's no better place" than this back patio serving "ice cold beer", BBQ, "good" hamburgers and "tamales if you're lucky"; you almost "forget you placed an order" with the "burger Nazi" as you "ogle sassy bike messengers", until the "tattooed" staff shouts your name over the "blaring" "punk rock" and "backyard bustle"; P.S. "tip the surly" cook.

ZUNI CAFÉ ●Ⓜ | 25 | 20 | 21 | $45 |
1658 Market St. (bet. Franklin & Gough Sts.), 415-552-2522

Having "defied the odds and lasted as a trendy spot" in a "desolate" Hayes Valley location since 1979, Judy Rodger's "Energizer Bunny" remains the "go-to" "hot spot" for "simple, but right on" "Mediterranean soul food" delivered by a staff that's "gracious, if a bit distracted"; join the "foodies", opera swells and "tourists" slurping "divine oysters" and "delicious drinks" at the "see-and-be-seen bar" or swoop upstairs to the "festive" "jigsaw of rooms" for "legendary" "roast chicken or "the best late-night burger", and you'll see why it's "worthy of all the fuss."

Zuppa | 20 | 19 | 19 | $42 |
564 Fourth St. (bet. Brannan and Bryant Sts.), 415-777-5900; www.zuppa-sf.com

What a "welcome addition" – this "industrial-chic SoMa" space offers the "same pizzazz that the owners established with Globe" agree *amici* who applaud the "balcony tables offering a great view of the scene" and "hearty portions of eclectic" Southern Italian, wood-fired pizzas and "well-presented" house-cured meats; but detractors sigh it's "disappointing after all the hype" what with "confused service" and "cold" climes (bring a "parka").

Zushi Puzzle | 26 | 10 | 18 | $33 |
1910 Lombard St. (Buchanan St.), 415-931-9319; www.zushipuzzle.com

"The secret is out" about the Marina's previously "undiscovered", "low-stress, high-taste" Japanese "gem" where "newly converted Puzzle fans" are "so taken with" the "sea-fresh" sashimi and "inventive rolls that they don't notice how ridiculously bad" the "'70s" decor is; join the "'in' crowd" at the "small bar" and watch "sushi god" chef-owner Roger, a "man who knows fish like no other", work his "magic" – you can really put away lots of "crazy" "combos", "they're so delicious."

East of San Francisco

Top Ratings East of SF

Excluding places with low voting, unless indicated.

Food

28 Chez Panisse	Gregoire/Socca Oven
27 Rivoli	Oliveto
Chez Panisse Café	PlumpJack Cafe
26 Erna's Elderberry	24 Zachary's Pizza
Kirala	Dopo
Lalime's	Soi Four
25 Bay Wolf	Prima
Wente Vineyards	À Côté
Great China	Cafe Esin
Uzen	Jojo

By Cuisine

American
24 Cafe Esin
23 Lark Creek
22 Forbes Mill Steak
Blackberry Bistro
Rick & Ann's

Californian
28 Chez Panisse
27 Rivoli
Chez Panisse Café
26 Erna's Elderberry
25 Wente Vineyards

Chinese
25 Great China
21 Rest. Peony
Shen Hua
17 Jade Villa
– Imperial/Berkeley Tea

French
25 Gregoire/Socca Oven
24 À Côté
Jojo
Soizic
23 Citron

Indian
24 Ajanta
Vik's Chaat Corner
23 Shalimar
21 Breads of India
19 Udupi Palace

Italian
25 Oliveto
24 Dopo
23 Postino
Rist. Raphael
Tratt. La Siciliana

Japanese
26 Kirala
25 Uzen
24 O'Chamé
23 Grasshopper
18 Yoshi's

Mediterranean
28 Chez Panisse
27 Rivoli
Chez Panisse Café
26 Lalime's
25 Bay Wolf

Mexican/Pan-Latin
24 Fonda Solana
23 Doña Tomás
22 Tacubaya
21 Picante Cocina
Cactus Taqueria

Southeast Asian
24 Soi Four
Pho 84
22 Nan Yang
21 Le Cheval
20 Cha Am Thai

By Special Feature

Breakfast/Brunch
25 Wente Vineyards
 Oliveto
24 Café Fanny
23 La Note
 Venus

Child-Friendly
25 Great China
24 Zachary's Pizza
22 Pizza Antica
20 Barney's
16 Pasta Pomodoro

Late Night
24 Fonda Solana
23 Koryo BBQ
21 Lanesplitter
20 Everett & Jones
19 Caspers Hot Dogs

Meet for a Drink
24 Va de Vi
 Fonda Solana
23 Zax Tavern
 César
 Townhouse B&G

Newcomers (Rated)
24 Tamarindo
21 Sea Salt
 Pappo▽
 Rist. Amorama▽
20 Café Gratitude

Outdoor Seating
25 Bay Wolf
 Wente Vineyards
 Oliveto
24 À Côté
23 La Note

People-Watching
27 Chez Panisse Café
24 À Côté
23 César
 Grasshopper
21 downtown

Romance
28 Chez Panisse
26 Erna's Elderberry
 Lalime's
25 Wente Vineyards
24 Soizic

Small Plates
24 Soi Four
 À Côté
 Va de Vi
 Fonda Solana
23 César

Trendy
24 À Côté
 Fonda Solana
23 Doña Tomás
 César
21 downtown

Views
25 Wente Vineyards
20 Blackhawk Grille
 Duck Club
19 Ahwahnee Din. Rm.
17 Jake's on the Lake

Winning Wine Lists
28 Chez Panisse
27 Chez Panisse Café
26 Erna's Elderberry
24 Va de Vi
23 César

By Location

Berkeley
28 Chez Panisse
27 Rivoli
 Chez Panisse Café
26 Kirala
 Lalime's

Oakland
26 Erna's Elderberry
25 Bay Wolf
 Uzen
 Gregoire/Socca Oven
 Oliveto

Top Decor

28 Ahwahnee Din. Rm.	Amber Rest.
26 Erna's Elderberry	**22** Mezze
Wente Vineyards	Venezia
25 Postino	O'Chamé
Bing Crosby's	Blackhawk Grille
24 Chez Panisse	Sunnyside Resort
Adagia	Zax Tavern
Bridges	Oliveto
23 Chez Panisse Café	Rist. Raphael
Rivoli	Bay Wolf

Top Service

28 Erna's Elderberry	Prima
26 Chez Panisse	**22** Cafe Esin
25 Rivoli	Oliveto
Chez Panisse Café	Postino
Bay Wolf	Mezze
24 Lalime's	Lark Creek
23 Zax Tavern	Rist. Raphael
PlumpJack Cafe	**21** Ajanta
Jojo	Soizic
Wente Vineyards	Venus

Top Bangs for the Buck

1. Caspers Hot Dogs
2. In-N-Out Burger
3. Arinell Pizza
4. Cactus Taqueria
5. Pho Hoa-Hiep II
6. Lanesplitter
7. Thai Buddhist Temple
8. Gioia Pizzeria
9. Fenton's Creamery
10. Picante Cocina
11. Tacubaya
12. Vik's Chaat Corner
13. House of Chicken/Waffles
14. Pho 84
15. Asqew Grill
16. Bette's Oceanview
17. Barney's
18. Juan's Place
19. Café Fanny
20. Zachary's Pizza

Other Good Values

Ajanta	Lo Coco's
Battambang	Marica
Bo's Barbecue	Nan Yang
Cafe Esin	Pizza Antica
César	Red/Nevada Red Hut
Chow/Park Chow	Shalimar
Dopo	Soi Four
Great China	Spettro
Koryo BBQ	Tratt. La Siciliana
La Méditerranée	Uzen

East of San Francisco

À Côté
24 21 20 $38

5478 College Ave. (Taft St.), Oakland, 510-655-6469;
www.acoterestaurant.com
A "young and hip crowd" has no reservations about "braving the wait or fighting for a place at the bar" to "eat, drink and be merry" at this "chic" Rockridge bistro; the French-Med "small plates" (including "addictive" mussels and frites) are "fabulous", as are the "kick-ass cocktails" and the "original wine" selection, all proffered with "friendly professionalism" in a "dimly lit room" that has a "great buzz."

Adagia Restaurant
21 24 19 $33

Westminster House, 2700 Bancroft Way (College Ave.), Berkeley,
510-647-2300; www.adagiarestaurant.com
In "a setting reminiscent of Hogwarts' dining hall in the Harry Potter movies", this "gorgeous" restaurant (with a "sunny patio") is "a rare adult eatery" near the UC Berkeley campus; although it "fills quickly with professors, MBAs and law students", you can still "hobnob with the liberal brain trust" or "take your parents" to sup on "light" Californian cuisine; just note that the "well-meaning" service is occasionally "amateurish."

AHWAHNEE DINING ROOM, THE
19 28 20 $53

Ahwahnee Hotel, 1 Ahwahnee Rd., Yosemite National Park,
209-372-1489; www.yosemitepark.com
"Every trip to Yosemite should include a visit" to this "breathtaking" "historic" Ahwahnee Hotel dining room perched at the base of Half Dome with the "granite walls of the valley" visible from the massive wood-beamed windows; although the "muddled" "wedding banquet"–quality Cal-American cuisine and "inattentive service" "lag miles behind the decor" (even when you splurge for the "over-the-top" Sunday brunch"), "let's face it", "you're there to take in the magnificent views"; N.B. jacket required.

Ajanta
24 19 21 $27

1888 Solano Ave. (bet. The Alameda & Colusa Ave.), Berkeley,
510-526-4373; www.ajantarestaurant.com
"Definitely not a curry-in-a-hurry" "hole-in-the-wall", this "upscale" subcontinental Berkeley "favorite" with a "calming ambiance" serves "tasty" monthly menus that "rotate by the seasons" and feature "regional dishes from all over India" incorporating "fresh, flavorful" hormone-free and free-range meats and poultry and sustainable seafood; with "courtesy and charm", the staff caters to spice preferences – "from mild to blast furnace", and the "welcoming" owner even suggests "superb wine pairings."

Amber Restaurant
21 23 20 $45

500 Hartz Ave. (Church St.), Danville, 925-552-5238;
www.amberbistro.com
For "city quality dining in Danville" locals head to this "intimate", "see-and-be-seen" "date-night" "hot spot" offering a "relaxed",

Zen-like setting and "outstanding presentations" of "well-prepared", "pretty" Asian fusion fare along with yuzu cocktails; if a few shout it's "super loud" and huff it "falls short of expectations", most retort it's "very sophisticated for the East Bay."

Amici's East Coast Pizzeria   20 | 12 | 17 | $19
4640 Tassajara Rd. (Dublin Blvd.), Dublin, 925-875-1600
See review in City of San Francisco Directory.

Arinell Pizza ⊄   24 | 5 | 12 | $7
2119 Shattuck Ave. (Center St.), Berkeley, 510-841-4035
With "an atmosphere like sitting next to a boom box on a subway", these "minuscule" "joints" in Berkeley and the Mission serving up "thin-enough-to-crack-when-you-fold-it-in-half" slices are "exactly what NYC-style pizzerias should be"; don't let the "alt-rocker" staff, lack of toppings ("no California froufrou here") or "limited seating" deter you – just belly up to the counter or "take it to go."

Asqew Grill   19 | 12 | 14 | $14
Bay Street Mall, 5614 Bay St. (Shellmound St.), Emeryville, 510-595-7471;
www.asqewgrill.com
See review in City of San Francisco Directory.

Balboa Cafe   19 | 18 | 18 | $34
1995 Squaw Valley Rd. (Squaw Peak Rd.), Olympic Valley, 530-583-5850;
www.balboacafe.com
See review in City of San Francisco Directory.

Barney's Gourmet Hamburgers ⊄   20 | 12 | 14 | $15
1600 Shattuck Ave. (Cedar St.), Berkeley, 510-849-2827
1591 Solano Ave. (Ordway St.), Berkeley, 510-526-8185
5819 College Ave. (Chabot Rd.), Oakland, 510-601-0444
4162 Piedmont Ave. (Linda Ave.), Oakland, 510-655-7180
www.barneyshamburgers.com
See review in City of San Francisco Directory.

Battambang ☒   20 | 11 | 17 | $19
850 Broadway (9th St.), Oakland, 510-839-8815
"Worth getting to know" in Oakland's Chinatown, this "homey" Cambodian "shines" with "heavenly", "flavorful" food including "great curries", all served by a "sweet", "accommodating" staff; the "small" space means you can "expect a wait", but the reward is an "excellent" experience at an "incredible value."

BAY WOLF   25 | 22 | 25 | $47
3853 Piedmont Ave. (Rio Vista Ave.), Oakland, 510-655-6004;
www.baywolf.com
"A winner since it opened" over 30 years ago, Michael Wild's "classy" Cal-Med in Oakland still sets the "East Bay gold standard" with "consistently fabulous" food ("order the duck") that "matches that of the most 'in' places in town" plus "well-priced" wines; the "charming" staff and "romantic" converted Victorian setting with a "beautiful enclosed deck" make it a "calming respite", and even if a few howl the menu "needs freshening", more insist decades of "experience" yields the "highest in fine dining."

Berkeley Teahouse   – | – | – | I
Epicurious Garden, 1511 Shattuck Ave. (bet. Cedar & Vine Sts.),
Berkeley, 510-540-8888; www.imperialtea.com
See Imperial Tea Court review in City of San Francisco Directory.

Bette's Oceanview Diner
| 22 | 15 | 18 | $17 |

1807 Fourth St. (Hearst St.), Berkeley, 510-644-3230;
www.bettesdiner.com
"Paradoxical" soufflé pancakes ("light but filling"), "perfect corned-beef hash" and the "best omelets in the Bay Area" atone for the "long lines", "haphazard service" and decided lack of ocean views at this "Berkeley landmark" for American eats with a "Cal twist"; a "colorful crowd" crams the "old-school diner" digs anticipating "big food" for breakfast and lunch, and those who deem the waits "not worth it" can mosey to the next-door take-out annex.

Bing Crosby's
| 19 | 25 | 18 | $49 |

1342 Broadway Plaza (S. Main St.), Walnut Creek, 925-939-2464;
www.bingcrosbysrestaurant.com
Der Bingle "would be pleased" by this "snazzy" homage in Walnut Creek where the "beautiful", "classy '50s"-style interior is festooned with "amazing" Crosby mementos, and the live piano music and "martinis galore" add to the "special-occasion" feel; the "pricey" American fare is all over the road, ranging from "great" to "mediocre", and the service "needs a little work", but its cronies croon over the "fun environment" that includes a "hopping bar" scene.

Bistro Liaison
| 20 | 19 | 20 | $36 |

1849 Shattuck Ave. (Hearst Ave.), Berkeley, 510-849-2155;
www.liaisonbistro.com
Berkeleyites "yearning for Paris" head to this "faithful "re-creation" of a corner French bistro, which despite being "only a few blocks from Downtown" "could be in the 6th arrondissement" given the "reasonably priced" *magnifique* cuisine delivered *sans* "pretensions" by a "charming" staff; *bien sûr*, the "cozy", "darkly lit" interior is a *oui* bit "cramped" and "noisy", but it provides "intimacy *pour la liaison*" or a "convivial" evening with friends "before the theater or movies."

Blackberry Bistro Ⓜ
| 22 | 15 | 14 | $19 |

4240 Park Blvd. (Wellington St.), Oakland, 510-336-1088;
www.blackberrybistro.com
"Sometimes you just gotta have" the "to-die-for" American food, including "Southern specialties" served at this wildly "popular", "cute neighborhood" cafe in Oakland that draws "long" lines on weekends; "church-goers still in their Sunday finery rub elbows with inked-up hipsters in Converse sneakers and tattered jeans", all jonesing for the "wonderful breakfast and brunch"; sure, most "hate the wait" and admit that the "pleasant" service can be "painfully slow", but basically, it's "worth" it.

Blackhawk Grille
| 20 | 22 | 19 | $48 |

The Shops at Blackhawk, 3540 Blackhawk Plaza Circle (Camino Tassajara), Danville, 925-736-4295; www.blackhawkgrille.com
One of the few "non–fast food restaurants in the area", this "upscale" Californian is a "favorite with locals" who find it "hard to beat" for "entertaining business and personal acquaintances"; the "ambitious kitchen" delivers "flavorful" fare, while the "spectacular setting" with a "wonderful view of the river walk at Blackhawk Plaza" and regional wine selection "never fail to impress"; but cynics squawk it's "inconsistent" and scoff that service is "inattentive."

Bo's Barbecue 🚫   24 | 12 | 16 | $22

3422 Mt. Diablo Blvd. (Brown Ave.), Lafayette, 925-283-7133
There's "nothin' like" this smokehouse where Lafayette "richie riches" "sink into the best rack of ribs west of the Mississippi" "washed down with the best vino while listening to Delta blues"; even with the "addition of the patio", takeout is an attractive option, given the "limited" "order-and-sit" "hole-in-the-wall setting", but cue-meisters insist Bo "McSwine's (can that really be his real name)?" "twinkle-eyed friendliness" "completes the meal."

Breads of India & Gourmet Curries   21 | 12 | 16 | $21

2448 Sacramento St. (Dwight Way), Berkeley, 510-848-7684 ⊅
948 Clay St. (bet. 9th & 10th Sts.), Oakland, 510-834-7684 🚫 Ⓜ
1358 N. Main St. (Cypress St.), Walnut Creek, 925-256-7684 ⊅
"Freshly baked" breads are "the name of the game" at this Indian trio, though the "mind-numbing curries" and "ever-changing" regional specialties are equally "tasty"; sure, the "bare-bones" decor at the Berkeley original, "long lines" and "indifferent service" are a naan-starter, but "great prices" for oft-organic "dishes you can't find anywhere else" make it "worth it" to tikka a chance.

Bridges Restaurant   21 | 24 | 21 | $56

44 Church St. (Hartz Ave.), Danville, 925-820-7200;
www.bridgesdanville.com
The "who's who of Danville" populates this "all-time favorite" for both "special events" or just a "quick dinner at the bar", drawn by the "upbeat" ambiance, "gorgeous" interior and "enchanting" garden; the "creative" (if "costly") Californian cuisine includes "excellent" Asian fusion dishes, and though there's dissent on the new management's imprint ("much improved" vs. "living on past glory"), bridge-builders can "see why it's a local classic."

Brigetender's Tavern   ▽ 18 | 16 | 13 | $21

30 W. Lake Blvd. (Rt. 89), Tahoe City, 530-583-3342
"Hang with the locals" at this "Tahoe classic" offering "mouth-watering burgers", "good sandwiches" and other "basic pub fare" washed down by "great margaritas" and "fine brews"; the "hunting-lodge atmosphere" is cozy for "casual group dinners" in winter but come summertime there's plenty of outdoor seating in a "beautiful" setting overlooking the Truckee River.

Bucci's 🚫   21 | 19 | 20 | $31

6121 Hollis St. (bet. 59th & 61st Sts.), Emeryville, 510-547-4725;
www.buccis.com
"A stalwart" since the days when "there were only train tracks and warehouses" in Emeryville, this "industrial" yet "welcoming" Cal-Med cafe continues to pull in "faithful locals" and the "techie crowd" for the "three food groups: pizza, salad and wine" that "shine" along with "delicious" pastas; you can also count on "wonderful" mama Bucci and the "friendly" staff to "greet you" while "rotating art" and "quotes on the chalkboards" "add flair."

Cactus Taqueria   21 | 13 | 15 | $11

1881 Solano Ave. (The Alameda), Berkeley, 510-528-1881;
www.cactustaqueria.com
5642 College Ave. (Keith Ave.), Oakland, 510-658-6180
For "fast food without the guilt", these "popular", oh-so-"very East Bay" Mexicans in Berkeley and Oakland offer a "terrific op-

tion" for "wonderful", "healthful" fare made with "fresh", "quality ingredients" including "humanely farmed" meats, all an "excellent value"; "those-in-the-know call in to order ahead" or "go during naptime" to avoid the "stroller blitzkrieg" and attendant "high-decibel experience", but "efficient" service will ensure you're in and out "quickly."

Cafe Cacao 19 17 15 $26

Scharffen Berger Chocolate Maker Factory, 914 Heinz Ave. (7th St.), Berkeley, 510-843-6000; www.cafecacao.biz

"Chocoholics" top off a tour of Berkeley's Scharffen Berger factory with this adjacent "little gem" that incorporates the "intoxicating" cocoa bean in savory and sugary American and French brunch (weekends) and lunch favorites including pastries, panini and "superb", "sinful" beverages and desserts; less sweet are "sullen" service and "expensive" tabs that have sourpusses saying "I shan't be back"; N.B. a recent redo may outdate the Decor score.

Cafe Esin ⊠Ⓜ 24 18 22 $40

2416 San Ramon Valley Blvd. (Crow Canyon Rd.), San Ramon, 925-314-0974; www.cafeesin.com

"Strip malls everywhere should be so lucky to have a place as good as" this "warm and happy" "gem" where the owners, a "friendly", "hardworking couple", deliver "exquisite" New American dishes with Mediterranean and "Turkish influences" "accompanied by superb wines" and "inspired" housemade desserts; if a few feel the "functional" decor "needs attention", most retort it's a "treat" in the "suburban desert" of San Ramon – "nothing else is even close!"

Café Fanny 24 12 14 $17

1603 San Pablo Ave. (Cedar St.), Berkeley, 510-524-5447

"Out-of-towners can't believe" "people queue up to sit" in a "chilly parking lot", comparing the experience to "eating from the tailgate of a truck", but "Berkeley-ites" "love" Alice Waters' "tiny" French stand-up bar "named after her daughter"; it's a "sure bet for a quick gourmet bite" – you'll "enjoy every expensive" drop of "absurdly good" "soup-sized bowls" of "Fair-Trade" café au lait, "simple" breakfast "sweets" and lunch fare made from "fresh, fresh, fresh" local organic ingredients, all served by "slightly precious Euro-chic counter help"; N.B. no dinner.

Café Fiore ▽ 26 23 25 $41

1169 Ski Run Blvd. (Tamarack Ave.), South Lake Tahoe, 530-541-2908; www.cafefiore.com

Though only a short drive from the honky-tonk of Casino Row, this "very romantic" destination is the ne plus ultra for couples to come pitch the woo while visiting South Lake Tahoe; the "charming" candlelit, wood-beamed Alpine-cabin–like room fits "only seven tables" so "reservations are hard to get but well worth" waiting for as the "outstanding" Northern Italian classics, impressive wine list and "impeccable service" add up to an "unforgettable dining experience"; N.B. summertime alfresco seating doubles capacity.

Café Gratitude 20 16 18 $21

1730 Shattuck Ave. (Virginia St.), Berkeley, 415-824-4652; www.cafegratitude.com

See review in City of San Francisco Directory.

Café Rouge | 21 | 19 | 19 | $37 |

Market Plaza, 1782 Fourth St. (bet. Hearst Ave. & Virginia St.), Berkeley, 510-525-1440; www.caferouge.net

"One part butcher plus one part restaurant plus one part bar equals happy Atkins-ites" calculate carnivores who canter over to this "companionable" "temple to red meat in Berkeley" ("it must be on the endangered species list"); also known for its charcuterie and "flavorful" French-Med menu, it's "one of the few" dinner options on Fourth Street – which compensates for "hoity-toity" service, "minuscule" servings and prices that have some seeing *rouge*.

Caffé Verbena ⊠ | 20 | 18 | 18 | $35 |

Walter Shorenstein Bldg., 1111 Broadway (bet. 11th & 12th Sts.), Oakland, 510-465-9300; www.caffeverbena.com

"Like a mirage in the desert", this "sophisticated setting" "in Downtown Oakland is easily the best choice around for a classy lunch" of "well-executed" Cal-Ital fare and a "sure bet", though lesser-known, "for weeknight dinners and afterwork snacks"; still, a few "business types" muse it's "maddeningly inconsistent" – "great one night, just ok the next", though most appreciate the "cheap wine on Monday" evenings; N.B. closed weekends.

Casa Orinda | 17 | 17 | 18 | $34 |

20 Bryant Way (Moraga Way), Orinda, 925-254-2981

A "throwback to Orinda in the cowboy era", replete with a "home-on-the-range atmosphere" and "gun collection" on the walls, this "vintage spot" dishes up "old-fashioned" American and Italian chuck wagon fare to the same "early-bird set" that's been eating at "The Casa" since it opened in 1932; youngsters stick to the "signature fried chicken" and tip their hats to the "fully stocked" "locals' bar", "the only place open late (by suburban standards)" in these parts.

Caspers Hot Dogs ⊅ | 19 | 7 | 16 | $6 |

545 San Pablo Ave. (bet. Brighton Ave. & Garfield St.), Albany, 510-527-6611
6998 Village Pkwy. (Dublin Blvd.), Dublin, 925-828-2224
951 C St. (bet. Main St. & Mission Blvd.), Hayward, 510-537-7300
21670 Foothill Blvd. (Grove Way), Hayward, 510-581-9064 ◗
5440 Telegraph Ave. (55th St.), Oakland, 510-652-1668
6 Vivian Dr. (Contra Costa Blvd.), Pleasant Hill, 925-687-6030 ◗
2530 Macdonald Ave. (Civic Center St.), Richmond, 510-235-6492
1280A Newell Hill Pl. (San Miguel Dr.), Walnut Creek, 925-930-9154

"Hot diggity!" shout frankfurter fanatics who "flock" to this "East Bay original", the Top Bang for the Buck in this *Survey*, for a "wiener fix" "with all the toppings" (try the "double cheese – it's pure heavenly bliss on a bun"); it "hasn't changed a bit" since opening in 1934 – which means it's still a "no-frills, cafeteria-style" "time warp", complete with "tons of Formica" and service from "old-fashioned gals" "who call you 'hon.'"

César | 23 | 20 | 19 | $32 |

1515 Shattuck Ave. (bet. Cedar & Vine Sts.), Berkeley, 510-883-0222
4039 Piedmont Ave. (bet. 40th & 41st Sts.), Oakland, 510-883-0222
www.barcesar.com

"Tapas is nearly reaching the strip-mall phase", nevertheless North Berkeley's "gourmet ghetto" progenitor is still "roaring with life and constantly packed" with "everybody from Wavy

Gravy and Gary Danko" to "scenesters" and "funky professors" who hail it as the "real deal", touting the Iberian-Mediterranean small plates and "fantastic" drinks that add up to "a big night out" at "not cheap" tabs; you may "stand shoulder to shoulder" "waiting outside" but few mind as "it's fun to sneak a peek" at what people are eating; N.B. the Oakland branch opened post-*Survey*.

Cha Am Thai   20 | 14 | 16 | $19
1543 Shattuck Ave. (Cedar St.), Berkeley, 510-848-9664
See review in City of San Francisco Directory.

CHEZ PANISSE 🅈   28 | 24 | 26 | $76
1517 Shattuck Ave. (bet. Cedar & Vine Sts.), Berkeley, 510-548-5525; www.chezpanisse.com
Little wonder it "caused NY foodies to face west", but with "oh-so-much history and aura surrounding" Alice Waters' Cal-Med "mecca" in Berkeley, visitors are "surprised how moved" they are "by the simplicity of it all", from the "wonderful Craftsman home setting" to the "stellar" staff that skips the "hovering and the fluff"; acolytes agree that the daily prix fixe menus "never disappoint", offering "fruits, vegetables, almost any living thing, in fact" "so fresh, perfectly selected" and prepared with such "reverence" that they "taste the way they're meant to."

CHEZ PANISSE CAFÉ 🅈   27 | 23 | 25 | $48
1517 Shattuck Ave. (bet. Cedar & Vine Sts.), Berkeley, 510-548-5049; www.chezpanisse.com
You can get anything you want at this "upstairs annex" of Alice's restaurant, a true "destination" where "urbane" Berkeleyites and "fussier eaters" enjoy the "Chez Panisse experience on their own terms"; exuding a "more casual" "clubhouse" air than the prix fixe "temple downstairs", this "less costly" à la carte cafe offers the "same inventive", "locally grown, ethically conscientious" Cal-Med creations, "so fresh you appreciate each ingredient", served by a "passionate" staff in that "charming Craftsman-design setting" – and it all comes "without the busy signals."

CHOW/PARK CHOW   20 | 15 | 18 | $22
La Fiesta Sq., 53 Lafayette Circle (Mt. Diablo Blvd.), Lafayette, 925-962-2469
See review in City of San Francisco Directory.

Christy Hill 🅈 Ⓜ   ∇ 22 | 22 | 26 | $49
115 Grove St. (Lake Blvd.), Tahoe City, 530-583-8551; www.christyhill.com
Situated just 100 feet above the shoreline of Lake Tahoe, this "small, but charming" waterside-wonder has been a crowd-pleaser for more than two decades, offering "amazing" panoramic views, a "creative menu" full of "fabulous" seasonally driven "nouveau" Cal fare and an international wine list; "get your reservation early" as it's difficult to get a table "during peak season" when everyone wants to dine on the deck over the blue.

Citron   23 | 20 | 21 | $46
5484 College Ave. (bet. Lawton & Taft Aves.), Oakland, 510-653-5484; www.citronrestaurant.biz
"Innovative" seasonal Cal–New French fare, coupled with an "excellent wine list" and a "well-trained" staff, continue to make this "romantic" Rockridge neighborhood bistro with a "nice pa-

tio" a "celebration"-worthy "retreat of quiet elegance"; the pro-
tracted prix fixe dinners remain an "excellent option", and may be
the "best deal in town", while morning mavens muse that newly
instituted "brunch is a must"; still, the "underwhelmed" feel it
doesn't "quite live up to the hype."

Cottonwood ▽ 17 | 20 | 20 | $37

Hilltop Lodge, State Hwy. 267 (Brockway Rd.), Truckee, 530-587-5711;
www.cottonwoodrestaurant.com
Perched atop the area's oldest ski lodge, this "rustic", "laid-
back" hilltop haunt with "stunning views of Downtown Truckee"
and the Sierras beyond offers a "solid" Eclectic menu and "atmosphere year-round", with fireside fare in winter and "picniclike"
lunches or sunset dinners on the "fantastic" deck in summer; try
the "eat-with-your-hands garlicky Caesar salad", then stay for
the live music that keeps the joint "crowded on weekends."

Doña Tomás 🛇 Ⓜ 23 | 17 | 18 | $31

5004 Telegraph Ave. (bet. 49th & 51st Sts.), Oakland,
510-450-0522
"Jumpin' with neighborhood foodies", all jonesing for the "haute
couture" of Mexican food, this "lively" must-stop in Oakland's
"trendy Temescal gourmet ghetto" is "expensive", but it ain't no
"taco shop"; "surprisingly complex, rich dishes" and "fresh lime
margaritas" are "pretty much mandatory" – your table will "fight
over the last bite of everything" – and for seats in the "fantastic"
courtyard; P.S. the carnitas are so "shockingly good" "you prac-
tically forget" about the "excessive noise" and "long waits."

Dopo 🛇 24 | 13 | 20 | $30

4293 Piedmont Ave. (Echo St.), Oakland, 510-652-3676
"Big things come in small packages" at this "tiny but titillating"
"cult" Italian in Oakland that delights diners with a "minuscule
menu" of "incredible artisan pizzas" and "amazing pastas" made
with "fresh" California ingredients, plus "cheap (but interesting)
wines" to "round out the night"; the "overflowing crowds" who
wish "they could add just one more table for me" may actually
"snag" one following a post-*Survey* expansion – now if only
they "accepted reservations."

downtown 21 | 20 | 20 | $44

2102 Shattuck Ave. (Addison St.), Berkeley, 510-649-3810;
www.downtownrestaurant.com
"The pride of Berkeley's Downtown scene", this "suave" "supper
club" with a "knowledgeable staff" is "ideally located for the theater or school concerts", offering "excellent" Cal-Med fare and
that "great feeling of being in the center of the whole community"; night owls get down with the "good late-night bar scene"
and hoot over the "frequently wonderful jazz"; still, quibblers
kvetch that live music is "a plus and a minus depending on where
you sit" in the "dimly" lit dining room.

Dragonfly ▽ 25 | 21 | 23 | $38

Porter Simmon Bldg., 10118 Donner Pass Rd. (Spring St.), Truckee,
530-587-0557; www.dragonflycuisine.com
"A real find in the Tahoe area", Downtown Truckee's "funky",
second-floor "local hang" is a Cal-Asian "oasis" pairing "great
creative food" ("similar to Wolfdale's'" from whence the chef
comes), "friendly" service and the "fairest wine prices above

6,000 feet"; "make reservations in the winter" or you may be "out in the cold" as it's "packed on ski weekends", while in warmer months, the "lovely" south-facing deck offers "views of the mountains" and doubles capacity.

Duck Club, The   20 | 20 | 20 | $47

Lafayette Park Hotel & Spa, 3287 Mt. Diablo Blvd. (Pleasant Hill Rd.), Lafayette, 925-283-3700; www.lafayetteparkhotel.com

See review in South of San Francisco Directory.

Eccolo   21 | 21 | 20 | $43

1820 Fourth St. (bet. Hearst Ave. & Virginia St.), Berkeley, 510-644-0444; www.eccolo.com

"There's always something intriguing" on the "small" menu at this "modern" trattoria on Fourth Street that's oh-so-"very Italian and Berkeley rolled into one"; chef-owner Christopher Lee, "progeny of Chez Panisse", "lovingly prepares" "house-cured meats", "homemade bread" and "comfort food" "like mama tried to make" from "local, fresh" ingredients, while "personable service" and "great martinis at the bar" underscore the "*simpatico* feel"; still, a frugal few feel "prices are large" for such "meager portions."

ERNA'S ELDERBERRY HOUSE   26 | 26 | 28 | $89

Chateau du Sureau, 48688 Victoria Ln. (Hwy. 41), Oakhurst, 559-683-6800; www.elderberryhouse.com

"For a bit of Europe in the Sierra" Nevada Mountains, gourmands make tracks to this "fairy-tale" manse nestled next to Château du Sureau hotel "amid the pines" of Oakhurst; it's an "amazing" "dining experience" "not to be missed", from the "imaginative" six-course Cal-French prix fixe menu and wine pairings to the "superior" staff that "never permits your glass to be empty" to the "magnificent" grounds; "sure, it's pricey, but you will never forget" your "magical evening."

Evan's American Gourmet Cafe   ▽ 27 | 21 | 24 | $53

536 Emerald Bay Rd. (15th St.), South Lake Tahoe, 530-542-1990; www.evanstahoe.com

Good Evans, despite its "small-town, forest setting" and "mom-and-pop feel", "there's nothing provincial" about this "surprisingly sophisticated" South Shore cabin-cum-"fine-dining" destination that's "way better than your typical tacky Tahoe" spot; unlike some of its brethren, boosters believe this "hidden gem" "would be successful anywhere" thanks to the "cosmopolitan-style" New American cuisine, "great" California-centric wine list, "wonderful ambiance and warm service" from a "knowledgeable" staff.

Everett & Jones Barbeque   20 | 9 | 11 | $19

296 A St. (Myrtle St.), Hayward, 510-581-3222 ●⊅
2676 Fruitvale Ave. (bet. Davis & 27th Sts.), Oakland, 510-533-0900
Jack London Sq., 126 Broadway (2nd St.), Oakland, 510-663-2350

It's a "coin toss" at these "no-frills" East Bay smokehouses; "on their best day, you think you've gone to BBQ heaven" with "finger-licking", "falling-off-the-bone ribs" ("who needs Wet Naps?"), "darn good" sides and "spicy" sauces ("hot is only for the brave" while "medium leaves you unscathed") to "complement the killer Q"; on the flip side, cynics scoff "don't need the attitude", "the looooong waits" or "dingy" digs (the "tonier" Jack London Square location" notwithstanding).

FatApple's 18 | 12 | 16 | $17
*1346 Martin Luther King Jr. Way (bet. Berryman & Rose Sts.),
Berkeley, 510-526-2260*
*7525 Fairmount Ave. (bet. Colusa & Ramona Aves.), El Cerrito,
510-528-3433*
"Stuff yourself" on "tasty" bakery goods, "thick burgers", "good
and hearty breakfasts" and other "four-square American" diner
"eats with home-cooked appeal" at this "standard family favorite" in Berkeley and El Cerrito; you can smell the "freshly baked
pastries" and pies that "even grandma can't beat" "from a mile
away", but don't be "in a hurry" to chow down because the
"friendly" service can be "slower than a snail on Valium."

Fenton's Creamery 19 | 15 | 14 | $13
*4226 Piedmont Ave. (Entrada Ave.), Oakland, 510-658-7000;
www.fentonscreamery.com*
A "throwback to the 1950s without the fakery", Oakland's "family-
friendly" "monument to ice cream" is an "old-style fountain"
dishing up "humongous" scoops and he-"man-sized sundaes"
like "black-and-whites to die for" at "dizzyingly modern prices";
you can also "stuff yourself" on "excellent sandwiches" from an
American menu that "goes beyond basic burgers", but dairy devotees declare they're best consumed with "your favorite milkshake"; P.S. "come ready to wait" on line.

Finfiné – | – | – | M
*2556 Telegraph Ave. (bet. Blake & Parker Sts.), Berkeley, 510-883-0167;
www.finfine.com*
Tucked away in Berkeley's little Village court, this little-known
East African eatery "stands out from other Ethiopian restaurants"
with "thoughtfully prepared" "tasty" stews including many "wonderful" fish and seafood specialties and "lovely" upscale digs
with white tablecloths and fresh flowers; it's still a roll-up-your-
sleeves affair but "shiver me timbers!" the "friendly waiters are
generous with the injera" and the Tej honey wine takes the edge
off the peppery preparations.

Fireside Pizza ▽ 20 | 18 | 16 | $23
*The Village at Squaw Valley, 1985 Squaw Valley Rd., Olympic Valley,
530-584-6150; www.firesidepizza.com*
Given that it's located "at a ski resort in Tahoe, as opposed to a
street corner in NYC", this unpretentious pizzeria right in The Village
at Squaw Valley is the "perfect post"-downhill prandial spot to
"bring the kids"; "it's great to sit on the piazza and people-watch
while you munch some pretty tasty" pies and salads, and afterwards, you can "cozy-up and warm your hands around the
big fire pit" outside.

Fonda Solana ◗ 24 | 21 | 20 | $34
*1501 Solano Ave. (Curtis St.), Albany, 510-559-9006;
www.fondasolana.com*
This "lively", late-night Pan-Latin hot spot offers "a little bit of San
Francisco hip in the sleepy town" of Albany, serving an "original",
"thoughtfully put-together" menu of "intensely tasty tapas" "shorn
of the clichés" that's "just the ticket for a nosh"; fond fans find this
"delightful" "joint's" "no slouch in the drink department" either and
also give a nod to the "sexy vibe" and "ebullient service", concluding it's "worth every penny of the somewhat steep prices."

Forbes Mill Steakhouse   22 | 21 | 21 | $58
200 Sycamore Valley Road W. (San Ramon Valley Blvd.), Danville,
925-552-0505; www.forbesmillsteakhouse.com
See review in South of San Francisco Directory.

Fresh Ketch Restaurant   ▽ 18 | 18 | 18 | $33
2435 Venice Dr. E. (off Tahoe Keys Blvd.), South Lake Tahoe,
530-541-5683; www.thefreshketch.com
Perched on Tahoe Keys Marina, this docksider "with excellent
views of the lake" reels in South Lake crowds with "consistently
good seafood"; "during the summer months", dive into your catch
on the "quaint back patio", and in cooler weather, head upstairs
to the recently renovated dining room or join the locals at the
"hipper" Seafood Bar "where there's always something going
on", be it live music or the "great sushi" night.

Garibaldis   23 | 21 | 20 | $42
5356 College Ave. (Manila Ave.), Oakland, 510-595-4000;
www.garibaldis-eastbay.com
See review in City of San Francisco Directory.

Gar Woods Grill & Pier   17 | 21 | 18 | $37
Carnelian Bay, 5000 N. Lake Blvd. (California St.), Carnelian Bay,
530-546-3366; www.garwoods.com
Although this year-round, "casual" Carnelian Bay "lakeside grill"
with a "retro ambiance" on North Tahoe's shores is "après-
heavenly" to the "ski crowd", "outdoorsy" folks who "arrive by
boat" can't imagine a "summer without sitting on the deck with
pitchers of Wet Woodys" (the "legendary" signature drink) and
soaking up the "fabulous views"; as to the Med–New American
grub, it's "good enough" for brunch, lunch or "sunset happy
hours", but it's the "atmosphere that's worth the visit."

Gioia Pizzeria ⓈⒺ   22 | 8 | 14 | $12
1586 Hopkins St. (McGee Ave.), Berkeley, 510-528-4692
Running "neck-in-neck" for the "distinction" of "best New York–
style pizza in the Bay Area", Berkeley's "hole-in-the-wall" "small
storefront" is reminiscent of the "Soup Nazi" – "you're locked
into" "just six different" choices of "unusual but delightful" combination pies, some with a "California twist"; "who cares if service is slow" and you have to "perch on a stool" or "walk away
munching" a slice – your "mouth will never be happier";
N.B. closes at 8 PM.

Grasshopper Ⓜ   23 | 19 | 18 | $32
6317 College Ave. (Claremont Ave.), Oakland, 510-595-3559;
www.grasshoppersake.com
"Cheap, chic and so exotic", this Pan-Asian hot spot at the "con-
fluence of Claremont and College" may be a "funky", "lower-cost
alternative" to the "Rockridge hustle" but it's still buzzing with
"high energy" – in fact, a few are bugged by the swarms of
"noisy" "Birkenstocks and Gen-Xers"; still, the "wide variety" of
"sublime", "tasty tapas" is reason enough to "take a gang and
order everything" or hang at the "sake bar to die for."

Great China   25 | 10 | 12 | $20
2115 Kittredge St. (Shattuck Ave.), Berkeley, 510-843-7996
"Despite its meek appearance", this Downtown "diamond in the
rough" near the UC Berkeley campus is "crowded" with "movie"-

goers, families and "homesick" Asian "academics" who flock for
the "exquisitely prepared", "very distinctive" modern Chinese
dishes; pay no mind to the "impossible waits" and "stone-faced",
"sullen servers" – once the "unusual bounteous platters" arrive
it's all "worth" it – or just "call ahead for takeout."

Gregoire   25 | 9 | 17 | $20
2109 Cedar St. (Shattuck Ave.), Berkeley, 510-883-1893
4001B Piedmont Ave. (40th St.), Oakland, 510-547-3444
www.gregoirerestaurant.com

Socca Oven
Epicurious Garden, 1511 Shattuck Ave. (bet. Cedar & Vine Sts.),
Berkeley, 510-548-6001
"Berkeley's best French restaurant" may be this "brilliant", "closet-
sized" gourmet ghetto take-out "shack" where devotees "battle"
over the "limited" sidewalk tables; "you could do this at home, in the
time" "it takes for them to cook" the "addictive potato puffs" and
organic specials but the "fun frantic stove activity" and Gregoire
Jacquet's "upbeat" "personality makes up for it"; N.B. there's a
new Oakland sidekick, plus a Socca Oven spin-off in Epicurious
Garden that sells soccas, pizzalike chickpea flour orbs, to go.

House of Chicken and Waffles ◑   18 | 13 | 19 | $15
444 Embarcadero W. (Broadway), Oakland, 510-836-4446;
www.hcwchickenandwaffles.com
Reminiscent of "SoCal's Roscoe's", this Southern–"soul food experience" in Downtown Oakland's Jack London Square lures the
"church"-bound and the hungover who come-a-"hankering" for
"rib-sticking food", including "evilous fried" or smothered
chicken and waffles that "hit the spot", all served by a "staff that
wants to please"; it's "worth a trip, if only for" the "charming
menu" and mural boasting dishes "named after family members",
"space-age" motif and Motown-and-gospel soundtrack.

IL FORNAIO   19 | 20 | 18 | $36
1430 Mt. Diablo Blvd. (bet. Broadway & Main St.), Walnut Creek,
925-296-0100; www.ilfornaio.com
See review in City of San Francisco Directory.

In-N-Out Burger ◑   22 | 9 | 17 | $8
8300 Oakport St. (Edgewater Dr.), Oakland, 800-786-1000;
www.in-n-out.com
See review in City of San Francisco Directory.

Jade Villa   17 | 9 | 12 | $20
800 Broadway (bet. 8th & 9th Sts.), Oakland, 510-839-1688
For a "huge variety of dim sum" that costs just a "few measly
dollars", the Oakland lunch- and brunch-bunch heads to this
"classic Chinese barn of a room", "chowing down" on dumpling
delights and other "fun" foods; but while fans find it a "true
cultural experience" right down to the "brisk staff", the jaded jibe
that the grande dame is "riding on its reputation" and overdue
"for a face-lift."

Jake's on the Lake   17 | 19 | 16 | $35
780 N. Lake Blvd. (Jackpine St.), Tahoe City, 530-583-0188;
www.jakestahoe.com
Should be renamed "Jewel on the Lake" quip admirers agog over
the "exceptional views" of the marina and the mountains afforded

by the "location, location, location" of this "'70s"-style mountain lodge with "great" deck seating; the Californian grub and grog is "better than expected", and the atmosphere is "family-friendly", adding to the "old standby's" "local favorite" appeal – just bear in mind that service can be on "Tahoe time."

Jimmy Bean's　　　　20 | 11 | 14 | $17

1290 Sixth St. (Gilman St.), Berkeley, 510-528-3435; www.jimmybeans.com
"A hidden gem in an industrial area of Downtown Berkeley", this "casual" counter-service cafe gets "crowded" with "earth-mother" types and "UC Haas" students who "go bonkers" over the "perfectly cooked" egg dishes and "must-try" silver-dollar pancakes as well as "gourmet" Californian lunches; "though better known" for its "leisurely" brunches and "excellent" coffee bevs, an "expanded seating area" makes for a "mellow dinner scene" as well.

Jodie's Restaurant Ⓜ⍢　　　　▽ 24 | 11 | 24 | $11

902 Masonic Ave. (Solano Ave.), Albany, 510-526-1109
Truly a "sui generis" "hole-in-the-wall", this "amazing" six-seater, unofficial "community center" near the Albany BART tracks, offers "delicious" New American–Eclectic fare "for meat eaters and vegetarians alike" including "excellent fried chicken" on weekends; dishes named for "frequent customers", "service with a smile" from the "charismatic proprietor" and "pleasant conversation" with "interesting" patrons transform breakfast and lunch into an "experience" that "soothes the soul."

Jojo Ⓢ Ⓜ　　　　24 | 18 | 23 | $44

3859 Piedmont Ave. (bet. 40th St. & Macarthur Blvd.), Oakland, 510-985-3003; www.jojorestaurant.com
A "labor of love from a great husband-and-wife team", this "small" "surprise" in Oakland offers "marvelous" French bistro fare "using the best ingredients" along with "thoughtfully chosen, value-priced wines" and "fabulous" desserts; "warm" service from an "excellent" staff and a "peaceful", "cozy" setting make it "delightful" for a "romantic" date , and "enthusiasts" consider the experience "on a par with more expensive" venues.

Jordan's　　　　▽ 22 | 25 | 23 | $49

Claremont Resort & Spa, 41 Tunnel Rd. (Claremont Ave.), Berkeley, 510-549-8510; www.claremontresort.com
"Million-dollar views of the Bay", a "beautiful", "elegant" setting and a "staff that treats you like royalty" are the "main draws" at this "grand old" dining room in Berkeley's Claremont Resort, luring "ladies who lunch", "out-of-towners" and "the prom crowd"; the Cal-French fare may be best at the "bountiful Sunday brunch", as some contend dinner, offered Wednesday–Saturday, "lacks that special something you expect."

Juan's Place　　　　17 | 12 | 17 | $15

941 Carleton St. (9th St.), Berkeley, 510-845-6904
"Juan and his family" have been serving "enormous portions" of "dependably tasty" and "cheap" Mexican "comfort food" including the "best homemade chips" (both corn and flour) "for generations" at this "institution" "hidden in the warehouses in West Berkeley"; "students and business types" "share tables" and quaff pitchers of "great wine margaritas" in a "nothing-fancy" setting lit by "Christmas lights 365 days of the year."

KIRALA   26 | 17 | 18 | $34
2100 Ward St. (Shattuck Ave.), Berkeley, 510-549-3486
KIRALA 2
Epicurious Garden, 1511 Shattuck Ave. (bet. Cedar & Vine Sts.),
Berkeley, 510-649-1384
www.kiralaberkeley.com
This no-reservations "Osaka transplant" "teaches" Berkeley "professors and bearded graduate students" a form of "Zen Buddhism" – the art of staying "patient until you're seated"; "who needs money when your taste buds are doing the cha-cha" over "outstanding sushi" and the "real attraction" – "fantastic robata" grill items; still, the recent addition of a "sake bar makes the waits" and "chaotic hash-slinging service" "tolerable" as does the take-out newcomer, Kirala 2 at Epicurious Garden.

Koryo Wooden Charcoal BBQ ◑   23 | 9 | 13 | $22
4390 Telegraph Ave. (Shattuck Ave.), Oakland, 510-652-6007
Oakland's Seoul food "standard" serving "copious" portions is a "perfect place to go for a meat feast" or to put an "early hangover defense system" into play – just don't "wear your Sunday best" because "you'll go home smelling like Korean BBQ"; "mini-mall decor" and "surly staff notwithstanding", "oh what a thrill" it is to devour this "straightforward delicious", "smoky" goodness.

Lalime's   26 | 21 | 24 | $45
1329 Gilman St. (bet. Neilson St. & Peralta Ave.), Berkeley, 510-527-9838;
www.lalimes.com
Even as the Krikorian family's culinary "empire has grown" (Jimmy Beans, Salt, T-Rex), the Berkeley "original" has "remained excellent" for more than 20 years, offering "first-class" seasonal fare from an "imaginative" Cal-Med menu at price points that add up to a "great deal"; the service is "low-key" but "thoughtful", the setting's "lovely" and "restful", and even though it may not "make headlines", it always makes for a "special" experience.

La Méditerranée   20 | 15 | 18 | $20
2936 College Ave. (Ashby Ave.), Berkeley, 510-540-7773;
www.cafelamed.com
See review in City of San Francisco Directory.

Lanesplitter Pub & Pizza   21 | 15 | 17 | $13
1051 San Pablo Ave. (Monroe St.), Berkeley, 510-527-8375
2033 San Pablo Ave. (University Ave.), Berkeley, 510-845-1652 ◑
4799 Telegraph Ave. (48th St.), Oakland, 510-653-5350 ◑
www.lanesplitterpizza.com
Keglers cry there's no "better place to indulge in carbs" than this "funky" converted Berkeley bowling alley and newer Oakland outpost where "tattooed hipsters", "aging bikers" and the "baby brigade" line up for "excellent" pizza (including a "great vegan" variation) and "tasty" microbrews; the staff's "super-friendly" if a bit "disorganized", and most striking are the "amazing" prices; N.B. take-out only at 1051 San Pablo.

La Note   23 | 22 | 19 | $24
2377 Shattuck Ave. (bet. Channing Way & Durant Ave.), Berkeley,
510-843-1535; www.lanoterestaurant.com
"Stellar" breakfasts starting with "lovely bowls of café au lait", "excellent", "authentic Provençal" salads and crôques for lunch

and "wonderful" dinners (Thursday–Saturday) with live accordion music ensure "you'll leave on a happy note" at this "sweet" French bistro in Berkeley; the "lovely" setting includes a "sunny patio" and the "cost-to-quality ratio is good", but the "painfully" long waits and sometimes "erratic" service are a bit off-key.

Lark Creek   23 | 20 | 22 | $42

1360 Locust St. (bet. Civic Dr. & Mt. Diablo Blvd.), Walnut Creek, 925-256-1234; www.larkcreek.com

Bradley Ogden's Walnut Creek offshoot attracts a faithful flock comprising "the famous, infamous and everyday folk" with "imaginative", "upscale" interpretations of "all-American favorites", many made in the wood-burning oven; the "pleasant" staff supplies "exceptional" service and the "lovely" setting is "cozy" (albeit "noisy" at times), and though it's "expensive" for "comfort food", it's "never a disappointment" – particularly the "decadent" desserts; P.S. it's "lovely" for weekend brunch too.

Le Cheval   21 | 14 | 16 | $21

1007 Clay St. (10th St.), Oakland, 510-763-8495; www.lecheval.com

Le Petit Cheval ☒⑂

2600 Bancroft Way (Bowditch St.), Berkeley, 510-704-8018

"Oakland bigwigs", "OPD officers" and "large parties" "hobnob" at this "universally adored", "lively", "barnlike" "warehouse" where the "modestly priced" Vietnamese fusion vittles arrive "seemingly seconds after you order it", even as the "throngs descend" for lunch and dinner; "starving students" gallop to the "cafeteria"-style Petit Cheval in Berkeley for "big, inexpensive lunches on the go", and while it's "not like the real Le Cheval", there's less of a line.

LEFT BANK   18 | 20 | 17 | $38

60 Crescent Dr. (Monument Blvd.), Pleasant Hill, 925-288-1222; www.leftbank.com

See review in North of San Francisco Directory.

Lo Coco's Restaurant & Pizzeria Ⓜ   22 | 14 | 20 | $23

1400 Shattuck Ave. (Rose St.), Berkeley, 510-843-3745
4270 Piedmont Ave. (Echo Ave.), Oakland, 510-652-6222 ⑂
www.lococospizzeria.com

"The decor is a bit worn, but that adds to the charm" of these 25-year-old, family-run red-sauce "staples" in Berkeley and Oakland specializing in "plentiful" portions of "hearty" meatballs and "*bellissimo*" pizza served "the classic Sicilian way" atop a checkered tablecloth by an "amiable, informed staff"; the dishes are "simple, but gosh it goes down well with" "families" and "dates" who "happily wait to sink their teeth" into the "solid", "sinful" dishes.

Luka's Taproom & Lounge   22 | 15 | 18 | $28

2221 Broadway (Grand Ave.), Oakland, 510-451-4677;
www.lukasoakland.com

"Surprisingly innovative" for an Oakland "beer paradise" – "what's not to love" about "off-the-hook mac 'n' cheese" and an "ambitious" New American–French bistro menu that mixes up "tasty, unusual dishes with comfort food" and, of course, an "extensive" brew selection; it's the "perfect after-work spot" and also "nice for late nights" choruses an "eclectic" "loud crowd" – but "don't even think of trying to have a conversation in here."

Mama's Royal Cafe ⊐   18 | 12 | 14 | $16
4012 Broadway (40th St.), Oakland, 510-547-7600;
www.mamasroyalcafeoakland.com
"Rain or shine there's always a line" at Oakland's "spunky, down-to-earth brunch" "institution" serving "tasty" Traditional American eats and staffed with "eclectic" servers that loyalists say are a "hoot"; "half the fun is the napkin art" contests – just ask the "whole generation of hipsters who grew up hanging out at the Royal and still meet old friends there"; but the pre-caffeinated pout it's "nothing special" "despite the rhetoric."

Marica   23 | 19 | 20 | $37
5301 College Ave. (Bryant Ave.), Oakland, 510-985-8388
"Sorry it took me so long" to catch on to this Oakland seafooder confide piscatorians who now fin their way over to this "deceptively modest", "brick-walled" "small eatery" for "beautifully prepared, pleasantly presented" "elegant and novel" fish dishes; "take advantage of the prix fixe specials – they're always a bargain and delish" – and relish the "hospitable" owners' "neighborhoody" air – you "feel like you're in Europe at your favorite corner restaurant."

Max's ⊠   17 | 13 | 16 | $24
Oakland City Ctr., 500 12th St. (bet. Broadway & Clay St.), Oakland,
510-451-6297; www.maxsworld.com
See review in City of San Francisco Directory.

Mezze   24 | 22 | 22 | $37
3407 Lakeshore Ave. (bet. Mandana Blvd. & Trestle Glen Rd.),
Oakland, 510-663-2500; www.mezze.com
Treasure-hunters in the Lake Merritt area prize this "chic" "jewel" for its "consistently delicious", thoroughly "memorable", "bright" Cal-Med entrees and small plates, "creative cocktails" and "great wine selection", commending the "expert bartenders who walk you through the list"; it's a "testament" to the "delightful owners" that it's "filled with regulars, not just those seeking the hippest new spot", so settle in for meze "on a warm East Bay night and forget all your troubles."

Moody's Bistro & Lounge   ▽ 25 | 22 | 22 | $45
Truckee Hotel, 10007 Bridge St. (off I-80), Truckee, 530-587-8688;
www.moodysbistro.com
Even if you didn't wing over to the Truckee Hotel's "fun, happening" 1950s-style speakeasy a few years ago the "night that Paul McCartney jammed with a local band", you'll still catch "great live music" here along with "inspired" Californian fare and an "impressive wine list"; the "enthusiastic staff aims to please", making it even more "worth the drive" from Tahoe; P.S. "make reservations" or you may be singing the 'Truckee Blues.'

Naan 'n Curry ⊐   19 | 7 | 10 | $13
2366 Telegraph Ave. (bet. Channing Way & Durant Ave.), Berkeley,
510-841-6226
See review in City of San Francisco Directory.

Naked Fish, The   ▽ 23 | 17 | 18 | $38
3940 Lake Tahoe Blvd. (bet. Hwy. 50 & Pioneer Trail), South Lake Tahoe,
530-541-3474
"Bring your flashlight because it's dark" at this "great find" decked out with a mermaid mural, nevertheless, the sushi is "ex-

cellent", "even in the dark" – in fact, some fin fans feel it may be the "best in Tahoe"; get in the swim with the "loud, hip crowd" and you're in for a "fun night out with friends"; still, a few quibble it's "expensive for such small portions."

Nan Yang Rockridge Ⓜ　　22　15　19　$23
6048 College Ave. (Claremont Ave.), Oakland, 510-655-3298
"Consistently tasty Burmese food" proffered by "efficient, welcoming" servers make this "neighborhood" "gem" a "Rockridge favorite"; "it's worth the trip to a different part of Asia" "when you're in the area" agree "adventurous diners" who dive into the "generous portions" of "unusual, delicious", "well-seasoned dishes" that are just right for a "nice change" of pace.

Nizza La Bella　　19　18　20　$31
825 San Pablo Ave. (bet. Solano & Washington Aves.), Albany, 510-526-2552
"*Zut alors!*" the "French Riviera on San Pablo Avenue" quip Euroseekers who covet the "consistently good" French-Italian fare at this "cozy neighborhood" bistro and sidewalk-style cafe in Albany; it's *très* "authentic" down to the "noise, crowds" and "tight" seating – which makes it all the easier to "meet folks" at the "gorgeous bar" staffed with "entertaining bartenders"; still, a "disappointed" few bella-eve it "lacks a little certain something."

North Beach Pizza ●　　18　9　14　$17
1598 University Ave. (California St.), Berkeley, 510-849-9800;
www.northbeachpizza.com
See review in City of San Francisco Directory.

O'Chamé ⊠　　24　22　20　$31
1830 Fourth St. (Hearst Ave.), Berkeley, 510-841-8783
At this unofficial "Zen center" of Berkeley's "Fourth Street corridor", diners escape the "frantic commercialism" outside to "meditate" over "nourishing" meals of "unbeatable noodle soups" and "fresh, clean" "Japanese nouvelle cuisine" ("everything but sushi") amid a "very healing", "serene" "tea garden" setting; still, "precious" small plates at "large prices" leave some diners dissatisfied; P.S. sip from a "wonderful selection" of "sake and rare green teas."

Oliveto Cafe & Restaurant　　25　22　22　$52
5655 College Ave. (Keith St.), Oakland, 510-547-5356; www.oliveto.com
Chef Paul Canales' "handcrafted salumi", "homemade pastas" and "classy, artisanal" Italian fare "regularly anointed with once-in-a-lifetime aceto balsamico and extra virgin olive oil" frenzy the faithful ("any more authentic, artistic and passionate it would be in the Vatican" instead of Oakland); however, heretics eschew "aggressive prices", "limited choices" and service that swings from "cheerful" to "snotty"; P.S. "if you can't get into the posh upstairs, the downstairs cafe" offers "good vino" and "artisanal" pizza and small plates.

Olivia ⊠ Ⓜ　　▽ 24　21　23　$39
1453 Dwight Way (Sacramento St.), Berkeley, 510-548-2322;
www.oliviaeats.com
It's "easy to miss if you're driving too fast", but discoverers "can't wait to go back" to this "charming little" "European-style" "bistro in a residential Berkeley neighborhood" for "delightful" Eclectic-

Med cuisine proffered by "chef-owners who take care of every detail so you feel pampered"; add in exclusive Kermit Lynch boutique French wine offerings and "jammed seating" and you feel like you've been "invited" to a "home in France, but at restaurant prices."

Pakwan �　　　　　　　　22 | 5 | 10 | $13 |
26617 Mission Blvd. (Sorenson Rd.), Hayward, 510-538-2401
See review in City of San Francisco Directory.

Pappo Ⓜ　　　　　　　∇ 21 | 19 | 18 | $36 |
2320 Central Ave. (bet. Oak & Park Sts.), Alameda, 510-337-9100;
www.papporestaurant.com
Residents reckon this cozy, brick-walled bistro in the tiny East Bay isle is a "great new addition to Alameda" thanks to chef/co-owner John Thiel's (ex Bay Wolf) ever-changing menu of "gourmet" Cal-Med "comfort food" incorporating organic ingredients; however, holdouts hint it's "got a ways to go", and budgeters believe it's "a bit pricey" for "small servings"; N.B. sidewalk seating and Sunday brunch are added enticements.

Pasta Pomodoro　　　　　16 | 13 | 16 | $19 |
5614 Shellmound St. (Powell St.), Emeryville, 510-923-1173
5500 College Ave. (Lawton Ave.), Oakland, 510-923-0900
www.pastapomodoro.com
See review in City of San Francisco Directory.

Pearl Oyster Bar & Restaurant　22 | 21 | 19 | $41 |
5634 College Ave. (bet. Keith Ave. & Ocean View Dr.), Oakland,
510-654-5426; www.pearloncollege.com
Surveyors who slurp at this "be-seen", "urban cool" "sliver of a restaurant" in Oakland savor "very fresh and inventive" weekly lineups of seafood "bites" (many "Asian"-accented) and "interesting" "fishing at the bar" (along with "good champagne by the glass, "soju and sake"); detractors, however, dis the "noise", "tiny portions" that "bring the small-plates concept into the realm of absurdity" and service that's "snooty" ("sometimes") and "rushed" when it's "crowded" ("always").

Pho 84　　　　　　　　24 | 11 | 18 | $16 |
354 17th St. (Franklin St.), Oakland, 510-832-1338
The "granddaddy of Vietnamese noodle shops", this "tiny" Downtown Oakland "bargain" joint serves "super-fast, super-abundant", super-"fresh" "authentic flavors of the Mekong" beyond the "outstanding" namesake soups, including "special rice" and spring rolls, making it the "way to pho" for phamished phans; phew are "put off" by the "bare-bones" "shabby interior", concurring "you're not going here for the looks", you're here for the "flavorful" phare.

Pho Hoa-Hiep II　　　　　21 | 6 | 13 | $10 |
1402 E. 12th St. (14th Ave.), Oakland, 510-533-0549
"A steaming hot bowl" of Vietnamese "comfort food" "is the perfect remedy for a rainy day" and a "cheap and delicious way to fill your stomach without emptying your wallet" any time of the year at this "no-nonsense" Oakland pho find (with outposts in Daly City and SF's Outer Sunset); "slurp-and-go" suggest old-hands, noting that the "no-frills" "time-warp" digs and "curt service" give little incentive to linger.

Pianeta
▽ 22 ⎤ 19 ⎤ 19 ⎤ $41 ⎤

10096 Donner Pass Rd. (off I-80), Truckee, 530-587-4694
For "dependable" "Italian rustica cuisine" locals brag "could compete in San Francisco" ("homemade ravioli is not to be missed") served by a "warm staff" in an "inviting", "dimly lit" faux old-world environment with stone and exposed-"brick walls", diners truck on over to this "upscale" trattoria that's arguably the "best" spot on the Downtown Truckee drag; for maximum "privacy, ask for a downstairs booth."

Piatti
18 ⎤ 19 ⎤ 19 ⎤ $34 ⎤

100 Sycamore Valley Rd. W. (San Ramon Valley Blvd.), Danville, 925-838-2082; www.piatti.com
This "popular", "pleasant" Pan–Bay Area Italian chain wins *amici* with its "welcoming" feel, "friendly" staff and "approachable", "fair-priced" Italian eats (featuring local organic produce) that "get the job done"; loyalists laud the "seasonal" "mainstays" as "better-than-average", but sterner surveyors sigh these "sophisticated suburbans" are so "predictable", though "if you've got to eat corporate, you could do worse"; P.S. "outdoor dining" at most locations "is a treat."

Picante Cocina Mexicana
21 ⎤ 13 ⎤ 15 ⎤ $14 ⎤

1328 Sixth St. (bet. Camelia & Gilman Sts.), Berkeley, 510-525-3121; www.picantecocinamexicana.com
"Very good Mexican fast food" that's been "Westernized and made healthy" draws "Berzerkeley" "families" to this "roaringly popular", "lived-in comfortable" "favorite" where there's "no table service" but "the long line always moves quickly"; still, buzzkills balk at "bland burritos" ("hello, flavor?") and caution the "kid-central" confines ("toddlers run screaming") can make for "mayhem" (though "strong margaritas" and the "great outside garden area" might help).

Pizza Antica
22 ⎤ 16 ⎤ 17 ⎤ $24 ⎤

3600 Mt. Diablo Blvd. (Dewing Ave.), Lafayette, 925-299-0500; www.pizzaantica.com
See review in South of San Francisco Directory.

Pizzaiolo ⊠ Ⓜ
23 ⎤ 18 ⎤ 16 ⎤ $31 ⎤

5008 Telegraph Ave. (51st St.), Oakland, 510-652-4888; www.pizzaiolo.us
"You'd think pizza was invented" at "Chez Panisse alum" Charlie Hallowell's "upbeat", "utterly Californian pizzeria" in Oakland, so "outrageous" are the crowds that amass "just about always" for "godly" pies with "crackerlike crusts" and "heavenly, fresh toppings" (and the rest of the "daily changing" Italian menu is "even better", accompanied by a "good-value wine list"); but the "prevalence of porcine products" limits "legions of vegetarians" – while the nightly "rush" for tables "really challenges the staff."

Pizza Rustica
19 ⎤ 10 ⎤ 14 ⎤ $18 ⎤

5422 College Ave. (bet. Kales & Manila Aves.), Oakland, 510-654-1601
6106 La Salle Ave. (Moraga Ave.), Oakland, 510-339-7878
www.caferustica.com
"Solid" "gourmet" pizza (like a Thai-style pie that's "hard to believe but deelish") or "rotisserie chicken almost as cheap as home cooking", lures hungry Oaklanders to this Italian duo – but they

don't always stay; while the "tiki"-themed Conga Lounge upstairs at the College Avenue site offers a "trip into the time tunnel", the otherwise "bare-bones decor" and "painfully slow service" make the "minor miracle" of delivery or "takeout the way to go."

Plearn Thai Cuisine | 19 | 13 | 17 | $19 |

2050 University Ave. (bet. Milvia St. & Shattuck Ave.), Berkeley, 510-841-2148

Since 1982, lunch and "pre-theater" crowds have flocked to this "inexpensive", "family-friendly" Siamese "standby" in Berkeley for "tasty" Thai comfort food" "with an extra touch of sweetness" that some say are a "pleasure to consume"; however, connoisseurs counter that the fare isn't "spicy enough" and lacks "nuanced flavors", concluding that, "like the Thailand posters on the wall, the glory has faded" from years past.

PlumpJack Cafe | 25 | 22 | 23 | $52 |

PlumpJack Squaw Valley Inn, 1920 Squaw Valley Rd. (Hwy. 89), Olympic Valley, 530-583-1576; www.plumpjackcafe.com

See review in City of San Francisco Directory.

Postino | 23 | 25 | 22 | $47 |

3565 Mt. Diablo Blvd. (Oak Hill Rd.), Lafayette, 925-299-8700; www.postinorestaurant.com

Lafayette "locals love" to "meet neighbors and friends" at this "spectacular" "brick château" (and "historical old post office!") for "tasty and varied" Italian fare featuring local produce, house-cured meats and homemade cheeses that "make your mouth demand more"; it's "a little pricey", but "personable service" compensates, while a "great wine selection" explains why the "cozy" "bar has become very popular."

Prima | 24 | 21 | 23 | $48 |

1522 N. Main St. (bet. Bonanza St. & Lincoln Ave.), Walnut Creek, 925-935-7780; www.primaristorante.com

The "'burbs broke out with a real restaurant to rival the city's" when this Northern Italian oenophiles' "hangout" opened in Walnut Creek three decades ago; it's "always a treat" to pore over the "priced-to-drink" list of 1,600 bottles, "unparalleled" in the East Bay along with the "solid" menu of "simply prepared", "elegantly plated" "fine food" delivered by a "well-versed" staff; N.B. check out the "really good jazz combos on weekends."

Red Hut Café ⊟ | ▽ 23 | 13 | 20 | $14 |

2749 Lake Tahoe Blvd. (Al Tahoe Blvd.), South Lake Tahoe, 530-541-9024

Nevada Red Hut Café ⊟

227 Kingsbury Grade (Deer Run Ct.), Lake Tahoe, NV, 775-588-7488

"You've just gotta love 'The Hut'", a "funky and fun" "little" "greasy" spoon serving what the weekend warriors who "crowd" in call the "best breakfast in Lake Tahoe", including pancakes "perfect for working off a late night in the casinos" and "lunch that is good and fast" (closing time is 2 PM); the Stateline location, however, boasts a "better view" and "easier parking in the snow."

Restaurant Peony | 21 | 15 | 12 | $24 |

Pacific Renaissance Plaza, 388 Ninth St. (bet. Franklin & Webster Sts.), Oakland, 510-286-8866

By day, "probably half of Oakland" swarms this "huge" Cantonese "dining hall" ("is it the world's largest?") in "big groups to adequately sample" the "authentic", "unique dim sum" – regulars recommend you "go early" (or "be prepared to wait") and "go with a native speaker" (or get ready for "guess-work"); conversely, frustrated diners who fantasize about "set-ting [themselves] on fire to attract a waiter" might find the "wonderful Hong Kong–style set dinners" "more enjoyable."

Rick & Ann's

22 | 15 | 18 | $20

2922 Domingo Ave. (bet. Ashby & Claremont Aves.), Berkeley, 510-649-8538; www.rickandanns.com

"Behold breakfast perfection" at this "always busy, always loud, always fun" "country kitchen"-esque "neighborhood fixture": "you can't get more Berkeley" than the "loyal following" gath-ered around the "communal table" over "newspapers" and "in-novative, organic" American "down-home cookin'" served "on the cheap"; outsiders "don't know if the long waits are worth it", but diehards declare "I would marry either Rick or Ann if they would promise to cook breakfast for me every morning."

Ristorante Amoroma

∇ 21 | 17 | 22 | $31

360 Park St. (Center St.), Moraga, 925-377-7662

"Finally, a first-rate" ristorante in "sleepy Moraga" agree *amici* who fall for this "real Roman" "hot spot" (whose name translates to 'I love Rome' in dialect) tucked into a shopping center – it's "so cute, so good" and such a "surprise" for the "'burbs"; add in a "homey" feel, "friendly service", a "great selection of Italian wines" and you've got a "delightful neighborhood favorite."

Ristorante Raphael Ⓜ

23 | 22 | 22 | $29

2132 Center St. (Shattuck Ave.), Berkeley, 510-644-9500; www.ristoranteraphael.com

"One of those only-in-Berkeley restaurants", this "dependable, creative" trattoria whips up "well-prepared", "excellent Italian food that happens to be kosher", offering "consistently great, tempting" fish and vegetarian choices – but no meat or poultry options; the "lovely, jaunty atmosphere" sets the stage for a "semi-elegant meal" "before the Rep" while the "extremely effi-cient service" "makes the meal even better."

River Ranch Restaurant & Lodge

∇ 18 | 23 | 19 | $38

2285 River Rd. (Alpine Meadows Rd.), Tahoe City, 530-583-4264; www.riverranchlodge.com

The Truckee "River runs through it", which adds to the "romantic lodge feel" of this Tahoe City slope standby that serves "solid" Californian fare; "don't expect much" in the way of "fine dining", but do treat yourself to one of "the best après ski scenes" by the fire and come summer, join the revelers having a "blast" downing "drinks on the deck" and "watching the rafters" as they "keep coming."

RIVOLI

27 | 23 | 25 | $46

1539 Solano Ave. (bet. Neilson St. & Peralta Ave.), Berkeley, 510-526-2542; www.rivolirestaurant.com

Truly the "highlight of Solano Avenue", Wendy and Roscoe's "East Bay find" with "polished service" is "wonderful without being pretentious"; "order anything" from the "innovative, high-caliber" menu "mixing Californian and Mediterranean" flavors and the "astounding wine list" and you'll "go home happy" – especially if you land a "window seat and watch the nocturnal animals poke about the garden" "in bloom"; just "book ahead" because everyone from "foodies" to "Nobel laureates and world-renowned scientists from UC Berkeley" are in on the same "secret."

Salute E Ristorante at Marina Bay ▽ 20 | 22 | 22 | $38
1900 Esplanade Dr. (Schnooner Dr.), Richmond, 510-215-0803;
www.salutemarinabay.com
A "dependable" marina mainstay in Richmond for over 20 years reveal viewmasters who vie for "spectacular" vistas "on a clear day"; the 100-year-old Victorian house with "bobbling sailboats" in the yacht harbor and "San Francisco in the distance" makes a "romantic" backdrop for supping on "surprisingly good", "solid Italian" dishes, all toted to table by a "professional staff."

Saul's Restaurant & Delicatessen 19 | 15 | 17 | $19
1475 Shattuck Ave. (bet. Rose & Vine Sts.), Berkeley, 510-848-3354;
www.saulsdeli.com
Corned beef–cravers and pastrami swamis file into Berkeley's "reliably good kosher-style deli" for a "bit of NY Jewish mama" food, including a "weekend brunch that could make your bubbe kvell"; it stays "true to its heritage" in spirit, serving up sandwiches like the "Lower East Side's", "only California-fresh with Niman Ranch" meats, so if the servers "move you through your meal very quickly" few mind, rejoining "keep the pickles coming."

Scott's Seafood 18 | 19 | 19 | $39
2 Broadway (Water St.), Oakland, 510-444-5969
1333 N. California Blvd. (Mt. Diablo Blvd.), Walnut Creek, 925-934-1300
www.scottsseafood.com
"Evokes times long past" muse admirers who "delight" in this "classic" Bay Area seafood chain with "old faithful" mother ships in Palo Alto and San Jose; aficionados champion the "plentiful" portions of "tastefully prepared" fish and American dishes and at the Oakland and Walnut Creek franchises, the "splendorous" Sunday jazz brunch "spread" too; but the less-enthused shrug it "does not disappoint, but it never dazzles" – though it may "impress parents from the Midwest."

Sea Salt 21 | 19 | 18 | $33
2512 San Pablo Ave. (Dwight Way), Berkeley, 510-883-1720;
www.seasaltrestaurant.com
"It feels like you're in the ocean with all the blue decor" at Berkeley's "attempt at New England seafood" with a "California sensibility", "well-meaning service" and no reservations; the "pretty presentations" of "imaginative" seafood and "off-the-beaten-track wine list" make it "worth the visit" for "old salts and others", while the "lobster roll beats a trip to Maine"; still, a few crab it "fails to wow", adding it's a "bit expensive."

Shalimar ⊘ 23 | 3 | 9 | $14
3325 Walnut Ave. (Paseo Padre Pkwy.), Fremont, 510-494-1919;
www.shalimarsf.com
See review in City of San Francisco Directory.

Shen Hua 21 | 17 | 17 | $24
2914 College Ave. (bet. Ashby Ave. & Russell St.), Berkeley, 510-883-1777
"Justifiably popular", this "semi-classy", "child-friendly" "requisite Berkeley experience" is "crowded every night of the week" with families clamoring for "spectacularly good" Szechuan "dishes that actually taste different"; "be prepared to share –

there are too many" "fresh, tasty and well-seasoned" Chinese "favorites" to "only pick one" – and expect "super-fast service" too; still, it's too speedy for a few who squawk they "shove you out the door" and get it "to go."

Soi Four ⊠   24 | 20 | 20 | $30 |

5421 College Ave. (bet. Kales & Manila Sts.), Oakland, 510-655-0889; www.soifour.com

Four-tify yourself – and your "out-of-town friends" too – with "fun, flavorful flavors" at this "modern", "sleek" "Thai heaven" serving "vibrant", "mouthwatering" small plates that are a "cut above and more interesting" than the "usual" Siamese offerings; the "date" digs may be "as noisy as Downtown Bangkok" but the high prices, "killer cocktails" and "trendy" crowd remind you that you're on the "chic side of Oakland."

Soizic Ⓜ   24 | 20 | 21 | $36 |

300 Broadway (3rd St.), Oakland, 510-251-8100; www.soizicbistro.com

The "warehouse"-like "exterior is forbidding" and "easy to miss", nevertheless once you "step inside" this "secret spot" "tucked away in the Oakland produce district" near Jack London Square, the "captivating", "quirky", "lovely" setting with "high ceilings" "catches your eye" while the "delicious", "ambitious" Cal-French fare and "unpretentious" staff "help you forget the neighborhood"; it's got a "lot of spirit" assert admirers who also confide it's a "great date place."

Sol y Lago   – | – | – | E |

Boatworks Mall, 760 N. Lake Blvd. (Red Cedar St.), Tahoe City, 530-583-0358

A "welcome addition", this "beautiful" Nuevo Latino newbie, set in the former home of Hacienda del Lago, "brings something different" to the "Tahoe City dining scene"; duck into the 30-seat lodge-pole pine bar to lap up a cocktail, then sample the "unique" fare inspired by mountainous regions of Spain, Argentina and Chile, created by avid snowboarder/chef Johnny Alamilla (ex SF's now-shuttered Alma) in the rustic yet contemporary setting, and relish the "lovely view of the lake."

Soule Domain   ▽ 25 | 25 | 25 | $49 |

9983 Cove St. (State Line Rd.), Kings Beach, 530-546-7529; www.souledomain.com

"Hands down the most romantic spot on the North Shore" – "how can you top a cozy log cabin" with "delicious" New American cuisine, "excellent service" and a West Coast wine list to boot bellow boosters; "ask for a table by the fireplace" and you'll see why chef-owner Charlie Soule's "lovely" Kings Beach forest hideaway is a "favorite place at the lake", and for hooked Crystal Bay diners, the sole domain of "special nights" out.

Spettro   19 | 15 | 20 | $23 |

3355 Lakeshore Ave. (Trestle Glen Rd.), Oakland, 510-451-7738

"You're home – or at least it feels that way" at this "kitschy" Lakeshore institution that's as "comfortable as a well-worn pair of shoes", turning out Eclectic "out-of-this-world" – even "freaky" – "original combos" "loved by Oaklanders"; "body ink on the staff" and a "funky interior" strung with skeletons may make you feel like you've "stepped into a *Día de Los Muertos* celebration" – but the "no corkage fee" lurches you back to earth.

Sunnyside Resort | 17 | 22 | 18 | $37 |
1850 W. Lake Blvd. (bet. Pineland Dr. & Tahoe Park Ave.), Tahoe City, 530-583-7200; www.sunnysideresort.com

"Be careful not to trip over the brides" at Tahoe's seafood-steakhouse, a "lakeside" "tradition" boasting a "beautiful setting on the water's edge"; sure, it's a "popular post-ski gathering place" for the "Bay Area second-home set", but "on a perfect day" it's "worth a trip" for a "relaxing" brunch or a "casual" "burger and beer" lunch – just "overlook the high prices" and go "before the crowds" turn the dockside deck into a "fraternity hangout."

Sushi Groove East ⍉Ⓜ | 23 | 19 | 18 | $37 |
1523 Giammona Dr. (bet. Locust & N. Main Sts.), Walnut Creek, 925-945-1400

See review in City of San Francisco Directory.

Tacubaya | 22 | 15 | 14 | $15 |
1788 Fourth St. (bet. Hearst Ave. & Virginia St.), Berkeley, 510-525-5160

"Just like *abuela's*" agree amigos who go to Berkeley's "authentic" Mexican cantina for an "incredibly fresh" taste of grandma – and then some; join the throngs of shoppers and "yuppies" lining up at the counter for the "lovely handmade", "high-end tacos" (no burritos) topped with "zesty, crunchy condiments" and "meticulously prepared" "addictive" tamales made with "healthy ingredients" – you may walk away convinced it's "better than the mother ship", Dona Tomas.

Tamarindo Antojeria Mexicana ⍉Ⓜ ▽ | 24 | 21 | 21 | $29 |
468 Eighth St. (bet. Broadway & Washington St.), Oakland, 510-444-1944; www.tamarindoantojeria.com

For "delightfully different" "regional" *cocina* that's like "a stylish guided tour of updated" Mexican–Nuevo Latino cooking, head to this "chic" new family-run "find in a totally up-and-coming commercial area" in Downtown Oakland; the "fresh, delicate" small plates, "spicy salsas and complex mole sauces" are "not of the bean and burrito genre" but they sure satisfy "cravings" while the "fantastic aquas frescas refresh the palate"; P.S. "go early because seats" "fill up quickly."

Thai Buddhist Temple Mongkolratanaram ⍉Ⓜ | 19 | 10 | 11 | $10 |
1911 Russell St. (bet. Martin Luther King Way & Otis St.), Berkeley, 510-849-3419

What a "scene" relay brunchers who compare the Sunday buffet in the courtyard of Downtown's Temple Mongkolratanaram to a "crazy", "chaotic" "street market in Bangkok"; "broke Berkeley students" and "dreadlocked" devotees "exchange money for tokens", then trade them for "wonderful", "homemade" Thai food doled out by "friendly Buddhist monks" before "staking out a seat" at the "picnic tables"; foodwise, it's-so so" but it's "an awesome way to spend the morning" and "a good cause" too.

Townhouse Bar & Grill ⍉ | 23 | 19 | 20 | $33 |
5862 Doyle St. (bet. 59th & Powell Sts.), Emeryville, 510-652-6151; www.townhousebarandgrill.com

"Martinis and steak? check . . . Porsches and Audis in the valet lot? check" – "don't a judge a book by its cover" because Emeryville's "former speakeasy" is actually the "power-lunch spot of the East Bay" filled with "techies" and politicos; have a drink in the "un-heralded bar", then "pretend you're running for mayor" and dine in the "cozy" digs or the "nice patio" on "delicious" Californian fare – it's a "menu you can rely on with experienced servers" to boot.

Trader Vic's | 17 | 21 | 18 | $44 |

9 Anchor Dr. (Powell St.), Emeryville, 510-653-3400;
www.tradervics.com

It's "not your daddy's Trader Vic's anymore" insist revelers who luau over to Emeryville's "South Seas concept", original home of the mai tai, for a touch of "tiki-tacky by the Bay"; it's "campy" "fun" to "nibble flaming pupu platters", but for most, it's the "exotic drinks that pack a wallop", "outshining" the "overpriced", "memory lane" Polynesian food; P.S. fans herald the Downtown SF branch's "welcome return" while "Palo Alto buzzes with the cocktail crowd."

Trattoria La Siciliana ⊘ | 23 | 15 | 14 | $29 |

2993 College Ave. (Ashby Ave.), Berkeley, 510-704-1474

If you've ever wondered "what it's like to have a big Italian family", make a beeline to this "cash-only" Berkeley trattoria that's as "loud and crowded" as a clan "reunion"; "cozy is an understatement" – "tight" and "tiny" is more like it – nevertheless, the "postage stamp–sized kitchen" churns out "hearty portions" of "garlic heaven" "comfort food" so "authentically Sicilian" you may "say grazie" to the "charmingly klutzy" staff.

T Rex Barbecue | 15 | 21 | 17 | $28 |

1300 10th St. (Gilman St.), Berkeley, 510-527-0099;
www.t-rex-bbq.com

Barbecue is hardly extinct in the East Bay but "can you name an-other BBQ place with class" besides this "stylish" "spin-off of Lalime's" ponder pundits who dig the "beautiful" "arty loft" look, "delicious drinks", "comforting" 'cue and "interesting sides" served in "massive portions" – it's a "great addition to the Berkeley scene"; still, for others who say it's "got potential", but is "still working out the kinks", it's not quite dino-mite yet.

Udupi Palace ⊘ | 19 | 6 | 12 | $14 |

1901-1903 University Ave. (Martin Luther King Jr. Way), Berkeley, 510-843-6600; www.udupipalace.net

"Stop, refuel" and "try new things" at this South Indian spot in the "heart of Berkeley" where the "many varieties of dosas and uttapams" with "sunny spices" are "designed for the heartier palate"; the "delicious", "filling" vegetarian fare is "appealing even to a dyed-in-the-wool carnivore" – and "so good you hardly notice" the "bare-bones decor" and "marginal", "robot"-like service; N.B. there is also a branch in Sunnyvale.

Uzen ⊠ | 25 | 13 | 19 | $31 |

5415 College Ave. (bet. Hudson St. & Kales Ave.), Oakland, 510-654-7753

"When the sushi mood strikes", Rockridge fin fans make a bee-line to this "laid-back hole-in-the-wall" Japanese "staple" for "beautifully presented" fish that's "stunningly fresh" doled out by an "experienced" counter chef; the "surroundings are sparse", prompting the put-off to pronounce it could use an "update" and fans to counter it's "so unassuming people pass right by" – "good for me" because there's "rarely a significant wait."

Va de Vi   24 | 21 | 20 | $44
1511 Mt. Diablo Blvd. (Main St.), Walnut Creek, 925-979-0100;
www.va-de-vi-bistro.com
Walnut Creek's "boisterous" "talk-of-the-town" "charmer" delivers
"suburban chic" vis-à-vis a "hot bar scene", "nice back patio"
and "delectable" Eclectic tapas; what "culinary bliss" – it's "easy
to get carried away" given the "clever", "savvy combinations"
served with "approachable, affordable wines by the glass or
flight"; if a few are "waiting for the service to settle", vaunters
"can't wait to return"; N.B. a sib called Pres a Vis is expected to
open this fall in the Presidio.

Venezia   21 | 22 | 20 | $30
1799 University Ave. (Grant St.), Berkeley, 510-849-4681;
www.caffevenezia.com
Go for the "festive" "piazza decor" that's "kind of like the Italian
Pirates of the Caribbean" with "laundry lines hanging from faux
balconies", murals and a "working fountain" – and stay for the
"hearty pasta" insist insiders who make this "atmospheric"
Berkeley "standby" their "'let's meet at' venue after virtually any
evening event"; it's a "great date place", but "families return time
after time" too, delighting in the "consistently delicious" fare.

Venus   23 | 18 | 21 | $25
2327 Shattuck Ave. (Durant Ave.), Berkeley, 510-540-5950;
www.venusrestaurant.net
"Out-of-this-world", "unusual" mostly organic morning fare may
make this "understated" cafe a Berkeley "brunch haven", but
"don't write it off" as just a "breakfast place" beg the moonstruck; the "savory", "soul-satisfying" Californian cuisine and
"informal" feel make it a "surprisingly good" lunchtime option for
the "Downtown business crowd" and a "reliable" dinnertime
stop too – plus the "lovely" "staff is good at getting you to
Zellerbach on time."

Vic Stewart's   21 | 20 | 20 | $50
850 S. Broadway (bet. Mt. Diablo Blvd. & Newell Ave.), Walnut Creek,
925-943-5666; www.vicstewarts.com
"Reserve a private", "romantic", "intimate" room in the attached
historic Pullman car and your evening is "transformed to dinner
on the Orient-Express" confide carnivores who hop onboard
this "unique" "true steakhouse" "set inside the old Walnut
Creek" depot; "bring out-of-town guests" for "gigantic" portions
of "high-quality tender meat", a "great wine list" and martinis
and "don't miss" the scalloped potatoes – just be "prepared to
mortgage the house."

Vik's Chaat Corner Ⓜ   24 | 4 | 9 | $11
726 Allston Way (bet. 4th & 5th Sts.), Berkeley, 510-644-4412;
www.vikdistributors.com
Yes, it's a "mob scene" and the "airplane hangar"–like setting
"doesn't encourage lingering", but Berkeley's self-service "bare-
bones operation" replete with "folding chairs and paper plates"
and a 6 PM closing time is actually a "mecca" for "solid Desi
treats"; the "vast selection can be disorienting" – just remember
"the thing to get here" is the "extremely authentic" chaat
("Indian street food and snacks"); P.S. it's "worth battling weekend crowds for the expanded menu."

WENTE VINEYARDS | 25 | 26 | 23 | $52 |

5050 Arroyo Rd. (Wetmore Rd.), Livermore, 925-456-2450;
www.wentevineyards.com

Whether you "save this stellar" "culinary gem in Livermore" for "special occasions" or "hike out" for a "romantic dinner" "after a full day of wine tasting", you're in for a "perfect" meal, complete with a staff that "describes dishes like a well-written poem" and allows you to "relax"; "on a warm day", sit outside with the "French doors open looking out on to the vineyards" and indulge in an "elegant lunch" of "seasonal" Cal-Med cuisine "married with a large selection" of "outstanding" vinos – it's simply "heaven."

Wild Goose Restaurant M | ▽ 22 | 24 | 22 | $49 |

7320 N. Lake Blvd. (Snowflake Ave.), Tahoe Vista, 530-546-3640;
www.wildgoosetahoe.com

The new owners of this "luxurious", recently remodeled water's edge venture are taking it a "step forward" honk habitués, hailing the ex-Postrio chef's "outstanding" New American fare; everything from the "wonderful" presentation to the "great sunset views across Lake Tahoe" is "geared toward complete enjoyment of the food and wine" – it may be the "first" in this location to do "everything right"; still, critics squawk that "portions are small."

Wolfdale's 🖼 M | ▽ 25 | 23 | 25 | $50 |

640 N. Lake Blvd., Tahoe City, 530-583-5700

For "big city elegance" in the Sierras, vacationers make tracks to the "casual" "but classy" waterfront "favorite" that "helped put Tahoe dining on the map" back in 1978 and still offers "gourmet on the lake" year-round; the Californian "flavor combos with an Asian twang" are "delightful" declare the doggedly devoted who also howl the praises of the "mountain ambiance."

Yoshi's at Jack London Square | 18 | 21 | 18 | $36 |

Jack London Sq., 510 Embarcadero W. (Washington St.), Oakland,
510-238-9200; www.yoshis.com

Yup, "the sushi is fresh and the jazz swingin'" at Oakland's "hip" Japanese joint with a "world-class" music club next door; it's a "combo you'd never think to partner", nevertheless it makes a "great one-stop" spot "for a night on the town" – and the pre-show prandial perch "makes it easy to scramble for good seats"; still, critics concur "skip" the "so-so" "meal, go for the show"; N.B. a branch is slated to open in SF's Fillmore District in 2007.

ZACHARY'S CHICAGO PIZZA ⊄ | 24 | 12 | 15 | $18 |

1853 Solano Ave. (The Alameda), Berkeley, 510-525-5950
5801 College Ave. (Oak Grove Ave.), Oakland, 510-655-6385
www.zacharys.com

"Pizza is an event" at the "undisputed king of Chicago" "deep dish that's the best this side of the Mississippi", if not "this side of the moon" opine pie-people who shuttle over to this Berkeley-Oakland duo (and soon San Ramon too) and endure "controlled chaos" to "stuff their mouths with amazing stuffed" sensations; "no need to brave the crowds" though – just "speed redial your" order and get a fully or partially baked "favorite" to go.

Zao Noodle Bar | 14 | 11 | 13 | $16 |

5614 Bay St. (Shellmound St.), Emeryville, 510-595-2888; www.zao.com
See review in City of San Francisco Directory.

Zatar 🅢🅜🖉　　　　▽ 22 | 20 | 20 | $34
1981 Shattuck Ave. (University Ave.), Berkeley, 510-841-1981;
www.zatarrestaurant.com
"What a wonderful discovery" – this "small storefront" "hopping" with locals is "worth seeking out" for its "rather eccentric" "atmosphere alone" vow Berkeleyites lured by the Moorish decor, "friendly" owners and "delicious", "innovative" Eclectic-Mediterranean fare; "take a moment to view the tangines decorating the walls" as you breathe in the "aroma of slow-cooked lamb and mint" – this is definitely "not a falafel place", in fact, much of the "lovely organic" produce is "homegrown" in their own garden.

Zax Tavern 🅜　　　　23 | 22 | 23 | $40
2826 Telegraph Ave. (bet. Oregon & Stuart Sts.), Berkeley, 510-848-9299;
www.zaxtavern.com
A Berkeley "neighborhood favorite that could hold its own anywhere", this "cozy" "go-to spot" "tucked way" from the "tromping" throngs of college students feels like a "third home" to East Bay "sophisticates" who laud the "lovely assortment" of "hearty", "carefully prepared" "tavern"-like Cal-Med fare, "excellent", "easygoing staff" and "bartenders who know how to make a drink"; you almost "feel like you're in the city (a high compliment)", nevertheless, the "bill won't flatten you."

North of San Francisco

Top Ratings North of SF

Excluding places with low voting.

Food

29 French Laundry	La Toque
28 Cyrus	Martini House
27 Terra	Syrah
Farmhouse Inn	Madrona Manor
Sushi Ran	Willi's Wine Bar
Redd Restaurant	**25** K&L Bistro
Mirepoix	Cole's Chop House
26 Fork	fig cafe & winebar
Cafe La Haye	Auberge du Soleil
Hana Japanese	Bistro Jeanty

By Cuisine

American
29 French Laundry
27 Terra
  Redd Restaurant
26 Martini House
24 Mustards Grill

Asian
27 Sushi Ran
26 Hana Japanese
23 Osake/Sake'O
  Royal Thai
22 Gary Chu's

Californian
27 Farmhouse Inn
26 Fork
  Cafe La Haye
  Syrah
25 Auberge du Soleil

Eclectic
26 Willi's Wine Bar
24 Picco
  Willow Wood Mkt.
23 Ravenous Cafe
  Celadon

French
28 Cyrus
27 Mirepoix
26 La Toque
  Madrona Manor
25 Bistro Jeanty

Italian
25 Cook St. Helena
  zazu
24 Pizzeria Picco
  Bistro Don Giovanni
  Tra Vigne

Mediterranean/Spanish
25 Zuzu
24 Pilar
  Insalata
23 Olema Inn
  Underwood Bar

Seafood/Steakhouses
25 Cole's Chop House
24 Willi's Seafood
22 Fish
  Press
  Scoma's

By Special Feature

Breakfast/Brunch

25 fig cafe & winebar
   Auberge du Soleil
   Downtown Bakery
24 Lark Creek Inn
   Willow Wood Mkt.

Child-Friendly

22 In-N-Out Burger
21 Pacific Catch
   Taylor's Automatic
20 Pizzeria Tra Vigne
17 Yankee Pier

Newcomers (Rated/Unrated)

27 Redd Restaurant
24 N.V.
22 Bovolo
– Rest. at Meadowood
– Wine Valley

Outdoor Seating

26 Martini House
   Madrona Manor
   Willi's Wine Bar
25 Auberge du Soleil
24 Lark Creek Inn
   John Ash & Co.

People-Watching

27 Redd Restaurant
26 Martini House
25 Bouchon
24 Bistro Don Giovanni
   Mustards Grill

Romance

28 Cyrus
27 Farmhouse Inn
26 Madrona Manor
25 Manka's
22 El Paseo

Small Plates

26 Fork
   Willi's Wine Bar
24 Willi's Seafood
23 Underwood Bar
18 Barndiva

Tasting Menus

29 French Laundry
28 Cyrus
27 Redd Restaurant
26 Fork
   Hana Japanese

Wine Bars

27 Sushi Ran
26 Martini House
   Willi's Wine Bar
25 fig cafe & winebar
18 Bounty Hunter

Winning Wine Lists

29 French Laundry
28 Cyrus
27 Terra
26 La Toque
   Martini House

By Location

Marin County

27 Sushi Ran
26 Fork
25 Marché aux Fleurs
   Manka's Inverness
24 Lark Creek Inn

Mendocino County

25 Cafe Beaujolais
24 Albion River Inn
23 Mendo Bistro
   955 Ukiah
22 MacCallum House

Napa County

29 French Laundry
27 Terra
   Redd Restaurant
26 La Toque
   Martini House

Sonoma County

28 Cyrus
27 Farmhouse Inn
   Mirepoix
26 Cafe La Haye
   Hana Japanese

Top Decor

28	Auberge du Soleil		John Ash & Co.
27	Cyrus	24	El Paseo
26	French Laundry		Terra
	Madrona Manor		Tra Vigne
	Étoile		Dry Creek Kitchen
	Martini House		Press
	Lark Creek Inn		N.V.
	Manka's Inverness	23	Wine Spectator
25	Farmhouse Inn		Albion River Inn
	Barndiva		Napa Wine Train

Top Service

28	French Laundry		Étoile
27	Cyrus		Press
26	Farmhouse Inn		El Paseo
	Terra		Cafe La Haye
	La Toque		Cole's Chop House
	Mirepoix		Martini House
	Madrona Manor		Syrah
25	Auberge du Soleil		Lark Creek Inn
	Redd Restaurant		Cafe Beaujolais
24	Marché aux Fleurs	23	Pilar

Top Bangs for the Buck

1. In-N-Out Burger
2. Downtown Bakery
3. Barney's
4. Taylor's Automatic
5. Joe's Taco Lounge
6. Model Bakery
7. Emporio Rulli
8. Jimtown Store
9. Alexis Baking Co.
10. Amici E. Coast Pizza
11. Pacific Catch
12. Dipsea Cafe/Flying Pig
13. Pizzeria Picco
14. Las Camelias
15. Royal Thai
16. Pizza Antica
17. Gordon's
18. Gira Polli
19. Lotus of India
20. Willow Wood Mkt.

Other Good Values

Avatars
Betty's Fish & Chips
Bistro Jeanty
Bistro Ralph
Bovolo
Cafe La Haye
Celadon
Christophe
Cindy's Backstreet
Fish
Foothill Cafe
girl & the fig
Insalata's
Market
Ravenous Cafe
Syrah
Tabla
Willi's Wine Bar
Zazu
Zuzu

North of San Francisco

ad hoc

– | – | – | E

6476 Washington St. (bet California Dr. & Oak Circle), Yountville, 707-944-2487

The doors haven't opened yet at Thomas Keller's casual temporary bistro, expected to debut in September 2006, but Yountville foodies are already clamoring for the French Laundry maestro's New American fare which will feature produce from its big sister's garden and an on-premises plot; the prix fixe menu, hovering at about $45, will cater to walk-ins in a setting that may conjure up déjà vu – little has changed decorwise since Wine Garden moved out, but expect a new look come 2007 when it's transformed into Burgers and Half Bottles, Keller's twist on a classic hamburger joint.

Albion River Inn

24 | 23 | 22 | $49

3790 North Hwy. 1 (Albion Little River Rd.), Albion, 707-937-1919; www.albionriverinn.com

Perched on a "magnificent ocean bluff" overlooking the Albion River, this "weekend trippers'" "special-occasion" favorite serves "memorable" Cal cuisine "showcasing local ingredients", but its daytime "panoramic Pacific vista" is what "shoots" its appeal "off the charts"; after sunset, a "warm fireplace" and "live piano player" "add to the ambiance", while "terrific service" and "notable" single malt scotch and spirits lists give it a more "cosmopolitan air than most options on the North Coast."

Alexis Baking Company

20 | 11 | 15 | $17

(aka ABC)

1517 Third St. (School St.), Napa, 707-258-1827; www.alexisbakingcompany.com

"Outstanding" "cinnamon bread", sandwiches and good "vibes" keep the "locals" "addicted" to this "small, quaint" bakery; "when it gets crowded, there is no seating" and the "confused (or is it laid-back?)" staff seems to "take twice as long to prepare" the "limited" selection of New American fare, "but there is no way you'll find a better breakfast in Napa"; P.S. they "also make incredible special-occasion cakes."

All Season's Cafe & Wine Shop

▽ 20 | 15 | 19 | $43

1400 Lincoln Ave. (Washington St.), Calistoga, 707-942-9111; www.allseasonsnapavalley.net

It's "fun to browse through the attached wine shop" confide oenophiles who gallop over to this "longtime fixture" in the "cowboy town of Calistoga" to "buy a bottle to be served" with the "good old standard" Californian fare; the "original storefront atmosphere" is "trumped by" the "tasty" eats made with the "freshest seasonal ingredients" while vaunters vow that vino "pricing is downright friendly."

Amici's East Coast Pizzeria

20 | 12 | 17 | $19

1242 Fourth St. (C St.), San Rafael, 415-455-9777; www.amicis.com
See review in City of San Francisco Directory.

Angèle   23 | 22 | 22 | $44

540 Main St. (3rd St.), Napa, 707-252-8115; www.angelerestaurant.com
There's "no need to go Up Valley" when this "angelic gem" perched
"at a bend in the river" in Downtown Napa offers a "perfect location
for an idyllic lunch" or a post-vino tasting dinner, plus a "lively
bar" "loaded with local wine talent"; add in a terrace, "comfort"
country French fare from "fantastic" new chef Tripp Mauldin and
"super-pro service" and it's little wonder day-trippers are "transported to the banks of the Seine" – *avec* "ooh-la-la-prices."

Annalien ⊠Ⓜ   ▽ 22 | 17 | 17 | $33

1142 Main St. (bet. 1st & Pearl Sts.), Napa, 707-224-8319
Napa "needed good Asian food" and this "intimate" Vietnamese
neophyte – outfitted with a dark-wood French colonial decor that's
more Saigon 1929 than Highway 29 – "fits the bill"; if a few find the
fare somewhat "bland" and Westernized, insiders retort it's "mostly
on the mark" – just ask the "ever-present, cheerful" Annalien to
"spice it up" and "they'll turn up the heat on any dish."

Applewood Inn & Restaurant ⊠Ⓜ   22 | 19 | 22 | $46

13555 Hwy. 116 (River Rd.), Guerneville, 707-869-9093;
www.applewoodinn.com
The "delightful hosts" of this "nicely appointed" hostelry "in the
heart of the Russian River Valley" "make you feel like you're dining in their home", albeit "a home with extraordinary food" that
showcases "delicious" market-driven Californian specialties of
the region and the seasons (romantics suggest it's "best in winter, when you can enjoy the two fireplaces"); it's worth the "long
drive each way" – though the "zinfully good" cellar might prompt
oenophiles to book a room.

AUBERGE DU SOLEIL   25 | 28 | 25 | $75

Auberge du Soleil, 180 Rutherford Hill Rd. (Silverado Trail), Rutherford,
707-967-3111; www.aubergedusoleil.com
It's "hard to imagine" a more "heavenly dining experience" than this
"extravagant" Rutherford resort; the Cal-French prix fixe dinners
are "fantastic", "but the real draw" is having "every whim catered
to while you look out over paradise" on the "patio with its panoramic views" of the vineyards; "it's definitely worth" the "mad-
dening prices" "if you want to impress the hell out of your date", so
go for a "romantic lunch" (the "very essence of summer in wine
country") or a sunset dinner – or just "have a drink on the balcony."

Avatars ⊠Ⓜ   ▽ 24 | 11 | 25 | $25

2656 Bridgeway (Harbor Dr.), Sausalito, 415-332-8083
"Despite the strip-mall setting", Sausalito locals insist "you have
only to eat" at this "self-described Marindian" "once to become a
committed fan"; although the "fusion" fare (part Marin County, "part
Indian, part Mexican and I think part Martian") served south-of-
the-border–style (think "Punjabi burritos" and enchiladas)
"doesn't sound like it would work", it's a "perfect amalgamation",
plus the "great" owner "welcomes everyone with enthusiasm."

Barndiva Ⓜ   18 | 25 | 17 | $42

231 Center St. (Matheson St.), Healdsburg, 707-431-0100;
www.barndiva.com
Yes, it's set in a "barnlike structure", but no one's singing "E-I-E-I-O"
at this "spectacular", "city-cool" Healdsburg "oasis" replete with

"beautiful" patio; though some cluck-cluck the self-described 'modern country' American fare is an "afterthought" (not to mention "pricey"), most maintain the small-plate offerings are "inventive", complemented by "whimsical" cocktails and "inspired" wines, and in a "town that closes early", it's moo-velous for a "late dinner."

Barney's Gourmet Hamburgers | 20 | 12 | 14 | $15 |
1020 Court St. (4th St.), San Rafael, 415-454-4594;
www.barneyshamburgers.com
See review in City of San Francisco Directory.

Betty's Fish & Chips ⊠ Ⓜ | ▽ 18 | 12 | 18 | $17 |
4046 Sonoma Hwy. (Streamside Dr.), Santa Rosa, 707-539-0899
Cod-noscenti crown the signature dish served at this "always-hopping" Santa Rosa stalwart the "best fish 'n' chips west of Liverpool"; the "friendly" staff and "low-key" digs stuffed to the gills with Brit bric-a-brac go down swimmingly with "unpretentious" sorts, but if its "off-the-highway" location doesn't appeal, "take-out's an alternative"; P.S. try a slice of "to-die-for homemade pie."

Bistro Don Giovanni | 24 | 22 | 22 | $44 |
4110 Howard Ln. (bet. Oak Knoll & Salvador Aves.), Napa, 707-224-3300;
www.bistrodongiovanni.com
"If you're not happy when you arrive, you will be" after ciaoing down at this "upbeat" wine country Italian serving "glorious", "reasonably priced" fare including "wonderful" pastas paired with "great" wines, all served by an "attentive" staff; the "idyllic" terrace overlooking vineyards and "bustling" dining room offer "loads of ambiance", but be warned: "rezzies are imperative" as it's "always packed" with the "Napa 'in' crowd" that treats this "Valley mainstay" like their "living room."

BISTRO JEANTY | 25 | 20 | 23 | $49 |
6510 Washington St. (Mulberry St.), Yountville, 707-944-0103;
www.bistrojeanty.com
"Berets" off to Monsieur Jeanty's original "oh-so-French bistro" in "the heart of wine country" in Yountville that's as "unchanging as the Arc de Triomphe", churning out "spectacular", "stick-to-the-ribs" *cuisine grand-mère* fare ferried by "friendly" *garçons*; the "welcoming" "sit-in-your-neighbor's-lap" experience in a "warm" setting costs less than "other top" spots, and the large "community table" where "drop-ins" can "get all the latest vintner dirt" epitomizes *égalité*.

Bistro Ralph ⊠ | 22 | 16 | 22 | $43 |
109 Plaza St. (Healdsburg Ave.), Healdsburg, 707-433-1380
At this "delightful place on the square" in Healdsburg, chef-owner Ralph Tingle still dishes up "reliably good" Cal–New American "comfort food" in a "jovial ambiance" that helped it "earn its place" as the "perfect wine country lunch" spot; the "small" "minimalist" digs remain full of "old-guard vintner types" who laud the "great classic martinis" as much as the "well-priced" "Sonoma-only" vino list, though kvetchers quibble it "needs to update its menu."

Bistro V | ▽ 21 | 15 | 19 | $38 |
2295 Gravenstein Hwy. (Bloomfield Rd.), Sebastopol, 707-823-1262;
www.bistro-v.com
Word is getting out about this "warm and friendly" Sebastopol sleeper, run by a "nice young couple" who "come out and talk" to

customers; their far-reaching "unique" French-Italian menu with a "contemporary" Peruvian "twist" showcases "local products" and offers some "great vegetarian choices" and "good desserts"; while a smattering of surveyors say service is "kind of slow", others shrug it "feels like it's still growing into itself."

Boca | 20 | 22 | 17 | $45 |

340 Ignacio Blvd. (Rte. 101), Novato, 415-883-0901; www.bocasteak.com
A "treat in an unexpected place", celeb-chef George Morrone's "relaxed" Cal-Argentinean "steakhouse with style" in Novato offers "cooked to perfection" beef served with "innovative" sauces and sides, plus "his old favorites" like "to-die-for tuna tartare" and "duck-fat-fried pomme frites that will certainly do you in"; Marinites are moooved by the "cool" "cowhide" decor and "warm feel", concurring that the "only minus" is "amateurish service" – perhaps they "need some time to get it all together."

Boonville Hotel | ▽ 21 | 18 | 19 | $38 |

Boonville Hotel, 14050 Hwy. 128 (Lambert Ln.), Boonville,
707-895-2210; www.boonvillehotel.com
"One of the best finds north of the city", this "quaint yet hip" hotel is like a mirage on the lonely road from San Francisco to Mendocino, where the owner "uses incredible fresh produce from his own backyard and family's farm" to fashion "clean" "creative" Californian cuisine; those "lucky to stay the night" can also rub elbows with the "local vintners" who hang out in the bar, stocked with "excellent Anderson Valley wines" and local Boonville beers.

BOUCHON ❶ | 25 | 23 | 23 | $51 |

6534 Washington St. (Yount St.), Yountville, 707-944-8037;
www.frenchlaundry.com
Keller's "perfect" "replica" of a Parisian bistro in "Thomasville" – aka Yountville – is more than just the "French Laundry's overflow room": the "handsome", "high-energy" "petite sibling" "for the rest of us" proffers "exquisitely prepared", "superbly presented" fare that's like "heaven on earth"; *oui*, the staff can get "stretched thin serving throngs" of "foodies", but it "doesn't spoil the magic" – *amis* "keep returning" for a lunch of "oysters and Sancerre" at the zinc bar or to hobnob into "late evening with area restaurateurs" – what a "treat"; P.S. stop by the adjacent bakery for "pastries and brioche."

Bounty Hunter | 18 | 17 | 18 | $32 |

975 First St. (Main St.), Napa, 707-255-0622
A "welcome antidote to Napa Valley pretentiousness", this "funky" wine bar and store has its "fun formula" down pat; while the "well-educated" staff helps the "eclectic crowd" "navigate" "unbeatable flights" from "Route 29" and beyond, everyone also has a "good time nibbling" the "always satisfying" beer-can chicken and house-smoked BBQ ribs (served Thursday–Saturday) from "communal tables"; still, a few locals dub it the "'Booty Hunter', 'cause it can be a meat market" on weekends.

Bovolo | 22 | 12 | 15 | $25 |

Plaza Farms, 106 Matheson St. (Healdsburg Ave.), Healdsburg,
707-431-2962
"Slow Food fast" is the conceit behind this Italian cafe in the Plaza Farms food cooperative, where Zuzu's owners proffer "fabulous home-cured salumi", "terrific pizzas", sandwiches and

"gelato that'll rock your socks off"; order your "casual" eats "cafeteria style" to go, or chow down in the back courtyard "away from the hubbub"; yes, it's "family-friendly" – "but only if your family name is Rockefeller" squawk critics who cry that's a "lot of money for bacon"; N.B. dinner Friday–Sunday only.

Brannan's Grill | 21 | 22 | 20 | $41 |

1374 Lincoln Ave. (Washington St.), Calistoga, 707-942-2233;
www.brannansgrill.com

"After a long day of wine tasting" and "mud baths", this "consistent" Calistoga "hangout" offers a "beautiful" bar and "relaxed atmosphere" augmented by "wonderful" live jazz on weekends; there's "excellent variety" on the menu of "delicious" American fare complemented by "good" vino and "mean" martinis, all served by a staff that "only seeks to make you happy", and even if a few whisper it's "nothing special for Napa", more retort "it rocks."

Brix | 21 | 22 | 21 | $49 |

7377 St. Helena Hwy./Hwy. 29 (Washington St.), Yountville, 707-944-2749;
www.brix.com

There's "no better way to start a meal than a stroll through the kitchen gardens" of this "solid performer" in Yountville offering "beautiful terrace dining" as well as a "lovely" interior, providing a fitting backdrop for "fabulous", "inspiring" Californian cuisine and "incredible" wines; though service can vary from "excellent" to "overwhelmed", most report a "pleasant experience", and the weekend brunch is one of the "best deals in the Bay Area"; P.S. the on-site shop offering local products is a "nice touch."

BUCKEYE ROADHOUSE | 23 | 22 | 21 | $42 |

15 Shoreline Hwy./Hwy. 1 (west of Hwy. 101), Mill Valley, 415-331-2600;
www.buckeyeroadhouse.com

"Terrific", "high-end" yet "down-home" Cal-inflected American cuisine (including "magnificent" BBQ ribs) and "excellent wines" are matched by the "stunning" "hunting lodge motif" with a "big fireplace" as focal point at this "winning" circa-1937 Mill Valley "institution" "right off the 101"; "friendly", "professional" service pleases "parents with kids" in tow, "celebrities" and "Marin trendies" "looking to network or score", though "expensive" tabs and "mandatory valet parking" buck the "casual" vibe.

Bungalow 44 | 21 | 19 | 20 | $39 |

44 E. Blithedale Ave. (Sunnyside Ave.), Mill Valley, 415-381-2500;
www.Bungalow44.com

"The mood, the food and the 'tude" is what makes this "bustling" Mill Valley "offshoot of the Buckeye" a "hot spot" – and one of the "best additions to Marin county in years"; join the "see-and-be-seen" set and "sidle up to the bar for enticing cocktails" or "grab a seat" by the "cozy fireplace in the enclosed patio" and enjoy "creative twists" on American "classics", served by a "courteous staff."

Cafe Beaujolais | 25 | 21 | 24 | $50 |

961 Ukiah St. (School St.), Mendocino, 707-937-5614;
www.cafebeaujolais.com

Connoisseurs confirm you can't "go to Mendocino without dining" at the area's de rigueur "special-occasion" "destination" that "lives up to its great reputation" ("even after all these years") for "magnificent", still-"intriguing" Cal-French cuisine accompanied by "perfect" *pain* and "excellent wines"; the "knowledge-able" staff supplies "superb" service in a "charming" converted Victorian setting with views of "lovely" gardens, though naysayers insist it's "overpriced"; N.B. new owners plan to offer lunch.

Cafe Citti
21 | 12 | 16 | $25

9049 Sonoma Hwy./Hwy. 12 (Shaw Ave.), Kenwood, 707-833-2690
When the "fog of all-day wine tasting hits, get a second wind at this roadside pit stop" "right on Highway 12, nestled in Kenwood"; "amble up to the counter and order" "succulent rotisserie chicken", "authentic Italian" pastas and "killer Caesar salad" ("it's not called 'Garlic Heaven' without reason"), paired with a "tumbler glass" of Chianti; sure, the decor "could use spiffing up, but then it wouldn't be the bargain it is."

CAFE LA HAYE ⊠M
26 | 19 | 24 | $48

140 E. Napa St. (bet. 1st & 2nd Sts.), Sonoma, 707-935-5994;
www.cafelahaye.com
"Hidden away among the tourist traps" on the Sonoma Square, this "itty-bitty" cafe is that elusive "great local wine country" spot, where "soulful" Cal–New American cuisine fit for "royalty" is prepared in an "open kitchen the size of a butler's pantry"; the "industrial" dining room is "small" (35 seats) and "sparse", "so don't expect the usual velvet-rope effect", "but Haye", the "accommodating" maitre d'/co-owner is a "hoot" and the "well-chosen list" boasts hard-to-find "boutique" vinos.

Cafe Z Epicerie
▽ 20 | 16 | 19 | $17

Bon Air Shopping Ctr., 282 Bon Air Ctr. (Sir Francis Drake Blvd.),
Greenbrae, 415-461-9444
If you want in on a "neighborhood secret let loose", check out this "nice little" "European"-like cafe tucked away in Greenbrae's Bon Air Shopping Center; while the "location is mundane", the New American crêpes, panini and salads are "really, really good" making it a "quick" stop for breakfast and lunch; come evening, the marble tables are topped with candles, the wine flows and newly added, more ambitious "home-cooked" dinner selections are served.

Caprice, The
▽ 22 | 25 | 21 | $49

2000 Paradise Dr. (Mar West St.), Tiburon, 415-435-3400
Marin's "expensive" "waterside" stalwart with "attentive service" may be "the last stop in Tiburon" but it's the first stop for "tourists" and "romantics" riveted by the "spectacular views of SF Bay and Golden Gate Bridge" ("you can watch yacht races right under your nose in late summer") as well as the "dark", "fireplace"-lit "muted interior"; however, its appeal is not solely "location, location, location" thanks to a new chef whose New American menu offers capricious "creative takes on French classics."

Carneros
22 | 21 | 20 | $44

The Lodge at Sonoma, 1325 Broadway (Leveroni Rd.), Sonoma,
707-931-2042; www.thelodgeatsonoma.com
Situated in the Lodge at Sonoma, this "special" "gathering place" "has it all" agree admirers who hail the "bar with seating", Californian bistro menu offering "excellent pizzas", "delicious" small plates and entrees made from regionally procured ingredients, and the "excellent wine list"; but while it's a "lovely place to hang out", a few find the service "lacking" and the fare "not inspired", citing "constantly changing chefs."

Celadon
23 | 21 | 22 | $44

The Historic Napa Mill, 500 Main St. (5th St.), Napa, 707-254-9690;
www.celadonnapa.com

"Let the tourists have the French Laundry" because "locals" are content to commandeer this "charming Napa" Mill "escape" near the river where Greg Cole (of Cole's Chop House) delights diners with "deftly spiced", globally inspired Eclectic–New American comfort food and a plethora of primo vinos; the setting is equally "comforting" both indoors or outside on the courtyard, blessed at any given time by "heat lamps or sunshine."

Chapter and Moon Ⓜ
∇ 23 | 16 | 21 | $38

32150 N. Harbor Dr. (Shoreline Hwy.), Fort Bragg, 707-962-1643

"Just the port in the storm I was looking for" quip moonstruck admirers about Fort Bragg's "funky", "froufrou"–free "local secret" tucked behind a trailer park; insiders well-versed on the "great views" of Noyo Harbor also note that the chef-owner "works wonders with local ingredients" and a wood stove, proffering Traditional American fare including "creatively" prepared fish and "outstanding salads", plus "fairly priced wines."

Charcuterie
21 | 16 | 19 | $31

335 Healdsburg Ave. (Plaza St.), Healdsburg, 707-431-7213

This "friendly", "petite" cafe just off the Healdsburg Square may "look like a coffee shop from the outside, but the kitchen really shines, turning out powerfully good" French bistro fare including "marvelous pastas" and, surprise, surprise, "the best charcuterie plate", plus vino at prices that won't "break the bank"; you can't help but feel in the pink – there are "pigs, pigs everywhere!" ("the owner is either a pig freak or a very serious Pink Floyd fan").

Christophe Ⓜ
21 | 18 | 22 | $33

1919 Bridgeway (Spring St.), Sausalito, 415-332-9244;
www.french-restaurant-marin.com

An "unbelievable bargain" – the "early-bird special is a steal" and so are the prix fixe and now à la carte offerings too exclaim enthusiasts of this "tiny" "Paris-like bistro" endowed with a "caring, careful staff"; while it "doesn't get the normal Sausalito tourist crowd", it's still way-"popular" with the locals who sometimes share this "quaint" find with "esteemed guests"; still, a few oenophiles whine that the "only knock is that the wine list isn't great."

Cindy's Backstreet Kitchen
24 | 20 | 22 | $40

1327 Railroad Ave. (bet. Adams & Hunt Sts.), St. Helena, 707-963-1200;
www.cindysbackstreetkitchen.com

"Rub shoulders" with Cindy Pawlcyn and the "Napa wine crowd" at "Mustards' St. Helena sister", a "homey but hip" "down-to-earth spot" serving "finger lickin' good" Cal–New American dishes (with Latin and Asian touches) that are "creative, yet seem like comfort food"; whether you sit on the "lovely" patio near the fig tree, sip "interesting" vinos at the zinc bar or "stretch weary wine-touring legs" in the "cozy" rooms, it's a "great place to hang out."

Cole's Chop House
25 | 22 | 24 | $56

1122 Main St. (bet. 1st & Pearl Sts.), Napa, 707-224-6328;
www.coleschophouse.com

"Prime beef from Chicago" and Montana, cult California Cabernets and "great" "classic sides" that seem straight outta Brooklyn's

"Peter Luger" total up to the "perfect" Downtown Napa "expense-account" dinner sure to "satisfy the hungriest cowpoke" at this old-stone "East Coast steakhouse with Western sensibilities"; if a few moan that "portions and prices both seem too big", most just "can't get enough" meat and find the "menu offers enough variety to keep things interesting."

Cook St. Helena ⊠ Ⓜ   25 | 14 | 20 | $40
1310 Main St. (Hunt Ave.), St. Helena, 707-963-7088
Chef Jude Wilmoth is "constantly making his first-class", "simple" yet "spectacular" Italian standards "better" at this rare "find" amid "the ersatz sophistication of the Napa Valley", a "low-key", "down-home" "hangout for Napa winemakers" in St. Helena offering "fair-priced" wines, "homemade pastas" and a "lively", "familylike environment"; insiders suggest it's even more "inviting" at lunch when the "friendly" staff is less "hectic" and the "cramped" room less crowded.

Cork   ▽ 21 | 17 | 26 | $27
317 Johnson St. (Bridgeway), Sausalito, 415-332-2975; www.corksf.com
Set "just off the beaten path" of Sausalito, this "wonderful neighborhood wine bar", modeled after Italian enotecas, "really treats people well", offering an "imaginative and well-chosen" array of "nibbles" like panini, crostini and tramezzini (finger sandwiches) paired with an "ever-changing list" of "top-quality" boutique vinos; "it's really fun to sit on the deck on a rare warm evening and just unwind" while enjoying the "tasty" "small bites" and "hospitality."

Cucina Paradiso ⊠   ▽ 24 | 12 | 22 | $34
Golden Eagle Shopping Ctr., 56 E. Washington St. (Petaluma Blvd.), Petaluma, 707-782-1130; www.cucinaparadisopetaluma.com
Beloved by Petaluma locals, this Southern Italian "diamond in the rough" "transcends" its pedestrian strip-mall provenance by way of "truly wonderful", "reasonably priced" *cucina* and "*autentico*" waiters with all their "unrestrained singing and old-country flair"; if the "homemade pasta" doesn't "send you straight" to "paradise", *Italia*-style, perhaps a glass of Chianti at the wine bar or an alfresco meal with views of the river will.

Cucina Restaurant & Wine Bar Ⓜ   22 | 16 | 20 | $35
510 San Anselmo Ave. (Tunstead Ave.), San Anselmo, 415-454-2942
Years after founding cult "city sibling Jackson Fillmore", owner "Jack can still do the trick" and work the floor like no other at his "bright, friendly" Downtown San Anselmo trattoria that cranks out "genuine" "rustic" Italian pastas that "sing" and "reliably excellent" wood-fired pizzas in a "neighborhoody sort of" atmosphere; settle into the "cozy wine bar" with the "really big, interesting list" and ask the staff to "help you find something amazing in your price range."

Cuvée   – | – | – | M
1650 Soscol Ave. (Vallejo St.), Napa, 707-224-2330; www.cuveenapa.com
Corks are once again popping at this handsome Napa venue, a decidedly more casual American update of the short-lived Restaurant Budo; aimed at locals, the moderately priced menu features simply presented comfort food (roasted chicken, skirt steak) that can be enjoyed in an inviting courtyard, plus there's an enlarged bar area that serves an affordable roster of draft wines and a late-night menu till midnight on Fridays and Saturdays.

CYRUS   28 | 27 | 27 | $98

Les Mars Hotel, 29 North St. (Healdsburg Ave.), Healdsburg, 707-433-3311; www.cyrusrestaurant.com

Nick Peyton and chef Douglas Keane, also of Market in St. Helena, deliver "an ultimate gastronomic experience" that's "as good as it gets for refinement" with "prices to match" at Healdsburg's "phenomenal" "new culinary destination" in Les Mars Hotel; "everything's over-the-top" – from the "dueling" "rolling champagne and caviar carts" and "fabulous" "formal" decor to the "orchestrated" presentation of "flawless" New French "flexible tasting menus" and "stellar wine pairings" – yet you "don't feel like you had to win the lottery to get in."

Della Fattoria Downtown Café Ⓜ   ▽ 27 | 19 | 19 | $25

141 Petaluma Blvd. N. (bet. Washington St. & Western Ave.), Petaluma, 707-763-0161; www.dellafattoria.com

This "charming cafe/bakery's" "regionally known" "bread of the gods" and "beautiful" pastries have prompted the "revitalization of Downtown Petaluma" and could "single-handedly destroy the low-carb craze"; while it "doesn't do dinners per se" (except Fridays, when it's open past 5:30 PM), the Eclectic menu provides "indulgences" aplenty, including "European-style breakfasts", "superb lunches" and "before-movie snacks" "without peer", made even sweeter by "amiable service."

Della Santina's   22 | 20 | 20 | $37

133 E. Napa St. (1st St. E.), Sonoma, 707-935-0576; www.dellasantinas.com

Like a "little corner of Lucca in Downtown Sonoma", this "amiable, family"-run Tuscan trattoria "knows the art of Italian cooking", luring locals "back again and again" with "old-world service" and "comfort food" "like my *nonna* used to make" (the "gnocchi makes us weak in the knees"); the chef-owner "takes a personal interest and it shows" right down to the "delightful patio" where you can "enjoy" your "pasta on a warm day" while "sipping good wine."

Deuce   ▽ 20 | 17 | 22 | $39

691 Broadway (Andrieux St.), Sonoma, 707-933-3823; www.dine-at-deuce.com

Loyalists "always count on a lovely dining experience" at this farmhouse-cum-restaurant located a few blocks from Sonoma Plaza, where the "wonderful" "husband-and-wife" owners "make you feel welcome", the county-centric wines and New American fare are "delicious" and the "great garden" is "delightful"; but while most consider it "cozy", it's less of a coup for a handful who find the art deco interior a bit "weird."

Dipsea Cafe, The   18 | 15 | 15 | $19

200 Shoreline Hwy./Hwy. 1 (Tennessee Valley Rd.), Mill Valley, 415-381-0298

Flying Pig

(fka Dipsea Cafe, The)

2200 Fourth St. (W. Crescent Dr.), San Rafael, 415-459-0700

Known for its "giant portions" of "unique" and Traditional American meals, Mill Valley's "sunny" "breakfast/brunch institution" is midweek HQ for Marin "mommies" and "retirees", and come weekend mornings, "crawling" with "fanny pack"–toting "hiking" and "biking troops" refueling "en route to Mt. Tam or

Stinson"; service, however, can range from "efficient" to "indifferent to nonexistent"; N.B. Dipsea's owners recently renamed the San Rafael outpost The Flying Pig and added BBQ to the coffee shop menu.

Downtown Bakery & Creamery ⊘   25 | 12 | 16 | $12
308A Center St. (Matheson St.), Healdsburg, 707-431-2719;
www.downtownbakery.net
"For what it is" – "a world-class bakery" known for "those sticky buns, that fabulous ice cream, those almond cookies" – "it doesn't get better than this" recently renovated, "always crowded" "small-town nugget" in Healdsburg that also supplies "indulgent" "picnic basket" provisions and now "excellent breakfasts" and "wonderful lunch entrees" too; sit at the new "copper tables" or "enjoy your goodies" with the local "bench bunch" out front.

Dry Creek Kitchen   23 | 24 | 20 | $63
Hotel Healdsburg, 317 Healdsburg Ave. (Matheson St.), Healdsburg,
707-431-0330; www.hotelhealdsburg.com
Charlie Palmer's "urbane" "mark is all over" this "divine" billet doux to wine country in the Hotel Healdsburg, from the "suave" setting to the "delectable" New American menu showcasing "original combinations" of local ingredients "matched with premier" bottlings ("love" the "no-corkage fee" on Sonoma vins); while acolytes crow it "exceeds expectations", it's an unrequited affair for others who leave it to "high-budget tourists", balking at "jumbo prices for tiny portions" of "pretty food (we want to eat it, not date it)" and "spotty" service.

Duck Club, The   20 | 20 | 20 | $47
Bodega Bay Lodge & Spa, 103 S. Hwy. 1 (Doran Park Rd.), Bodega,
707-875-3525; www.bodegabaylodge.com
See review in South of San Francisco Directory.

E&O Trading Company   19 | 21 | 17 | $34
2231 Larkspur Landing Circle (Old Quarry Rd. S.), Larkspur, 415-925-0303;
www.eotrading.com
See review in City of San Francisco Directory.

El Dorado Kitchen   22 | 21 | 20 | $50
El Dorado Hotel, 405 First St. W. (W. Spain St.), Sonoma, 707-996-3030;
www.eldoradosonoma.com
"A diamond in the making on the Sonoma Square", the El Dorado Hotel's "posh" Cal-Med newcomer is making waves – "as you'd expect" with "French Laundry grad" chef Ryan Fancher "heading up an ambitious open kitchen"; but while enthusiasts exclaim over an "eclectic menu", with "gutsy" dishes showing "flashes of brilliance", fence-sitters feel the fare "lacks flair" and find service "earnest, but not yet expert" – but even they concede that with time, it should "hit its stride."

El Paseo Ⓜ   22 | 24 | 24 | $53
17 Throckmorton Ave. (bet. Blithedale & Sunnyside Aves.), Mill Valley,
415-388-0741
Never mind the Spanish surname – Mill Valley's "go-to date place for romance, fine wine and finer food" made with Californian ingredients is one of the "loveliest" destinations around for "true French food lovers"; follow the "cobblestone walkway" to "soft-lit"

rooms where you can "coo without shouting" over "excellent", "pricey" fare while an "attentive" staff uncorks "phenomenal" vinos (from a 1,400 bottle cellar); if trendsters tut it's "stuffy" and "out of date", supporters retort "you will not be disappointed."

Emporio Rulli 21 | 22 | 14 | $20

464 Magnolia Ave. (bet. Cane & Ward Sts.), Larkspur, 415-924-7478; www.rulli.com

A "simple" "alfresco" "coffee break turns into" a *"magnifico"* "memory" of those "languorous days in Rome" at this "perfect replica of an Italian *pasticceria*" in Larkspur, with Downtown SF and Marina outposts; the *"bella"* "baristas" and "painted ceiling" add to the "charm", while the "scrumptious" pastries, "crispy panini" and "modest" dinner offerings are "prepared perfectly"; but even dolce vita-ites assert service can be "confounding."

ÉTOILE 25 | 26 | 24 | $65

(fka Domaine Chandon)

1 California Dr. (Hwy. 29), Yountville, 707-944-2892; www.chandon.com

"My God, the view, the food, the intoxicating bubbly" – "who knew there were so many sparkling" vintages gush guests agog over Domaine Chandon's winery "delight", which recently uncorked a new look and name, but remains the "quintessential" Yountville experience; whether you sit inside the "sumptuous environment" where a "jacket is not out of place" or "decompress with a bottle" outside, the Californian fare is "heavenly" and the setting "fabulous"; N.B. the updated wine bar offers flights and nibbles.

FARMHOUSE INN & 27 | 25 | 26 | $63
RESTAURANT, THE

Farmhouse Inn, 7871 River Rd. (Wohler Rd.), Forestville, 707-887-3300; www.farmhouseinn.com

"Foodies rejoice at this secluded, intimate" Russian River farmhouse in Forestville, a "must-stop for a romantic evening in wine country" that captures the "essence of Sonoma living"; from the Californian fare "so fresh it just screams farmer's market", "amazing cheese cart" and "well-assembled" vino list spotlighting "local growers" to the "quaint", "definitely country" surroundings with a "sense of home" and a staff that pays "superb attention to little details", "all of the elements fuse into that oh-so-rare special dining experience"; N.B. open for Thursday–Sunday dinner only.

fig cafe & winebar 25 | 20 | 23 | $34

(fka the girl & the gaucho)

13690 Arnold Dr. (Warm Springs Rd.), Glen Ellen, 707-938-2130; www.thefigcafe.com

Glen Ellen's "casual sister" to the girl and the fig is "less-crowded and not as pricey" as the "tourist" "scene at the Sonoma Plaza", making it a "fabulous place for foodies" – including "locals" – to "grab a bite"; "just walk in for down-home" yet "inventive" French country fare and "excellent pizzas" paired with "intriguing" wine options – or "bring your own" because there's "no corkage fee."

Fish 22 | 13 | 13 | $29

350 Harbor Dr. (foot of Clipper Yacht Harbor), Sausalito, 415-331-3474; www.331fish.com

"High-fives" to this "bare-bones bayfront warehouse" for "embracing the sustainable fish movement" that "makes you feel good about what you're eating"; the "consistently delicious" Pacific

Northwest fin fare "takes a gourmet approach" to "simplicity", and while there's "no atmosphere" inside, it's "nice" to perch on a "perfect picnic table" outdoors on a "sunny day in Saucylito", dive into an "expensive sandwich that's worth every cent" and "watch the harbor activity"; P.S. "plastic isn't welcome."

Flavor ⊠   19 | 18 | 15 | $29
96 Old Courthouse Sq. (Santa Rosa Ave.), Santa Rosa, 707-573-9600; www.flavorbistro.com
About the "best thing to happen in Downtown Santa Rosa in years", this "high-decibel" "locals'" "sidewalk cafe" run by "engaging owners" is "always hopping" with worker-bees and families; "visit, socialize" then devour the "outta-this-world breakfast and brunch" fare and come dinner time, the "truly flavorful", "unique" large and small plates of Sonoma-sourced Eclectic eats combining Pacific Rim, Mediterranean and European influences; still, a few squawk that service is "uneven."

Foothill Cafe Ⓜ   ▽ 23 | 11 | 20 | $38
J&P Shopping Ctr., 2766 Old Sonoma Rd. (Foothill Blvd.), Napa, 707-252-6178
"A little gem known to the locals" yet rarely "revealed to tourists", this "friendly" Napa nook is "beset" by an "obscure", "out-of-the-way" strip-mall location, "but buoyed" by the "best" BBQ "this side of Oakland"; never mind the "tight seating" and "limited menu" – the lines form early for the "mind-blowing prime rib" and "knockout ribs" served with a petite selection of Carneros wines; N.B. longtime chef-owner Jerry Shaffer sold the cafe post-*Survey.*

FORK ⊠Ⓜ   26 | 18 | 23 | $50
198 Sir Francis Drake Blvd. (bet. Bank St. & Tunstead Ave.), San Anselmo, 415-453-9898; www.marinfork.com
Marinites "who prefer to graze" consider San Anselmo's "upscale yet folksy" "small dish joint" "bluegrass", savoring the "forkalicious" Cal-French "morsels in cramped quarters" with boutique wines; whether you nibble the "perfect-size portions" packed with "remarkable flavors" or choose the "always imaginative tasting menu", it's a "treat every time" – "it's a wonder" that there's such "surprising excellence" given its "store-front setting" – and that it's "weathered" the departure of the founding chef – and a successor too, who left post-*Survey.*

Frantoio   21 | 20 | 19 | $41
152 Shoreline Hwy./Hwy. 1 (west of Hwy. 101), Mill Valley, 415-289-5777; www.frantoio.com
This "hidden find" in Mill Valley may be "oddly housed" next to a Holiday Inn Express, but once inside the "pleasant room" with "lofty ceilings" and "accommodating service" "you forget where you are" and concentrate on the Northern Italian dishes; while carboloaders commend the "interesting pastas" and chitchatters chime in "normal conversation is possible", the "real treat" is the "functioning olive press, with which they make their own oil."

FRENCH LAUNDRY, THE   29 | 26 | 28 | $254
6640 Washington St. (Creek St.), Yountville, 707-944-2380; www.frenchlaundry.com
"Heaven on earth" gush "gourmands" after "an indulgent five hours" of a "near-religious dining experience" that's "about so much more than eating" and "worth every hundred dollar bill" at

Thomas Keller's "outrageously" priced "holy grail of haute" French–New American cuisine "nestled in Yountville"; from the "mind-bending", "sublime" tasting menus and the "phone book–size wine list" to the "impeccable" "staff that treats you like royalty" it's everything it's "hyped up to be" – no wonder "foodies" "would be willing to sell a family member to get a reservation"; N.B. jacket required.

Fumé Bistro & Bar   21 | 18 | 21 | $37
4050 Byway St. E. (Wine Country Ave.), Napa, 707-257-1999;
www.fumebistro.com
Until recently, this "*non*-nonsense" Napa bistro with a "charming" patio was "one of the Valley's undiscovered gems" "bustling" with "vintners", but now even "tourists" are taking notice of the "excellent" New American cuisine emerging from the wood-burning ovens; "you feel like you're in a different world once you go inside" muse folks who even "love" the "bar action."

Gary Chu's Ⓜ   22 | 19 | 22 | $29
611 Fifth St. (bet. D & Mendocino Sts.), Santa Rosa, 707-526-5840;
www.garychus.com
Although "the North Bay is not a bastion of great" Asian food, this "stylish" Sino in Santa Rosa delivers "outstanding", "nouveau-gourmet" fare that proves it's "not your ordinary Chinese restaurant"; a Chu-sy crowd covets dishes that "allow each ingredient to shine" and prices "reasonable enough to bring the young 'uns for a feast"; still, a handful huff it's "reliable, if unexciting."

Gaylord India Ⓢ Ⓜ   18 | 16 | 16 | $33
201 Bridgeway (bet. Princess & Richardson Sts.), Sausalito,
415-339-0172; www.gaylords.com
See review in City of San Francisco Directory.

General Café   ▽ 20 | 14 | 17 | $27
Napa General Store, 540 Main St. (5th St.), Napa, 707-259-0762;
www.napageneralstore.com
Set inside a "funky" Napa Mill's general store specializing in wine country bric-a-brac, this mostly daytime cafe serves a Cal-Eclectic collection of pizza, sandwiches and Vietnamese small plates "well-executed with love"; "dining on the deck overlooking the river" is the "perfect" perch for lunch, but a few generally feel that the "decidedly deli atmosphere" inside lacks "dinner-spot" appeal on Fridays and Saturdays when it stays open until 8 PM.

Gira Polli   20 | 12 | 17 | $22
590 E. Blithedale Ave. (Camino Alto), Mill Valley, 415-383-6040
"Sorry to see the North Beach original" close, "but thank goodness" the Mill Valley sibling remains, as it's the only place to procure "delicious" "wood-oven spit-roasted chicken" at "reasonable prices"; there's "lots more" seating nowadays, still, the takeout-happy sigh "why cook when the succulent" Sicilian-style "signature" dish and "delicious" Italian "sides are at your beck and call"; N.B. the Decor rating may not reflect a recent expansion.

girl & the fig, the   22 | 20 | 21 | $42
Sonoma Hotel, 110 W. Spain St. (1st St.), Sonoma, 707-938-3634;
www.thegirlandthefig.com
Don't give a fig if you "bring your girl to the girl, or your boy to the girl" – just visit this "charming" French bistro on the Square in the

Sonoma Hotel; whether you "cozy" up near the "cool paintings" or dine in the "delightful" garden, "it's the perfect spot" to "enjoy" "hearty" Provence-inspired dishes and a "killer cheese course" with an "all-Rhône wine" selection that screams "South of France"; still, a "disappointed" handful opt for "cocktails at the old, wooden bar" instead.

Gordon's   21 | 14 | 15 | $22
6770 Washington St. (Madison St.), Yountville, 707-944-8246

"The best breakfasting spot in the area" located "just downwind from the French Laundry" is a "Yountville institution" in its own right; "a mix of local characters" "stand in line" for Sally Gordon's "warm hospitality" and "fabulous sour cream coffee cake before it disappears each morning", plus "super" "made-to-order" American sandwiches and salads; there's a "good reason" why it "gets mighty crowded", so "relax" and pay no mind to counter service that can be "lackadaisical."

Guaymas   18 | 21 | 17 | $33
5 Main St. (Tiburon Blvd.), Tiburon, 415-435-6300;
www.spectrumrestaurantgroup.com

"Worth a ferry trip to Marin on a pretty day", Tiburon's "imaginative Mexican", blessed with "killer views of the Bay" and a "happening" vibe, "goes beyond the standard options", tempting "tourists" and locals with "terrific margaritas" and "solid, satisfying" seafood dishes that reveal a "different" coastal "flair"; but while it's "fun" to "bask in the sun" on the dock, a few feel the fare misses the boat, sighing "so much potential", but it "tastes ordinary."

HANA JAPANESE RESTAURANT Ⓜ   26 | 15 | 21 | $41
Doubletree Plaza, 101 Golf Course Dr. (Roberts Lake Rd.), Rohnert Park, 707-586-0270; www.hanajapanese.com

For "the best Japanese" food "north of the Gate", "put yourself in owner Ken's hands" at this "pleasant surprise" in Rohnert Park; "ok, it's located in an upscale strip mall", but it's "where the chefs eat" and little wonder since his "creative presentations" of "pristine" sushi and sashimi "flown in straight from Japan" and fused with "fresh" Sonoma ingredients along with "excellent" hot offerings like "foie gras wonton soup" "astonish your every sense."

Harmony Restaurant   ▽ 22 | 25 | 19 | $52
Ledson Hotel, 480 First St. E. (Napa St.), Sonoma, 707-996-9779;
www.ledsonhotel.com

What with its sidewalk cafe tables and "great" opulent ambiance, replete with marble floors and a fireplace, you "could be in Paris" declare devotees of this Eclectic small-plates destination inside Sonoma Square's Ledson Hotel; if the "expensive" prices strike a disharmonious chord with a few, for most the "winner of a new menu", live piano music and recently expanded global wine list make it one of the few "super-fun" spots around.

Hurley's Restaurant & Bar   21 | 18 | 22 | $44
6518 Washington St. (Yount St.), Yountville, 707-944-2345;
www.hurleysrestaurant.com

"You've gotta be good to survive in Yountville" and while this "casual" family-friendly "locals' place" may not stir up the hurly-burly of its higher profile neighbors, customers nonetheless confer "kudos" to the chef-owner and "super-accommodating" staff; compatriots concur it's a "pleasure" to partake of "perfectly prepared" Cal-Med dishes and Napa wines on the patio, particularly on a "warm day" – and don't forget to "hit it for late-night munchies"; P.S. "wild game week is truly wild."

Il Davide   21 | 17 | 19 | $35
901 A St. (bet. 3rd & 4th Sts.), San Rafael, 415-454-8080;
www.ildavide.net
"Always good, always consistent" Tuscan fare along with a "creative wine list" draw locals to this "ideally located", "friendly" ristorante in Downtown San Rafael done up with colorful murals and a "beautiful outside sidewalk dining area"; aficionados salute the "well-presented", "excellent pasta" and seafood dishes, commending the "fresh ingredients" and "flavorful sauces" but others concede that while it's a "nice neighborhood Italian, I'm not sure what the fuss is about."

IL FORNAIO   19 | 20 | 18 | $36
Corte Madera, 223 Corte Madera Town Ctr. (Madera Blvd.),
Corte Madera, 415-927-4400; www.ilfornaio.com
See review in City of San Francisco Directory.

In-N-Out Burger ●   22 | 9 | 17 | $8
798 Redwood Hwy. (Belvedere Dr.), Mill Valley, 800-786-1000
820 Imola Ave./Hwy. 121 (Napa Valley Hwy.), Napa, 800-786-1000
www.in-n-out.com
See review in City of San Francisco Directory.

Insalata's   24 | 21 | 21 | $41
120 Sir Francis Drake Blvd. (Barber Ave.), San Anselmo, 415-457-7700;
www.insalatas.com
Chef-owner Heidi Krahling has a "heart of gold" gush groupies who feel they've hit the "unbelievably scrumptious" Mediterranean jackpot at this San Anselmo "gem"; the "delicious", "creative, original cooking" using seasonal ingredients coupled with the "vibrant colors of the paintings and walls" make this "noisy, happy place" "fun for a convivial dinner" – plus it "looks even better following" a recent face-lift; if a few quibble about "erratic service", regulars retort it's "excellent."

Izzy's Steaks & Chops   19 | 16 | 17 | $38
55 Tamal Vista Blvd. (Madera Blvd.), Corte Madera, 415-924-3366;
www.izzyssteaksandchops.com
See review in City of San Francisco Directory.

Jimtown Store   20 | 17 | 16 | $19
6706 Hwy. 128 (1 mi. east of Russian River), Healdsburg,
707-433-1212; www.jimtown.com
If you're driving on the back roads to or from Healdsburg, "don't pass by" this "cute", "old-fashioned country store" purveying "exceptional" "gourmet" sandwiches and "treats", wine and coffee that's perfect for packing a "picnic lunch" to enjoy while vineyard-"hopping" or on the "attractive" patio; it's also "fun to poke around" the shop "stuffed" with candy, antiques and "oddball" offerings.

Joe's Taco Lounge & Salsaria   20 | 16 | 16 | $18
382 Miller Ave. (Montford Ave.), Mill Valley, 415-383-8164
"Bikers down from the trails" and Mill Valley "locals with kids" "line up" for the "fresh", "excellent" and "authentic" "Baja-

style" coastal *cocina* at this "casual" tacqueria; the "colorful", "kitschy" digs, "quick" service and "reasonable" prices (not to mention "wonderful" margaritas) ensure that it's "busy from early until late" – no wonder amigos assert it's a "cool hangout."

John Ash & Co. | 24 | 25 | 23 | $55 |

4330 Barnes Rd. (River Rd.), Santa Rosa, 707-527-7687;
www.johnashrestaurant.com

"Santa Rosa's special-occasion" destination is an "oasis" for "excellent presentations" of "terrific" Californian cuisine paired with "killer" wines; "stylish new decor" by Pat Kuleto complements the "beautiful" setting by the Vintner's Inn overlooking "gorgeous vineyard views", and the "attentive" staff contributes to the "soothing" experience; though a few find the food "overpriced" and feel the former gold "standard for Sonoma dining" has "lost its edge", more maintain it "still hits the right notes."

Julia's Kitchen | 24 | 20 | 22 | $51 |

COPIA, 500 First St. (bet. Silverado Trail & Soscol Ave.), Napa,
707-265-5700; www.copia.org

"Quite the experience" crow acolytes who consider dinner at the late Mrs. Child's namesake Cal-French restaurant a "step into Julia's world" – and a "great way to end the day" after touring COPIA's food museum, "gourmet gardens" and kitchen store; enjoy "top toque" Victor Scargle's "masterly prepared" dishes and a "marvelous wine list" on the "sublime terrace" overlooking where the "fresh ingredients" grow or in the "contemporary" (some say "institutional") quarters; P.S. the "locals' cut-rate" prix fixe Thursday night dinner is a "steal."

K&L Bistro ⊠ | 25 | 17 | 22 | $42 |

119 S. Main St. (Bodega Hwy./Hwy. 12), Sebastopol, 707-823-6614

"Quite a surprise" for the area, this "tiny", "noisy", "bustling, typical Parisian bistro" imports a "sophisticated" slice of France to "earthy Sebastopol" serving "well-executed" Gallic dishes in "hearty portions" complemented by "interesting wines" and "friendly service" that makes you feel part of their "extended family"; peer into the open kitchen where the husband-and-wife owner-chefs "produce" their fare from "excellent local ingredients" with a "deft touch" – it almost "feels like home."

Kenwood Ⓜ | 23 | 21 | 22 | $46 |

9900 Sonoma Hwy./Hwy. 12 (Warm Springs Rd.), Kenwood,
707-833-6326; www.kenwoodrestaurant.com

There's "nothing like sitting outside" on a "sunny day" on the "lovely" patio of this "upscale roadhouse" in Kenwood and dining on "simple, fresh, great" French–New American fare "without all the nouveau glitz"; whether you dine alfresco or cram into the "noisy" bar area for a "well-prepared", "casual" meal, this "pleasant" "locals' fave" with "attentive service" "always delivers" – think of it as "comfort food for wine fanatics."

Kitchen at 868 Grant | 23 | 17 | 20 | $38 |

868 Grant Ave. (Sherman Ave.), Novato, 415-892-6100;
www.kitchen868.com

"Fine dining finally comes to Downtown Novato" at this "happening, little" storefront that delivers a missing link to the "foodie-laden Bay Area"; "don't get hooked on anything" because the "fresh, organic and novel" Cal eats "presented by an enthusiastic staff" "change on a daily basis"; still, a handful confide "for a leisurely" meal, "it's great but if you're on a schedule, choose another place"; N.B. a post-*Survey* chef change may impact the Food score.

La Ginestra ⓂⓂ ▽ | 18 | 13 | 20 | $31 |

127 Throckmorton Ave. (Miller Ave.), Mill Valley, 415-388-0224
"Relax and refuel the family" at this "old-time" Mill Valley "haunt" dishing up "consistently good" "but not fancy", "home-style" trattoria dishes and pizza; "sure, it's anything but Marin-upscale" – it's more like "eating in my grandma's kitchen" (the only thing "missing are candles in Chianti bottles") – but for many, it's "still a favorite"; however, a modernist minority tuts "this is what Beaver Cleaver thought [Southern] Italian dining was all about."

LARK CREEK INN, THE | 24 | 26 | 24 | $53 |

234 Magnolia Ave. (Madrone Ave.), Larkspur, 415-924-7766;
www.larkcreek.com
"As romantic a setting as you could imagine", this "lovely" Larkspur longtimer is "worth the drive" just for the "charming" converted Victorian digs and "gorgeous surroundings"; but better yet, the "superb", "seasonal" "haute American cuisine", "fine wines" and "divine" desserts including the signature butterscotch pudding are ferried by a "fantastic" staff, and though it's decidedly "pricey" and a few wish Bradley Ogden "would come home", it's still one of the "best" "special-occasion" destinations "north of the Golden Gate Bridge."

LaSalette Ⓜ | 23 | 18 | 21 | $39 |

Sonoma Plaza, 452 First St. E. (bet. Napa & Spain Sts.), Sonoma,
707-938-1927; www.lasalette-restaurant.com
"Explorers" extol the "intriguing", "superb" Portugeuse specialties that are "beautifully prepared" in an open kitchen at this "delightful" Sonoma Plaza storefront; "exceptional" service from the "congenial" staff, a "small" but "warm" and "charming" space and moderate prices also make it "worth the hunt"; P.S. the sweet and savory breakfast crêpes, omelets and "heavenly" breads are a "great way to start the day."

Las Camelias | 20 | 16 | 18 | $23 |

912 Lincoln Ave. (bet. 3rd & 4th Sts.), San Rafael, 415-453-5850;
www.lascameliasrestaurant.com
"Terrific" traditional Mexican fare including "standard-setting" guacamole as well as "outstanding", "unique" dishes "with a twist" make this San Rafael veteran one of the "best in Marin"; it's "perfect for family gatherings", thanks to "good-value" prices and "homey" digs featuring "interesting" artwork by the owner – not to mention "excellent" sangria for *madre y padre*.

LA TOQUE Ⓜ | 26 | 22 | 26 | $102 |

Rancho Caymus Inn, 1140 Rutherford Rd. (east of Hwy. 29), Rutherford,
707-963-9770; www.latoque.com
"Master chef" Ken Frank's "exquisite", "exciting" French cuisine plus "brilliant" sommelier Scott Tracy's "phenomenal" wine pairings equal an "extraordinary dining experience" that's "worthy of the terrain" at this Rutherford "treasure"; the meal is complemented by "intelligent" service, and the "elegant", "romantic" room is warmed by a "roaring fire"; even if "you'll have to take out a second mortgage" to pay for the prix fixe–only tasting dinner

(vino is extra), it's still "considered a bargain" compared with some of its Napa neighbors; N.B. closed Monday and Tuesday.

Ledford House Ⓜ   ▽ 23 | 22 | 24 | $45

3000 N. Hwy. 1 (Spring Grove Rd.), Albion, 707-937-0282;
www.ledfordhouse.com

"Stunning panoramic Pacific vistas" and "soulful" Cal-Med creations are the hallmarks of this "friendly", "coastline" restaurant in the Albion headlands; add in "relaxed service", "spot-on wine guidance" and a setting that "feels like home" and you've got a "great" way to "wind up a day in Mendocino"; if you don't want to "fork over" the dough for dinner, stop by the bar for live jazz and the same "breathtaking views"; N.B. dinner Wednesday–Sunday.

LEFT BANK   18 | 20 | 17 | $38

Blue Rock Inn, 507 Magnolia Ave. (Ward St.), Larkspur, 415-927-3331;
www.leftbank.com

Roland Passot "re-creates the experience of a Left Bank brasserie" at his "stylish" Larkspur "haunt" (with branches South and East of SF) where "madames and monsieurs" rendezvous for "satisfying" *"grand-mère* cuisine" amid "vintage posters and live jazz"; but while *amis* say the "food shines", likening it to an "old-growth Bordeaux beginning to peak as the tannins mellow", detractors counter it's like that "box of chocolates – you never know what you're going to get."

Little River Inn   22 | 21 | 23 | $43

Little River Inn, 7901 N. Hwy. 1 (Little River Airport Rd.), Little River,
707-937-5942; www.littleriverinn.com

Truly an "inn, not some pretentious chichi spot", this "lovely" turn-of-the-century Little River resort with "friendly service" offers "straightforward" "real" Californian seafood that's "better than mom's ever was"; "do yourself a favor" and kick off your meal by "hanging with the locals at Ole's Whale Watch Bar" and taking in the "dramatic ocean views" and incredible sunsets; P.S. with the arrival of chef Marc Dym (ex The Restaurant at Stevenswood), the kitchen may "reach a higher level."

Lotus Cuisine of India   21 | 18 | 20 | $28

704 Fourth St. (bet. Lincoln & Tamalpais Aves.), San Rafael,
415-456-5808; www.lotusrestaurant.com

For some of the "best Indian food this side of Mumbai" ("you wouldn't know you were in Marin"), San Rafaelites sit under the "cool" retractable roof that "makes warm nights a pleasure" and order up "tasty" subcontinental eats made with "fresh ingredients"; "I could bathe in their masala sauce" quip patrons who also stand behind the "great lunch buffet" and the "welcoming staff."

Lucy's   ▽ 18 | 17 | 16 | $34

6948 Sebastopol Ave. (bet. Main St. & Petaluma Ave.), Sebastopol,
707-829-9713; www.lucysrestaurant.com

Downtown Sebastopol's "hometown" haunt "has grown from its storefront roots across the street" into a "very popular", "happy" "West County" "social scene" luring a "hometown and sophisticated clientele"; loyal sorts still rally for the "very good wood-oven pizzas", and "healthy", organic Cal-Med dishes made from "excellent quality" ingredients, but grumblers balk that "prices have jumped", and are bereft it's "no longer the cute neighborhood" spot it once was.

MacCallum House
22 | 20 | 21 | $42

*MacCallum House Inn, 45020 Albion St. (bet. Kasten & Lansing Sts.),
Mendocino, 707-937-5763; www.maccallumhouse.com*

Set in a "quaint" "19th-century house", this "charming"
Mendocino village inn and restaurant is a "favorite spot for out-
of-towners and locals" who gather for "creative" "seasonal"
Californian fare and "unusual wines"; with its "classical rooms"
and fireplaces, the "lovely" setting is a "Victorian treat" while the
Gray Whale Bar allows you to "save a bunch"; still, a "disappointed" few find the fare "good, but not special."

MADRONA MANOR
26 | 26 | 26 | $61

*Madrona Manor, 1001 Westside Rd. (W. Dry Creek Rd.), Healdsburg,
707-433-4231; www.madronamanor.com*

For a bit of "wine country paradise" and a "true" New American–
French "gourmet experience", largely sourced "from the garden
outside your window", head to this "elegant Victorian"
Healdsburg B&B filled with antiques and set on "spectacular
terraced" grounds "a-ways out of town"; it's "hard to beat the
beautiful setting", plus the vino-tasting dinners are "worth
planning your calendar around", while service is both "friendly
and refined"; P.S. "spend the night to make your occasion
even more special!"

MANKA'S INVERNESS LODGE
25 | 26 | 21 | $74

*Manka's Inverness Lodge, 30 Callendar Way (Argyle St.), Inverness,
415-669-1034; www.mankas.com*

Feels like you're "walking into someone's living room" confide the
cabin-bound who "cozy" up to this "magical" Inverness mountain lodge complete with "an old dog that covets bacon from table
to table" when not napping by the "blazing fire"; settle in for a
"sensational", "on-the-wild-side" Californian "tour de force" prix
fixe meal that integrates "local elements" from the "rustic" environs and "knocks your hiking boots off"; bear in mind, however,
that dinner lasts for hours and the staff can be "imperious."

Manzanita Ⓜ
21 | 17 | 20 | $42

336 Healdsburg Ave. (North St.), Healdsburg, 707-433-8111

"Unpretentious, honest" pizza and "savory" Cal-Med entrees
"kissed by the wood-burning oven" and made with organic ingredients lure diners to this "comfortable, inviting" Healdsburg haunt;
it's a "great place for a sunny day" and a "nice way to end the day
after wine tasting", plus the "staff makes everyone feel welcome";
still, a few fence-sitters are not yet sure how it will "fare under
the new ownership."

Marché aux Fleurs Ⓢ Ⓜ
25 | 21 | 24 | $45

*23 Ross Common (off Lagunitas Rd.), Ross, 415-925-9200;
www.marcheauxfleursrestaurant.com*

Not your garden-variety restaurant but rather a "highly personal-
ized" husband-and-wife affair, this "elegant" yet "rustic hideaway" in the "sleepy village of Ross" enchants diners with
"fabulous" New French fare made from local ingredients that
"reflect the seasons and moods of Marin county", an "imaginative wine" trove of international boutique bottlings and "service
that's friendly without being overbearing"; kicking the "charm"
factor up a notch: the "tree-canopied" "romantic patio" – it's truly
"delightful on summer evenings."

Maria Manso World Cuisine Ⓜ   ▽ 24 | 19 | 22 | $38
1613 Fourth St. (F St.), San Rafael, 415-453-7877;
www.mariamanso.com
San Rafael's "undiscovered star" "gives the chef license to ex-
periment" with "interesting flavors" from "all over the world" –
there's "some creative thinking going on" at this Eclectic "wonderful spot" agree acolytes who also globe-trot over for Korean soju
cocktails, Cuban flan and American jazz; an "attentive staff" and
a "backyard that's delightful in the summer" cement its "winner"
status; N.B. a late-night menu is served on weekends until 2 AM.

Market   22 | 20 | 23 | $38
1347 Main St. (bet. Adam & Spring Sts.), St. Helena, 707-963-3799;
www.marketsthelena.com
"Put aside regrets that you missed out on Napa Valley's impossible-
to-access" "food temples" and sidle up to the "welcoming, hopping
bar" at St. Helena's "down-to-earth" "Main Street keeper" set in
a historic building and staffed with "sassy" servers; expect
"Cyrus food without Cyrus prices" – makes sense as it's the same
owners – nevertheless the "chic", "inspired, gourmet takes on
American" home cooking and an "extensive wine list" seem
"way too affordable" for this "neck of the woods."

MARTINI HOUSE   26 | 26 | 24 | $58
1245 Spring St. (bet. Main & Oak Sts.), St. Helena, 707-963-2233;
www.martinihouse.com
"Don't worship your meal – just enjoy it" at St. Helena's "celebratory" spot where you may reach "nirvana" supping in the "fairy-lit
garden" or in the historic "Craftsman home beautifully renovated"
to a 'T' with a "hunting lodge feel"; "mycologists" trip out watching
"mushroom freak" chef Todd Humphries prepare his 'Fall Fungus
Frenzy' and "innovative" New American "works of art", proffered
by a "flat-out outstanding" staff; skip the stiff ones and slip into the
walk-in cellar bar hidden downstairs for the "fun-to-read" wine list.

Max's   17 | 13 | 16 | $24
60 Madera Blvd. (Hwy. 101), Corte Madera, 415-924-6297;
www.maxsworld.com
See review in City of San Francisco Directory.

Meadowood Grill   22 | 20 | 21 | $55
Meadowood Resort, 900 Meadowood Ln. (Howell Mountain Rd., off
Silverado Trail), St. Helena, 707-963-3646; www.meadowood.com
"Savor Meadowood's peace" at this St. Helena grill "tucked away
in the resort" where "you feel as if you're part of the country-club
set" lunching on the "deck overlooking the croquet lawn and
nine-hole course"; the "preppy" "space is more golf"-house–
"casual than dining room", but the "lovely wooded area",
"delightful" Californian fare, "fantastic" Valley-centric cellar and
"attentive service" still make it a "treat."

Mendo Bistro   23 | 19 | 22 | $33
The Company Store, 301 N. Main St., 2nd fl. (Redwood Ave.), Fort Bragg,
707-964-4974; www.mendobistro.com
A "youthful exuberance" reigns at this "zany place full of charac-
ters" led by "ringleader" chef Nicholas Petti and his wife, Jaimi,
who make "everyone feel like the most important customers";
kick back in the "open" upstairs bistro overlooking Fort Bragg and

"feel in command" as you "choose the method and the sauce" you prefer for your entree from the "creative" New American menu, plus a bottle from the "excellent wine list."

Mendocino Hotel
19 | 21 | 19 | $39

Mendocino Hotel, 45080 Main St. (off Rte. 1), Mendocino, 707-937-0511;
www.mendocinohotel.com

"Victorian delights abound" at this "charming, period" Mendocino Hotel restaurant kitted out with a "dark-wood" interior and a Californian menu that's "right on the mark"; order "small plates" – or "if nothing else, a cocktail" and "hang out in the bar" under a stained-glass dome and "drink in the lovely", "Old West ambiance" – you may glimpse the ghost who reportedly haunts tables six and eight; N.B. the Garden Room offers less expensive breakfast and lunch.

MIREPOIX Ⓜ
27 | 20 | 26 | $48

275 Windsor River Rd. (Honsa Ave.), Windsor, 707-838-0162;
www.restaurantmirepoix.com

"Like finding a truffle in the woods" sigh the starstruck who've stumbled upon Windsor's "tiny pillbox", an "intimate" former home with floor-to-ceiling windows and a heated patio that doubles its capacity; the "absolutely fantastic" French fare "goes way beyond bistro food in its originality, but competes well for value", and it's served "sans attitude" "rejoice foodies" who also pop their corks over the "energetic staff that loves wine"; *oui*, "we'll definitely go back again" – it's "always a memorable experience."

Model Bakery Ⓜ
19 | 10 | 11 | $14

1357 Main St. (bet. Adams & Spring Sts.), St. Helena, 707-963-8192;
www.themodelbakery.com

It "smells fantastic when walking in" and you feel "sinful" walking out after downing "fussy pastries" and the "best bread in the Valley" at this "crowded", "unpretentious" art deco bakery in St. Helena; "wake up and read the paper" with "real people" sharing tables, go for "simple" sandwiches" or "pick up a picnic baguette" – it's worth putting up with the "slow" staff (heck, "who needs good service when the goodies are this good?").

Monti's Rotisserie & Bar
20 | 18 | 16 | $38

Montgomery Village Shopping Ctr., 714 Village Ct. (Farmers Ln.), Santa Rosa, 707-568-4404; www.montisroti.net

Santa Rosa residents get one "whiff" of the wood-burning rotisserie while "banking" in the shopping center and hotfoot it over to this American-Med "favorite" (from the Willi's folks) to indulge in "perfectly cooked" spit-fare and "creative" small plates; "it's fun to sit at the wine bar" where every bottle on the Sonoma-centric list is available by the glass or on the "lovely" rustic patio – you almost "forget about" the "inattentive" service.

Moosse Cafe
21 | 19 | 19 | $36

390 Kasten St. (Albion St.), Mendocino, 707-937-4323;
www.themoosse.com

"Don't let the quirky name fool you": this "pleasant little Mendo cafe" "always offers pleasure for the palate" serving Coastal Californian cuisine "for grown-ups" in "bright and airy" digs; it "really shines at lunchtime", so "kick back and enjoy" the "nice salads and sandwiches" and "organic specialties" served in portions big enough "to satisfy" on the "sunny deck facing the garden."

Mustards Grill
24 | 18 | 21 | $43

7399 St. Helena Hwy./Hwy. 29 (bet. Oakville Grade Rd. & Washington St.), Yountville, 707-944-2424; www.mustardsgrill.com

"Better than an '85 Cab", Cindy Pawlcyn's "iconic" Yountville "roadhouse" feels like a "throwback" to Napa before the wine train and snooty limos", yet her "inventive" Californian–New American fare "brings new meaning to comfort food"; the "tasty treats" made with the "best of everything" "stir the soul" ("two words: pork chops"), especially when paired with the "outstanding wine list"; sure, you'll find "day-trippers" "'unwine'ding" – the bar's "a must" "after hitting the vineyards"; N.B. a sib named Go Fish is slated to open this fall at 611 Main Street.

Napa Valley Grille
21 | 20 | 21 | $40

Washington Sq., 6795 Washington St. (off Hwy. 29), Yountville, 707-944-8686; www.napavalleygrille.com

A "nice relaxing stop after a day of wine tasting", this "casual", "lively" Yountville outpost of a mini-chain serves up "creative", "consistent quality" Californian eats in "peaceful surroundings"; "service is friendly and helpful – they give you plenty of time to lounge in the sun" and they don't "rush the courses" – so kick back on the patio and enjoy the "lovely view of the vineyards."

Napa Valley Wine Train
16 | 23 | 20 | $70

1275 McKinstry St. (bet. 1st St. & Soscol Ave.), Napa, 707-253-2111; www.winetrain.com

"Tourists" find it "entertaining" to "ride on an opulent old train" "looking at the grapevines" and the "great scenery as it rolls" through Napa while dining on Californian cuisine and "tasting lots of" vino (especially on Friday when a guest "vintner is onboard"); however, "locals" quip it should be renamed the "whine train" noting "foodie types will be sorely disappointed" with the "over-priced" "banquet-quality" fare and oenophiles may be steamed that "wine isn't included in the ticket price."

955 Ukiah Ⓜ
23 | 19 | 21 | $37

955 Ukiah St. (School St.), Mendocino, 707-937-1955; www.955restaurant.com

Although this "fantastic little restaurant" tucked off the street along a serpentine pathway may "often be lost in the shadow" of Mendocino's "big boys", admirers insist that it's "not to be missed"; the owners and their "great" staff "put their heart and soul into" proffering "consistently good", "witty" New American–New French menus using regional ingredients in a "charming" dining room that's "both casual and elegant" – little wonder loyalists "look forward to every visit."

North Coast Brewing Co. Tap Room & Grill
▽ 18 | 13 | 18 | $26

444 N. Main St. (Pine St.), Fort Bragg, 707-964-3400; www.northcoastbrewing.com

Mendocino coast cruisers suggest "try the tasting" of "great craft beers" ("oh my!") at Fort Bragg's microbrewery tavern, "an amazing way to expand a rookie's mind about darker, richer brews"; many locals "don't even bother with the dining room", heading straight to the "easygoing" bar for "great fish 'n' chips", maintaining most of the "affordable" but "typical" Cal-Eclectic eats are "just there to soak up the beer."

N.V. ☒   24 | 24 | 22 | $56

1106 First St. (Main St.), Napa, 707-265-6400
Its initials shout wine country, but this "new" "hot spot" "for grown-ups" actually brings a "bit of New York to Napa" with a "hip" vibe that's decidedly "N(ot) V(allejo)"; if a few mutter the "food needs a little work for the price", most muse "it's about time" we "got a sophisticated" Californian bistro that "doesn't cost the diner a fortune"; P.S. the "upscale lounge" serves "top-shelf cocktails" and tapas till 2 AM Thursday–Saturday.

Olema Inn   23 | 22 | 21 | $46

Olema Inn, 10000 Sir Francis Drake Blvd. (Hwy. 1), Olema, 415-663-9559; www.theolemainn.com
A "delightful" "way station on your way along the Western Marin coast", this "charming" "old hotel" (circa 1876) offers "clean, fresh and creative" Cal-Med meals with "organic local" ingredients paired with a "lovely" wine selection; service is "average" but "allows for a leisurely meal" amid the "comfortable" "rustic" rooms with floors from an old tobacco barn; N.B. weekend lunch is served too.

Ora Ⓜ   ▽ 20 | 21 | 19 | $43

(fka Mi Casa)
24 Sunnyside Ave. (Blithedale Ave.), Mill Valley, 415-381-7500; www.oramv.com
"A wonderful addition" to Mill Valley, this moderately priced Pan-Asian exudes a Zen-like aura with a soothing waterfall on the patio and bamboo ceilings; chef Van Nguyen (ex Masa's) lassoes the big flavors of Thailand, Japan and China on his "original", "fun menu" of seasonal "small plates" paired with an "esoteric wine list" and extensive sake flights; N.B. the lounge projects silent black-and-white Japanese monster flicks.

Osake ☒   23 | 19 | 21 | $33

2446 Patio Ct. (Farmers Ln.), Santa Rosa, 707-542-8282
Sake 'O Ⓜ
505 Healdsburg Ave. (Piper St.), Healdsburg, 707-433-2669
www.garychus.com
Sated Santa Rosans are "thankful" that chef-owner "Gary Chu is everywhere", particularly at the sushi bar of this Japanese outpost where "he makes some fun things that are not on the menu", including "beautifully prepared" entrees; "sit back and relax" as you sip "sake poured to overflowing" or a selection from the all–Sonoma County wine list in the somewhat "dated" dining room; N.B. the Sake 'O offshoot opened post-*Survey*.

Pacific Catch   21 | 12 | 16 | $20

133 Corte Madera Town Ctr. (off Hwy. 101), Corte Madera, 415-927-3474; www.pacificcatch.com
See review in City of San Francisco Directory.

Pangaea Ⓜ   ▽ 24 | 20 | 23 | $46

39165 S. Hwy. 1 (east side of the Hwy.), Gualala, 707-884-9669; www.pangaeacafe.com
Gualala's "unpretentious" Cal-French cafe channels the "funky aesthetic" of the coastal artist community in its canvas-filled, "1960s" country home setting; "huge portions" of "soulful" "haute" "comfort food" "based on local, mostly organic ingredi-

ents" (from a farm named Oz – how perfect is that?) are paired with a "strong, eclectic wine list" (favoring biodynamic bottlings) and "friendly service" – just be aware of early closing hours.

Pearl ⓈⓂ   ▽ 23 | 17 | 22 | $40

1339 Pearl St. (bet. Franklin & Polk Sts.), Napa, 707-224-9161; www.therestaurantpearl.com
"Proof that the town of Napa is equal to the rest of the Valley" laud locals who string together a "comforting" meal of "delicious" Californian fare at this "wonderfully quaint" "secret" that's a "little hard to find but worth the trouble"; "caring" service and a "low-key" vibe enhance its "charming" appeal – it almost "feels like you're at your best friend's house for dinner."

Piatti   18 | 19 | 19 | $34

625 Redwood Hwy. (Hwy. 101), Mill Valley, 415-380-2525; www.piatti.com
See review in East of San Francisco Directory.

Piazza D'Angelo   19 | 20 | 19 | $35

22 Miller Ave. (bet. Sunnyside & Throckmorton Aves.), Mill Valley, 415-388-2000; www.piazzadangelo.com
Mill Valley's "happening spot" boasts a "bustling and friendly" feel with "owners who are always there to greet and schmooze" the "many regulars" munching "well-prepared", "starch-friendly Italian favorites" priced for "value"; naysayers note it's "noisy" and "inconsistent" and tire of the "old formula" (25 years), and phobes "avoid the Friday and Saturday night crush" at the "middle-aged pickup bar", but players consider the "people-watching" "a sport."

Picco   24 | 19 | 20 | $47

320 Magnolia Ave. (King St.), Larkspur, 415-924-0300
"Small plates again?" – perhaps, but Bruce Hill's "sophisticated", perma-"packed" "California equivalent of a tapas bar" "hits big" with its Eclectic menu of "fun" "mini-burgers, mini-shakes" and other clever nibbles (paired with "carefully chosen wines"), giving "small-town Larkspur" a dose of "big-city attitude"; "the only downside" is the "noise" emanating from a "bar that attracts the non-geriatric Marin set" – decibel-detesters might prefer the daytime quiet of adjacent Pizzeria Picco.

Pilar ⓈⓂ   24 | 18 | 23 | $49

807 Main St. (3rd St.), Napa, 707-252-4474; www.pilarnapa.com
With a great "husband-wife team at the creative controls", this "small" "storefront" is "the best-kept secret in Downtown Napa – but it shouldn't be", because the "seasonal" Californian food with "innovative Latin touches" "definitely competes with the best Up Valley", and what's more, the "servers really know their stuff" (including a wine list that balances local and foreign wines); it's "not fancy", but it sure is an "affordable", "relaxing respite" from the area's "more famous eateries."

Pine Cone Diner ⌷   ▽ 19 | 14 | 16 | $21

60 Fourth St. (bet. 3rd & 5th Sts.), Point Reyes Station, 415-663-1536
Although this "classic old-time diner" looks a lot like the Point Reyes truck stop it once was, the "huge" "traditional" breakfasts and lunches are prepared "with a twist" (and "virtually all local and organic ingredients"); "you might be the only person there who

does not know everyone else" and "the service can be prickly" (some "call this 'color'"), but "don't take yourself too seriously" and you'll have a "fun" "stopover when driving up the Coast."

Pizza Antica 22 | 16 | 17 | $24

Strawberry Vlg., 800 Redwood Hwy., #705 (Belvedere Dr.), Mill Valley, 415-383-0600; www.pizzaantica.com
See review in South of San Francisco Directory.

Pizza Azzurro ⌧ ▽ 23 | 11 | 17 | $21

1400 Second St. (Franklin St.), Napa, 707-255-5552
At this "nondescript" Napa hang, a modest meal composed of a personal-sized, wood-fired pizza with a "great crisp crust", an "interesting, tasty salad" and a glass of California wine is "the perfect foil for too much gourmet food" according to binged-out tourists; the locals concur, concluding it's a "nice spot that delivers good flavors – if not the pizza to your door."

Pizzeria Picco & Wine Shop ⊅ 24 | 15 | 17 | $23

316 Magnolia Ave. (King St.), Larkspur, 415-945-8900
Picco's sidekick is "one of the great eat-and-run stops in Marin", rolling out "crust so thin it makes your shoe sole look thick" – "but it's what's on top that counts": "local, seasonal and organic" goodies; "high-quality ingredients" also distinguish the salads and ice cream, while "lesser-known producers" grace the "smart wine list"; still, "limited and cramped seating" can lead to "chaos", prompting many patrons to "grab the 'za to go."

Pizzeria Tra Vigne 20 | 14 | 17 | $26

Inn at Southbridge, 1016 Main St. (Pope St.), St. Helena, 707-967-9999; www.travignerestaurant.com
Sometimes "hungry travelers" "just need" "a change from the gourmet routine" – and this "spacious" St. Helena pizzeria provides just that: "one of the only" "family-oriented" places in the Valley (there's even "a pool table for the kids"), it serves up "quality" pizzas, piadines and salads "without breaking the bank" (a "no corkage" policy helps); too bad it "resembles a chain" rather than its famed namesake – you could be "in any suburb."

P.J. Steak 21 | 19 | 19 | $53

(fka PèreJeanty)
6725 Washington St. (Madison St.), Yountville, 707-945-1000; www.pjsteak.com
"If you're looking for a steakhouse in Napa Valley", Philippe Jeanty's "renamed", revamped "antidote to fancy-pants cuisine" "is it", dishing up "darn tasty" chops "without pretensions", plus a soupçon of classic bistro fare; but what good-time Charlies find "fun" and "not stuffy" strikes foodies as "noisy" and "half-baked" – so "if you only have time for one 'Jeanty' restaurant in Yountville", "make it the other one."

Poggio Ristorante 22 | 23 | 19 | $43

Casa Madrona, 777 Bridgeway (Bay St.), Sausalito, 415-332-7771; www.poggiotrattoria.com
"From the creator of Il Fornaio" comes, well, "Il Fornaio on steroids" – a "charming" Sausalito trattoria in the Casa Madrona hotel that's "far more than a tourist trap" thanks to its "seaside setting", "beautifully decorated rooms", "solid wine list" and "earthy country Italian" fare; "opt for an outdoor table at lunch" –

it's a "perfect" perch for "people-watching" – "you feel like you're in a small" Tuscan village; still, a few feel the fare "misses the mark and service is so-so."

Press 22 | 24 | 24 | $72 |

587 St. Helena Hwy. (White Ln.), St. Helena, 707-967-0550; www.pressthelena.com

"What a delightful mix of unexpected tastes" concur carnivores, "winemakers" and "VIPs" who canter over to this "upscale" American steakhouse in a "prime" St. Helena location for "outstanding" fare, including "straightforward slabs o' meat" from the rotisserie "carved at the table" by "impeccable waiters"; but "you'll be pressed to find a bargain" (the "impressive wine list" is "waaay out of line"), so leave it for "special occasions" or cocktails "by the fireplace"; N.B. a post-*Survey* change of chef may impact the Food score.

Ravenous Cafe Ⓜ 23 | 17 | 19 | $39 |

420 Center St. (North St.), Healdsburg, 707-431-1302

"Absent of all wine-country pretensions", this "quirky", "laid-back" Healdsburg "hangout" hidden "off the tour bus path" in "an old family home" with "funky decor, including acid-orange walls" and "odd seating arrangements" plus an outdoor patio, has "savvy locals" a-raving over "oversized" portions of "adventurous" Cal-Eclectic fare that's "pure Sonoma"; at meal's end, "diner prices" compensate for "sometimes slow service."

Ravens Restaurant, The ▽ 26 | 25 | 24 | $40 |

Stanford Inn & Spa, Coast Hwy. & Comptche Rd. (Hwy. 1), Mendocino, 707-937-5615; www.stanfordinn.com

At this eco-"nirvana" set in a spa on the Mendocino coast, conscientious diners happily confront "the ultimate contradiction: healthy indulgence" in the form of "innovative" organic vegetarian fare, including vegan dishes, "even carnivores can enjoy" ("don't miss the sea-palm strudel") – all made with ingredients "fresh from the garden" you can see from the dining-room window; meanwhile, oenophiles might ask their "delightful", "pet-friendly" hosts about the wine list's "organic choices"; N.B. breakfast and dinner only.

REDD RESTAURANT ● 27 | 21 | 25 | $65 |

6480 Washington St. (California Dr.), Yountville, 707-944-2222; www.reddnapavalley.com

A "new star has risen in Yountville" attest admiring "tourists", "vintners" and "the Napa chic" awed by (ex Masa's and Auberge du Soleil) chef-owner Richard Reddington's "stylish" New American "masterpiece"; every "divine" dish on his "wine-friendly" à la carte and tasting menus "hits the high notes – very high" and it's all "beautifully presented" by a "flawless" staff; a few find it too "hard edged and noisy", but most give it the green light, insisting the "very architectural", "minimalist" setting allows the "lavish food" "to shine."

Rendezvous Inn & Restaurant Ⓜ ▽ 28 | 22 | 25 | $47 |

647 N. Main St. (Bush St.), Fort Bragg, 707-964-8142; www.rendezvousinn.com

A "magical evening" awaits guests of Kim Badenhop, a "classically trained" chef-owner and "wonderful host" whose "little" New French "gem tucked away in Fort Bragg" is the "nicest place for miles and miles"; "stopping by to chat with" "all comers" to the "romantic", redwood-paneled spot, he handpicks wines to complement the "fabulous", "organically inflected", "creatively presented" fare (of course, the "outgoing staff" really "knows the menu" too); bottom line: it's "worth every dollar" "for anniversaries, birthday dinners" or even "once a month."

Restaurant, The   ▽ 25 | 18 | 25 | $36

418 N. Main St. (W. Laurel St.), Fort Bragg, 707-964-9800; www.therestaurantfortbragg.com

"When visitors ask for the locals' favorite restaurant", the answer "is easy: The Restaurant", joke regulars of this Fort Bragg "institution", where chef-owner Jim Larsen ("a character" in his own right) has been whipping up "consistently top-notch" New American fare for over 30 years; meanwhile, his wife ensures "excellent service" in the dining room – where, culture vultures observe, "you're surrounded" with "a huge collection" of paintings by California artist Olaf Palm.

Restaurant at Meadowood ⑤Ⓜ   – | – | – | E

Meadowood Napa Valley, 900 Meadowood Ln. (Howell Mountain Rd., off Silverado Trail), St. Helena, 707-967-1205; www.meadowood.com

After a three-year hiatus, the culinary cognoscenti are once again descending on the Meadowood resort's flagship restaurant, where chef Joseph Humphrey (ex Auberge du Soleil) offers lavish three-, four- and seven-course prix fixe menus showcasing Napa Valley larder, as well as a comprehensive regional wine list with some international highlights; the dark-wood and leather-accented setting was designed by Howard Backen (Cyrus, Kokkari) and offers a 10-seat 'Vintner's Table' and a fair-weather terrace overlooking the tree-lined fairways.

Restaurant at Stevenswood, The   ▽ 22 | 22 | 22 | $60

Stevenswood Lodge, 8211 Shoreline Hwy./Hwy. 1 (1.5 minutes south of Mendocino), Little River, 707-937-2810; www.stevenswood.com

"Tucked away off Highway 1" amid redwoods on the Mendocino coast, this "surprisingly urbane" Little River inn bids guests to dine in armchairs by the fire on "fancy" Mediterranean fare paired with "wonderful wines"; following the departure of "great chef Marc Dym", however, what was "once the most innovative" menu "in the area" now strikes some as "limited" and "overpriced", especially considering the "inconsistent" service – "attentive" here, "perfunctory" there.

Ristorante Fabrizio ⑤   18 | 15 | 20 | $33

455 Magnolia Ave. (Cane St.), Larkspur, 415-924-3332

"Always packed with loyal locals", this "neighborly" nook in Downtown Larkspur may offer "no surprises", nevertheless, customers "keep coming back" for "real home-cooked" Northern Italian cuisine served in a "cozy dining room that's quiet enough for conversation – even when it's busy"; you can count on "warm, welcoming host Fabrizio" to "make you feel special" – this is a "comfort-food place" where you can "restore yourself."

Robata Grill & Sushi   20 | 16 | 18 | $32

591 Redwood Hwy./Hwy. 101 (Seminary Dr. exit), Mill Valley, 415-381-8400; www.robatagrill.com

For "creatively presented, very fresh" rolls and sashimi, Mill Valley maki-seekers fin their way over to this "laid-back", "modest" Japanese eatery; for "something different" sit at the robata and order "tasty grilled items", including fish and vegetables – it's "quite fun", plus "service is especially friendly"; if a few land-locked locals lament "it doesn't compare to Japantown", even they admit "who's driving all that way for sushi?"

Royal Thai   23 | 16 | 19 | $25
610 Third St. (Irwin St.), San Rafael, 415-485-1074;
www.royalthaisanrafael.com
When it's high time for Siamese supping, San Rafaelites ascend the stairs to this "delightful" house and clamor for "interesting house specials and reliable favorites"; it's the "benchmark for Thai in the Bay Area" vow loyalists who consider the "good 'n' cheap" "tried-and-true" cuisine "consistently" "wonderful" and also dig the "cute digs and "friendly service."

Rutherford Grill   22 | 18 | 20 | $36
1180 Rutherford Rd. (Hwy. 29), Rutherford, 707-963-1792;
www.houstons.com
"Are there that many people that like to stuff themselves?" ponder pundits who endure "long waits" to eat at this "hopping" Houston's offspring, an "unpretentious" place with a "party atmosphere" serving up "hearty" Traditional American vittles, including "ribs that put others to shame"; diners "don't care that it's part of a chain" – the "comforting grub" "hits the mark", service is "attentive" – and you're bound to "strike up new conversations" in the "lively bar."

Sabor of Spain Ⓜ   17 | 20 | 16 | $35
1301 Fourth St. (C St.), San Rafael, 415-457-8466; www.saborofspain.com
A "refreshing change from the usual Marin dining scene" declare diners who descend on this "stylish", "cosmopolitan" San Rafael vinoteca for "authentic" *alta cocina* tapas and "inventive" en-trees made from local ingredients, complemented by "superb Spanish wines"; still, some squawk about "painfully slow" service – "hope it picks up" with time; P.S. duck into the "specialty shop next door" to buy a bottle, plus food and tchotchkes from the Iberian Peninsula.

Sam's Anchor Cafe   14 | 18 | 15 | $31
27 Main St. (Tiburon Blvd.), Tiburon, 415-435-4527; www.samscafe.com
The "frat" "party never stops" at this "touristy" Tiburon "institu-tion" that's "ferociously" crowded on "sunny weekends" with "hootchy waitresses" and drunken "single-watchers" hoping to catch bait on the "justly famous dock patio" while "soaking up" "views of the city"; after "ingesting a margarita", no one notices the "nothing special" American seafood and burger grub, that is, until the "seabirds" "bomb-dive and take" it away.

Santé   ▽ 21 | 21 | 22 | $75
Fairmont Sonoma Mission Inn & Spa, 100 Boyes Blvd. (Sonoma Hwy.),
Sonoma, 707-939-2415; www.fairmont.com
This "comfortable, quiet" Californian with "Mission-style" decor in the Fairmont Sonoma Mission Inn offers an "expectedly expen-sive" "great dining experience" that "aspires not to be hotel food"; the prix fixe and à la carte fare is "pretty unique and flavor-ful" while service is "solicitous"; still, a handful sigh it "doesn't disappoint though at times it fails to thrill" and feels too "formal" for "wine country."

Santi
23 | 19 | 21 | $46

21047 Geyserville Ave. (Hwy. 128), Geyserville, 707-857-1790;
www.tavernasanti.com
It's "the best unexpected surprise in wine country" crow the cogna-
santi who head to this "plain-fronted" Geyserville "delight" in a
"tiny burg" "that time long forgot" for "sophisticated" Italian *cucina*
and vino; the "adventurous" dishes – "robust pasta", "wonderful
homemade sausages" and cured meats – make you feel like you're
"touring rural Italy", especially when you lounge on the "large
courtyard patio"; P.S. the 707-set comes round for Wednesday
Locals' Nights and "martinis to die for."

Scoma's
22 | -18 | 19 | $41

588 Bridgeway (Princess St.), Sausalito, 415-332-9551;
www.scomassausalito.com
See review in City of San Francisco Directory.

Sea Ranch Lodge Restaurant
▽ 22 | 21 | 22 | $51

Sea Ranch Lodge, 60 Sea Walk Dr. (Hwy. 1), Sea Ranch, 707-785-2371;
www.searanchlodge.com
The rustic redwood "decor is early '70s Sea Ranch", but with new
owners and an "excellent" new chef "onboard", expect "nothing
but better things to come" at this seaside "showplace" "perched
above Sonoma's cliffs"; while some tout lunch and before sunset
as the "best time to enjoy" the "panoramic Pacific views" and
"much improved", "creatively presented" Californian-seafood
fare, smitten surveyors say it's a "spectacular" spot to "eat, visit,
stay or get married" anytime.

Seaweed Café Ⓜ
▽ 25 | 19 | 19 | $44

1580 Eastshore Rd. (Hwy. 1), Bodega Bay, 707-875-2700;
www.seaweedcafe.com
Coastal denizens "drive fast to get to this Slow Food" bistro "hidden" in a Bodega Bay shopping mall, serving "superb", "fresh,
fresh, fresh" Cal-French fare; the "wonderful" food has eco lean-
ings, showcasing the "best of local ingredients", while the "excellent" vino list focuses on Sonoma "wines from west of
Highway 101"; even after expanding, the "wildly wacky" dining
room and open kitchen exude a "small" salon vibe where the
owners "mingle" with guests; N.B. dinner Thursday–Sunday only.

Sharon's By the Sea
▽ 21 | 14 | 19 | $32

Noyo Harbor, 32096 N. Harbor Dr. (Hwy. 1), Fort Bragg, 707-962-0680;
www.sharonsbythesea.com
"Plenty" of "wonderful" Italian seafood is your "reward for
checking out what's under the bridge" at this "accommodating"
"upscale fish shack" at Noyo Harbor near Fort Bragg; everyone
"hankers" for seats on the "deck in the sunshine" but even the
"slightly cramped interior" is tolerable because the "views of the
wildlife, the fishermen and the Pacific sunset" "make it worthwhile"; N.B. the owners pulled up anchor at Mendocino's Hill
House Inn branch in 2005.

Sonoma Meritage & Oyster Bar
20 | 19 | 20 | $40

165 West Napa St. (bet. 1st & 2nd Sts.), Sonoma, 707-938-9430;
www.sonomameritage.com
"Quite a gathering spot for local winemakers" muse admirers
who blend right in at this "lively", "friendly", "warm dining expe-

rience" "right off the Sonoma Square"; if you're "craving a good drink, a little shellfish", "reasonably priced" French–Northern Italian fare and a "comfortable" ambiance with a "nice garden" to boot, this "pleasant surprise" is the "place for you"; still, a few harrumph the cocktails are more "memorable" than the meals.

Station House Cafe, The

16 | 14 | 15 | $29

11180 State Rte. 1 (4th St.), Point Reyes Station, 415-663-1515; www.stationhousecafe.com

"Cap off a marvelous Point Reyes National Seashore day with a relaxed" "impromptu" dinner of "homey", "well-prepared" Cal fare on the "lovely patio" at this "busy" "West Marin oasis" suggest wayfarers who also "stop in" for the "outstanding breakfast"; the "local, organic food" is "definitely not gourmet" and service can be "sketchy", but it's nonetheless "memorable" on those "sunny days" when you can "enjoy the gardens."

St. Orres

∇ 25 | 25 | 25 | $52

36601 Shoreline Hwy./Hwy. 1 (2 mi. north of Gualala), Gualala, 707-884-3303; www.saintorres.com

"If you're within 100 miles" of the "sleepy town of Gualala", take thee to this "charmingly bizarre" Mendocino hotel for a "memorable" meal and feast on "uniquely Californian" cuisine in a "rustic","onion-domed" dining room boasting "distinctly Russian architecture"; "love the dedicated staff" confide disciples who also fall for the "wild game, locally foraged mushrooms" and "excellent local wine list"; still, a few heretics huff after "nearly 30 years", it's "time to reinvigorate" the setting.

SUSHI RAN

27 | 19 | 20 | $47

107 Caledonia St. (bet. Pine & Turney Sts.), Sausalito, 415-332-3620; www.sushiran.com

"Run don't walk" to this "higher-class" "nirvana" "tucked away in Sausalito" that feels like a "neighborhood spot" but cranks out "unbelievable" Japanese–Pacific Rim creations "every bit as good as Masa's" for a "buzzy crowd"; expect "more than the usual suspects" – the "sushi chefs take great pride" in "skillfully" presenting raw fish "basics done to perfection" along with "delicious dishes" and "Kobe beef that melts in your mouth" – and "don't be discouraged if you have to sit" in the wine bar next door – it's a "good alternative."

Syrah

26 | 20 | 24 | $45

205 Fifth St. (Davis St.), Santa Rosa, 707-568-4002; www.syrahbistro.com

Napa no more agree Santa Rosans who "leave the French Laundry to the tourists" and anoint chef/co-owner Josh Silver "Mr. Sonoma County" at this "supreme locals' favorite" with a "delightful staff" in Railroad Square; he's got a "lot of energy and fun ideas" – the "exceptional" Cal–French bistro fare, offset by an "eclectic" Rhône-centric wine list", is always "warm and homey – in spite of the industrial chic decor" – and it "never lets us down"; P.S. the "tasting menu is the best."

Tabla ⚅ Ⓜ

∇ 26 | 13 | 19 | $18

1167 Magnolia Ave. (Estrelle Rd.), Larkspur, 415-461-6787

The "delicious dosai are not to be missed" declare denizens who make tracks to this "little" Larkspur cafe in a strip mall for Indian-inspired Cali-style "delicate" crêpe "favorites" "brimming with interesting combinations" of "organic, locally sourced" "meats, cheese and vegetables and served with remarkable chutneys"; "wish they could find a bigger nicer space", but hey, the "take-away options are fantastic, as are the seasonal salads."

Taylor's Automatic Refresher   21 | 12 | 15 | $16
933 Main St. (bet. Charter Oak Ave. & Pope St.), St. Helena, 707-963-3486; www.taylorsrefresher.com

A "must-stop for lunch" in St. Helena, this "upscale California version of an old-fashioned fountain" delivers "2000s-style" Traditional American food in a "1950s-style outdoor diner" setting; "brave the lines for the tuna burger" and a "milkshake to break up a day of drinking" – or just go for an "interesting" vino selection (you can't "beat a drive-in that serves wine"); P.S. the Ferry building spin-off delivers some of the "best chic fast food" in SF.

TERRA   27 | 24 | 26 | $64
1345 Railroad Ave. (bet. Adams & Hunt Sts.), St. Helena, 707-963-8931; www.terrarestaurant.com

"Hiro is our hero" and he "makes beautiful music" in his St. Helena "hideaway", "blending disparate cuisines" from Northern Italian to Southern French into an "incredible" New American menu offset by "excellent wines" chorus fans of chef Sone; the "complete experience" is orchestrated by a "formal but friendly" staff that "describes every ingredient" in every "revelatory" bite, and it's served in a "gorgeous restored farmhouse" – talk about "romantic"; N.B. the chef and his co-owner wife recently opened Ame in SF.

TRA VIGNE   24 | 24 | 22 | $53
1050 Charter Oak Ave. (Hwy. 29), St. Helena, 707-963-4444; www.travignerestaurant.com

For a "taste of Tuscany" in St. Helena, join the "crowds pouring in" the "massive, impressive doors" of this "forever favorite"; you "never get tired of the earthy", "marvelous" Northern Italian fare and "artful wine pairings" agree *amici*, equally transported by the "delightful atmosphere that evokes the old country" and "lovely" courtyard offering a bit of "heaven" – "this is what a night out in Napa is all about"; still, a minority says it's "lost the magic" – positing it's "time for a rethink."

Underwood Bar & Bistro Ⓜ   23 | 22 | 20 | $40
9113 Graton Rd. (Edison St.), Graton, 707-823-7023; www.underwoodgraton.com

There "doesn't seem to be a soul" in Graton "until you part the velvet curtains" at this "stylish", "high-energy" "West County hangout" and find locals, "winery workers" and "tony weekenders packing the stools and tiny tables" with "resultant noise" "to match"; "what a rare find" – "city-style drinks" and "delicious" Mediterranean tapas and entrees made from local "bounty" – "just enjoy the people, food and atmosphere" – and overlook the "spotty" service; P.S. there's "more elbow room" to the rear.

Uva Trattoria & Bar Ⓜ   ▽ 23 | 17 | 23 | $34
1040 Clinton St. (Main St.), Napa, 707-255-6646; www.uvatrattoria.com

"The moment you walk in the door you're in for a special treat" exclaim locals who fall for the "lively" "neighborhood feel" of this "comfortable" trattoria "just off Main Street"; "vintage photographs of stars from way back when" set the "welcoming" stage for "delicious, but not pretentious" Southern Italian dishes and "interesting wines at reasonable prices", all served by a "caring staff"; "great jazz" in the "beautiful bar" Wednesday–Sunday "cinches" the deal: this is a Napa "must-do."

Wappo Bar Bistro
| 22 | 20 | 19 | $38 |

1226 Washington St. (Lincoln Ave.), Calistoga, 707-942-4712; www.wappobar.com

"Take a trip around the world" at this "oh-so-delightful", "Eclectic to the extreme" wine country bistro with a "low-key staff" serving a "wide range" of "innovative", "wonderfully delectable" globally inspired cuisines and a "nice" vino list to boot; the redwood interior with copper-topped tables is "seductive anytime", but "on warm Calistoga evenings" "nothing beats" relaxing on the "great" brick patio under the "large outdoor arbor."

Water Street Bistro ⊄
| ▽ 23 | 15 | 20 | $25 |

100 Petaluma Blvd. N. (Western Ave.), Petaluma, 707-763-9563

"What a delight" – "there's no better" breakfast or lunch place for Petaluma "foodies" agree *amis* who head to this French bistro and sit "right on the river bank" with a "latte and a properly made scone" or "perfect" sandwiches and soups "made with love" – and the "freshest local products"; chef-owner Stephanie Rastetter is such a "wonder" that her "themed prix fixe" dinners served once a month and on summer weekends "sell out" instantly, so call in advance.

Willi's Seafood & Raw Bar
| 24 | 20 | 19 | $43 |

403 Healdsburg Ave. (North St.), Healdsburg, 707-433-9191; www.willisseafood.net

Head to this "happening" Healdsburg seafood "adventure" for "small plates so delicious" and "creative" you "always end up ordering more than you planned" – little wonder why your tab "rises faster than the Titanic sinks"; the "spirited, lively" Havana-meets–New Orleans atmosphere is further fueled by a "raw bar for the purists" and a "joy" of a wine list, all delivered by an "engaging" staff that enhances the "memorable dining experience."

Willi's Wine Bar
| 26 | 18 | 20 | $42 |

Orchard Inn, 4404 Old Redwood Hwy. (River Rd.), Santa Rosa, 707-526-3096; www.williswinebar.net

"Borrow, beg or steal" to "experience" the "sensational" Eclectic small plates packed "with big flavors" inspired by "faraway lands" declare diehards – all it takes is a "single visit" to Santa Rosa's "slightly funky", "quintessential wine country" "roadhouse" to turn you into a "raving proselytizer"; "it's easy to spend far too much" on the "intriguing" dishes and "super selection" of vinos "but you won't be disappointed" – the "unique" nibbles may earn a "special place in the epicurean corner" of your mind.

Willow Wood Market Cafe
| 24 | 17 | 19 | $28 |

9020 Graton Rd. (Brush St.), Graton, 707-522-8372

Recently "renovated and ready to go" with an expanded wine bar, Underwood's "lovable" Eclectic-Mediterranean wine country sibling, set in Graton's "funky old general store" with "off-the-wall stuff for sale", serves a "great Sunday brunch", some of the "best sandwiches on the planet" and "upscale" dinner delights like "creamy polenta"; "add a cold pear cider and backyard patio and what more could you ask for?"; just "don't be in a hurry", because service is also "relaxed."

Wine Spectator Greystone   23 | 23 | 23 | $51
Culinary Institute of America, 2555 Main St. (Deer Park Rd.), St. Helena, 707-967-1010; www.ciachef.edu
"Take the tour" of St. Helena's CIA school, then head up to the "beautiful historic restaurant" in the "old Christian Brothers winery", a "big, noisy", "festive" "foodie's" destination where "hot chef Jimmy Corwell" (not students) prepares "outstanding" Californian fare and the staff "aims to please"; for a "real treat", dine on the outside terrace or sit by the open kitchen for a "bird's-eye view of the action" – what a "culinary show!"; still, a few grumblers grouse "expected more."

Wine Valley Restaurant   – | – | – | M
1146 Main St. (Pope St.), St. Helena, 707-963-3371
In a county brimming with high-end restaurants, this homey locals' joint in Downtown St. Helena offers refreshingly affordable, unpretentious Cal-Italian lunch and dinner fare; the chef hails from the now-shuttered Green Valley Cafe, and diners familiar with that venture will recognize some carryovers on the menu; as expected, local vino, with a smattering of Chiantis, comprises the wine list.

Yankee Pier   17 | 15 | 17 | $32
286 Magnolia Ave. (bet. King St. & William Ave.), Larkspur, 415-924-7676; www.yankeepier.com
For "New England crab shack fun", head to Bradley Ogden's "informal", "kid-friendly" Larkspur and Santana Row outposts and "feast" on "chowda", "fried clams as big as your fist" and lobster rolls that "fill the fish niche nicely" in digs so "East Coast preppy" you can almost "hear a foghorn on a rainy day"; but the less-finatical deem it "disappointing" – you can't "pretend to be a Yankee" in California; N.B. there's a SFO branch too.

Zaré   ▽ 21 | 14 | 21 | $44
5091 Solano Ave. (Oak Knoll Ave.), Napa, 707-257-3318; www.zarenapa.com
"Don't let the gypsy decor" or the "funky" locale "fool you", because Hoss Zaré's "hidden gem" is not only "one of the most interesting places in Napa" – some say it's even "better" than his now-defunct Downtown SF restaurant, especially if you eat "outdoors with the jazz trio"; this chef "aims to please", "personally greeting and hobnobbing with his guests" while the Cal-Med combos are "fantastic, interesting and creative"; N.B. a new building is going up on the grounds, with an on-site wine bar to follow.

zazu   25 | 20 | 23 | $45
3535 Guerneville Rd. (Willowside Rd.), Santa Rosa, 707-523-4814; www.zazurestaurant.com
What a "special feeling" – you'll get the "warmest reception in the Valley" at Santa Rosa's "bohemian", "somewhat rustic roadhouse" where a "quirky chef couple" puts plenty of "heart into their craft", "zazounding" even "jaded palates" with "original", "always gourmet takeoffs" on New "Americana"–Northern Italian dishes including "delicious" "homemade pastas and salumi"; check out the "wonderful" 'Pinot and Pizza Nights' – it's a "very reasonable alternative to a regular dinner" – and "be sure to hit their Healdsburg" offshoot, Bovolo.

Zin 20 | 17 | 20 | $38

344 Center St. (North St.), Healdsburg, 707-473-0946;
www.zinrestaurant.com

For "down-home goodness in Sonoma County", take ze to this
"locals' favorite" in Healdsburg and dine in "industrial digs" on
"robust" New American fare made with produce "fresh from the
Zin garden"; "it's all about the blue-plate specials" – and they "go
really well" with a wine list that spotlights "never-heard-of"
Zinfandels and "varietals not starting with 'Z'"; a handful, however,
huff that the combos are "bizarre" and the staff "too casual."

Zinsvalley ⊠ ▽ 19 | 15 | 18 | $37

Browns Valley Shopping Ctr., 3253 Browns Valley Rd. (bet. Austin &
Larkin Sts.), Napa, 707-224-0695; www.zinsvalley.com

The "closest thing to a neighborhood-comfortable joint in Napa",
this "quaint", "homey" haunt lures Browns Valleyites to its "obscure" strip-mall location with "solid" New American vittles and
an "unexpected" plus: a "lovely outdoor" deck next to a creek;
two fireplaces, an "interesting selection of wines" including
(what else) "great" Zinfandels and "no corkage" fee give locals
even more rea-Zins to make this spot their "relaxed" "hangout."

Zuzu 25 | 19 | 21 | $36

829 Main St. (bet. 2nd & 3rd Sts.), Napa, 707-224-8555;
www.zuzunapa.com

You'll "feel like you're in San Sebastian, Spain", instead of
Downtown Napa at this "tapatastic" small-plate "heaven with atmosphere" aplenty and "fair prices" to boot; it's a "fun place" "to
relax Spanish-style" thanks to a "creative" menu with a Latin
American–Iberian "bent" and a vino list that boasts "fantastic"
Southern Hemisphere selections, "considering" you're in California
wine country; P.S. it's less of a "crowded" zu at lunchtime.

South of San Francisco

Top Ratings South of SF

Excluding places with low voting, unless indicated.

Food

28 Marinus
Kaygetsu
27 Manresa
Le Papillon
Sierra Mar
L'Auberge Carmel
26 Tamarine
La Forêt
Cafe Gibraltar
Marché

Oswald
Pacific's Edge
Bouchée
Fresh Cream
25 Evvia
Koi Palace
Village Pub
Bistro Elan
John Bentley's
Amber India

By Cuisine

American
27 Manresa
26 Pacific's Edge
25 Village Pub
John Bentley's
24 Flea St. Café

Asian
26 Tamarine
25 Alexander's Steak
24 Flying Fish Grill
22 Three Seasons
21 Straits Café

Californian
27 Sierra Mar
L'Auberge Carmel
26 Oswald
Bouchée
25 Parcel 104

Chinese
25 Koi Palace
O'mei
22 Fook Yuen Seafood
Hunan Home's
21 Chef Chu's

Continental
26 Fresh Cream
24 Chantilly
23 Anton & Michel
Ecco
20 Maddalena's

French
28 Marinus
27 Le Papillon
26 La Forêt
Marché
25 Emile's

Italian
24 Osteria
22 Casanova
Pizza Antica
Pasta Moon*
21 La Strada

Japanese
28 Kaygetsu
24 Flying Fish Grill
22 Fuki Sushi
21 Blowfish Sushi
18 Juban

Mediterranean
26 Cafe Gibraltar
25 Evvia
23 Stokes
Brigitte's▽
Café Marcella

Seafood
25 Passionfish
24 Flying Fish Grill
22 Pisces
20 Sardine Factory
19 Barbara Fishtrap

By Special Feature

Breakfast/Brunch
26 La Forêt
25 Koi Palace
24 Flea St. Café
   Navio
   Gayle's

Outdoor Seating
27 Sierra Mar
25 Bistro Elan
24 Roy's at Pebble Beach
   Anton & Michel
   Casanova

People-Watching
26 Tamarine
25 Evvia
   Village Pub
22 Spago Palo Alto
20 Zibibbo

Romance
28 Marinus
27 Le Papillon
   Sierra Mar
   L'Auberge Carmel
26 La Forêt

Singles Scenes
23 Seven
20 Zibibbo
19 Cascal
   E&O Trading Co.
17 Kingfish

Small Plates
26 Tamarine
23 Stokes
22 Three Seasons
21 Straits Cafe
   Zucca

Tasting Menus
28 Marinus
   Kaygetsu
27 Manresa
   Le Papillon
   L'Auberge Carmel

Winning Wine Lists
28 Marinus
27 Le Papillon
   Sierra Mar
   L'Auberge Carmel
26 Bouchée

By Location

Carmel/Monterey
28 Marinus
27 Sierra Mar
   L'Auberge Carmel
26 Pacific's Edge
   Bouchée

Half Moon Bay/Coast
26 Cafe Gibraltar
24 Navio
22 Pasta Moon
   Cetrella Bistro
21 Taqueria 3 Amigos

Palo Alto/Menlo Park
28 Kaygetsu
26 Tamarine
   Marché
25 Evvia
   Bistro Elan

Peninsula
25 Koi Palace
   Village Pub
   John Bentley's
24 Chantilly
23 Viognier

Santa Cruz/Capitola
26 Oswald
25 O'mei
24 Gayle's Bakery
22 Gabriella Café
20 Shadowbrook

Silicon Valley
27 Manresa
   Le Papillon
26 La Forêt
25 Amber India
   Emile's

Top Decor

28	Sierra Mar		Nepenthe
	Pacific's Edge		Tamarine
27	Navio		Manresa
	Shadowbrook		Village Pub
26	Marinus		Cetrella Bistro
	Roy's at Pebble Beach	23	Marché
	La Forêt		Fresh Cream
25	Sino		Evvia
	L'Auberge Carmel		Seven
24	Le Papillon		Casanova

Top Service

27	Le Papillon		Pacific's Edge
	L'Auberge Carmel		Marché
	Marinus		Sent Sovi
26	Manresa	24	Navio
	Kaygetsu		Bella Vista
25	Fresh Cream		Oswald*
	Emile's		Chantilly
	La Forêt*		Village Pub
	Sierra Mar		Plumed Horse
	Chez TJ	23	Anton & Michel

Top Bangs for the Buck

1. In-N-Out Burger	11. jZcool
2. Taqueria 3 Amigos	12. Udupi Palace
3. La Taqueria	13. Amici E. Coast Pizza
4. Pancho Villa	14. Dish Dash
5. Pho Hoa-Hiep II	15. Pasta Pomodoro
6. La Cumbre Taqueria	16. North Beach Pizza
7. Burger Joint	17. Shalimar
8. Gayle's Bakery	18. Zao Noodle
9. Cool Café	19. Passage to India
10. Patxi's Chicago Pizza	20. Pizza Antica

Other Good Values

Basque Cultural Ctr.	Mezza Luna
Cetrella Bistro	Montrio Bistro
Da Kitchen	Passionfish
Flea St. Café	Stokes
Flying Fish Grill	Straits Cafe
Hong Kong Flower	Tamarine
Juban	Taqueria Tlaquepaque
Koi Palace	Tarpy's Roadhouse
La Victoria Taqueria	Three Seasons
Lure	Turmeric

South of San Francisco

F	D	S	C

Alexander's Steakhouse
25 | 23 | 23 | $63

Vallco Shopping Ctr., 10330 N. Wolfe Rd. (Wolfe Rd.), Cupertino, 408-446-2222; www.alexanderssteakhouse.com

Despite "cow carcasses" hanging around and "$100 Kobe beef" specials (for "when you hit the lottery"), "steakhouse is a misnomer" for this "showy, stylish" Cupertino Asian meatery whose "menu goes far beyond" "basic offerings to awesome" East-West small plates; add in an "impeccable" wine-savvy staff that "caters to Japanese businessmen" and "Silicon Valley–casual" expense-accounters and it's no wonder a meal "feels like an event"; still, a few malcontents moo that it's a "lot of bucks for simple bull."

Amber Café
25 | 19 | 20 | $32

600 W. El Camino Real (Castro St.), Mountain View, 650-9698-1751

Amber India
Olive Tree Shopping Ctr., 2290 W. El Camino Real (Rengstorff Ave.), Mountain View, 650-968-7511
377 Santana Row (Olsen Dr.), San Jose, 408-248-5400
www.amber-india.com

"Northern Indian food is served with an extra helping of class" at this Mountain View original and "trendier", "swankier" Santana Row locale that "stand apart from the hoi-polloi"; the "luncheon buffet is very satisfying, but it really comes to life in the evening" when "unique creations" including curries and tandoori that are "spicy without being four-alarm mouth burners" take center stage; N.B. the Amber Café spin-off, serving chaats and small bites, opened post-*Survey*.

Amici's East Coast Pizzeria
20 | 12 | 17 | $19

790 Castro St. (Church St.), Mountain View, 650-961-6666
226 Redwood Shores Pkwy. (Twin Dolphin Dr.), Redwood Shores, 650-654-3333
69 Third Ave. (San Mateo Dr.), San Mateo, 650-342-9392
www.amicis.com

See review in City of San Francisco Directory.

Anton & Michel Restaurant
23 | 22 | 23 | $51

Mission St. (bet. Ocean & 7th Aves.), Carmel, 831-624-2406;
www.antonandmichel.com

For more than 25 years, this "quaint" "Carmel must" has represented the ne plus ultra in "old-world Cal-Continental dining", where veteran waiters prepare "Caesar salad for two and carve Châteaubriand tableside like the days" of "your grandparents" and uncork treasures from the "unusually superior" 700-bottle wine cellar; though a few feel the formula "needs rejuvenation", romantics concede the "elegant", "peaceful" "courtyard" setting, replete with a reflecting pool and fountains, compensates for any "lack of pizzazz in the food."

A.P. Stump's   21 | 22 | 21 | $49 |
163 W. Santa Clara St. (bet. Almaden Blvd. & San Pedro St.), San Jose, 408-292-9928; www.apstumps.com

"It's hard to say what's prettier – the staff", the "clubby decor" or the "exquisitely presented", "signature steaks" – at San Jose's "beautiful" "businessman's" chophouse "a short stroll from the HP Pavillion"; while a few foodies beef that it's "lost its edge" now that it "no longer produces the imaginative" dishes on the "original Stump's menu", for most it still delivers an "exceptional dining experience" though at "stratospheric", "special-occasion" prices.

Arcadia   23 | 21 | 21 | $53 |
San Jose Marriott, 100 W. San Carlos St. (Market St.), San Jose, 408-278-4555; www.michaelmina.net

"A fine choice for a business dinner" "when you crave" Michael Mina's "imaginative" New American food without the drive or "the wait", this "sleek" San Jose Marriott offshoot offers "great wines" and "decadent", "down-home" signature dishes like lobster pot pie and "tasty corn dogs" that "make people clog up the SF" mother ship; still, cynics snap it's "rather austere" ("feels like a hotel restaurant, wait – it is") and "marred by" "slow service."

A Tavola   20 | 21 | 19 | $36 |
1041 Middlefield Rd. (Jefferson St.), Redwood City, 650-995-9800; www.atavoladining.com

Still a "crowd-pleaser" following a post-fire move in 2005 from San Carlos, this "welcome addition to the RWC dining scene" boasts a "lovely dark" ambiance with "well-chosen" wines, a "revamped" Cal-Italian menu of "hearty" fare and a staff so "friendly" you feel like you're "eating at your long-lost cousin's"; if a few table their enthusiasm, claiming the eats lack "zip" and "service is inconsistent", for most it's "so much better" than before.

Barbara's Fishtrap ⌀   19 | 12 | 16 | $22 |
281 Capistrano Rd. (Hwy. 1), Princeton by the Sea, 650-728-7049

For fish 'n' chips "better than in all of the U.K.", drop anchor at "Bab's" "cheesy" "strictly cash" "coastal dive" overlooking Princeton Harbor where there's "always a wait" for fried "seafood served on patterned oilcloth by casual wait-folk"; if you want your "fresh" catch "in a flash", sidle up to the "take-out window" and savor it with a brew on the "picnic tables."

Basin, The   20 | 19 | 22 | $40 |
14572 Big Basin Way (5th St.), Saratoga, 408-867-1906; www.thebasin.com

The "personable" staff supplies "excellent" service at this "upscale" yet "comfortable" Saratoga "hangout" that also lures "locals" with "creative", "tasty" Spanish-accented New American fare along with "well-made cocktails" and "good finds" on the wine list; the "lovely patio" canopied by a 120-year-old oak tree is "great for small celebrations", and though a few pout it's "pricey", more deem it a "favorite" for "fun in the suburbs."

Basque Cultural Center Ⓜ   19 | 13 | 18 | $28 |
599 Railroad Ave. (bet. Orange & Spruce Aves.), South San Francisco, 650-583-8091; www.basqueculturalcenter.com

This South San Francisco banquet hall may resemble an "Elks Lodge" and its patrons are more "old-timers" than "Gen-X", but diners "eat high on the hog" on "good", "classic", daily changing Basque specialties, washed down with "great" French or Spanish wines; even if the atmosphere's "not conducive to romance", the "hearty" "family-style portions and "unbeatable" prices give "bargain-hunters" a lot to love.

Bella Vista ⑤ Ⓜ   22 | 21 | 24 | $48 |

13451 Skyline Blvd. (5 mi. south of Rte. 92), Woodside, 650-851-1229; www.bvrestaurant.com
"Nestled high in the woods", this "old-style" Woodside "destination" is "hard to beat" for its "majestic" South Bay and cityscape views and "wonderful" service from a tuxedeo-clad staff that prepares flambéed dishes tableside; the French-Italian cuisine is "outstanding", the soufflés are the "best" and the wines from the 600-bottle list are "excellent", and even if "getting there is a trip" and the "drive back down the hill is sobering" (along with the prices), most report the "warm ambiance" makes it "worth" the effort.

Bistro Elan ⑤ Ⓜ   25 | 18 | 22 | $47 |

448 S. California Ave. (El Camino Real), Palo Alto, 650-327-0284
Peninsula diners would "prefer that you not tell anyone" about this "small, hidden neighborhood" bistro because it's already "crowded" to the rafters with Palo Alto's "movers and shakers" who recognize that the "limited" selection of "seasonal", "divine" Cal-French fare and the "well-priced wines" proffered by an "informed" staff "make up for any deficiency in size" and dining room "din"; it's "fun to sit at the bar", but in warm weather, nothing compares to the "beautiful garden out back."

Bistro Vida   18 | 19 | 19 | $35 |

641 Santa Cruz Ave. (El Camino Real), Menlo Park, 650-462-1686
Montmarte "comes to Menlo Park" at this "lovely", independently operated Parisian-inspired bistro that offers Francophiles a "more authentic" yet "low-key" spin on the chalkboard menu of "classics" than the "well-known" chainster next door; although the food and "service can falter", few mind as the "friendliest" proprietor and "comfortable" interior inspires *amis* to "catch up" over an alfresco brunch or "linger" "over a glass of wine" with a "copy of *Le Monde*."

Blowfish Sushi To Die For   21 | 20 | 16 | $38 |

335 Santana Row (off Stevens Creek Blvd.), San Jose, 408-345-3848; www.blowfishsushi.com
See review in City of San Francisco Directory.

Bouchée   26 | 21 | 21 | $65 |

Mission St. (bet. Ocean & 7th Aves.), Carmel, 831-626-7880; www.boucheecarmel.com
Still "holding on to the 'best in Carmel' designation nicely", L'Auberge Carmel's "smart", "small" "romantic" older sibling and "connected wine boutique" delights sophisticates; chef Walter Manzke's "very creative" Californian cuisine, including "killer" prix fixe dinners, is "artfully plated" and worth "lingering over", especially when offset by "brilliantly-thought-out" and -priced vintages, plus the "owner makes you feel like you're the most important customers he has"; still, a few fret about "snaillike service", opining that the "pace needs to be picked up."

Brigitte's French Mediterranean Gourmet & Healthy Cuisine ⑤ Ⓜ
▽ 23 | 14 | 21 | $38

351 Saratoga Ave. (Pruneridge Ave.), Santa Clara, 408-246-2333; www.brigittescuisine.com

"A breath of French air" in Santa Clara, this "authentic" "charmer" also delivers a "lovely", "flavorful" taste of the Mediterranean in "seasonal" dishes that are "as billed, healthy" (if *un peu* "pricey"); though a few find the strip-mall setting "slightly odd", the "personal" service and "doting" attention from Brigitte herself make it "easy to overlook" the "simple" decor and "small" space.

Buca di Beppo
14 | 16 | 16 | $25

Pruneyard Shopping Ctr., 1875 S. Bascom Ave. (Campbell Ave.), Campbell, 408-377-7722
643 Emerson St. (bet. Forest & Hamilton Aves.), Palo Alto, 650-329-0665
Oakridge Mall, 925 Blossom Hill Rd. (Santa Teresa Blvd.), San Jose, 408-226-1444
www.bucadibeppo.com

Though they "wouldn't admit it in public", bands of Bay Area *paesani* pack this "raucous", "red-checkered-tablecloth" chain to "yell across the table", imbibe "big bottles of wine" and share "tubs" of "decent", "old-school Italo-American" in "warrens" of "kitsch-filled" rooms that, like the "energetic" staff, either "amuse or horrify"; it's "fun" for "birthday parties", "family get-togethers" and folks "on a budget", but certainly "not a place for snobs."

Burger Joint ⚫
19 | 13 | 14 | $12

San Francisco Int'l Airport, Int'l Terminal, Boarding Area A, South San Francisco, 650-583-5863
See review in City of San Francisco Directory.

CAFE GIBRALTAR Ⓜ
26 | 21 | 22 | $38

425 Ave. Alhambra (Palma St.), El Granada, 650-560-9039; www.cafegibraltar.com

"Walk through those magical doors" to reach this "unexpected coastal pleasure" in El Granada that "conjures up a bazaar in Morocco", serving "imaginative" Mediterranean fare that's a "joy to experience"; "recline on pillows at booths", tuck into "luscious bread and meze dips" that marry "sweet and savory flavors" with "fresh ingredients" and watch the chefs "perform a ballet of steaming pots and pans"; if a few find the service "typical Half Moon Bay" – "friendly" but "spotty" – most gladly make "the drive over the hill."

Cafe Grillades
▽ 18 | 11 | 18 | $13

(fka Crepes du Monde)
Bayhill Shopping Ctr., 851 Cherry Ave. (San Bruno Ave.), San Bruno, 650-589-3778; www.cafegrillades.com

This casual, butter-yellow Bretonne-style eatery in San Bruno recently changed its name from Crepes du Monde after opening a Hayes Valley outpost and expanded its Mediterranean menu too; while the "terrific" crêpes remain a highlight, with over 40 different types of "authentic", "unusual" savory and sweet fillings, diners can also choose from affordable omelets (served all day), plus the namesake 'grillades' (charcoal-grilled steak, chicken or burgers), kebabs, panini and North African halal dinners.

Café Marcella Ⓜ | 23 | 19 | 21 | $45 |
368 Village Ln. (bet. N. Santa Cruz & University Aves.), Los Gatos,
408-354-8006; www.cafemarcella.com
Los Gatos locals dub this long-running "bustling" cafe "the 'everyday Manresa'" thanks to its "high-gourmet" French-Med meals, prepared with the "freshest ingredients" and paired with an "excellent" list of "reasonably priced" wines; despite "changes in the kitchen" it remains a "top choice" for lunch, when "big windows" let in "lots of sunlight" and at night, when the "huge bar" radiates with "activity"; still, a noise-sensitive few say it's "a bit loud when full."

Casanova | 22 | 23 | 21 | $50 |
Fifth Ave. (Mission St.), Carmel, 831-625-0501;
www.casanovarestaurant.com
Casanovas looking "to impress their sweetie" book a table at this "darling" Northern Italian–French destination in Carmel with a "comprehensive" 1,700-bottle wine list, "charming", "cozy feel", "funky rooms and patios" and "warm service" that pays "attention to details" – "add the right person and you have a romantic experience to die for"; but the less-smitten find the vinos "wildly overpriced" and fare "just average", sighing it "used to be better."

Cascal | 19 | 21 | 18 | $33 |
400 Castro St. (California St.), Mountain View, 650-940-9500;
www.cascalrestaurant.com
"Plentiful sangria", "tasty tapas", "vibrant" "Vegas-like" decor and "live jazz on the weekends" keep the "'in' crowd" "happy" at this "energetic" Pan-Latin Mountain Viewer that "brings a bit of class to a street overrun with cheap dives"; "make reservations or you'll literally be out in the cold warming your hands on the heaters" as the joint is jumpin' "later than most Peninsula" haunts; however, it's "too loud" for others who also find the fare "mediocre at best."

Cetrella Bistro & Café | 22 | 24 | 20 | $45 |
845 Main St. (Monte Vista Ln.), Half Moon Bay, 650-726-4090;
www.cetrella.com
With its "absolutely lovely" "Tuscan farmhouse" interior, "well-prepared" Northern Mediterranean bistro fare, "fairly extensive wine list" and "top-flight" jazz, this "ambitious" Half Moon Bay "favorite" could "be a star in wine country or a mainstay in the city"; that said, "locals" are "truly glad it's hidden away in my corner of the coast" – the only thing "missing is an ocean-front view" and a "consistent" staff – unfortunately, "it varies wildly between attentive and snotty."

Chantilly Ⓢ | 24 | 23 | 24 | $56 |
3001 El Camino Real (Selby Ln.), Redwood City, 650-321-4080;
www.chantillyrestaurant.com
"It doesn't get much more old-school" than this "rare formal option" in Redwood City that "turns back the hands of time to when dining out was a special occasion"; while the "remembrances of the 1970s" Continental menu is lost on the "Generation X"–set, proponents insist "look past the wealthy" "blue-hairs" and "stuffy atmosphere" – heck, "take your grandmother if you have to" – but do come here to "celebrate" in style – down to a complimentary rose for the ladies at the end.

CHEESECAKE FACTORY, THE   16 | 16 | 15 | $26

925 Blossom Hill Rd. (bet. Oakridge Mall & Winfield Blvd.), San Jose, 408-225-6948 Ⓢ Ⓜ
Westfield Shoppingtown Valley Fair, 3041 Stevens Creek Blvd.
(bet. S. Redwood Ave. & Winchester Blvd.), Santa Clara, 408-246-0092;
www.thecheesecakefactory.com ●
See review in City of San Francisco Directory.

Chef Chu's   21 | 14 | 18 | $26

1067 N. San Antonio Rd. (El Camino Real), Los Altos, 650-948-2696;
www.chefchu.com
For "authentic, delicious" Chinese in Silicon Valley, Chu-hounds feel "you can't do better" "without traveling to SF" than this "go-to" Los Altos Sino "old reliable" that "continues to shine", luring "crowds" with an "extensive menu of traditional and new dishes"; if the less-enthralled feel it's "like an aging starlet" that "hasn't upgraded in years" and could "really use a face-lift", they may want to reassess since it was renovated in 2006.

Chez Shea Ⓢ Ⓜ   – | – | – | I

408 Main St. (Mill St.), Half Moon Bay, 650-560-9234
Globe-trotters feel right at home at Cafe Gibraltar's new Downtown Half Moon Bay sibling, a thimble-sized, casual, counter-service all-day eatery serving an Eclectic, ethnically varied menu of organic comfort food; start with chilequilles or green eggs and ham scramble for weekend brunch, then make your way around the world during the week with dishes like chile verde, Asian pasta, falafel and even Slow Food–inspired stews.

Chez TJ Ⓢ Ⓜ   24 | 22 | 25 | $80

938 Villa St. (bet. Castro St. & Shoreline Blvd.), Mountain View, 650-964-7466; www.cheztj.com
Mountain View's "über-special occasion" dinner house, set in a "charming Victorian" dating back to 1890, continues to impress "friends – rich friends", that is, with its "informed staff", "romantic setting" and "tremendously good" New French prix fixe tasting menu from a "talented new chef" (with "improved wine pairings" to boot); still, a handful huff that it's "all shake but no bake", citing "nano"-sized portions and "sporadic service", which makes it hard to "justify the extremely high prices."

Club XIX   ▽ 22 | 24 | 22 | $72

The Lodge at Pebble Beach, 17 Mile Dr. (Hwy. 1), Pebble Beach, 831-625-8519; www.pebblebeach.com
"If you're over 60 play golf and drive a large, showy car", this Lodge restaurant "looking over the 18th green at Pebble Beach" delivers a "delightful dining experience, in a retro" jacket-suggested "sort of way" complete with "impeccable" Cal-French fare, cigars and vintage cognacs; if you're not, "bring somebody else's wallet" and enjoy a drink on the patio or in the less-formal Stillwater Bar and Grill upstairs; N.B. a chef change in early 2006 may impact the Food score.

Cool Café Ⓜ   21 | 18 | 13 | $17

Stanford Univ. Cantor Arts Ctr., 328 Lomita Dr. (Museum Way), Palo Alto, 650-725-4758; www.cooleatz.com
"What's better than eating on a veranda" or in the "sublime" Stanford "campus lunch" cafe "overlooking the fabulous Rodin

Sculpture Garden" muse "socially conscious foodies" and Cantor Art Center exhibit-goers who also put chef Jesse Cool's (Flea St. Café, jZcool) "inventive", organic Californian fare on a pedestal; if a few find the "long" counter lines "rather cafeteria-ish", supporters retort the "sandwiches are greater works of art than anything in the museum next door"; N.B. dinner served on Thursdays.

Da Kitchen ☒ ▽ 18 | 9 | 16 | $14 |

1477 Plymouth St. (Shoreline Blvd.), Mountain View, 650-960-6906; www.da-kitchen.com
For "a taste of old Hawaii without the palm trees or the isolation", this Mountain View outpost of the popular Maui cheap "grindz" chain is "da place", scooping up the "most authentic" "mixed-plate lunches" (kalua pork, Spam fried rice) "east of the islands" complete with "gigantic" portions and "relaxed island service"; the "tacky decorations and plastic lawn chairs" merely enhance the "onolicious" experience; N.B. closes 3 PM on Saturday.

Dasaprakash ▽ 21 | 20 | 20 | $19 |

2636 Homestead Rd. (bet. Kiely Blvd. & San Tomas Expwy.), Santa Clara, 408-246-8292; www.dasaprakash.com
You can even "bring omnivore friends" to this vegetarian Southern Indian restaurant (affiliated with outposts abroad and Southern California) hidden in a Santa Clara strip mall that also delights expats and "American palates"; the menu offers a "good cross-section" of the "bright flavors of Bangalore" including "amazing dosas" and Thali plates while the "attractive, calm interior and very accommodating staff" make for a "nice evening out."

Dish Dash ☒ 24 | 17 | 19 | $23 |

190 S. Murphy Ave. (Washington Ave.), Sunnyvale, 408-774-1889; www.dishdash.net
Middle Eastern mavens "love lunching" at this "bustling" "favorite" crowning it "Silicon Valley's falafel champion", while other savvy Sunnyvalers "wade through" the meze and "head straight to the *mansaf*" (the signature lamb stew), one of several "pleasing" dinner options proffered in the "hookah bar expansion" next door; if a handful dish about "long waits" and the "cacophony of concurrent conversations", acolytes dash back it's "worth putting up with."

Duarte's Tavern 19 | 12 | 17 | $26 |

202 Stage Rd. (Pescadero Rd.), Pescadero, 650-879-0464; www.duartestavern.com
"It sounds like a broken record, but it remains true": stick to the "legendary soups" ("amazing artichoke, green chile"), "freshest of fish" (crab cioppino, abalone) and the seasonal olallieberry "pie to die for" and "you won't regret" the "drive down the coast" to get to this "fourth-generation" Pescadero "roadside dive"; Traditional American eats aside, the "mobbed" "Wild West cowboy bar" lures an "eclectic customer base" while service is the "salt-of-the-earth sort" – no wonder this "old standby keeps rocking."

Duck Club, The 20 | 20 | 20 | $47 |

Stanford Park Hotel, 100 El Camino Real (Sand Hill Rd.), Menlo Park, 650-330-2790; www.stanfordparkhotel.com
Monterey Plaza Hotel & Spa, 400 Cannery Row (Wave St.), Monterey, 831-646-1700; www.woodsidehotels.com
This archipelago of "conservative" Bay Area country clubs is "just ducky" for "impressing business associates with your good

taste" in "fancy" New American fare, a "substantial wine list and a substantial check" and you can turn them onto a "hidden jewel of a bar" too; but squawkers quack about "mundane" fare and a "hotel feeling" – looks like it was "decorated by the Audubon Society."

E&O Trading Company   19 | 21 | 17 | $34
96 S. First St. (San Fernando St.), San Jose, 408-938-4100;
www.eotrading.com
See review in City of San Francisco Directory.

Ecco Restaurant ⑤   23 | 21 | 22 | $47
322 Lorton Ave. (Burlingame Ave.), Burlingame, 650-342-7355;
www.eccorestaurant.com
A "secret" despite being around since "the '80s", this "pricey" Burlingamer makes an "excellent" go-to spot on the mid-Peninsula for "business lunches and dinners" thanks to its "elegant atmosphere", "attractive garden" and "professional" staff; insiders insist it's "worth going out of your way" for the "creative" Cal-Continental cuisine and "sublime desserts", but others shrug there aren't "many surprises."

Emile's ⑤Ⓜ   25 | 19 | 25 | $54
545 S. Second St. (bet. Reed & William Sts.), San Jose, 408-289-1960;
www.emiles.com
"It's all about" the Swiss Mister "Emile Mooser – his style, presence and personal touch" proclaim patrons who are "delighted" when the "charming" chef "stops tableside to chat" – he "makes any occasion a special one" at his "fabulous" fine-dining establishment in San Jose; while "delicious" offerings like fondue reveal his "roots", soufflés and entrees have an "elegant" French flair, making for an experience that's "outstanding in every way."

Eulipia Restaurant & Bar Ⓜ   22 | 19 | 20 | $38
374 S. First St. (bet. San Carlos & San Salvador Sts.), San Jose,
408-280-6161; www.eulipia.com
Conveniently located near the California Theatre, this long-running New American maintains its rep as a "good choice before a San Jose Rep play", with a "congenial staff" working the massive dining room large enough to hold a cast of 200; season ticket holders insist "you gotta 'lava' the chocolate volcano" and the "well-executed" "standards", but critics "yearn for the opening days" when this performer had a bit more "edge."

EVVIA   25 | 23 | 23 | $46
420 Emerson St. (bet. Lytton & University Aves.), Palo Alto, 650-326-0983;
www.evvia.net
A "festive" "big fat Greek wedding of an atmosphere" "delights" visitors to this "noisy" Hellenic-Med taverna where "briskly served sensations" "fit for the gods" are ferried to table by "flirty" waiters; the "cozy" ambiance sets an "inviting" stage to "savor" a "hearty" meal whether you "come for lunch and see all the Palo Alto power players" or take a dinner "date – chicks love it", "linger over" the "equally fabulous vinos" and plan your "next visit."

Fahrenheit Ultra Lounge ⑤Ⓜ   ▽ 19 | 23 | 18 | $31
99 E. San Fernando St. (3rd St.), San Jose, 408-998-9998;
www.fahrenheitultralounge.com
"Hip", "trendy and different", this new San Jose "hangout" offers "surprisingly good" "creative" Eclectic tapas to the afternoon

business set and DJs, jazz and karaoke nights for the "good-looking" "after-work" and after-hours "club crowd" who come to "mingle" over cocktails as the "evening wears on and it becomes more a lounge"; however, a few quip that it still "doesn't know what it wants to be when it grows up."

Fandango　　　　23｜21｜23｜$41

223 17th St. (bet. Laurel & Lighthouse Aves.), Pacific Grove, 831-372-3456; www.fandangorestaurant.com

It's "like meandering into a French cottage" coo acolytes who fandango over to this Pacific Grove "staple" on the Monterey Peninsula that "never fails to please" with "flawlessly prepared" Mediterranean fare and international wines served with a dose of "old-world hospitality" by "European waiters who add to the ambiance"; "for a quieter experience, sit in one of the smaller" areas – the "fireplace room is always full, therefore noisier" – then "treat" yourself to a "wonderful dining experience."

Flea St. Café Ⓜ　　　　24｜18｜21｜$42

3607 Alameda de las Pulgas (Avy Ave.), Menlo Park, 650-854-1226; www.cooleatz.com

Jesse Cool's "long-standing" Menlo Park pioneer ("the original restaurant to go organic") continues to please Peninsula patrons with "delicious", "innovative", "sustainable" and "local" Cal–New American fare that's "as satisfying to the palate as to the conscience"; "once you find" this "lovely intimate" "hideaway", you "keep coming back" for the "top-grade preparations" that "highlight the best of the season", as well as the "excellent wine selection", "wonderful friendly service" and weekend brunch to boot.

Flying Fish Grill　　　　24｜20｜23｜$41

Carmel Plaza, Mission St. (bet. Ocean & 7th Aves.), Carmel, 831-625-1962

When "feeling fishy", locals "fly" to this "ichiban" "treasure" of Downtown Carmel with a "Japanese speakeasy" feel to get "Kenny'd" by "warm, friendly" "host/owner/chef/comedian/musician" Kenny Fukomoto whose "pithy comments" make you feel like a "V.I.P."; duck into this "secret lair" (still "undiscovered by tourists – yeah!)" for "imaginative, delicious" Cal-Asian dishes "based on the freshest seafood" and you'll "feel like you got your money's worth" in this "expensive town."

Flying Fish Grill Ⓜ　　　▽ 21｜12｜17｜$20

99 San Mateo Rd. (bet. Main St. & Rte. 92), Half Moon Bay, 650-712-1125; www.flyingfishgrill.net

Although this "kitschy", "hole-in-the-wall", "deep-fried seafood" roadside shack (and adjacent fish market) would be "more at home in Hawaii than the foggy coast of Half Moon Bay", surfer dudes and road-trippers swear the "fish tacos are the best north of Baja"; while the decor is reel "divey", the "quick, cheap" fin fare is "surprisingly well prepared", making it "well worth the visit when out on the coast."

Fook Yuen Seafood　　　　22｜10｜13｜$25

195 El Camino Real (Victoria Ave.), Millbrae, 650-692-8600

"Swarming with families on weekends", this "wildly popular" "Millbrae landmark" and Singaporean–Hong Kong import is definitely "not your typical cheap Chinese" standby; "fresh ingredients translate" into excellent "dim sum" and "awesome" fish dishes (the "prawns were probably swimming when you arrived"), all so "enjoyable" you're willing to "tolerate the service" (you'll "wish you had an interpreter"), "showroom/warehouse surroundings" and "crowds" ("wait it out").

Forbes Mill Steakhouse   22 | 21 | 21 | $58
206 N. Santa Cruz Ave. (Royce St.), Los Gatos, 408-395-6434;
www.forbesmillsteakhouse.com
"Definitely for the high-roller carnivore crowd" ("take the boss from out of town, as long as he's paying"), this "clubby, darkly lit", "lively" American steakhouse in Los Gatos and its new Danville sidekick "can set you up with some fine" Kobe beef bred in the U.S. that's a "cut above" with "tasty sides" and a "good wine list to complement the experience"; still, cynics carp that the "deal-making chatter makes it too noisy" and mutter it's a "mite too pricey."

Fresh Cream   26 | 23 | 25 | $64
Heritage Harbor, 99 Pacific St. (bet. Artillery & Scott Sts.),
Monterey, 831-375-9798; www.freshcream.com
"Worth the hunt" for the "views of evening sunlight on boats at anchor, sea lions, seals" and the "sun setting" over Monterey Bay, this "romantic splurge" "still knows how to pamper guests", plying them with "reliable" French-Continental standards "prepared to perfection" and served by a "warm, inviting" staff that's "second to none"; while it's far from "trendy", it's remains an "all-time favorite", especially for "special occasions" – no wonder diehards declare "don't miss this culinary delight."

Fuki Sushi   22 | 20 | 19 | $37
4119 El Camino Real (bet. Arastradero & Page Mill Rds.), Palo Alto,
650-494-9383; www.fukisushi.com
Way-"authentic", from the "traditional" setting ("reserve a tatami room") in Palo Alto "right down to the prices of Tokyo", this "high-end" Japanese offers a "solid sushi experience" that "reminds natives of home"; the "beautifully prepared" fish is "so fresh I'm afraid it might swim off the plate", making it "perfect for a business lunch" or a "casual evening with the family", though a few caution it's best when you "have all day" as service can be "slow and erratic."

Gabriella Café   22 | 20 | 19 | $36
910 Cedar St. (bet. Church & Locust Sts.), Santa Cruz, 831-457-1677;
www.gabriellacafe.com
An "intimate and cozy slice of the Mediterranean right in Downtown Santa Cruz", this "funky" Cal-Italian gem makes it easy to "temporarily forget you're right in the middle of the city" in this "romantic setting"; acolytes crow that the "delightful", "wonderfully prepared dishes" showcase "local flavors" while the "personable staff makes dining here a pleasure"; still, a few Gab-bers gripe seating is "cramped", "especially outdoors", and say service can "spotty."

Gayle's Bakery & Rosticceria   24 | 13 | 18 | $17
504 Bay Ave. (Capitola Ave.), Capitola, 831-462-1200;
www.gaylesbakery.com
"One of the few spots where busting the diet feels oh-so-worth it" reveal road-trippers who brake at this Capitola "must-stop" bakery for "dangerously addictive" pastries and Traditional American "blue-plate specials" when "heading south on Highway 1"; while the counter staff "has the number system

down", the "cafeteria-style" "cozy seaside cottage" gets as crowded as "Grand Central Station", prompting insiders to tote "excellent sandwiches" to the "garden patio" or take out "scrumptious picnic" provisions for the beach.

Gaylord India | 18 | 16 | 16 | $33 |
1706 El Camino Real (Encinal Ave.), Menlo Park, 650-326-8761; www.gaylordmenlo.com
See review in City of San Francisco Directory.

Grasing's Coastal Cuisine | 22 | 19 | 21 | $47 |
Jordan Ctr., Sixth St. (Mission St.), Carmel, 831-624-6562; www.grasings.com
Graze on "truly creative", coastal-inspired, "slow-cooked" Cal cuisine at restaurateur Kurt Grasing's little cottage hidden "on a back, quiet street" of Carmel; "the warm atmosphere", "friendly" service and "dog-friendly" patio make it a "real find" for lunch, while the "bargain" prix fixe dinners "make for a lovely evening", but what really gets tails wagging is co-owner Narsai David's "marvelous", "well-priced" 1,000-bottle cellar.

Happy Cafe Restaurant ⌷ | ▽ 20 | 4 | 10 | $16 |
250 S. B St. (bet. 2nd & 3rd Aves.), San Mateo, 650-340-7138
For an "assortment" of "cheap" but "tasty" "Shanghainese street food" including the best "*xiao long bao*" (dumplings) and noodle dishes "this side of the Pacific", bargain-hunters head to this "small" San Mateo "hole-in-the-wall" lunch counter and take-out shop; but while enthusiasts are happy to withstand the "slow lines and brusque service", many are downright sad that "dinner is only available Wednesday nights."

Hunan Garden | 22 | 10 | 17 | $22 |
3345 El Camino Real (bet. Fernando & Lambert Aves.), Palo Alto, 650-565-8868

Hunan Home's Restaurant
4880 El Camino Real (Showers Dr.), Los Altos, 650-965-8888
See review in City of San Francisco Directory.

Iberia | 20 | 20 | 15 | $44 |
1026 Alma St. (bet. Oak Grove & Ravenswood Aves.), Menlo Park, 650-325-8981; www.iberiarestaurant.com
You "won't leave stuffed, but you'll leave satisfied" assert adventurers who feel "transported back to my days on the Ramblas" promenade at this "overlooked gem" in Menlo Park; whether you "partake of real tapas" and the "extensive wine list" in the "comfortable lounge" or "interesting entrees" in the "homey" dining room with a "Spanish cellar"-feel, you'll be glad you wandered "off the beaten path"; the "only downside": "slow service"; P.S. the "attached bodega" lets you "bring Iberia home."

IL FORNAIO | 19 | 20 | 18 | $36 |
327 Lorton Ave. (bet. Burlingame Ave. & California Dr.), Burlingame, 650-375-8000
The Pine Inn, Ocean Ave. (Monte Verde St.), Carmel, 831-622-5100
Garden Court Hotel, 520 Cowper St. (bet. Hamilton & University Aves.), Palo Alto, 650-853-3888
Sainte Claire, 302 S. Market St. (San Carlos St.), San Jose, 408-271-3366
www.ilfornaio.com
See review in City of San Francisco Directory.

Il Postale
| 22 | 17 | 20 | $30 |

127 W. Washington St. (bet. S. Murphy & S. Sunnyvale Aves.), Sunnyvale, 408-733-9600

"You're treated like family" at this "quaint", "compact" Sunnyvale "favorite" where you "always discover" "hearty" Italian dishes worth "savoring"; it's "always packed", so you can't help but "get cozy with fellow diners" in the "loftlike" space, but few mind as the "comfortable atmosphere", "generous" portions and "cute" patio offer a "pleasant respite from Silicon Valley."

In-N-Out Burger ●
| 22 | 9 | 17 | $8 |

11 Rollins Rd. (Millbrae Ave.), Millbrae
1159 N. Rengstorff Ave. (bet. Charleston Rd. & Leghorn St.), Mountain View
260 Washington St. (bet. Rte. 280 & Sullivan Ave.), Daly City
53 W. El Camino Real (bet. Bay St. & Grant Rd.), Mountain View ⊕
5611 Santa Teresa Blvd. (bet. Blossom Hill Rd. & Summerbrook Ln.), San Jose
800-786-1000; www.in-n-out.com
See review in City of San Francisco Directory.

Izzy's Steaks & Chops
| 19 | 16 | 17 | $38 |

525 Skyway Rd. (off Hwy. 101), San Carlos, 650-654-2822; www.izzyssteaksandchops.com
See review in City of San Francisco Directory.

John Bentley's ⊠
| 25 | 21 | 22 | $53 |

2915 El Camino Real (bet. Dumberton Ave. & Selby Ln.), Redwood City, 650-365-7777
2991 Woodside Rd. (bet. Cañada & Whiskey Hill Rds.), Woodside, 650-851-4988 Ⓜ
www.johnbentleys.com

Chef John Bentley delivers "some of the Peninsula's best" cuisine in two locations that offer "fantastic" New American–Continental fare served by an "excellent" staff; a "well-heeled" clientele celebrates "special occasions" in the "countrified" confines of the "Woodside original", while a "younger (and louder) crowd" prefers the bar-centric Redwood City "power spot" where "you're overdressed if you aren't in jeans" but "still pay coat-and-tie prices."

Juban
| 18 | 15 | 16 | $31 |

1204 Broadway (bet. California Dr. & El Camino Real), Burlingame, 650-347-2300
712 Santa Cruz Ave. (El Camino Real), Menlo Park, 650-473-6458
www.jubanrestaurant.com

"Benihana for the wealthy", these "interactive" "family-oriented" "Japanese *yakiniku* joints" in Burlingame and Menlo Park (and Japantown too) are "crowd-pleasers" for kids and "do-it-yourself" types who find it "fun" to grill "piles of meat" and seafood in "sweet and spicy barbecue sauces" "on tabletop hibachis"; but while "you can't blame the chef if it's too done", the easily "bored" believe you may not find it a "memorable dining experience" either.

Junnoon ⊠
| – | – | – | E |

150 University Ave. (High St.), Palo Alto, 650-329-9644; www.junnoon.com

Haute Hindi haunts are hot in the South Bay as this Bollywood-inspired newcomer attests; the dramatic red-and-black dining room sets the stage for modern Indian fare, including a wildly inventive selection of housemade chutneys, tandoori and naan, crafted by an all-star lineup of consulting chefs hailing from NYC's Tabla and London's Cinnamon Club, among others; belly up to the backlit bar for fusion cocktails such as the Drunken Darjeeling.

jZcool
20 | 11 | 14 | $16

827 Santa Cruz Ave. (bet. Crane St. & University Dr.), Menlo Park, 650-325-3665; www.cooleatz.com

"Do your health a favor" and "treat" yourself to a "perfect happy lunch" or takeout from Jessie Cool's Flea St. Café sidekick in Downtown Menlo Park where you order "creative", organic Californian "comfort food" "cafeteria-style", then dig in at a "big trestle table with benches"; if a few grumble it's a "bit pricey" ("money does not organically grow on trees!"), most believe it "beats by a mile the usual" "fast food"; N.B. no dinner served.

KAYGETSU
28 | 20 | 26 | $73

Sharon Hts. Shopping Ctr., 325 Sharon Park Dr. (Sand Hill Rd.), Menlo Park, 650-234-1084; www.kaygetsu.com

Prized for its "elegant kaiseki meals", a "seasonally changing creative feast for the senses" that "leaves you breathless with its beauty and quality", this "extraordinary gem" with "amazing service" in a Menlo Park strip mall makes you feel "like you're on the panel of *Iron Chef*"; sure, you'll find some of the most "pristine" sushi on the à la carte menu, but the multicourse tasting menu is where owner "Toshi really works his magic" – it's "an experience not to be missed."

Kingfish
17 | 19 | 16 | $36

201 S. B St. (2nd Ave.), San Mateo, 650-343-1226; www.kingfish.net

"If you're looking for a quiet place", mosey on, because this "happening" Creole–New American "standby" in San Mateo and its SF sidekick "convenient to the ballpark" "take you right to New Orleans" with their "jazz vibe", "lively" ambiance (the "bar rocks") and "interesting seafood"; but the disheartened declare that while the setting is "bustling, the service is snail-land"; in fact, what with "uninspiring", "inconsistent food", "lately it has lost its crown."

Koi Palace
25 | 17 | 12 | $32

Serramonte Plaza, 365 Gellert Blvd. (bet. Hickey & Serramonte Blvds.), Daly City, 650-992-9000; www.koipalace.com

"Wake up early" if your heart is set on "fantastic dim sum" at this "undisputed emperor of Cantonese cuisine in the Bay Area"; it's "well worth" enduring a "ridiculous wait" that "seems endless" (an "experience in itself") as well as servers who make you feel like "you're bothering them" because there's an "incredible" pay-off: the "mysteries behind the Great Wall delivered right to your table."

Kuleto's
20 | 18 | 20 | $41

1095 Rollins Rd. (Broadway), Burlingame, 650-342-4922; www.kuletostrattoria.com
See review in City of San Francisco Directory.

Kurt's Carmel Chop House
▽ 19 | 19 | 20 | $55

Fifth Ave. & San Carlos St., Carmel, 831-625-1199; www.carmelchophouse.com

Carnivores on the coast with "meat on the mind" canter over to this "lovely" chophouse with "delightful service" "in the heart of

Carmel's gallery-hopping and shopping area" for Kurt Grasing's "tasty" porterhouse steaks, Kobe beef burgers and a handful of fish dishes; no matter your preference, everyone benefits from the chef's Kurt-ship with radio personality Narsai David, whose on-site cellar features stunning Santa Barbara County wines.

La Cumbre Taqueria | 20 | 8 | 14 | $11 |
28 N. B St. (bet. 1st & Tilton Aves.), San Mateo, 650-344-8989
See review in City of San Francisco Directory.

LA FORÊT ☒ | 26 | 26 | 25 | $61 |
21747 Bertram Rd. (Almaden Rd.), San Jose, 408-997-3458;
www.laforetrestaurant.com
"You feel like you are in a deep forest treehouse" at this "charming", "woodsy" "wonderful historic building" "tucked back in the Almaden Valley" with a "nice view" of the "running creek" and "first-rate" service concur acolytes who crown this French "gem" "one of the South Bay's most romantic restaurants"; the "excellent tasting menus" are also "worth the drive", especially if you're hunting for "game dishes galore"– just bear in mind it's a "very high-class, high-style and high-priced" "eating experience."

La Strada | 21 | 19 | 20 | $37 |
335 University Ave. (bet. Bryant & Waverly Sts.), Palo Alto, 650-324-8300;
www.lastradapaloalto.com
"Not your typical Italian", this "inviting" "hot spot" on Palo Alto's main Downtown *strada* showcases "joyous" chef Donato Scotti's "recipes from his [native] Bergamo" as well as "innovative" pastas and pizzas and "irresistible house-cured meats"; with a "wonderful" outdoor area and "polished" service, it's "great for a date", though be warned: it's *molto* "crowded on weekends."

La Taqueria ☒⊘ | 24 | 7 | 13 | $10 |
15 S. First St. (Santa Clara Ave.), San Jose, 408-287-1542
See review in City of San Francisco Directory.

L'AUBERGE CARMEL | 27 | 25 | 27 | $106 |
L'Auberge Carmel, Monte Verde St. (7th Ave.), Carmel, 831-624-8578;
www.laubergecarmel.com
This "small", "top-flight" "Carmel charmer" may be the "most expensive" "dining experience" in this "relaxed town" but it's well "worth it" for a "special occasion"; gourmands "settle in" for an "intimate" "event" that lasts for hours (hint: "not a pre-activity dinner") and luxuriate in Walter Manzke's (also of Bouchée) "inventively presented", "truly inspired" Cal tasting menu with "delightful wine pairings", best capped off with a stay at the adjoining hotel where you can "dream of your meal"; N.B. the lobby's salon offers an à la carte bistro menu.

Lavanda | 20 | 20 | 19 | $44 |
185 University Ave. (bet. Emerson & High Sts.), Palo Alto, 650-321-3514;
www.lavandarestaurant.com
A "wine list that shines" and a "stylish" Med menu make this Palo Alto "favorite" a "popular" "Silicon Valley meeting place"; "grab a glass on the way to a movie" – the "waiters are generous with their pours" – or "sit down" for "some fine cookin'" that "combines ingredients smartly without trying too hard"; but those less lavish with praise feel the large plates are "well-executed but without the wow factor" and arrive at "glacial speeds."

La Victoria Taqueria ●
▽ 23 | 8 | 11 | $9

140 W. San Carlos St. (Almaden Blvd.), San Jose, 408-298-5335
Head to this "great" taqueria offers "wonderful" burritos, tacos and quesadillas doused with a "secret"-recipe sauce that's "deservedly its claim to fame", all at "cheap" tabs; Mex mavens warn "getting a table is a challenge during feeding times, which is all the time" considering its location "next to San Jose State" and the fact that this "dive" is "one of the only places" Downtown open till 2 AM.

LEFT BANK
18 | 20 | 17 | $38

635 Santa Cruz Ave. (Doyle St.), Menlo Park, 650-473-6543
377 Santana Row (S. Winchester Blvd.), San Jose, 408-984-3500
Bay Meadows, 1100 Park Pl. (Saratoga Dr.), San Mateo, 650-345-2250
www.leftbank.com
See review in North of San Francisco Directory.

LE PAPILLON
27 | 24 | 27 | $68

410 Saratoga Ave. (Kiely Blvd.), San Jose, 408-296-3730;
www.lepapillon.com
"Don't let the neighborhood fool you – walk inside" San Jose's "hideaway" for "gastronomes" and "expense-accounters" and you "feel like you've arrived in Oz" declare the spellbound who deem it "outstanding in every way"; if the "stellar" New French tasting menus "beautifully presented" with "increasingly inspired wine pairings" don't bewitch, the "friendly", "flawless service" that "anticipates your needs" will; sure, it's "sticker-shock" city, but this "old-school" "butterfly just gets better with age."

Lion & Compass ⌂
19 | 18 | 19 | $42

1023 N. Fair Oaks Ave. (Weddell Dr.), Sunnyvale, 408-745-1260;
www.lionandcompass.com
Although "quieter" than during its "tech boom" "heyday", this "unassuming old villa" with a "tropical" feel remains a "Sunnyvale institution", satisfying power brokers dining on the company's dime with its "professionally prepared" New American fare; but while loyalists say it "never disappoints", a few roar that the "elegant but boring interior" "could use some updating."

Lure ⌂ M
▽ 22 | 25 | 21 | $50

204A Second Ave. (S. Ellsworth Ave.), San Mateo, 650-340-9040;
www.lurerestaurant.com
This "edgy, contemporary" "San Francisco–style" seafooder may be a fish out of water in suburban San Mateo, but it's a "welcome addition to the Peninsula dining scene" nonetheless, luring locals with its "inventive" "crudo with bright flavors" and "delicious" crustaceans prepared by a Malaysian-born chef; the "staff seems to anticipate what you need" and the digs are "well appointed", but the catch is it all comes at big-city prices.

MacArthur Park
16 | 18 | 17 | $37

27 University Ave. (El Camino Real), Palo Alto, 650-321-9990;
www.spectrumfoods.com
See review in City of San Francisco Directory.

Maddalena's & Café Fino ⌂
20 | 20 | 22 | $43

544 Emerson St. (bet. Hamilton & University Aves.), Palo Alto,
650-326-6082
"Just when you thought there were no quiet, intimate restaurants left" to "take your mother-in-law", you flashback to this "tradi-

tional old-school Continental-style" standby in Palo Alto that's "been there forever"; if you're looking for a more up-tempo night out, however, head to Café Fino next door with a "1940s feel", jazz on the weekends and the "best martini in town" – you can't help but have "fun with Freddie as your host."

MANRESA ⌧ Ⓜ   27 | 24 | 26 | $94 |
320 Village Ln. (bet. N. Santa Cruz & University Aves.), Los Gatos, 408-354-4330; www.manresarestaurant.com
"Dollars fly from wallets" at this "romantic" "hideaway" in Los Gatos where diners "throw frugality and culinary prejudices to the wind" after indulging in "daring chef" David Kinch's "avant-garde", "physics"-inspired New American–New French tasting menus with "provocative wine pairings"; "no celebrity blarney here" – instead, a "supremely delicious" "spa for your taste buds" that "elicits many wows", though a few cynics quibble about "tight tables" and a "staff that could be more seasoned"; N.B. dinner Tuesday–Saturday only.

Mantra   ▽ 19 | 24 | 16 | $52 |
632-636 Emerson St. (Hamilton Ave.), Palo Alto, 650-322-3500; www.mantrapaloalto.com
Palo Altans find culinary enlightenment – sans deep-fryer or Vegas-style buffet – at this "premier destination" with a chic lounge; the East "Indian–influenced Cal" cuisine reveals a dedication to fresh ingredients, served in a contemporary setting done up with gold wallpaper and a waterfall; if a few squawk the "food falls short of expectations", defenders declare we'll "try again"; N.B. the original chef departed post-*Survey,* which may impact the Food score.

MARCHÉ ⌧ Ⓜ   26 | 23 | 25 | $68 |
898 Santa Cruz Ave. (University Dr.), Menlo Park, 650-324-9092; www.restaurantmarche.com
"San Francisco dining, without the drive to the city" confirm "foodies, not trendies" who "march" to this "glorious" New French Peninsula destination that brings "suave", "urbane sophistication to Menlo Park"; chef Howard Bulka has earned a "loyal and deserved following" with his "dazzling" cuisine, prepared in an open kitchen, and accolades for his "truly wonderful tasting menu" and "great wine pairings"; nevertheless, a few fail to fall in line finding it "too pricey" for the area.

MARINUS   28 | 26 | 27 | $80 |
Bernardus Lodge, 415 Carmel Valley Rd. (Laureles Grade Rd.), Carmel, 831-658-3500; www.bernardus.com
It's a "longer drive than you might expect" to get to Carmel Valley's "luxurious" Bernardus Lodge in "the middle of nowhere" but "wow!" what an "incredible setting" – this is where "SF foodies visiting the Monterey Peninsula" come to splurge; chef Cal Stamenov's "sublime" derring-do with New French fare "speaks volumes" – pair it with the "tremendous wine list" for a "not-so-cheap thrill" you'll talk about long after dining by the "gorgeous fireplace"; "stroll the grounds before" dinner – or stay overnight – "you won't be sorry."

Max's   17 | 13 | 16 | $24 |
1250 Old Bayshore Hwy. (Broadway), Burlingame, 650-342-6297 Stanford Shopping Ctr., 711 Stanford Shopping Ctr. (Sand Hill Rd.), Palo Alto, 650-323-6297

(continued)

Max's

1001 El Camino Real (James Ave.), Redwood City, 650-365-6297
Westgate Shopping Ctr., 1620 Saratoga Ave. (Prospect Rd.), San Jose,
408-379-8886
www.maxsworld.com
See review in City of San Francisco Directory.

Mezza Luna | 20 | 16 | 20 | $33 |

459 Prospect Way (Capistrano Rd.), Princeton by the Sea,
650-728-8108; www.mezzalunabythesea.com
"*Mangia*" on "inventive, beautifully presented" Italian dishes
"authentic" "in every detail" (down to the "attentive staff's" "accents!") at this seaside trattoria "tucked away by the ocean";
soak up the "lovely view" of the Princeton Harbor during the day
and come nightfall, sit beside the "cozy fireplace that warms the
barroom" (it has "more life than the main dining room") and dive
into the "fresh fish dishes."

Mistral ☒ | 20 | 19 | 19 | $38 |

370-6 Bridge Pkwy. (Marine World Pkwy.), Redwood Shores,
650-802-9222; www.mistraldining.com
When you're craving "gourmet" French-Italian food and a
"homey atmosphere" that's ideal for an "expense-account lunch",
head to this "bustling" "Oracle hangout" from the owners of A
Tavola; sink into the "comfy chairs and sofa" on the "lovely patio"
and "check out the waterview" "on a clear day" of Redwood
Shores – "it's a great romantic place for drinks and appetizers";
still, a few sing the blues about "inconsistent service."

Montrio Bistro | 21 | 21 | 19 | $42 |

414 Calle Principal (Franklin St.), Monterey, 831-648-8880;
www.montrio.com
"Enjoyable in every way" enjoin enthusiasts who blaze a trail to
this "casual, hip" "unique" converted firehouse in Monterey for
"inspired, whimsical" "small plates that are great for grazing"
and Californian "creations" with a Southwestern spin delivered
by a "warm" staff; still, insiders suggest "go early" or for "late-
night snacks" as it can get a "little loud for quiet conversation"
during prime time when service "isn't very attentive."

NAVIO | 24 | 27 | 24 | $70 |

Ritz-Carlton Half Moon Bay, 1 Miramontes Point Rd. (Hwy. 1),
Half Moon Bay, 650-712-7000; www.ritzcarlton.com
For a "civilized dining experience unmarred by reality", put yourself in the "pampering" hands of the "efficient staff" at this "glorious" Ritz-Carlton Half Moon Bay nautical-inspired "gem"; "it's
hard to beat the knockout views" of the Pacific as you "indulge"
in the "wild" Sunday brunch "spread that caters to every possible
taste" or a "perfect post-golf romantic dinner" – but all eyes are
now also on the "open kitchen" where chef Aaron Zimmer
(ex CityZen in Washington, DC's Mandarin Oriental), who arrived
post-*Survey,* crafts a New American menu.

Nepenthe | 14 | 24 | 16 | $33 |

Hwy. 1, 3rd fl. (¼ mi. south of Ventana Inn & Spa), Big Sur, 831-667-2345;
www.nepenthebigsur.com
"Who's kidding who": day-trippers driving "down Highway 1"
stop at this Big Sur perch for its "movie-set" vistas of the "Pacific

Ocean as waves crash on the rocky shore" sure to bring back "memories of Orson Welles and Rita Hayworth" whose cabin once stood on this "dramatic" setting; the "views are so perfect you overlook" the "average" American "pub food" and "wavering" service – heck, even "a Whopper would taste good" "sitting on the deck."

North Beach Pizza ◐   18 | 9 | 14 | $17
240 E. Third Ave. (B St.), San Mateo, 650-344-5000;
www.northbeachpizza.com
See review in City of San Francisco Directory.

Oak City Bar & Grill   19 | 18 | 18 | $37
1029 El Camino Real (Menlo Ave.), Menlo Park, 650-321-6882;
www.oakcitybarandgrill.com
You'll find "something for everyone" at this neighborhood grill in Menlo Park that puts a New American "spin on classic favorites" like mac 'n' cheese and burgers at "moderate prices"; "busy business folks" log in midday for the "fixed-price lunch", families gather for a "relaxing dinner" and local Oakies belly up to the "long bar, a pleasant watering hole"; still, the less-floored find the fare "uneven" and the environs "boring."

O'mei   25 | 14 | 18 | $26
2316 Mission St. (King St.), Santa Cruz, 831-425-8458;
www.omeifood.com
There are "lots of good things to sample" – and it's better done with more folks" suggests the "laid-back Santa Cruz" crowd that frequents this "unassuming", "oh-so-trendy" Chinese "must"-visit; what a "sumptuous mix of traditional Szechuan" and "exciting", "spicy" Sino flavors sigh insiders who extol the virtues of the "varied selection – it's a "great dining experience", in spite of "indifferent service" and the "nondescript strip-mall" setting.

Original Joe's ◐   18 | 13 | 19 | $28
(aka Joe's, OJ's)
301 S. First St. (San Carlos St.), San Jose, 408-292-7030;
www.originaljoes.com
See review in City of San Francisco Directory.

Osteria ⊠   24 | 14 | 19 | $33
247 Hamilton Ave. (Ramona St.), Palo Alto, 650-328-5700
"Homemade pastas" are "al dente perfecto" and "piping hot" at this "boisterous" Palo Alto "matchbox", still "busy, busy, busy" "for casual dates" and Stanford "business lunches"; *si*, "you're squished in and there's no decor to speak of", but the "homey", "stalwart Italian" "*cucina*" is "worthy of a North Beach address" – and you gotta love that both the "brusque" waiters and "wallet-friendly" prices "have more or less stayed the same forever."

OSWALD Ⓜ   26 | 20 | 24 | $44
1547 Pacific Ave., Ste. D (Cedar St.), Santa Cruz, 831-423-7427
"Tucked away where you won't notice it", this "charming" "gem" is the "most together", "upscale" "restaurant in Santa Cruz" with "edgy, creative" seasonal Californian dishes "utilizing local raised and picked foods" "that rival most top-notch restaurants in a large, sophisticated city"; add in "stellar service" and a "tempting" wine list and you've got the "perfect place to take a visiting foodie"; N.B. a move may be in the works.

PACIFIC'S EDGE   26 | 28 | 25 | $76
Highlands Inn, 120 Highlands Dr. (Hwy. 1), Carmel, 831-620-1234;
www.pacificsedge.com
"A window-side seat is worth a bribe" for a "surreal" "view of the
greatest meeting of land and sea on earth" that will "leave you
speechless" at this "aptly named", "romantic" Carmel "gem"; the
"unmatched culinary experience" combines "divine" French-
New American prix fixe menus, an "encyclopedic" 1,700-strong
wine list, "outstanding service" and "fabulous" decor – though
frugal foodies suggest if you aren't "comfortable writing a blank
check", "enjoy a cocktail at the adjoining bar" for the same "fantastic sunsets" and "bat show."

Pancho Villa Taqueria   23 | 9 | 13 | $11
365 S. B St. (bet. 3rd & 4th Aves.), San Mateo, 650-343-4123
See review in City of San Francisco Directory.

Parcel 104   25 | 21 | 21 | $55
Santa Clara Marriott, 2700 Mission College Blvd. (Great America Pkwy.),
Santa Clara, 408-970-6104; www.parcel104.com
"Bradley Ogden does Silicon Valley" at this "elegant" Santa Clara
Californian wooing worshipers with "fantastic", "farm-fresh"
seasonal fare (organic "veggies right out of the earth – cleaned, of
course") and "perfect" vino pairings from a master sommelier; the
spacious setting "full of gorgeous woodwork" and a "professional"
staff that "makes you feel at home" prompt queries of "can you
believe it's in a Marriott?"; but those less-impressed with the whole
package pout that the wine list is "outrageously expensive."

Passage to India   19 | 14 | 15 | $21
1991 W. El Camino Real (Clark Ave.), Mountain View, 650-969-9990;
www.passagetoindia.net
"Don't wear tight pants" to this Mountain View "mainstay" if
you're planning to indulge in the "monstrously popular", "stuff-
your-gills" buffet (lunch and late-week dinner) representing "the
whole subcontinent"; some surveyors say "no particular dish
stands out" in the "eclectic mix" that includes "Desi-Chinese"
choices, but it's a "deal" and "good for groups" – just overlook
the "poor service"; P.S. you can also "order off the menu" too.

Passionfish   25 | 17 | 23 | $40
701 Lighthouse Ave. (Congress Ave.), Pacific Grove, 831-655-3311;
www.passionfish.net
Pacific Grove "locals" "hate to let on" about this "casual fine-
dining" "favorite" featuring "passionately made", "adventurous"
and "sustainable" Californian seafood "as fresh and appealing as
the aquarium down the road" with a wine list that's "stunning, both
for its breadth and low markup"; service is "professional yet
friendly" and "fair prices" make it a fish out of water on the spendy
Monterey Peninsula – so few mind the "upgraded" "diner" decor.

Pasta Moon   22 | 19 | 19 | $36
315 Main St. (Mills St.), Half Moon Bay, 650-726-5125;
www.pastamoon.com
Half Moon Bay's 20-year-old trattoria "favorite" serves "fresh,
light" seasonal Italian including "some of the tastiest pasta
around" and "wonderful daily specials" "complemented by a fine
Italian wine list"; the "quaint bistro-style" setting is a "good bet

after browsing" Main Street or "visiting nearby beaches", though the less-moonstruck muse "it's a bit pricey for pasta", plus the "slow" staff seems comprised of "Maverick [surfer] wannabes."

Pasta Pomodoro | 16 | 13 | 16 | $19 |

Evergreen Mkt., 4898 San Felipe Rd. (Yerba Buena Blvd.), San Jose, 408-532-0271; www.pastapomodoro.com
See review in City of San Francisco Directory.

Patxi's Chicago Pizza ⓜ | 21 | 14 | 17 | $18 |

441 Emerson St. (bet. Lytton & University Aves.), Palo Alto, 650-473-9999; www.patxispizza.com
For "excellent" Windy City deep-dish pizza without the "trek across the Bay", homesick "Chicagoans" get "stuffed" on the "closest to the real thing" at this "upscale" Palo Alto pizzeria (pronounced PAH-cheese); pies are available to go, but a "Left Coast atmosphere" and a "nice range of beers" and wine invite dining in – just brace yourself for service "kinks" and waits that take "forever", "even if they're empty"; N.B. there's a Hayes Valley branch too.

Pearl Alley Bistro | ▽ 21 | 20 | 19 | $35 |

110 Pearl Alley, 2nd fl. (bet. Lincoln & Walnut Sts.), Santa Cruz, 831-429-8070; www.pearlalley.com
It's "really bounced back" over alley cats who ascend the "secret steps to this private", "cozy", "friendly" French bistro with a "beautiful marble-topped" central bar in an "old" Santa Cruz building; the "always innovative", "delicious" dishes are made with "top ingredients" while the wine list reveals some "gems" – it's a "perfect" place for a "group to share and taste everyone's food"; still, some scoff that service is "slow and erratic."

Pho Hoa-Hiep II | 21 | 6 | 13 | $10 |

85 Southgate Ave. (bet. Palmcrest & Park Plaza Drs.), Daly City, 650-992-3814
See review in East of San Francisco Directory.

Piatti | 18 | 19 | 19 | $34 |

Sixth Ave. (Junipero St.), Carmel, 831-625-1766
3905 Rivermark Plaza (Montague Expwy.), Santa Clara, 408-330-9212
www.piatti.com
See review in East of San Francisco Directory.

Pisces ⊠ ⓜ | 22 | 19 | 21 | $52 |

1190 California Dr. (Broadway), Burlingame, 650-401-7500; www.piscesrestaurant.com
The "food is plentiful, but space is limited" at this Cal-French seafooder set in a "funky" "old Burlingame railroad station"; sure, it's "not in the same league as its sister, Aqua", nevertheless, it brings a "touch of class" to the Peninsula with "creative" cuisine presented by an "outstanding" staff – just steel yourself for "trains roaring past the windows – it's a bit of a shock the first time" but it's "more charming than annoying" and "adds to the ambiance."

Pizza Antica | 22 | 16 | 17 | $24 |

334 Santana Row (Stevens Creek Blvd.), San Jose, 408-557-8373; www.pizzaantica.com
"Artisanal" pies prepared "the Italian way" – "cracker-thin" – and "seasonal vegetable offerings" "that make even Brussels sprout-haters swoon" are the signatures of this "convivial" pair

of parlors in San Jose and Lafayette, rivaling even those of "white-tablecloth restaurants"; not so the "bustling" environs, often "frantic with children", but luckily there's "sidewalk dining in fair weather" (following "long waits at peak" times); N.B. a Mill Valley branch opened post-*Survey*.

Plumed Horse ⧄ | 23 | 21 | 24 | $56 |

14555 Big Basin Way (4th St.), Saratoga, 408-867-4711;
www.plumedhorse.com

"Enjoyed by generations" of guests since 1952, this "classic" Cal-French thoroughbred in Saratoga still "exudes class and elegance", thanks to a "staff in tuxedos" that "remembers what patrons like and how they like it" – namely "old standards" (like "Caesars served tableside") paired with wines from a "stunning" 750-bottle list; some whippersnappers, however, warn the "quite expensive" "menu could stand some updating", and ditto the decor.

Rio Grill | 21 | 18 | 19 | $38 |

Crossroads Shopping Ctr., 101 Crossroads Blvd. (Rio Rd.), Carmel,
831-625-5436; www.riogrill.com

Twenty-three years after igniting Carmel's wood-burning-oven craze, this "old standby" continues to lure the "lunch"-bunch and "casual" crowd on "sightseeing breaks" to its "energetic", "strip-mall" adobe digs, serving up "solid" Californian eats with "Tex-Mex overtones" in a "kitschy Southwestern" setting; it's "still packed with locals" – "which is a good thing" – in fact, most rio-lize it's "never lost its appeal."

Ristorante Capellini | 19 | 19 | 18 | $39 |

310 Baldwin Ave. (B St.), San Mateo, 650-348-2296; www.capellinis.com

"Amazingly consistent", this "noisy" San Mateo trattoria is packed "each and every day" with "cheerful" regulars who "go, eat, shout and enjoy" themselves, reveling in the "reasonably priced" Italian standbys and one of "the best bars in town"; but while optimistas insist the "always enjoyable food and service" "stand the test of time", a wistful few find you're "never surprised by the chef's inspirations", suggesting the whole fandango "needs a redo."

Robert's Whitehouse Ⓜ | ▽ 23 | 24 | 21 | $50 |

649 Lighthouse Ave. (19th St.), Pacific Grove, 831-375-9626;
www.robertswhitehouse.com

For a "tasty surprise" head to chef Robert Kincaid's "extremely romantic", antiques-filled, white Victorian mansion in Downtown Pacific Grove; partisans opine that the ex–Fresh Cream chef "hasn't lost his touch" – he "beats the better-known places by a mile" – currying favor with a "diverse" French menu of "delicious", downright "dreamy" dishes ranging from Dover sole to duckling; but electorates are split on service, tsking "it can be attentive one visit" and "lacking" the next.

Rogue Chefs Ⓜ | ▽ 20 | 16 | 18 | $36 |

730 Main St. (Correas St.), Half Moon Bay, 650-712-2000;
www.roguechefs.com

"There's a new kid" in this "seaside" town confide foodies who pass the "crown" to "this bright Half Moon Bay" bungalow serving "adventurous" Californian small and large plates made with "local, sustainable and organic ingredients"; it's "still getting it's footing" "after being transformed from a take-out" spot, nevertheless, voyeurs vow it's "fun" to "sit at the chef's table" overlooking the exhibition kitchen – "you feel like part of the *mise en place*"; N.B. open Wednesday–Saturday for dinner, and brunch on Sunday.

ROY'S AT PEBBLE BEACH | 24 | 26 | 23 | $52 |

The Inn at Spanish Bay, 2700 17 Mile Dr. (Congress Rd.), Pebble Beach, 831-647-7423; www.pebblebeach.com

The "quintessential Pebble Beach experience", Roy Yamaguchi's Hawaiian Regional "favorite" delivers "just what you want in a resort meal": a "wonderful setting at the edge of Spanish Bay" with "table views overlooking the golf links and the Pacific", "smart, prompt service" and "awesome food"; "get a reservation just after sunset, listen to the bagpipe player serenade you – and enjoy the magic"; P.S. it's "more formal than its strip-mall counterparts", making it a must for "special occasions."

Sardine Factory | 20 | 20 | 21 | $52 |

701 Wave St. (Prescott Ave.), Monterey, 831-373-3775; www.sardinefactory.com

Fans of the finned swim downstream to this New American seafooder in Monterey for the "signature abalone bisque", served in a "beautiful" multi-room setting that's a "little over the top" with "old-time attention to service", prompting literary types to postulate "Steinbeck's Doc never had Cannery Row so good"; but critics carp it's a "tourist trap" and "a bit on the expensive side" to boot, suggesting "bar tapas, yes, dining room, no!"

Scott's of Palo Alto | 18 | 19 | 19 | $39 |

#1 Town & Country Vlg. (Embarcadero Rd.), Palo Alto, 650-323-1555; www.scottsseafood.com

Scott's of San Jose

185 Park Ave. (Almaden Blvd.), San Jose, 408-971-1700; www.scottsseafoodsj.com

See Scott's Seafood review in East of San Francisco Directory.

Sent Sovi Ⓜ | 23 | 21 | 25 | $62 |

14583 Big Basin Way (5th St.), Saratoga, 408-867-3110; www.sentsovi.com

David Kinch may have ceded his toque but the "young new chef"-owner at this "cozy" cottage "tucked away in the beautiful village of Saratoga" is winning plaudits for his "excellent", "contemporary" takes on French-inflected Cal dishes accompanied by "creative wine pairings"; what a "memorable meal" exclaim enthusiasts – "every morsel" on the tasting menu is "tasty" while the staff is "exceptional"; still, a few holdouts feel that while Josiah Stone has "promise" he may need time to "find his voice."

Seven Restaurant & Lounge Ⓢ | 23 | 23 | 21 | $41 |

754 The Alameda (Bush St.), San Jose, 408-280-1644; www.7restaurant.us

More "Silicon Alley than Silicon Valley", this "edgy", "cosmopolitan" spot may be "out of the way", but it's "always hopping" with the "young" and the restless, "especially before Pavilion events"; "thought I was in Manhattan" muse the "see-and-be-seen" who dig the "jazzy", "upmarket" French–New American fare and the "ultracool lounge" where "unique drinks are a highlight"; still, "lots of *vivre*" means "lots of noise" so if you want to "talk with your date", pick another number.

71 Saint Peter 🛇

23 | 18 | 22 | $40

71 N. San Pedro St. (bet. Santa Clara & St. John Sts.), San Jose,
408-971-8523; www.71saintpeter.com

"Channeling" a "quaint Euro-style" vibe, this "hidden haunt" set at the end of San Jose's San Pedro Square is a "tried-and-true" choice for an alfresco meal "before a Sharks game" or on "theater nights"; the "inviting atmosphere", complete with "plants winding around indoor trellises", plus the "incredible value", "superior quality" Cal-Med tasting menus with "generous wine pairings" and "personable service" "keep bringing diners back."

SHADOWBROOK

20 | 27 | 22 | $45

1750 Wharf Rd. (Capitola Rd.), Capitola, 831-475-1511;
www.shadowbrook-capitola.com

For 60 years, this Capitola "showplace" with "excellent" service has been "one of the best places to propose" confide acolytes; take a funicular "down the steep incline" to this "magical" "multi-roomed" "lovers' paradise" "nestled" next to Soquel Creek and "enjoy" the "seasonally changing" "great greenery" and "gorgeous gardens" – the "perfect dressing" for "surprisingly good" New American–Continental cuisine; still, a few would rather "just look at the grounds" than brook the "less than inspiring food."

Shalimar 🛇 Ⓜ

23 | 3 | 9 | $14

1146 El Camino Real (bet. Jackson & Main Sts), Santa Clara, 408-530-0300
See review in City of San Francisco Directory.

SIERRA MAR

27 | 28 | 25 | $83

Post Ranch Inn, Post Ranch/Hwy. 1 (30 mi. south of Carmel), Big Sur,
831-667-2800

"Words cannot describe" "the experience of dining in God's living room" – the "terrific service" and "epic view" from your "perch" "high on the hills" above the Pacific in Big Sur is almost "too spectacular to recall" the Californian cuisine confirm fklempt foodies who fawn over the "drop-dead gorgeous everything"; tear yourself away from "watching the whale migration below" as a "dreamy mist creeps up the window" and you'll find yourself "dining with multimillionaires" on equally "stunning food" while "sipping" "great wines" from the 1,800-bottle list.

Sino

18 | 25 | 18 | $41

Santana Row, 377 Santana Row (Olin Ave.), San Jose, 408-247-8880;
www.sinorestaurant.com

Step inside Chris Yeo's (Straits Cafe) new Santana Row Chinese venture for a peek at the "beautiful, sleek" decor boasting "lots of sexy black lacquer and red all over" – but "don't leave without eating the dim sum" or the "exotic" entrees; still, a real sign o' where the action is lies in the "bustling" lounge where "old kung fu movies are shown" on a scrim and "pretty" "singles" swill "pretty cocktails with names like 'Mineral', 'Rain' and 'Wood'."

Spago Palo Alto 🛇

22 | 22 | 21 | $56

265 Lytton Ave. (bet. Bryant & Ramona Sts.), Palo Alto, 650-833-1000;
www.wolfgangpuck.com

"Palo Alto is no Beverly Hills", but it's still "wonderful" to dress up" for a "luxury" meal at Wolfgang Puck's brainchild confide loyalists who laud an ambiance that's "sophisticated with a sense of playfulness" and the "creative" Cal-Med fare (they do "deft and delicate things with fish"); but Spago's a no-go for nixers who shrug "all in all, it wasn't so impressive" – it's time to "spiff up the environment" and "sometimes disappointing" dishes.

St. Michael's Alley Ⓜ

23 | 19 | 22 | $40

806 Emerson St. (Homer Ave.), Palo Alto, 650-326-2530; www.stmikes.com
"What a treat to go back" to Palo Alto's "cozy" "little charmer" for "wonderfully fresh" Cal fare that still "takes advantage of current local produce" under a new chef; the "amazing Sunday brunch", "friendly, knowledgeable service" and "homey" "atmosphere that promotes convivial conversation" is also up fans' alley, imparting a "real feeling of satisfaction"; N.B. a move to 140 Homer Avenue is slated for fall 2006.

Stokes Restaurant & Bar

23 | 21 | 22 | $44

500 Hartnell St. (bet. Madison & Polk Sts.), Monterey, 831-373-1110; www.stokesrestaurant.com
This "beautifully restored", rambling "171-year-old Mexican pueblo" ("with its own ghost" to stoke the imagination) and a "wonderful" menu of small and large plates showcasing "the sunny flavors of the Mediterranean" and California sets the stage for a "marvelous" meal in Downtown Monterey; the "service always lives up to my expectations", plus the "taste treats" are "affordable" for tourist-central ("try lunch" – it's an "unbelievable value").

STRAITS CAFE

21 | 19 | 17 | $35

1100 Burlingame Ave. (Highland Ave.), Burlingame, 650-373-7883
3295 El Camino Real (Lambert Ave.), Palo Alto, 650-494-7168
333 Santana Row (bet. Olin Ave. & Tatum Ln.), San Jose, 408-246-6320
www.straitsrestaurants.com
"Rhymes with great" quip patrons who head straightaway to this Bay Area–wide outfit for Singaporean food you'll want to "share with friends" and "talk about later"; "walk through the door into another hemisphere" – chef Chris Yeo's "highly creative" Pan-Asian dishes boast flavors "fused right"; still, the "noise"-sensitive shout it's "like trying to eat in the middle of a club" at some locales; N.B. the Geary Boulevard branch closed and a new branch is set to open fall 2006 in Downtown's Westfield San Francisco Centre.

TAMARINE

26 | 24 | 22 | $46

546 University Ave. (Tasso St.), Palo Alto, 650-325-8500; www.tamarinerestaurant.com
A "tough reservation" "hot spot with the big bucks crowd", this "ideal date locale" with a "beautiful, sexy environment" and "great art" in Palo Alto "puts upscale Vietnamese on the gourmet map"; it's "dining heaven" all the way, from the parade of "unusual", "elegant plates" to the "inviting atmosphere" and "smooth service"; P.S. "eat at the bar and meet fellow foodies" while also enjoying "well-matched wines" and "cocktails that rock."

Taqueria 3 Amigos Ⓢ Ⓜ

21 | 11 | 14 | $10

200 S. Cabrillo Hwy. (Kelly Ave.), Half Moon Bay, 650-347-4513
243 S. B St. (bet. 2nd & E. 3rd Aves.), San Mateo, 650-347-4513
Day-trippers and "locals adore" this "classic taqueria", a "tasty, cheap fill 'er up" joint in Half Moon Bay cranking out "hearty" Mexican, from "great burritos" to "delicious fish tacos"; a recent remodeling may have turned the "frenetic" spot from "charming hole-in-the-wall to semi-fancy hole-in-the-wall" with expanded

seating, nonetheless, these "three friends" "haven't lost what has made them famous"; N.B. there's a second Amigo in San Mateo.

Taqueria Tlaquepaque   ▽ 22 | 13 | 16 | $17

2222 Lincoln Ave. (bet. Curtner & Franquette Aves.), San Jose, 408-978-3665
699 Curnter Ave. (Canoas Garden Ave.), San Jose, 408-448-1230
721 Willow St. (Delmas Ave.), San Jose, 408-287-9777 🅢 🅜

"One of the best Mexican restaurants in Silicon Valley" vow vaunters who join the throngs at this "budget" taqueria trio in San Jose for "no-frills cooking" priced to "fit a tight budget" and elevated by the owner's "very hot salsa"; match the "perfect flavors" with a Chevelas cocktail, a frozen chalice filled with beer and lemon juice, rimmed with salt and a shot of tequila, while gazing at tile paintings depicting doomed Aztec lovers.

Tarpy's Roadhouse   22 | 22 | 22 | $38

2999 Monterey-Salinas Hwy. (Canyon Del Rey Blvd.), Monterey, 831-647-1444; www.tarpys.com

"Fun" is the operative word at this "out-of-the-way", "quaint roadhouse", a "favorite" stopover for locals and tourists "on the way home from Monterey Peninsula"; the "beautiful old stone house "with a courtyard and "all-around" Traditional American eats are "more refined than you might expect", but the "quaint" setup with "crayons on the butcher-paper–covered tabletops" and a "friendly staff" appeal "to all ages."

Thea Mediterranean Cuisine   22 | 21 | 18 | $38

3090 Olsen Dr. (Stephen's Creek Blvd.), San Jose, 408-260-1444; www.thearestaurant.com

At this "festive" Greco-Mediterranean arrival, "flaming cheese", gyrating belly dancers (on Fridays) and a "lovely garden atmosphere" inside and out, not to mention an olive tree standing guard, provide "distraction" aplenty for "hip" revelers; but thea's another reason why it's a "new favorite on Santana Row": (ex Boulevard) chef Alex Padilla's food boasts "interesting combinations of ingredients" and it's all super-"scrumptious", right down to the "homemade pita bread and dips."

Three Seasons   22 | 20 | 19 | $34

518 Bryant St. (University Ave.), Palo Alto, 650-838-0353; www.threeseasonsrestaurant.com
See review in City of San Francisco Directory.

Trader Vic's   17 | 21 | 18 | $44

Dina's Garden Hotel, 4269 El Camino Real (bet. Charleston & San Antonio Rds.), Palo Alto, 650-849-9800; www.tradervicspaloalto.com
See review in East of San Francisco Directory.

Turmeric   ▽ 21 | 17 | 17 | $26

141 S. Murphy St. (bet. Evelyn & Washington Aves.), Sunnyvale, 408-617-9100; www.turmericrestaurant.com

"Sumptuous subcontinental smorgasbords" make this Sunnyvale Indian the "toast of the town" for Silicon Valley's lunch-bunch; you'll be "tempted by the delicious aromas" report insiders who've discovered this "pretty", saffron-washed dining room – "once word gets around it will be a class act"; still, spice-seekers say it "doesn't stand out" yet; N.B. the expat chef who has cooked for VIPs like President Clinton took over ownership post-*Survey*.

231 Ellsworth 🗷 | 22 | 19 | 21 | $59 |

231 S. Ellsworth Ave. (bet. 2nd & 3rd Aves.), San Mateo, 650-347-7231; www.231ellsworth.com

Like its clientele, the "elegant" New American tasting menus at this San Mateo sophisticate are "rich but quite good" – add in "doting service", a "magnificent wine list" and a "pricey, private club atmosphere" and you've got a "nice surprise" if "you're romancing your love or trying to close an important business deal"; but others opine it "over-promises and under-delivers", comparing the "stuffy", "impersonal dining room" to a "banquet hall."

Udupi Palace | 19 | 6 | 12 | $14 |

976 E. El Camino Real (Poplar Ave.), Sunnyvale, 408-830-9600; www.udupipalace.net

See review in East of San Francisco Directory.

Village Pub, The | 25 | 24 | 24 | $57 |

2967 Woodside Rd. (Whiskey Hill Rd.), Woodside, 650-851-9888; www.thevillagepub.net

"Not like a pub at all", this "swank setting" with a "fancy men's club feel" including Bordeaux-colored mohair walls is actually "the most elegant restaurant" in Woodside, serving "ingredient-driven", "innovative" New American "high-end comfort food" that "sparkles" and a "wine list that's a treasure trove for oenophiles"; "bring a full wallet" as you'll be flanked by the "abundantly affluent", but remember "this is where all of your culinary desires" will be "fulfilled" by a "stellar" staff.

Viognier | 23 | 22 | 21 | $55 |

Draeger's Mktpl., 222 E. Fourth Ave. (bet. B St. & Ellsworth Ave.), San Mateo, 650-685-3727; www.viognierrestaurant.com

"Wander around" the gourmet goods below to "work up an appetite" advise "foodies" who ascend the stairs for "impressive" Californian-French fare at this "hidden gem in San Mateo" above the "high-end" Draeger's Market; "what a great concept" – the dishes are "enticing", the "setting beautiful" and the sommelier a "wealth of information"; if a few fret it's in an "odd" location, others shrug you "can do your shopping on the way home"; N.B. a post-*Survey* chef change may impact the Food score.

Yankee Pier | 17 | 15 | 17 | $32 |

378 Santana Row (S. Winchester Ave.), San Jose, 408-244-1244
San Francisco Int'l Airport, United Domestic Departure Terminal, South San Francisco, 650-821-8938
www.yankeepier.com

See review in North of San Francisco Directory.

Zao Noodle Bar | 14 | 11 | 13 | $16 |

261 University Ave. (bet. Bryant & Ramona Sts.), Palo Alto, 650-328-1988; www.zao.com

See review in City of San Francisco Directory.

Zibibbo | 20 | 21 | 19 | $41 |

430 Kipling St. (bet. Lytton & University Aves.), Palo Alto, 650-328-6722; www.restaurantlulu.com

Join the "pretty people" at Restaurant LuLu's "big", "buzzy", "bustling" brother in Palo Alto, one of the "sexiest" Peninsula spots with a "great indoor-outdoor layout that really makes you feel like you're in Europe" and a "tempting" Mediterranean menu, including small plates, to "satisfy a variety of cravings"; the "wine bar is unreal – who can keep track" of all the "awesome" vinos by the glass – while the patio with "twinkling lights" adds to the "wonderful experience."

Zucca Ristorante

21 | 18 | 21 | $36

186 Castro St. (bet. Central & Villa Sts.), Mountain View, 650-864-9940; www.zuccaristorante.com

"Perfect for grazers like me" – the seasonal "menu is right up my alley" with "tasty small plates" and "imaginative" entrees inspired by "bordering countries along the Mediterranean sea" opine patrons of this "popular" Downtown Mountain View "staple"; a "bargain" "pre-theater" prix fixe menu, "fresh" ingredients that "shine", a "fun cocktail list" and "wonderful outdoor seating" with "heaters for nippier nights" further "distinguish" this "friendly place" from other Castro Street spots.

Indexes

CUISINES
LOCATIONS
SPECIAL FEATURES

Places outside of San Francisco are marked as follows:
E=East of SF; N=North; and S=South.

CUISINES

Afghan
Helmand

American
Alfred's Steak
Bing Crosby's/E
Bungalow 44/N
Burger Joint
Cafe Divine
Cafe Grillades
Cafe Grillades/S
Cuvée/N
Giordano Bros.
House
Kookez Café
Max's
MoMo's
Monti's Rotisserie/N
Oola

American (New)
ad hoc/N
Alexis Baking Co./N
Ame
Arcadia/S
Basin/S
Beach Chalet
Big 4
Bistro Ralph/N
Blue Plate
Boonville Hotel/N
Boulette's Larder
Boulevard
Brick
Cafe Esin/E
Cafe La Haye/N
Cafe Z Epicerie/N
Campton Place
Caprice/N
Celadon/N
Chenery Park
Chow/Park Chow
Chow/Park Chow/E
Cindy's Backstreet/N
Cosmopolitan

Crave
Deuce/N
Dottie's True Blue
Dry Creek Kitchen/N
Duck Club/E/N/S
Eulipia/S
Evan's American/E
Flea St. Café/S
Fog City Diner
French Laundry/N
Frisson
Fumé Bistro/N
Gar Woods Grill/E
Gary Danko
Gordon's/N
Indigo
Jodie's Rest./E
John Bentley's/S
Kenwood/N
Kingfish
Kingfish/S
Lion & Compass/S
Luka's Taproom/E
Luna Park
Madrona Manor/N
Manresa/S
Martini House/N
Mecca
Mendo Bistro/N
Michael Mina
Moose's
Mustards Grill/N
Myth
Navio/S
955 Ukiah/N
Oak City B&G/S
One Market
Pacific's Edge/S
Park Chalet
Park Grill
Pine Cone Diner/N
Postrio
Range
Redd Restaurant/N

Restaurant/N
rnm
Rotunda
Sardine Factory/S
Seven/S
Shadowbrook/S
Slow Club
Soule Domain/E
Street
Tablespoon
Terra/N
Town Hall
Town's End
2223
231 Ellsworth/S
Universal Cafe
Village Pub/S
Washington Sq. B & G
Wild Goose Rest./E
Woodward's Garden
XYZ
zazu/N
Zin/N
Zinsvalley/N

American (Regional)
Forbes Mill Steak/S
Green Chile Kitchen
Maverick
Sea Salt/E
Woodhouse Fish Co.
Yankee Pier/N/S

American (Traditional)
Ahwahnee Din. Rm./E
Balboa Cafe
Balboa Cafe/E
Barndiva/N
Bette's Oceanview/E
Bistro Boudin
BIX
Blackberry Bistro/E
Brannan's Grill/N
Brazen Head
Brigetender's Tavern/E
Buckeye Roadhse./N
Carnelian Room

Casa Orinda/E
Chapter & Moon/N
Cheesecake Factory
Cheesecake Factory/S
Chloe's Cafe
Dipsea Cafe/Flying Pig/N
Duarte's Tavern/S
Ella's
Forbes Mill Steak/E
Gayle's Bakery/S
Goat Hill Pizza
Hard Rock Cafe
Home
In-N-Out Burger/N/S
Lark Creek/E
Lark Creek Inn/N
Liberty Cafe
MacArthur Park
MacArthur Park/S
Mama's Wash. Sq.
Mama's Royal Cafe/E
Market/N
Maverick
Mo's
Nepenthe/S
Original Joe's
Original Joe's/S
Pluto's Fresh Food
Pork Store Café
Press/N
Q
Red/Nevada Red Hut/E
Red's Java House
Rick & Ann's/E
Rosamunde Grill
Rutherford Grill/N
Sam's Anchor/N
Sauce
Scott's/E/S
Sears Fine Food
Tarpy's Roadhouse/S
Taylor's Automatic
Taylor's Automatic/N

Argentinean
Boca/N
El Raigon

Asian

Alexander's Steak/S
Asia de Cuba
Azie
Bridges/E
butterfly embarcadero
CAFÉ KATi
Circolo
Dragonfly/E
Eos Rest./Wine Bar
Hawthorne Lane
Limón
Sparrow
SUMI
Wolfdale's/E

Asian Fusion

Amber Rest./E
AsiaSF
Bridges/E
CAFÉ KATi
Eos Rest./Wine Bar
Flying Fish Grill/S
House
Koo
Silks
SUMI

Bakeries

Alexis Baking Co./N
Bistro Boudin
Boulange
Cafe Cacao/E
Citizen Cake
Downtown Bakery/N
Gayle's Bakery/S
Il Fornaio
Il Fornaio/E/N/S
Liberty Cafe
Mama's Wash. Sq.
Model Bakery/N
Tartine Bakery
Town's End

Barbecue

Bo's Barbecue/E
Bounty Hunter/N

Buckeye Roadhse./N
Everett & Jones/E
Foothill Cafe/N
Memphis Minnie's
Q
T Rex Barbecue/E
Zeitgeist

Belgian

Frjtz Fries

Brazilian

Espetus Churrascaria
Mangarosa

British

Betty's Fish & Chips/N
Lovejoy's Tea Rm.

Burmese

Burma Super Star
Mandalay
Nan Yang/E

Cajun

Andrew Jaeger's
Elite Cafe

Californian

Abigail's Bakery
Adagia/E
Ahwahnee Din. Rm./E
Albion River Inn/N
All Season's Cafe/N
Americano
Annabelle's
Anton & Michel/S
Applewood Inn/N
Aqua
A. Sabella's
AsiaSF
Asqew Grill
Asqew Grill/E
A Tavola/S
Auberge du Soleil/N
bacar
Bar Tartine
Bay Wolf/E

Bistro Aix
Bistro Elan/S
Bistro Ralph/N
Bistro 1689
Blackhawk Grille/E
Boca/N
Boonville Hotel/N
Bouchée/S
Boulevard
Bridges/E
Brix/N
Bucci's/E
butterfly embarcadero
Cafe Beaujolais/N
Cafe La Haye/N
Caffé Verbena/E
Canteen
Carneros/N
Chez Panisse/E
Chez Panisse Café/E
Christy Hill/E
Cindy's Backstreet/N
Citizen Cake
Citron/E
Cliff House Bistro
Club XIX/S
Coco 500
Coi
Cool Café/S
de Young Cafe
downtown/E
Dragonfly/E
Ecco/S
El Dorado Kitchen/N
Eliza's
El Paseo/N
Enrico's Sidewalk
Eos Rest./Wine Bar
Erna's Elderberry/E
Étoile/N
Farmhouse Inn/N
1550 Hyde Café
Firecracker
Flavor/N
Flea St. Café/S
Fleur de Lys
Flying Fish Grill/S

Flying Fish Grill/S
Foreign Cinema
Fork/N
Fournou's Ovens
Frascati
Gabriella Café/S
Garden Court
Garibaldis
Garibaldis/E
General Café/N
Globe
Grand Cafe
Grasing's Coastal/S
Hawthorne Lane
Hurley's/N
Jack Falstaff
Jake's on the Lake/E
Jardinière
Jimmy Bean's/E
John Ash & Co./N
Jordan's/E
Julia's Kitchen/N
jZcool/S
Kitchen at 868 Grant/N
Lalime's/E
La Scene Café
L'Auberge Carmel/S
Ledford House/N
Little River Inn/N
Lucy's/N
MacCallum House/N
Manka's Inverness/N
Mantra/S
Manzanita/N
Meadowood Grill/N
Mendocino Hotel/N
Mezze/E
Modern Tea
Montrio Bistro/S
Moody's Bistro/E
Moosse Cafe/N
Mustards Grill/N
Napa Valley Grille/N
Napa Wine Train/N
Nectar Wine
NoPa
North Coast Brewing/N

N.V./N
Olema Inn/N
Osake/Sake 'O/N
Oswald/S
Pangaea/N
Pappo/E
Parcel 104/S
Passionfish/S
Pearl/N
Pilar/N
Pisces/S
Plumed Horse/S
PlumpJack Cafe
PlumpJack Cafe/E
Public
Ravenous Cafe/N
Rest. at Meadowood/N
Richmond Rest.
Rio Grill/S
River Ranch Rest./E
Rivoli/E
Rogue Chefs/S
Rubicon
Rue Saint Jacques
Saha
Santé/N
Scott Howard
Sea Ranch Lodge/N
Seasons
Seaweed Café/N
Senses Rest.
Sent Sovi/S
71 Saint Peter/S
Sierra Mar/S
Silks
Soizic/E
Spago Palo Alto/S
Station House Cafe/N
St. Michael's/S
Stokes/S
St. Orres/N
Sutro's at Cliff Hse.
Syrah/N
Tabla/N
Townhouse B&G/E
2223
Venus/E

Viognier/S
Waterfront
Wente Vineyards/E
Wine Spectator/N
Wine Valley Rest./N
Wolfdale's/E
Zaré/N
Zax Tavern/E

Cambodian
Angkor Borei
Battambang/E

Caribbean
Cha Cha Cha
Charanga

Caviar
Tsar Nicoulai

Central American
Platanos

Cheese Steaks
Jay's Cheesesteak

Chinese
(* dim sum specialist)
Alice's
Imperial/Berkeley Tea
Imperial/Berkeley Tea/E
Brandy Ho's
Chef Chu's/S
Dragon Well
Eliza's
Eric's
Firecracker
Fook Yuen Seafood/S*
Gary Chu's/N
Great China/E
Great Eastern*
Happy Cafe/S*
Henry's Hunan
House of Nanking
Hunan Home/Garden
Hunan Home/Garden/S
Jade Villa/E*
Jai Yun
Koi Palace/S*

Mandarin
Mayflower*
O'mei/S
R & G Lounge
Rest. Peony/E*
San Tung
Shanghai 1930
Shen Hua/E
Sino/S*
Tommy Toy's
Ton Kiang*
Yank Sing*
Yuet Lee

Coffee Shops/Diners
Bette's Oceanview/E
FatApple's/E
Jimmy Bean's/E
Mel's Drive-In
Pine Cone Diner/N
Sears Fine Food
St. Francis
Taylor's Automatic

Continental
Anton & Michel/S
Chantilly/S
Ecco/S
Fresh Cream/S
John Bentley's/S
Maddalena's/S
O'Reilly's Holy Grail
Shadowbrook/S

Creole
Andrew Jaeger's
Elite Cafe
Kingfish
Kingfish/S
PJ's Oyster Bed

Cuban
Asia de Cuba
Cafe Lo Cubano

Delis
California St. Deli
Jimtown Store/N

Max's
Max's/E/N/S
Moishe's Pippic
Saul's Rest./Deli/E

Dessert
Boulange
Cafe Cacao/E
Café Tiramisu
Cheesecake Factory
Cheesecake Factory/S
Citizen Cake
Downtown Bakery/N
Emporio Rulli
Emporio Rulli/N
Fenton's Creamery/E
Tartine Bakery

Eclectic
Andalu
Avatars/N
Avenue G
Celadon/N
Chez Shea/S
Cottonwood/E
Delancey St.
Della Fattoria/N
Fahrenheit Ultra/S
Firefly
Flavor/N
General Café/N
Harmony Rest./N
Jodie's Rest./E
Levende
Lime
Mantra/S
Maria Manso/N
North Coast Brewing/N
Olivia/E
Picco/N
Pomelo
Ravenous Cafe/N
Spettro/E
supperclub
Teatro ZinZanni
Va de Vi/E
Wappo Bar/N

Willi's Wine Bar/N
Willow Wood Mkt./N

Eritrean
Massawa

Ethiopian
Axum Cafe
Finfiné/E
Massawa

French
À Côté/E
Angèle/N
Annalien/N
Aqua
Auberge du Soleil/N
Bella Vista/S
Bistro 1689
Bistro V/N
BIX
Bodega Bistro
Boulange
Boulevard
Brannan's Grill/N
Cafe Beaujolais/N
Café Fanny/E
Cafe Grillades
Cafe Grillades/S
Cafe Jacqueline
Café Marcella/S
Caprice/N
Casanova/S
Chez Spencer
Club XIX/S
Coi
Couleur Café
El Paseo/N
Emile's/S
fig cafe & winebar/N
French Laundry/N
Fresh Cream/S
Gregoire/Socca Oven/E
Isa
Jardinière
Jordan's/E
Julia's Kitchen/N

Kenwood/N
La Folie
La Forêt/S
L'Amour/le Four
La Provence Rest.
La Toque/N
Luna Park
Madrona Manor/N
Mistral/S
Nizza La Bella/E
Pacific's Edge/S
Pangaea/N
Pisces/S
P.J. Steak/N
Plumed Horse/S
Rest. LuLu/Petite
Robert's Whitehouse/S
Scott Howard
Seasons
Seaweed Café/N
Senses Rest.
Seven/S
Soizic/E
Sonoma Meritage/N
Sparrow
Tao Cafe
Viognier/S

French (Bistro)
Abigail's Bakery
Alamo Square
Anjou
Baker St. Bistro
Bistro Aix
Bistro Clovis
Bistro Elan/S
Bistro Jeanty/N
Bistro Liaison/E
Bistro Vida/S
Bouchon/N
Brigitte's/S
Butler & Chef Cafe
Cafe Bastille
Café Claude
Café de la Presse
Café Rouge/E
Chapeau!

Charcuterie/N
Chez Maman
Chez Papa Bistrot
Chou Chou
Christophe/N
Clémentine
Côté Sud
Eguna Basque
Florio
Fringale
girl & the fig/N
Grand Cafe
Hyde St. Bistro
Jeanty at Jack's
Jojo/E
K&L Bistro/N
La Note/E
Le Central Bistro
Le Charm Bistro
Le Petit Robert
Le Zinc
Luka's Taproom/E
Mirepoix/N
Oola
Pearl Alley Bistro/S
Plouf
Rue Saint Jacques
Scala's Bistro
Sent Sovi/S
South Park Cafe
Syrah/N
Ti Couz
Water St. Bistro/N
Zazie

French (Brasserie)
Absinthe
Left Bank/E/N/S

French (New)
Ana Mandara
Azie
Chaya Brasserie
Chez TJ/S
Citron/E
Cyrus/N
Erna's Elderberry/E

Fifth Floor
Fleur de Lys
Fork/N
Le Colonial
Le Papillon/S
Les Amis
Manresa/S
Marché/S
Marché aux Fleurs/N
Marinus/S
Masa's
955 Ukiah/N
Quince
Rendezvous Inn/N
Rigolo
Ritz-Carlton Din. Rm.
Rubicon
SUMI

German
Suppenküche
Walzwerk

Greek
Evvia/S
Kokkari Estiatorio
Thea Mediterranean/S

Hamburgers
Balboa Cafe
Balboa Cafe/E
Barney's
Barney's/E/N
Burger Joint
Burger Joint/S
FatApple's/E
In-N-Out Burger
In-N-Out Burger/E/N/S
Joe's Cable Car
Mel's Drive-In
Mo's
Taylor's Automatic
Taylor's Automatic/N

Hawaiian
Da Kitchen/S
Hukilau
Moki's Sushi

Roy's
Roy's at Pebble Beach/S

Hawaii Regional
Roy's
Roy's at Pebble Beach/S

Health Food
Café Gratitude
Café Gratitude/E
jZcool/S
Lettus: Cafe Organic
Mixt Greens

Hot Dogs
Caspers Hot Dogs/E

Indian
Ajanta/E
Amber India/S
Breads of India/E
Dasaprakash/S
Dosa
Gaylord India
Gaylord India/S
Indian Oven
Junnoon/S
Lotus of India/N
Mantra/S
Naan 'n Curry
Naan 'n Curry/E
Passage to India/S
Rotee
Shalimar
Shalimar/E
Turmeric/S
Udupi Palace/E/S
Vik's Chaat Corner/E
Zante

Italian
(N=Northern; S=Southern)
Acquerello
Albona Rist. (N)
Alioto's (S)
Americano
Amici E. Coast Pizza
Amici E. Coast Pizza/E/N/S

Antica Trattoria
Aperto
A 16 (S)
A Tavola/S
Bella Trattoria (S)
Bella Vista/S
Bistro Don Giovanni/N
Bistro V/N
Bovolo/N
Brindisi Cucina (S)
Buca di Beppo
Buca di Beppo/S
Cafe Citti/N (N)
Café Fiore/E (N)
Café Tiramisu (N)
Caffe Delle Stelle
Caffe Macaroni (S)
Caffè Museo
Caffé Verbena/E
Casanova/S (N)
Casa Orinda/E
Cook St. Helena/N (N)
Cork/N
Cucina Paradiso/N (S)
Cucina Rest./Wine Bar/N
Delfina (N)
Della Santina's/N (N)
Dopo/E
E'Angelo
Eccolo/E (N)
Emmy's Spaghetti
Emporio Rulli
Emporio Rulli/N
Fior d'Italia (N)
Fireside Pizza/E
Florio
Frantoio/N (N)
Frascati
Gabriella Café/S (N)
Gioia Pizzeria/E
Gira Polli/N
Globe
Il Davide/N (N)
Il Fornaio
Il Fornaio/E/N/S
Il Postale/S
Incanto (N)

Jackson Fillmore
Joe DiMaggio's
Kuleto's (N)
Kuleto's/S (N)
La Ciccia
La Ginestra/N (S)
La Strada/S
Last Supper Club (S)
Lo Coco's/E (S)
L'Osteria del Forno (N)
Mangarosa
Mario's Bohemian (N)
Mescolanza (N)
Mezza Luna/S (S)
Mistral/S
Nizza La Bella/E
Nob Hill Café (N)
North Beach Rest. (N)
Oliveto/E
Original Joe's
Original Joe's/S
Osteria/S (N)
Ottimista Enoteca
Palio d'Asti
Pane e Vino (N)
Pasta Moon/S
Pasta Pomodoro
Pasta Pomodoro/E/S
Pazzia
Pesce (N)
Pianeta/E
Piatti/E/N/S
Piazza D'Angelo/N
Pizza Antica/E/N/S
Pizza Azzurro/N
Pizzaiolo/E (S)
Pizza Rustica/E
Pizzeria Delfina (N)
Pizzeria Picco/N (S)
Pizzeria Tra Vigne/N
Poggio/N (N)
Postino/E
Prima/E (N)
Quince
Rist. Amoroma/E (S)
Rist. Bacco
Rist. Capellini/S (N)

Rist. Fabrizio/N (N)
Rist. Ideale (S)
Rist. Milano (N)
Ristorante Parma
Rist. Raphael/E
Rist. Umbria (N)
Rose Pistola (N)
Rose's Cafe (N)
Salute E Ristorante/E
Santi/N (N)
Scala's Bistro (N)
Scoma's/N
Sharon's By Sea/N
Sociale
Sonoma Meritage/N (N)
Tommaso's (S)
Tratt. Contadina
Tratt. La Siciliana/E (S)
Tra Vigne/N (N)
Uva Trattoria/N (S)
Venezia/E
Venticello (N)
Vivande Porta Via (S)
Washington Sq. B & G
Wine Valley Rest./N
zazu/N (N)
Zuppa (S)

Japanese
(* sushi specialist)
Ace Wasabi's*
Anzu*
Blowfish Sushi*
Blowfish Sushi/S*
Chaya Brasserie*
Deep Sushi*
Ebisu*
Flying Fish Grill/S
Fuki Sushi/S*
Godzila Sushi*
Grandeho Kamekyo*
Grasshopper/E
Hamano Sushi*
Hana Japanese/N*
Hotei*
Isobune*
Juban

Cuisines

Juban/S
Kabuto*
Kaygetsu/S*
Kirala/E*
Koo*
Kyo-Ya*
Maki
Medicine Eatstation
Mifune
Moki's Sushi*
Naked Fish/E*
Nihon
O'Chamé/E
Osake/Sake 'O/N*
Ozumo*
Robata Grill/N*
Sanraku*
Sebo*
Shabu-Sen
Sushi Groove*
Sushi Ran/N*
Takara*
Ten-Ichi*
Tokyo Go Go*
Tsunami Sushi*
Uzen/E*
Yoshi's/E*
Yuzu*
Zushi Puzzle*

Jewish
California St. Deli
Saul's Rest./Deli/E

Korean
(* barbecue specialist)
Brother's Korean*
Koryo BBQ/E*
RoHan Lounge
San Tung

Kosher
California St. Deli
Rist. Raphael/E

Mediterranean
Absinthe
À Côté/E

bacar
Baraka
Bar Tartine
Bay Wolf/E
Belden Taverna
Brigitte's/S
Bucci's/E
Cafe Esin/E
Cafe Gibraltar/S
Café Marcella/S
Café Rouge/E
Caffè Museo
Cav Wine Bar
Cetrella Bistro/S
Chez Nous
Chez Panisse/E
Chez Panisse Café/E
Coco 500
Cortez
downtown/E
El Dorado Kitchen/N
Enrico's Sidewalk
Evvia/S
Fandango/S
1550 Hyde Café
Foreign Cinema
Fournou's Ovens
Garibaldis
Garibaldis/E
Gar Woods Grill/E
Goood Frikin' Chicken
Hurley's/N
Insalata's/N
Lalime's/E
La Méditerranée
La Méditerranée/E
La Scene Café
Lavanda/S
Ledford House/N
Lucy's/N
Luella
Manzanita/N
MarketBar
Mezze/E
Monti's Rotisserie/N

Olema Inn/N
Olivia/E
Ottimista Enoteca
Pappo/E
paul k
PlumpJack Cafe
PlumpJack Cafe/E
Public
Rest. at Stevenswood/N
Rest. LuLu/Petite
Ritz-Carlton Terrace
Rivoli/E
Savor
71 Saint Peter/S
Spago Palo Alto/S
Stokes/S
Terzo
Thea Mediterranean/S
Truly Mediterranean
Underwood Bar/N
Wente Vineyards/E
Willow Wood Mkt./N
Zaré/N
Zatar/E
Zax Tavern/E
Zibibbo/S
Zucca/S
Zuni Café

Mexican

Cactus Taqueria/E
Colibrí Mexican
Doña Tomás/E
El Balazo
El Metate
Guaymas/N
Joe's Taco Lounge/N
Juan's Place/E
La Cumbre Taqueria
La Cumbre Taqueria/S
Las Camelias/N
La Taqueria
La Taqueria/S
La Victoria Taqueria/S
Mamacita
Maya

Mijita
Nick's Crispy Tacos
Pancho Villa
Pancho Villa/S
Papalote Mexican
Picante Cocina/E
Puerto Alegre
Roosevelt Tamale
Tacubaya/E
Tamarindo Antojeria/E
Taqueria Can-Cun
Taqueria 3 Amigos/S
Taqueria Tlaquepaque/S
Tortilla Heights
Tres Agaves
Velvet Cantina

Middle Eastern

Dish Dash/S
Goood Frikin' Chicken
Kan Zaman
La Méditerranée
La Méditerranée/E
Saha
Truly Mediterranean
YaYa
Yumma's

Moroccan

Aziza
Belden Taverna
Medjool
Zagora

Nepalese

Little Nepal

Noodle Shops

Citizen Thai
Citrus Club
Hotei
Mifune
Osha Thai Noodles
San Tung
So
Zao Noodle
Zao Noodle/E/S

Nuevo Latino
Asia de Cuba
Circolo
Destino
Platanos
Sol y Lago/E
Tamarindo Antojeria/E
Velvet Cantina

Pacific Northwest
Fish/N
Flavor/N

Pacific Rim
Pacific Catch
Pacific Catch/N
Silks
Sushi Ran/N
Tonga Room

Pakistani
Naan 'n Curry
Naan 'n Curry/E
Pakwan
Pakwan/E
Rotee
Shalimar
Shalimar/E

Pan-Asian
Bambuddha
Betelnut Pejiu Wu
Citrus Club
(415) Asian
Gaylord India/N
Grasshopper/E
Ora/N
Poleng Lounge
Ponzu
RoHan Lounge
Straits Cafe/S
Tonga Room
Zao Noodle
Zao Noodle/E/S

Pan-Latin
Cascal/S
Charanga
Fonda Solana/E

Persian/Iranian
Maykadeh

Peruvian
Destino
Fresca
Limón
Mochica

Pizza
Amici E. Coast Pizza
Amici E. Coast Pizza/E/N/S
Arinell Pizza
Arinell Pizza/E
Bistro Boudin
Giorgio's Pizzeria
Goat Hill Pizza
La Ginestra/N
Lanesplitter/E
Little Star Pizza
Lo Coco's/E
Nicky's Pizzeria Rustica
North Beach Pizza
North Beach Pizza/E/S
Palio d'Asti
Patxi's Chicago Pizza
Patxi's Chicago Pizza/S
Pauline's Pizza
Pazzia
Pizza Antica/E/N/S
Pizza Azzurro/N
Pizzaiolo/E
Pizza Rustica/E
Pizzeria Delfina
Pizzeria Picco/N
Pizzeria Tra Vigne/N
Pizzetta 211
Postrio
Tommaso's
Zachary's Pizza/E
Zante

Polynesian
Trader Vic's
Trader Vic's/E/S

Portuguese
LaSalette/N

Pub Food
Brigetender's Tavern/E

Russian
Katia's Tea Rm.
Tsar Nicoulai

Sandwiches
Cafe Divine
Citizen Cake
Downtown Bakery/N
Gayle's Bakery/S
Giordano Bros.
Jimtown Store/N
Mario's Bohemian
Max's
Max's/E/N/S
Model Bakery/N
Pluto's Fresh Food
Rest. LuLu/Petite
Saigon Sandwiches

Seafood
Alamo Square
Alioto's
Aqua
A. Sabella's
Barbara Fishtrap/S
Bar Crudo
Catch
Farallon
Fish/N
Flying Fish Grill/S
Flying Fish Grill/S
Fook Yuen Seafood/S
Great Eastern
Guaymas/N
Hayes St. Grill
Hog Island Oyster
Koi Palace/S
Little River Inn/N
Lure/S
Marica/E
Mayflower
McCormick & Kuleto
O'Reilly's Holy Grail
Pacific Café

Pacific Catch
Pacific Catch/N
Passionfish/S
Pearl Oyster Bar/E
Pesce
Pisces/S
PJ's Oyster Bed
Plouf
Sam's Anchor/N
Sam's Grill
Sardine Factory/S
Scoma's
Scoma's/N
Scott's/E/S
Sea Ranch Lodge/N
Sears Fine Food
Sea Salt/E
Sharon's By Sea/N
Sonoma Meritage/N
Sunnyside Resort/E
Swan Oyster Depot
Tadich Grill
Tsar Nicoulai
Waterfront
Willi's Seafood/N
Woodhouse Fish Co.
Yabbies Coastal
Yankee Pier/N/S
Yuet Lee

Singaporean
Straits Cafe/S

Small Plates
(See also Spanish tapas specialist)
À Côté/E (French-Med)
Andalu (Eclectic)
AsiaSF (Cal-Asian)
Baraka (Mediterranean)
Barndiva/N (American)
Betelnut Pejiu Wu (Pan-Asian)
Cascal/S (Pan-Latin)
Cav Wine Bar (Mediterranean)
César/E (Spanish)

Cha Cha Cha (Caribbean)
Charanga (Latin-Carib.)
Chez Nous (Mediterranean)
Citizen Thai (Thai)
Cortez (Mediterranean)
Crave (New American)
E&O Trading Co. (SE Asian)
Eos Rest./Wine Bar (Cal-Asian)
Fonda Solana/E (Pan-Latin)
Fork/N (Cal-New French)
General Café/N (Cal-Eclectic)
Grasshopper/E (Pan-Asian)
Isa (French)
Levende (Eclectic)
Le Zinc (French)
Lime (Eclectic)
Medjool (Med-Middle Eastern)
Ora/N (Pan-Asian)
Ottimista Enoteca (Italian-Med)
Pearl Oyster Bar/E (Seafood)
Pesce (Italian)
Platanos (Central American)
Ponzu (Asian)
rnm (American-French)
Rogue Chefs/S (Californian)
RoHan Lounge (Pan-Asian)
Saha (Cal-Middle Eastern)
Soi Four/E (Thai)
Stokes/S (Cal-Med)
Straits Cafe/S (Pan-Asian)
Tamarine/S (Vietnamese)
Terzo (Mediterranean)
Three Seasons (Vietnamese)
Three Seasons/S (Vietnamese)
Underwood Bar/N (Med)
Va de Vi/E (Eclectic)
Willi's Seafood/N (Seafood)
Willi's Wine Bar/N (Eclectic)
Zibibbo/S (Mediterranean)
Zucca/S (Mediterranean)

Soul Food
farmerbrown
House of Chicken/Waffles/E
Powell's Place

Southeast Asian
Ana Mandara
Annalien/N
Bambuddha
Basil Thai
Bodega Bistro
Cha Am Thai
Cha Am Thai/E
Citizen Thai
Crustacean
E&O Trading Co.
E&O Trading Co./N/S
Khan Toke
King of Thai
Koh Samui
Le Cheval/E
Le Colonial
Le Soleil
Mangosteen
Manora's Thai
Marnee Thai
Osha Thai Noodles
Pho 84/E
Pho Hoa-Hiep II
Pho Hoa-Hiep II/E/S
Plearn Thai/E
Royal Thai/N
Slanted Door
Soi Four/E
Tamarine/S
Tao Cafe
Thai House
Thanh Long
Thep Phanom Thai
Three Seasons
Three Seasons/S
Tu Lan

Southern
Blue Jay Cafe
Everett & Jones/E
House of Chicken/Waffles/E
Kate's Kitchen
Powell's Place

Spanish
(* tapas specialist)
Alegrias*
Basque Cultural Ctr./S
B44
Bocadillos*
Cafe Lo Cubano
César/E*
Esperpento*
Iberia/S*
Iluna Basque*
Picaro*
Piperade
Ramblas*
Sabor of Spain/N*
Zarzuela*
Zuzu/N*

Steakhouses
Acme Chophouse
Alexander's Steak/S
Alfred's Steak
Anzu
A.P. Stump's/S
Boca/N
Cole's Chop House/N
El Raigon
Espetus Churrascaria
Harris'
House of Prime Rib
Izzy's Steak
Izzy's Steak/N/S
Joe DiMaggio's
Kurt's Carmel Chop House/S
Morton's Steak
P.J. Steak/N
Press/N
Ruth's Chris Steak
Sunnyside Resort/E
Vic Stewart's/E

Swiss
Emile's/S
Matterhorn Swiss

Tearooms
Imperial/Berkeley Tea
Imperial/Berkeley Tea/E

Lovejoy's Tea Rm.
Modern Tea
Poleng Lounge

Thai
Basil Thai
Cha Am Thai
Cha Am Thai/E
Citizen Thai
Khan Toke
King of Thai
Koh Samui
Kwanjai Thai
Manora's Thai
Marnee Thai
Osha Thai Noodles
Plearn Thai/E
Royal Thai/N
Soi Four/E
Suriya Thai
Thai Buddhist Temple/E
Thai House
Thep Phanom Thai

Turkish
A La Turca

Vegetarian
(* vegan)
Café Gratitude*
Café Gratitude/E*
Fleur de Lys
French Laundry/N
Greens
Herbivore*
Medicine Eatstation*
Millennium*
Ravens Rest./N*
Saha*
Udupi Palace/E/S

Vietnamese
Ana Mandara
Annalien/N
Bodega Bistro
Bong Su

Crustacean
Le Cheval/E
Le Colonial
Le Soleil
Mangosteen
Pho 84/E
Pho Hoa-Hiep II
Pho Hoa-Hiep II/E/S

Saigon Sandwiches
Slanted Door
Tamarine/S
Tao Cafe
Thanh Long
Three Seasons
Three Seasons/S
Tu Lan

LOCATIONS

CITY OF SAN FRANCISCO

AT&T Park/South Beach
Acme Chophouse
Amici E. Coast Pizza
Kingfish
MoMo's
Tres Agaves

Bernal Heights
Angkor Borei
Blue Plate
Chez Maman
Emmy's Spaghetti
Liberty Cafe
Little Nepal
Moki's Sushi
Taqueria Can-Cun
Zante

Castro
Asqew Grill
Catch
Chow/Park Chow
Côté Sud
Crave
Destino
Home
La Méditerranée
Lime
Mecca
Pasta Pomodoro
SUMI
Thai House
2223
Woodhouse Fish Co.

Chinatown
Brandy Ho's
Great Eastern
House of Nanking
Henry's Hunan
Hunan Home/Garden
Jai Yun
R & G Lounge
Yuet Lee

Cow Hollow
Amici E. Coast Pizza
Balboa Cafe
Betelnut Pejiu Wu
Brazen Head
Chez Maman
Boulange
L'Amour/le Four
Ottimista Enoteca
Pane e Vino
Pasta Pomodoro
PlumpJack Cafe
Rose's Cafe
Terzo
YaYa

Downtown
Alfred's Steak
Anjou
Anzu
Aqua
Asia de Cuba
Bar Crudo
Belden Taverna
B44
BIX
Brindisi Cucina
Cafe Bastille
Café Claude
Café de la Presse
Café Tiramisu
Campton Place
Canteen
Carnelian Room
Cheesecake Factory
Citizen Cake
Coi
Colibrí Mexican
Cortez
E&O Trading Co.
Emporio Rulli
Farallon
Frisson

Garden Court
Globe
Grand Cafe
Henry's Hunan
Jeanty at Jack's
King of Thai
Kokkari Estiatorio
Kuleto's
Kyo-Ya
La Scene Café
Le Central Bistro
Le Colonial
Les Amis
MacArthur Park
Masa's
Max's
Medicine Eatstation
Michael Mina
Millennium
Mixt Greens
Morton's Steak
Myth
Naan 'n Curry
Palio d'Asti
Park Grill
Piperade
Plouf
Ponzu
Postrio
Rotunda
Rubicon
Sam's Grill
Sanraku
Scala's Bistro
Scott Howard
Sears Fine Food
Seasons
Silks
Tadich Grill
Taqueria Can-Cun
Tommy Toy's
Trader Vic's
Yank Sing

Embarcadero
Americano
Boulette's Larder
Boulevard
butterfly embarcadero
Chaya Brasserie
Delancey St.
Fog City Diner
Gaylord India
Hog Island Oyster
Il Fornaio
Imperial/Berkeley Tea
MarketBar
Mijita
North Beach Pizza
One Market
Ozumo
Pancho Villa
Red's Java House
Rest. LuLu/Petite
Shanghai 1930
Slanted Door
Taylor's Automatic
Teatro ZinZanni
Town's End
Tsar Nicoulai
Waterfront

Excelsior
Joe's Cable Car
North Beach Pizza

Fisherman's Wharf
Alioto's
Ana Mandara
A. Sabella's
Bistro Boudin
Gary Danko
Grandeho Kamekyo
Hard Rock Cafe
In-N-Out Burger
Mandarin
McCormick & Kuleto
Scoma's

Forest Hills/West Portal
Chou Chou
Fresca

Glen Park
Chenery Park

Haight-Ashbury/Cole Valley
Asqew Grill
Boulange
Cha Cha Cha
Citrus Club
El Balazo
Eos Rest./Wine Bar
Grandeho Kamekyo
Kan Zaman
Massawa
North Beach Pizza
Pork Store Café
Zazie

Hayes Valley/Civic Center
Absinthe
Bistro Clovis
Cafe Grillades
Caffe Delle Stelle
Cav Wine Bar
Citizen Cake
Espetus Churrascaria
Fritz Fries
Hayes St. Grill
Indigo
Jardinière
Max's
Mel's Drive-In
Modern Tea
Moishe's Pippic
Patxi's Chicago Pizza
paul k
Sauce
Sebo
Suppenküche
Zuni Café

Inner Richmond
Avenue G
Bella Trattoria
Brother's Korean
Burma Super Star
Chapeau!
Clémentine
Giorgio's Pizzeria
Hukilau

Katia's Tea Rm.
King of Thai
Le Soleil
Mandalay
Mel's Drive-In
Q
Richmond Rest.
RoHan Lounge

Inner Sunset
Café Gratitude
Chow/Park Chow
Ebisu
Hotei
Koo
Marnee Thai
Naan 'n Curry
PJ's Oyster Bed
Pluto's Fresh Food
Pomelo
Yumma's

Japantown
CAFÉ KATi
Isobune
Juban
Maki
Mifune
Pasta Pomodoro
Shabu-Sen
Takara

Laurel Heights/ Presidio Heights
Cafe Lo Cubano
California St. Deli
Ella's
(415) Asian
Garibaldis
Pasta Pomodoro
Rigolo
Sociale

Lower Haight
Axum Cafe
Burger Joint
Indian Oven
Kate's Kitchen

Memphis Minnie's
rnm
Rosamunde Grill
Rotee
Thep Phanom Thai

Marina
Abigail's Bakery
Ace Wasabi's
Alegrias
A 16
Asqew Grill
Baker St. Bistro
Barney's
Bistro Aix
Dragon Well
E'Angelo
Emporio Rulli
Greens
Home
Isa
Izzy's Steak
Kwanjai Thai
Lettus: Cafe Organic
Mamacita
Mel's Drive-In
Nectar Wine
Pacific Catch
Pluto's Fresh Food
Ristorante Parma
Three Seasons
Yuzu
Zushi Puzzle

Mission District
Andalu
Arinell Pizza
Bar Tartine
Blowfish Sushi
Burger Joint
Café Gratitude
Cha Cha Cha
Charanga
Chez Spencer
Circolo
Delfina
Dosa

El Metate
Esperpento
Firecracker
Foreign Cinema
Goood Frikin' Chicken
Herbivore
Jay's Cheesesteak
La Cumbre Taqueria
La Provence Rest.
Last Supper Club
La Taqueria
Levende
Limón
Luna Park
Maverick
Medjool
Nihon
Osha Thai Noodles
Pakwan
Pancho Villa
Papalote Mexican
Pauline's Pizza
Picaro
Pizzeria Delfina
Platanos
Pork Store Café
Puerto Alegre
Ramblas
Range
Roosevelt Tamale
Senses Rest.
Slow Club
St. Francis
Suriya Thai
Tao Cafe
Taqueria Can-Cun
Tartine Bakery
Ti Couz
Tokyo Go Go
Truly Mediterranean
Universal Cafe
Velvet Cantina
Walzwerk
Woodward's Garden
Zagora
Zeitgeist

Nob Hill

Big 4
Crustacean
Fleur de Lys
Fournou's Ovens
Nob Hill Café
Ritz-Carlton Din. Rm.
Ritz-Carlton Terrace
Rue Saint Jacques
Ruth's Chris Steak
Shalimar
Sparrow
Swan Oyster Depot
Tonga Room
Venticello

Noe Valley

Alice's
Barney's
Bistro 1689
Chloe's Cafe
Deep Sushi
Eric's
Firefly
Fresca
Hamano Sushi
Incanto
Kookez Café
La Ciccia
Le Zinc
Lovejoy's Tea Rm.
Pasta Pomodoro
Pomelo
Rist. Bacco
Savor

North Beach

Albona Rist.
Andrew Jaeger's
Bocadillos
Cafe Divine
Cafe Jacqueline
Caffe Macaroni
Citizen Thai
Eguna Basque
El Raigon
Enrico's Sidewalk
Fior d'Italia

Giordano Bros.
Helmand
House
Iluna Basque
Joe DiMaggio's
Boulange
L'Osteria del Forno
Mama's Wash. Sq.
Mangarosa
Mario's Bohemian
Maykadeh
Moose's
Mo's
Naan 'n Curry
North Beach Pizza
North Beach Rest.
Pasta Pomodoro
Rist. Ideale
Rose Pistola
Tommaso's
Tratt. Contadina
Washington Sq. B & G

Outer Richmond

Aziza
Cliff House Bistro
Kabuto
Khan Toke
King of Thai
Mayflower
Mescolanza
Pacific Café
Pizzetta 211
Sutro's at Cliff Hse.
Ton Kiang

Outer Sunset

Beach Chalet
de Young Cafe
King of Thai
Marnee Thai
Park Chalet
Pasta Pomodoro
Pho Hoa-Hiep II
San Tung
So
Thanh Long

Locations

Pacific Heights
Boulange
Chez Nous
Eliza's
Florio
Godzila Sushi
Quince
Tortilla Heights
Vivande Porta Via

Potrero Hill
Aperto
Baraka
Chez Maman
Chez Papa Bistrot
Couleur Café
Eliza's
Goat Hill Pizza

Russian Hill
Acquerello
Antica Trattoria
Boulange
1550 Hyde Café
Frascati
Harris'
House of Prime Rib
Hyde St. Bistro
La Folie
Le Petit Robert
Luella
Matterhorn Swiss
Nick's Crispy Tacos
Nicky's Pizzeria Rustica
O'Reilly's Holy Grail
Pesce
Rist. Milano
Street
Sushi Groove
Tablespoon
Yabbies Coastal
Zarzuela

SoMa
Ame
Annabelle's
AsiaSF

Azie
bacar
Basil Thai
Bong Su
Buca di Beppo
Butler & Chef Cafe
Caffè Museo
Cha Am Thai
Coco 500
Cosmopolitan
Fifth Floor
Fringale
Goat Hill Pizza
Hawthorne Lane
Henry's Hunan
Jack Falstaff
Koh Samui
Le Charm Bistro
Manora's Thai
Maya
Mel's Drive-In
Mochica
Mo's
Oola
Pazzia
Public
Rest. LuLu/Petite
Rist. Umbria
Roy's
Sanraku
South Park Cafe
supperclub
Sushi Groove
Town Hall
Tu Lan
XYZ
Yank Sing
Zuppa

Tenderloin
A La Turca
Bambuddha
Bodega Bistro
Brick
Dottie's True Blue
farmerbrown
Mangosteen

Naan 'n Curry
Original Joe's
Osha Thai Noodles
Pakwan
Saha
Saigon Sandwiches
Shalimar
Thai House

Upper Fillmore
Elite Cafe
Fresca
Jackson Fillmore
La Méditerranée
Powell's Place

Ten-Ichi
Zao Noodle

Western Addition
Alamo Square
Blue Jay Cafe
Green Chile Kitchen
Herbivore
Jay's Cheesesteak
Little Star Pizza
NoPa
Papalote Mexican
Poleng Lounge
Tsunami Sushi

EAST OF SAN FRANCISCO

Alameda
Pappo

Albany
Caspers Hot Dogs
Fonda Solana
Jodie's Rest.
Nizza La Bella

Berkeley
Adagia
Ajanta
Arinell Pizza
Barney's
Imperial/Berkeley Tea
Bette's Oceanview
Bistro Liaison
Breads of India
Cactus Taqueria
Cafe Cacao
Café Fanny
Café Gratitude
Café Rouge
César
Cha Am Thai
Chez Panisse
Chez Panisse Café
downtown
Eccolo
FatApple's

Finfiné
Gioia Pizzeria
Great China
Gregoire/Socca Oven
Jimmy Bean's
Jordan's
Juan's Place
Kirala
Lalime's
La Méditerranée
Lanesplitter
La Note
Le Cheval
Lo Coco's
Naan 'n Curry
North Beach Pizza
O'Chamé
Olivia
Picante Cocina
Plearn Thai
Rick & Ann's
Rist. Raphael
Rivoli
Saul's Rest./Deli
Sea Salt
Shen Hua
Tacubaya
Thai Buddhist Temple
Tratt. La Siciliana

T Rex Barbecue
Udupi Palace
Venezia
Venus
Vik's Chaat Corner
Zachary's Pizza
Zatar
Zax Tavern

Carnelian Bay
Gar Woods Grill

Danville
Amber Rest.
Blackhawk Grille
Bridges
Forbes Mill Steak
Piatti

Dublin
Amici E. Coast Pizza
Caspers Hot Dogs

El Cerrito
FatApple's

Emeryville
Asqew Grill
Bucci's
Pasta Pomodoro
Townhouse B&G
Trader Vic's
Zao Noodle

Fremont
Shalimar

Hayward
Caspers Hot Dogs
Everett & Jones
Pakwan

Kings Beach
Soule Domain

Lafayette
Bo's Barbecue
Chow/Park Chow
Duck Club

Pizza Antica
Postino

Lake Tahoe
Red/Nevada Red Hut

Livermore
Wente Vineyards

Moraga
Rist. Amoroma

Oakland
À Côté
Barney's
Battambang
Bay Wolf
Blackberry Bistro
Breads of India
Cactus Taqueria
Caffé Verbena
Caspers Hot Dogs
César
Citron
Doña Tomás
Dopo
Everett & Jones
Fenton's Creamery
Garibaldis
Grasshopper
Gregoire/Socca Oven
House of Chicken/Waffles
In-N-Out Burger
Jade Villa
Jojo
Koryo BBQ
Lanesplitter
Le Cheval
Lo Coco's
Luka's Taproom
Mama's Royal Cafe
Marica
Max's
Mezze
Nan Yang
Oliveto
Pasta Pomodoro
Pearl Oyster Bar

Pho 84
Pho Hoa-Hiep II
Pizzaiolo
Pizza Rustica
Rest. Peony
Scott's
Soi Four
Soizic
Spettro
Tamarindo Antojeria
Uzen
Yoshi's
Zachary's Pizza

Olympic Valley
Balboa Cafe
Fireside Pizza
PlumpJack Cafe

Orinda
Casa Orinda

Pleasant Hill
Caspers Hot Dogs
Left Bank

Richmond
Caspers Hot Dogs
Salute E Ristorante

San Ramon
Cafe Esin

South Lake Tahoe
Café Fiore
Evan's American
Fresh Ketch Rest.

Naked Fish
Red/Nevada Red Hut

Tahoe City
Brigetender's Tavern
Christy Hill
Jake's on the Lake
River Ranch Rest.
Sol y Lago
Sunnyside Resort
Wolfdale's

Tahoe Vista
Wild Goose Rest.

Truckee
Cottonwood
Dragonfly
Moody's Bistro
Pianeta

Walnut Creek
Bing Crosby's
Breads of India
Caspers Hot Dogs
Il Fornaio
Lark Creek
Prima
Scott's
Sushi Groove East
Va de Vi
Vic Stewart's

Yosemite-Oakhurst
Ahwahnee Din. Rm.
Erna's Elderberry

NORTH OF SAN FRANCISCO

Bodega/Bodega Bay
Duck Club
Seaweed Café

Calistoga
All Season's Cafe
Brannan's Grill
Wappo Bar

Corte Madera
Il Fornaio
Izzy's Steak
Max's
Pacific Catch

Forestville
Farmhouse Inn

Geyserville
Santi

Glen Ellen/Kenwood
Cafe Citti
fig cafe & winebar
Kenwood

Greenbrae
Cafe Z Epicerie

Guerneville
Applewood Inn

Healdsburg/Windsor
Barndiva
Bistro Ralph
Bovolo
Charcuterie
Cyrus
Downtown Bakery
Dry Creek Kitchen
Jimtown Store
Madrona Manor
Manzanita
Mirepoix
Ravenous Cafe
Osake/Sake 'O
Willi's Seafood
Zin

Larkspur
E&O Trading Co.
Emporio Rulli
Lark Creek Inn
Left Bank
Picco
Pizzeria Picco
Rist. Fabrizio
Tabla
Yankee Pier

Mendocino County
Albion River Inn
Boonville Hotel
Cafe Beaujolais
Chapter & Moon
Ledford House

Little River Inn
MacCallum House
Mendo Bistro
Mendocino Hotel
Moosse Cafe
955 Ukiah
North Coast Brewing
Pangaea
Ravens Rest.
Rendezvous Inn
Restaurant
Rest. at Stevenswood
Sea Ranch Lodge
Sharon's By Sea
St. Orres

Mill Valley
Buckeye Roadhse.
Bungalow 44
Dipsea Cafe/Flying Pig
El Paseo
Frantoio
Gira Polli
In-N-Out Burger
Joe's Taco Lounge
La Ginestra
Ora
Piatti
Piazza D'Angelo
Pizza Antica
Robata Grill

Napa
Alexis Baking Co.
Angèle
Annalien
Bistro Don Giovanni
Bounty Hunter
Celadon
Cole's Chop House
Cuvée
Foothill Cafe
Fumé Bistro
General Café
In-N-Out Burger
Julia's Kitchen
Napa Wine Train

N.V.
Pearl
Pilar
Pizza Azzurro
Uva Trattoria
Zaré
Zinsvalley
Zuzu

Novato
Boca
Kitchen at 868 Grant

Petaluma
Cucina Paradiso
Della Fattoria
Water St. Bistro

Ross
Marché aux Fleurs

Rutherford
Auberge du Soleil
La Toque
Rutherford Grill

San Anselmo
Cucina Rest./Wine Bar
Fork
Insalata's

San Rafael
Amici E. Coast Pizza
Barney's
Dipsea Cafe/Flying Pig
Il Davide
Las Camelias
Lotus of India
Maria Manso
Royal Thai
Sabor of Spain

Santa Rosa/Rohnert Park
Betty's Fish & Chips
Flavor
Gary Chu's
Hana Japanese
John Ash & Co.
Monti's Rotisserie

Osake/Sake 'O
Syrah
Willi's Wine Bar
zazu

Sausalito
Avatars
Christophe
Cork
Fish
Gaylord India
Poggio
Scoma's
Sushi Ran

Sebastopol/Graton
Bistro V
K&L Bistro
Lucy's
Underwood Bar
Willow Wood Mkt.

Sonoma
Cafe La Haye
Carneros
Della Santina's
Deuce
El Dorado Kitchen
girl & the fig
Harmony Rest.
LaSalette
Santé
Sonoma Meritage

St. Helena
Cindy's Backstreet
Cook St. Helena
Market
Martini House
Meadowood Grill
Model Bakery
Pizzeria Tra Vigne
Press
Rest. at Meadowood
Taylor's Automatic
Terra

Tra Vigne
Wine Spectator
Wine Valley Rest.

Tiburon
Caprice
Guaymas
Sam's Anchor

West Marin/Olema
Manka's Inverness
Olema Inn
Pine Cone Diner
Station House Cafe

Yountville
ad hoc
Bistro Jeanty
Bouchon
Brix
Étoile
French Laundry
Gordon's
Hurley's
Mustards Grill
Napa Valley Grille
P.J. Steak
Redd Restaurant

SOUTH OF SAN FRANCISCO

Big Sur
Nepenthe
Sierra Mar

Burlingame
Ecco
Il Fornaio
Juban
Kuleto's
Max's
Pisces
Straits Cafe

Campbell
Buca di Beppo

Carmel/Monterey Peninsula
Anton & Michel
Bouchée
Casanova
Club XIX
Duck Club
Fandango
Flying Fish Grill
Fresh Cream
Grasing's Coastal
Il Fornaio
Kurt's Carmel Chop House
L'Auberge Carmel
Marinus

Montrio Bistro
Pacific's Edge
Passionfish
Piatti
Rio Grill
Robert's Whitehouse
Roy's at Pebble Beach
Sardine Factory
Stokes
Tarpy's Roadhouse

Cupertino
Alexander's Steak

Half Moon Bay/Coast
Barbara Fishtrap
Cafe Gibraltar
Cetrella Bistro
Chez Shea
Duarte's Tavern
Flying Fish Grill
Mezza Luna
Navio
Pasta Moon
Rogue Chefs
Taqueria 3 Amigos

Los Altos
Chef Chu's
Hunan Home/Garden

Los Gatos
Café Marcella
Forbes Mill Steak
Manresa

Menlo Park
Bistro Vida
Duck Club
Flea St. Café
Gaylord India
Iberia
Juban
jZcool
Kaygetsu
Left Bank
Marché
Oak City B&G

Millbrae
Fook Yuen Seafood
In-N-Out Burger

Mountain View
Amber India
Amici E. Coast Pizza
Cascal
Chez TJ
Da Kitchen
In-N-Out Burger
Passage to India
Zucca

Palo Alto
Bistro Elan
Buca di Beppo
Cool Café
Evvia
Fuki Sushi
Hunan Home/Garden
Il Fornaio
Junnoon
La Strada
Lavanda
MacArthur Park
Maddalena's
Mantra
Max's
Osteria

Patxi's Chicago Pizza
Scott's
Spago Palo Alto
St. Michael's
Straits Cafe
Tamarine
Three Seasons
Trader Vic's
Zao Noodle
Zibibbo

Redwood City
A Tavola
Chantilly
John Bentley's
Max's

Redwood Shores
Amici E. Coast Pizza
Mistral

San Bruno
Cafe Grillades

San Carlos
Izzy's Steak

San Jose
Amber India
A.P. Stump's
Arcadia
Blowfish Sushi
Buca di Beppo
Cheesecake Factory
E&O Trading Co.
Emile's
Eulipia
Fahrenheit Ultra
Il Fornaio
In-N-Out Burger
La Forêt
La Taqueria
La Victoria Taqueria
Left Bank
Le Papillon
Max's
Original Joe's
Pasta Pomodoro

Pizza Antica
Scott's
Seven
71 Saint Peter
Sino
Straits Cafe
Taqueria Tlaquepaque
Thea Mediterranean
Yankee Pier

San Mateo
Amici E. Coast Pizza
Happy Cafe
Kingfish
La Cumbre Taqueria
Left Bank
Lure
North Beach Pizza
Pancho Villa
Rist. Capellini
Taqueria 3 Amigos
231 Ellsworth
Viognier

Santa Clara
Brigitte's
Cheesecake Factory
Dasaprakash
Parcel 104
Piatti
Shalimar

Santa Cruz/Aptos/Capitola
Gabriella Café
Gayle's Bakery
O'mei
Oswald
Pearl Alley Bistro
Shadowbrook

Saratoga
Basin
Plumed Horse
Sent Sovi

South San Francisco/Daly City
Basque Cultural Ctr.
Burger Joint
In-N-Out Burger
Koi Palace
Pho Hoa-Hiep II
Yankee Pier

Sunnyvale
Dish Dash
Il Postale
Lion & Compass
Turmeric
Udupi Palace

Woodside
Bella Vista
John Bentley's
Village Pub

SPECIAL FEATURES

(Indexes list the best in each category. Multi-location restaurants' features may vary by branch.)

Breakfast
(See also Hotel Dining)
Alexis Baking Co./N
Bette's Oceanview/E
Blackberry Bistro/E
Boulange
Boulette's Larder
Butler & Chef Cafe
Cafe Cacao/E
Café Fanny/E
Cafe Lo Cubano
Chloe's Cafe
Dipsea Cafe/Flying Pig/N
Dottie's True Blue
Downtown Bakery/N
Ella's
Emporio Rulli
FatApple's/E
Gayle's Bakery/S
General Café/N
Gordon's/N
Il Fornaio
Il Fornaio/N
Jimmy Bean's/E
Jimtown Store/N
Kate's Kitchen
Koi Palace/S
La Note/E
Mama's Wash. Sq.
Mama's Royal Cafe/E
Mel's Drive-In
Model Bakery/N
Mo's
Oliveto/E
Pork Store Café
Red's Java House
Rick & Ann's/E
Rigolo
Rose's Cafe
Savor
Sears Fine Food
Tartine Bakery
Town's End
Venus/E
Water St. Bistro/N
Willow Wood Mkt./N
Zazie

Brunch
Absinthe
Adagia/E
Ahwahnee Din. Rm./E
Alexis Baking Co./N
Americano
Anzu
Baker St. Bistro
Balboa Cafe
Beach Chalet
Bistro Liaison/E
Bistro V/N
Bistro Vida/S
Blackberry Bistro/E
Blackhawk Grille/E
Blue Jay Cafe
Brix/N
Buckeye Roadhse./N
Cafe Cacao/E
Campton Place
Canteen
Carnelian Room
Catch
Cetrella Bistro/S
Chez Maman
Chloe's Cafe
Chow/Park Chow
Citizen Cake
Delancey St.
Dipsea Cafe/Flying Pig/N
Dottie's True Blue
Duck Club/E/S
Elite Cafe
Ella's
Erna's Elderberry/E

Fandango/S
fig cafe & winebar/N
Flea St. Café/S
Foreign Cinema
Fresca
Gabriella Café/S
Garden Court
Garibaldis/E
Gayle's Bakery/S
girl & the fig/N
Gordon's/N
Grand Cafe
Greens
Home
Insalata's/N
John Ash & Co./N
Jordan's/E
Kate's Kitchen
La Forêt/S
La Note/E
Lark Creek/E
Lark Creek Inn/N
Last Supper Club
Le Petit Robert
Levende
Le Zinc
Liberty Cafe
Luna Park
Memphis Minnie's
MoMo's
Moose's
Navio/S
Nob Hill Café
Park Chalet
Pesce
Piazza D'Angelo/N
Picante Cocina/E
PJ's Oyster Bed
Q
Rest. LuLu/Petite
Rick & Ann's/E
Rio Grill/S
Ritz-Carlton Terrace
Rose's Cafe
Santi/N
Savor
Scott's/E

Seasons
Seaweed Café/N
Shadowbrook/S
Slow Club
St. Michael's/S
Tarpy's Roadhouse/S
Ton Kiang
Town's End
Trader Vic's/E
2223
Universal Cafe
Venus/E
Viognier/S
Washington Sq. B & G
Wente Vineyards/E
Willow Wood Mkt./N
Yank Sing
Zazie
Zibibbo/S
Zucca/S
Zuni Café

Business Dining

Acme Chophouse
Alexander's Steak/S
Alfred's Steak
Amber India/S
Ame
Americano
Anzu
A.P. Stump's/S
Aqua
Azie
bacar
Basin/S
Belden Taverna
Big 4
Bing Crosby's/E
Bistro V/N
Boca/N
Bong Su
Boulevard
Café de la Presse
Caffé Verbena/E
Campton Place
Carnelian Room
Cha Am Thai

Chantilly/S
Chaya Brasserie
Chef Chu's/S
Coco 500
Cole's Chop House/N
Colibrí Mexican
Cool Café/S
Cosmopolitan
Duck Club/S
E&O Trading Co./S
Emile's/S
Evvia/S
Farallon
Flea St. Café/S
Fournou's Ovens
Fresh Cream/S
Fuki Sushi/S
Gaylord India
Gaylord India/S
Grand Cafe
Harris'
Hawthorne Lane
House of Prime Rib
Iberia/S
Il Fornaio
Il Fornaio/E/N/S
Izzy's Steak
Jack Falstaff
Jeanty at Jack's
Joe DiMaggio's
Junnoon/S
Kaygetsu/S
Kokkari Estiatorio
Kuleto's
Kuleto's/S
Kyo-Ya
La Forêt/S
Lavanda/S
Le Central Bistro
Le Papillon/S
Les Amis
Lion & Compass/S
MacArthur Park/S
Mandarin
Marinus/S
MarketBar
Masa's

Max's/E
Meadowood Grill/N
Mijita
Mistral/S
Mixt Greens
MoMo's
Moose's
Morton's Steak
Myth
Oak City B&G/S
One Market
Osteria/S
Ozumo
Palio d'Asti
Park Grill
Pazzia
Picco/N
Piperade
Poggio/N
Ponzu
Postrio
Press/N
Rest. LuLu/Petite
Rist. Umbria
Ritz-Carlton Din. Rm.
Roy's
Rubicon
Ruth's Chris Steak
Sam's Grill
Sanraku
Scott Howard
Seasons
71 Saint Peter/S
Shanghai 1930
Silks
Sino/S
South Park Cafe
Spago Palo Alto/S
St. Michael's/S
Tadich Grill
Tommy Toy's
Townhouse B&G/E
231 Ellsworth/S
Viognier/S
Waterfront
Yank Sing
Zibibbo/S

Zuni Café
Zuppa

Catering
Acquerello
Adagia/E
Alexis Baking Co./N
All Season's Cafe/N
Americano
Aqua
AsiaSF
Asqew Grill
Asqew Grill/E
Azie
Barndiva/N
Betelnut Pejiu Wu
Bistro Liaison/E
Bistro V/N
BIX
Blowfish Sushi
Blowfish Sushi/S
Bocadillos
Boonville Hotel/N
Buckeye Roadhse./N
Cafe Cacao/E
Cafe Esin/E
CAFÉ KATi
Caffé Verbena/E
César/E
Cetrella Bistro/S
Cha Cha Cha
Charanga
Chaya Brasserie
Chef Chu's/S
Chenery Park
Chez Nous
Chez Papa Bistrot
Chez Spencer
Citron/E
Coco 500
Colibrí Mexican
Cool Café/S
Cucina Paradiso/N
Della Santina's/N
Destino
downtown/E
Ebisu

Emile's/S
Emporio Rulli
Emporio Rulli/N
Eos Rest./Wine Bar
Evvia/S
fig cafe & winebar/N
Frascati
Fresca
Fringale
Gabriella Café/S
Gayle's Bakery/S
Gaylord India/S
General Café/N
Globe
Grasing's Coastal/S
Greens
Hana Japanese/N
Iberia/S
Il Davide/N
Il Fornaio/S
Insalata's/N
Jack Falstaff
Jimtown Store/N
Julia's Kitchen/N
jZcool/S
Kingfish
Kokkari Estiatorio
La Méditerranée
La Méditerranée/E
La Strada/S
Lavanda/S
Left Bank/E/N/S
Manresa/S
Manzanita/N
Marché/S
Marinus/S
Max's
Memphis Minnie's
Mochica
Moki's Sushi
Monti's Rotisserie/N
Nick's Crispy Tacos
Ozumo
Pangaea/N
Piatti/E/N/S
Piazza D'Angelo/N
Picante Cocina/E

Pilar/N
Pizza Antica/E
Pizza Rustica/E
PJ's Oyster Bed
Platanos
Pomelo
Q
Rest. LuLu/Petite
Rick & Ann's/E
Rose Pistola
Rose's Cafe
Roy's
Sabor of Spain/N
Santi/N
Saul's Rest./Deli/E
Seaweed Café/N
Shalimar
Shalimar/E
Slanted Door
Sociale
Spago Palo Alto/S
St. Michael's/S
Stokes/S
Straits Cafe/S
Tacubaya/E
Town Hall
Town's End
Tratt. La Siciliana/E
Tra Vigne/N
Truly Mediterranean
2223
Vik's Chaat Corner/E
Village Pub/S
Vivande Porta Via
Wappo Bar/N
Washington Sq. B & G
Wente Vineyards/E
Willi's Seafood/N
Willi's Wine Bar/N
Willow Wood Mkt./N
Woodward's Garden
Yabbies Coastal
Yank Sing
YaYa
Yumma's
Zao Noodle
Zao Noodle/E/S

Zatar/E
zazu/N
Zibibbo/S
Zin/N
Zuppa

Celebrity Chefs

Acme Chophouse, *Traci Des Jardins*
Ame, *Hiro Sone*
Andrew Jaeger's, *Andrew Jaeger*
Aqua, *Laurent Manrique*
Arcadia/S, *Michael Mina*
bacar, *Arnold Eric Wong*
Bistro Jeanty/N, *Philippe Jeanty*
Boca/N, *George Morrone*
Bocadillos, *Gerald Hirigoyen*
Bouchée/S, *Walter Manzke*
Bouchon/N, *Thomas Keller*
Boulevard, *Nancy Oakes*
Chef Chu's/S, *Lawrence Chu*
Chez Panisse/E, *Alice Waters*
Cindy's Backstreet/N, *Cindy Pawlcyn*
Citizen Cake, *Elizabeth Falkner*
Coco 500, *Loretta Keller*
Coi, *Daniel Patterson*
Cool Café/S, *Jesse Cool*
Cyrus/N, *Douglas Keane*
Delfina, *Craig Stoll*
Dry Creek Kitchen/N, *Charles Palmer*
Eos Rest./Wine Bar, *Arnold Eric Wong*
Farallon, *Mark Franz*
Fifth Floor, *Melissa Perello*
Flea St. Café/S, *Jesse Cool*
Fleur de Lys, *Hubert Keller*
(415) Asian, *John Beardsley*
French Laundry/N, *Thomas Keller*
Gary Danko, *Gary Danko*
Jardinière, *Traci Des Jardins*
Jeanty at Jack's, *Philippe Jeanty*

La Folie, *Roland Passot*

Lark Creek Inn/N, *Bradley Ogden*

La Toque/N, *Ken Frank*

L'Auberge Carmel/S, *Walter Manzke*

Left Bank/E/N/S, *Roland Passot*

Market/N, *Douglas Keane*

Martini House/N, *Todd Humphries*

Masa's, *Gregory Short*

Michael Mina, *Michael Mina*

Mijita, *Traci Des Jardins*

Mustards Grill/N, *Cindy Pawlcyn*

NoPa, *Laurence Jossel*

Oliveto/E, *Paul Bertolli*

Parcel 104/S, *Bradley Ogden*

Picco/N, *Bruce Hill*

Pilar/N, *Pilar Sanchez*

Piperade, *Gerald Hirigoyen*

Pizzeria Delfina, *Craig Stoll*

Pizzeria Picco/N, *Bruce Hill*

P.J. Steak/N, *Philippe Jeanty*

Postrio, *Wolfgang Puck*

Redd Restaurant/N, *Richard Reddington*

Ritz-Carlton Din. Rm., *Ron Siegel*

Roy's, *Roy Yamaguchi*

Roy's at Pebble Beach/S, *Roy Yamaguchi*

Rubicon, *Stuart Brioza*

Scott Howard, *Scott Howard*

Sino/S, *Chris Yeo*

Slanted Door, *Charles Phan*

Sol y Lago/E, *Johnny Alamilla*

Spago Palo Alto/S, *Wolfgang Puck*

Straits Cafe/S, *Chris Yeo*

Terra/N, *Hiro Sone*

Town Hall, *Steven and Mitchell Rosenthal*

Yankee Pier/S, *Bradley Ogden*

Zuni Café, *Judy Rodgers*

Child-Friendly

(Alternatives to the usual fast-food places; * children's menu available)

Acme Chophouse

Adagia/E*

Ahwahnee Din. Rm./E*

Alexis Baking Co./N

Alice's

Alioto's*

Amici E. Coast Pizza*

Amici E. Coast Pizza/E/N/S*

Aperto*

Arcadia/S*

A. Sabella's*

Asqew Grill*

Asqew Grill/E*

Barbara Fishtrap/S*

Barney's*

Barney's/E/N*

Basque Cultural Ctr./S*

Beach Chalet*

Bella Trattoria*

Bette's Oceanview/E

Bistro Boudin

Boulange

Brandy Ho's

Brannan's Grill/N

Brigitte's/S

Buca di Beppo*

Buca di Beppo/S*

Bucci's/E

Buckeye Roadhse./N*

Bungalow 44/N*

Burger Joint

Burma Super Star

Cactus Taqueria/E*

Cafe Cacao/E

Cafe Citti/N

Cafe Lo Cubano

Caffe Delle Stelle

Caffe Macaroni

Caffè Museo

Casa Orinda/E

Caspers Hot Dogs/E

Cetrella Bistro/S*

Cha Am Thai

Cha Am Thai/E
Cheesecake Factory
Cheesecake Factory/S
Chenery Park*
Chez Spencer
Chow/Park Chow*
Chow/Park Chow/E*
Cindy's Backstreet/N
Citrus Club
Cliff House Bistro
Cook St. Helena/N
Cool Café/S
Delancey St.
Dipsea Cafe/Flying Pig/N*
Dottie's True Blue
Downtown Bakery/N
Duarte's Tavern/S*
El Balazo*
Eliza's
Ella's*
Emmy's Spaghetti*
Emporio Rulli
Emporio Rulli/N
Enrico's Sidewalk
Eric's
Everett & Jones/E
FatApple's/E*
Fenton's Creamery/E*
Fireside Pizza/E*
Fish/N
Flavor/N*
Fog City Diner*
Fook Yuen Seafood/S
Foothill Cafe/N
Forbes Mill Steak/E*
Fournou's Ovens*
Garibaldis/E*
Gar Woods Grill/E*
General Café/N
Giordano Bros.
Giorgio's Pizzeria
Gira Polli/N
Goat Hill Pizza
Goood Frikin' Chicken
Great China/E
Great Eastern
Guaymas/N*

Hard Rock Cafe*
Henry's Hunan
Home
Hunan Home/Garden
Hunan Home/Garden/S
Hurley's/N*
Il Fornaio*
Il Fornaio/E/N/S*
In-N-Out Burger
In-N-Out Burger/N/S
Insalata's/N*
Jade Villa/E
Jay's Cheesesteak
Jimmy Bean's/E*
Jimtown Store/N*
Joe's Cable Car
Joe's Taco Lounge/N
Juan's Place/E
Juban
Juban/S
jZcool/S*
King of Thai
Koi Palace/S
Kookez Café*
Koryo BBQ/E
Kuleto's
Kuleto's/S
La Cumbre Taqueria
La Méditerranée*
La Méditerranée/E
Lark Creek/E*
Left Bank/E/N/S*
Lo Coco's/E
Lovejoy's Tea Rm.*
Lucy's/N
Mama's Wash. Sq.
Market/N
Max's*
Max's/E/N/S*
Mel's Drive-In*
Memphis Minnie's
Mifune
Model Bakery/N
Mo's*
Napa Valley Grille/N*
Nepenthe/S*
Nick's Crispy Tacos

North Beach Pizza
North Beach Pizza/E/S
North Beach Rest.
O'mei/S
Original Joe's
Original Joe's/S*
Pancho Villa
Pancho Villa/S
Parcel 104/S*
Park Chalet*
Pasta Pomodoro*
Pasta Pomodoro/E/S*
Pauline's Pizza
Piatti/E/N/S*
Picante Cocina/E*
Pizza Antica/E/S*
Pizza Azzurro/N
Pizza Rustica/E
Pizzeria Picco/N
Pizzeria Tra Vigne/N*
Pork Store Café
Powell's Place*
Q
R & G Lounge
Rest. Peony/E
Rick & Ann's/E*
Rigolo*
Robata Grill/N
Saul's Rest./Deli/E*
Savor*
Scoma's*
Scoma's/N*
Sears Fine Food
Sharon's By Sea/N*
Shen Hua/E
Taqueria Can-Cun
Tarpy's Roadhouse/S*
Taylor's Automatic
Taylor's Automatic/N
Tommaso's
Ton Kiang
Venezia/E*
Waterfront
Willow Wood Mkt./N
Yankee Pier/N/S*
Yank Sing
Yumma's

Zachary's Pizza/E
Zao Noodle*
Zao Noodle/E/S*

Critic-Proof
(Gets lots of business despite so-so food)
Beach Chalet
Buca di Beppo
Buca di Beppo/S
Mel's Drive-In
Zao Noodle
Zao Noodle/E/S

Dancing
Andrew Jaeger's
AsiaSF
Bambuddha
Frisson
Jordan's/E
Kan Zaman
Levende
Luka's Taproom/E
Maddalena's/S
Medjool
Plumed Horse/S
Shanghai 1930
Straits Cafe/S
Tonga Room
XYZ

Delivery
Ajanta/E
Alexis Baking Co./N
Amici E. Coast Pizza
Amici E. Coast Pizza/N/S
Angkor Borei
Asqew Grill
Asqew Grill/E
Barney's
Barney's/E/N
Basil Thai
Brandy Ho's
Buca di Beppo/S
Cha Cha Cha
Cortez
Dish Dash/S
Emporio Rulli

Fuki Sushi/S
Gary Chu's/N
Giordano Bros.
Goat Hill Pizza
Henry's Hunan
Insalata's/N
Jimtown Store/N
King of Thai
La Méditerranée
La Méditerranée/E
Mandalay
Max's
Max's/E/N
Mescolanza
North Beach Pizza
North Beach Pizza/E/S
Pakwan/E
Pho Hoa-Hiep II/E
Piatti/S
Pizza Antica/S
Pizza Rustica/E
Pork Store Café
Powell's Place
Rio Grill/S
Seven/S
Swan Oyster Depot
Ton Kiang
Vivande Porta Via
Yank Sing
Zante
Zatar/E

Dining Alone
(Other than hotels and places with counter service)
Absinthe
Ace Wasabi's
Acme Chophouse
Amber India/S
Andalu
Arinell Pizza
Arinell Pizza/E
Asqew Grill
Avatars/N
bacar
Bar Crudo
Barney's/N

Bar Tartine
Bette's Oceanview/E
Bistro Jeanty/N
Bistro Ralph/N
Blowfish Sushi
Blue Jay Cafe
Bocadillos
Bodega Bistro
Bong Su
Bouchon/N
Boulange
Boulevard
Bovolo/N
Breads of India/E
Buckeye Roadhse./N
Bungalow 44/N
Burger Joint
Cafe Bastille
Cafe Citti/N
Café Claude
Café de la Presse
Café Gratitude
Café Gratitude/E
Cafe Grillades
Cafe Grillades/S
Cafe Lo Cubano
Café Rouge/E
Cafe Z Epicerie/N
California St. Deli
Cascal/S
Cav Wine Bar
César/E
Cetrella Bistro/S
Cha Cha Cha
Chez Maman
Chez Papa Bistrot
Chou Chou
Citizen Cake
Coco 500
Coi
Cook St. Helena/N
Cork/N
Couleur Café
Cuvée/N
Da Kitchen/S
Della Fattoria/N
de Young Cafe

Dish Dash/S
Dosa
Duarte's Tavern/S
E&O Trading Co./S
Ebisu
Emporio Rulli/N
Enrico's Sidewalk
Eos Rest./Wine Bar
Evvia/S
farmerbrown
FatApple's/E
1550 Hyde Café
Firefly
Fog City Diner
Fringale
Frjtz Fries
General Café/N
Gioia Pizzeria/E
Godzila Sushi
Grandeho Kamekyo
Green Chile Kitchen
Gregoire/Socca Oven/E
Hamano Sushi
Hog Island Oyster
House of Chicken/Waffles/E
Hurley's/N
Jack Falstaff
Jodie's Rest./E
Kabuto
Kaygetsu/S
King of Thai
Kirala/E
Koo
Lanesplitter/E
La Note/E
Last Supper Club
La Victoria Taqueria/S
Left Bank/E/S
Le Petit Robert
Lettus: Cafe Organic
Le Zinc
Mario's Bohemian
MarketBar
Matterhorn Swiss
Maverick
Max's/S
Medicine Eatstation

Medjool
Mel's Drive-In
Mixt Greens
Modern Tea
Mustards Grill/N
Myth
Naan 'n Curry
Naked Fish/E
Nicky's Pizzeria Rustica
Nizza La Bella/E
North Coast Brewing/N
N.V./N
Ora/N
O'Reilly's Holy Grail
Ottimista Enoteca
Pacific Catch/N
Pancho Villa
Papalote Mexican
Pasta Pomodoro
Pasta Pomodoro/E
Patxi's Chicago Pizza
Patxi's Chicago Pizza/S
Pearl Oyster Bar/E
Pho Hoa-Hiep II
Pho Hoa-Hiep II/E
Pine Cone Diner/N
Piperade
Pizza Antica/E/S
P.J. Steak/N
Pluto's Fresh Food
Powell's Place
Redd Restaurant/N
Red/Nevada Red Hut/E
rnm
Robata Grill/N
Osake/Sake 'O/N
Sebo
Shabu-Sen
Sino/S
So
Sonoma Meritage/N
Suppenküche
Sushi Ran/N
Swan Oyster Depot
Tabla/N
Tablespoon
Taqueria Can-Cun

Taqueria 3 Amigos/S
Taqueria Tlaquepaque/S
Terzo
Thai House
Ti Couz
Tokyo Go Go
Tommaso's
Tortilla Heights
Town Hall
Tra Vigne/N
Tres Agaves
T Rex Barbecue/E
Tsunami Sushi
Viognier/S
Vivande Porta Via
Wild Goose Rest./E
Willi's Seafood/N
Woodhouse Fish Co.
Yank Sing
Yoshi's/E
Zatar/E
Zazie
Zeitgeist
Zibibbo/S
Zuni Café
Zushi Puzzle

Entertainment
(Call for days and times of performances)
Ahwahnee Din. Rm./E (piano)
Albion River Inn/N (piano)
Ana Mandara (jazz)
Anzu (jazz)
Asia de Cuba (Latin house)
AsiaSF (gender illusionists)
bacar (jazz)
Bambuddha (DJ)
Beach Chalet (jazz)
Big 4 (piano)
Bing Crosby's/E (piano)
Bistro Liaison/E (jazz)
BIX (jazz)
Blowfish Sushi/S (DJ)
Blue Jay Cafe (jazz)
butterfly embarcadero (DJ)
Cafe Bastille (jazz)

Café Claude (jazz)
Cascal/S (Spanish band)
Catch (jazz/piano)
Cetrella Bistro/S (jazz)
Chaya Brasserie (jazz)
Circolo (DJ)
Cosmopolitan (piano/vocals)
Deep Sushi (DJ)
downtown/E (jazz)
Emmy's Spaghetti (DJ)
Enrico's Sidewalk (jazz)
Everett & Jones/E (varies)
Foreign Cinema (movies)
Frisson (DJ)
Frjtz Fries (DJ)
Garden Court (harp/jazz)
Giordano Bros. (varies)
Harmony Rest./N (piano)
Harris' (jazz/piano)
Jardinière (jazz)
Jordan's/E (jazz)
Kan Zaman (varies)
Katia's Tea Rm. (accordion)
La Note/E (accordion)
Ledford House/N (jazz)
Left Bank/N (jazz/vocals)
Levende (varies)
Lime (DJ)
Maddalena's/S (jazz)
Marinus/S (jazz)
Max's (singing waiters)
Max's/S (singing waiters)
Mecca (DJ)
Moose's (jazz)
Navio/S (jazz)
Olema Inn/N (varies)
Pearl/N (varies)
Plumed Horse/S (jazz/piano)
Powell's Place (gospel)
Prima/E (jazz)
Puerto Alegre (mariachi trio)
Ramblas (flamenco guitar)
Ravenous Cafe/N (varies)
Ritz-Carlton Din. Rm. (harp)
RoHan Lounge (DJ)
Rose Pistola (jazz)
Rose's Cafe (guitar)

Santé/N (piano)
Sardine Factory/S (piano)
Scott's/E (jazz/piano)
Seasons (piano)
Shadowbrook/S (jazz)
Shanghai 1930 (jazz)
Slanted Door (DJ)
Straits Cafe/S (DJ/jazz)
Sushi Groove (DJ)
Tonga Room (live music)
Townhouse B&G/E (jazz)
Uva Trattoria/N (jazz)
Vic Stewart's/E (piano)
Wappo Bar/N (jazz)
Washington Sq. B & G (jazz)
XYZ (DJ)
Yoshi's/E (jazz)
Zaré/N (jazz)
Zuni Café (piano)

Fireplaces

Adagia/E
Albion River Inn/N
Alexander's Steak/S
Ame
Anton & Michel/S
Applewood Inn/N
A. Sabella's
Asia de Cuba
Auberge du Soleil/N
Barney's/E
Bella Vista/S
Betelnut Pejiu Wu
Big 4
Bistro Don Giovanni/N
Bistro Jeanty/N
Boca/N
Boonville Hotel/N
Bouchée/S
Boulange
Brannan's Grill/N
Brix/N
Buckeye Roadhse./N
Cafe Citti/N
Café Gratitude/E
Caprice/N
Casanova/S

Casa Orinda/E
Catch
Cetrella Bistro/S
Chantilly/S
Chez TJ/S
Chow/Park Chow
Chow/Park Chow/E
Christy Hill/E
Cottonwood/E
Cuvée/N
Della Santina's/N
Dipsea Cafe/Flying Pig/N
Duck Club/N/S
E&O Trading Co./N
El Paseo/N
Erna's Elderberry/E
Étoile/N
Evvia/S
Fandango/S
Farmhouse Inn/N
Fleur de Lys
Flying Fish Grill/S
Foreign Cinema
French Laundry/N
Fresh Cream/S
Gaylord India/S
Guaymas/N
Harmony Rest./N
Harris'
Home
House of Prime Rib
Hurley's/N
Iberia/S
Il Fornaio/E/N/S
Jake's on the Lake/E
John Ash & Co./N
Kenwood/N
Kokkari Estiatorio
Lark Creek Inn/N
La Toque/N
Ledford House/N
Left Bank/N
Lion & Compass/S
MacArthur Park
MacArthur Park/S
MacCallum House/N
Madrona Manor/N

Manka's Inverness/N
Marinus/S
Martini House/N
Mezza Luna/S
Moosse Cafe/N
Navio/S
Nepenthe/S
N.V./N
Oliveto/E
Olivia/E
Pacific's Edge/S
Parcel 104/S
Park Chalet
Piatti/E/N/S
Piazza D'Angelo/N
Plouf
Plumed Horse/S
PlumpJack Cafe/E
Poleng Lounge
Postino/E
Press/N
Prima/E
Ravenous Cafe/N
Rendezvous Inn/N
Rest. at Stevenswood/N
Rio Grill/S
River Ranch Rest./E
Robert's Whitehouse/S
Rutherford Grill/N
Salute E Ristorante/E
Santé/N
Santi/N
Sardine Factory/S
Sea Ranch Lodge/N
Seasons
Seaweed Café/N
Shadowbrook/S
Shanghai 1930
Sierra Mar/S
Spago Palo Alto/S
Stokes/S
St. Orres/N
Tarpy's Roadhouse/S
Terzo
Townhouse B&G/E
Vic Stewart's/E
Village Pub/S

Viognier/S
Wine Spectator/N
Zibibbo/S
Zinsvalley/N

Historic Places

(Year opened; * building)
1800 Côté Sud*
1800 Market/N*
1829 Cindy's Backstreet/N*
1844 Celadon/N*
1848 La Forêt/S*
1849 Tadich Grill
1857 Little River Inn/N*
1860 Mandarin*
1860 Pizza Antica/E*
1863 Cliff House Bistro
1864 Jeanty at Jack's*
1864 Pisces/S*
1865 O'Reilly's Holy Grail*
1866 Cole's Chop House/N*
1867 Sam's Grill
1875 Garden Court*
1875 La Note/E*
1876 Gordon's/N*
1876 Olema Inn/N*
1878 A.P. Stump's/S*
1878 Mendocino Hotel/N*
1879 Il Fornaio/S*
1880 Deuce/N*
1880 Pianeta/E*
1881 Madrona Manor/N*
1882 MacCallum House/N*
1884 General Café/N*
1884 Terra/N*
1886 Fior d'Italia
1886 Mendo Bistro/N*
1886 Willi's Wine Bar/N*
1889 Boulevard*
1889 Lark Creek Inn/N*
1889 Pacific Café*
1890 Chez TJ/S*
1890 Scoma's/N*
1893 Cafe Beaujolais/N*
1893 Jimtown Store/N*
1894 Duarte's Tavern/S*
1894 Fenton's Creamery/E

1894 Robert's Whitehouse/S*	1925 Alioto's
1895 Restaurant/N*	1925 John Bentley's/S*
1897 Rendezvous Inn/N*	1927 Ahwahnee Din. Rm./E
1900 Cha Cha Cha*	1927 Bella Vista/S*
1900 French Laundry/N*	1927 Townhouse B&G/E*
1900 La Ginestra/N*	1928 Alfred's Steak
1900 MacArthur Park*	1929 L'Auberge Carmel/S*
1900 Pauline's Pizza*	1930 Big 4*
1900 Salute E Ristorante/E*	1930 Caprice/N*
1902 Santi/N*	1930 Foreign Cinema*
1904 Moosse Cafe/N*	1930 Lalime's/E*
1904 paul k*	1930 Lo Coco's/E*
1905 Model Bakery/N*	1932 Casa Orinda/E*
1905 Postino/E*	1933 Luka's Taproom/E*
1905 Public*	1934 Caspers Hot Dogs/E
1906 Coco 500*	1934 Trader Vic's/E
1906 Imperial/Berkeley Tea*	1935 Tommaso's
1906 Pork Store Café*	1937 Buckeye Roadhse./N
1907 Town Hall*	1937 Original Joe's
1910 Campton Place*	1937 231 Ellsworth/S*
1910 Catch*	1938 Sears Fine Food
1910 Harris'*	1945 Tonga Room
1910 Poleng Lounge*	1947 Shadowbrook/S
1910 Rest. LuLu/Petite*	1949 House of Prime Rib
1912 Swan Oyster Depot	1949 Nepenthe/S
1913 Annabelle's*	1949 Taylor's Automatic/N
1913 Balboa Cafe	1950 Axum Cafe*
1913 Zuni Café*	1951 Trader Vic's
1914 Red's Java House*	1952 Plumed Horse/S
1915 Jordan's/E*	1953 Mel's Drive-In*
1915 MacArthur Park/S*	1955 Breads of India/E*
1915 Napa Wine Train/N*	1956 Original Joe's/S
1917 Manka's Inverness/N*	
1917 Pacific's Edge/S*	**Hotel Dining**
1917 Tarpy's Roadhouse/S*	Adagio Hotel
1918 Olivia/E*	Cortez
1918 St. Francis	Ahwahnee Hotel
1919 Albion River Inn/N*	Ahwahnee Din. Rm./E
1919 Sauce*	Auberge du Soleil
1920 Acquerello*	Auberge du Soleil/N
1920 A. Sabella's	Bernardus Lodge
1920 Kingfish/S*	Marinus/S
1920 Rist. Capellini/S*	Blue Rock Inn
1920 Sam's Anchor/N	Left Bank/N
1922 Hawthorne Lane*	Boonville Hotel
1923 Martini House/N*	Boonville Hotel/N
1925 Adagia/E*	

Campton Place Hotel
  Campton Place
Carlton Hotel
  Saha
Casa Madrona
  Poggio/N
Chateau du Sureau
  Erna's Elderberry/E
Claremont Resort & Spa
  Jordan's/E
Clift Hotel
  Asia de Cuba
Commodore Hotel
  Canteen
Dina's Garden Hotel
  Trader Vic's/S
Doubletree Plaza
  Hana Japanese/N
El Dorado Hotel
  El Dorado Kitchen/N
Fairmont Hotel
  Tonga Room
Fairmont Sonoma Mission
  Santé/N
Farmhouse Inn
  Farmhouse Inn/N
Four Seasons Hotel
  Seasons
Garden Court Hotel
  Il Fornaio/S
Highlands Inn
  Pacific's Edge/S
Hilltop Lodge
  Cottonwood/E
Hotel Healdsburg
  Dry Creek Kitchen/N
Hotel Monaco
  Grand Cafe
Hotel Nikko
  Anzu
Hotel Palomar
  Fifth Floor
Hotel Vintage Ct.
  Masa's
Hotel Vitale
  Americano

Huntington Hotel
  Big 4
Inn at Southbridge
  Pizzeria Tra Vigne/N
Inn at Spanish Bay
  Roy's at Pebble Beach/S
Lafayette Park Hotel & Spa
  Duck Club/E
L'Auberge Carmel
  L'Auberge Carmel/S
Ledson Hotel
  Harmony Rest./N
Les Mars Hotel
  Cyrus/N
Little River Inn
  Little River Inn/N
Lodge at Pebble Beach
  Club XIX/S
Lodge at Sonoma
  Carneros/N
MacCallum House Inn
  MacCallum House/N
Madrona Manor
  Madrona Manor/N
Mandarin Oriental Hotel
  Silks
Manka's Inverness Lodge
  Manka's Inverness/N
Meadowood Napa Valley
  Rest. at Meadowood/N
Meadowood Resort
  Meadowood Grill/N
Mendocino Hotel
  Mendocino Hotel/N
Monterey Plaza Hotel & Spa
  Duck Club/S
Olema Inn
  Olema Inn/N
Palace Hotel
  Garden Court
  Kyo-Ya
Park Hyatt Hotel
  Park Grill
Phoenix Hotel
  Bambuddha
Pine Inn, The
  Il Fornaio/S

PlumpJack Squaw Valley Inn
  PlumpJack Cafe/E
Post Ranch Inn
  Sierra Mar/S
Prescott Hotel
  Postrio
Rancho Caymus Inn
  La Toque/N
Renaissance Stanford Ct.
  Fournou's Ovens
Ritz-Carlton Half Moon Bay
  Navio/S
Ritz-Carlton Hotel
  Ritz-Carlton Din. Rm.
  Ritz-Carlton Terrace
Sainte Claire
  Il Fornaio/S
San Jose Marriott
  Arcadia/S
San Remo Hotel
  Fior d'Italia
Santa Clara Marriott
  Parcel 104/S
Savoy Hotel
  Millennium
Sea Ranch Lodge
  Sea Ranch Lodge/N
Serrano Hotel
  Ponzu
Sir Francis Drake Hotel
  Scala's Bistro
Sonoma Hotel
  girl & the fig/N
Stanford Inn & Spa
  Ravens Rest./N
Stanford Park Hotel
  Duck Club/S
Stevenswood Lodge
  Rest. at Stevenswood/N
St. Regis Hotel
  Ame
Truckee Hotel
  Moody's Bistro/E
Villa Florence Hotel
  Kuleto's
Warwick Regis
  La Scene Café

Westin St. Francis
  Michael Mina
W Hotel
  XYZ

Jacket Required
Ahwahnee Din. Rm./E
Fleur de Lys
French Laundry/N
Masa's
Tommy Toy's

Late Dining
(Weekday closing hour)
Absinthe (12 AM)
Andrew Jaeger's (1:45 AM)
Avenue G (12 AM)
Bouchon/N (12:30 AM)
Brazen Head (1 AM)
Brick (12 AM)
Brother's Korean (varies)
Caspers Hot Dogs/E (varies)
Everett & Jones/E (varies)
Fonda Solana/E (12:30 AM)
Globe (1 AM)
Great Eastern (1 AM)
House of Chicken/Waffles/E
  (varies)
In-N-Out Burger (1 AM)
In-N-Out Burger/E/N/S (1 AM)
King of Thai (varies)
Koryo BBQ/E (12 AM)
Lanesplitter/E (varies)
La Victoria Taqueria/S (2:00 AM)
Lime (varies)
Mamacita (12:00 AM)
Mel's Drive-In (varies)
Naan 'n Curry (varies)
Nihon (12 AM)
NoPa (1 AM)
North Beach Pizza (varies)
North Beach Pizza/E/S (varies)
Oola (1 AM)
Original Joe's/S (varies)
Osha Thai Noodles (varies)
Pancho Villa (varies)
Redd Restaurant/N (12 AM)

Sauce (12 AM)
Scala's Bistro (12 AM)
Taqueria Can-Cun (varies)
Thai House (varies)
Tortilla Heights (2 AM)
Tres Agaves (1 AM)
Tsunami Sushi (12 AM)
Zeitgeist (2 AM)
Zuni Café (12 AM)

Meet for a Drink

Absinthe
Alexander's Steak/S
Amber Rest./E
Americano
Ana Mandara
Andalu
Andrew Jaeger's
Annabelle's
AsiaSF
Azie
bacar
Balboa Cafe
Bambuddha
Barndiva/N
Bar Tartine
Beach Chalet
Belden Taverna
Betelnut Pejiu Wu
Big 4
Bing Crosby's/E
Bistro Clovis
Bistro Don Giovanni/N
Bistro V/N
Bistro Vida/S
BIX
Blowfish Sushi
Bong Su
Bouchon/N
Boulevard
Brazen Head
Brick
Brigetender's Tavern/E
Buckeye Roadhse./N
Bungalow 44/N
butterfly embarcadero
Cafe Bastille

Café Claude
Café de la Presse
Café Rouge/E
Carnelian Room
Cascal/S
Catch
Cav Wine Bar
Celadon/N
César/E
Cetrella Bistro/S
Cha Cha Cha
Chaya Brasserie
Citizen Thai
Cliff House Bistro
Coi
Colibrí Mexican
Cool Café/S
Cork/N
Cortez
Cosmopolitan
Cottonwood/E
Crave
Cuvée/N
Cyrus/N
Delfina
Doña Tomás/E
Dragonfly/E
E&O Trading Co.
E&O Trading Co./N/S
Elite Cafe
Enrico's Sidewalk
Eos Rest./Wine Bar
Fahrenheit Ultra/S
Farallon
farmerbrown
1550 Hyde Café
fig cafe & winebar/N
Florio
Fonda Solana/E
Foreign Cinema
(415) Asian
Fresh Ketch Rest./E
Frisson
Garibaldis
Garibaldis/E
Gar Woods Grill/E
Grasshopper/E

Guaymas/N
Harmony Rest./N
Home
Hukilau
Hurley's/N
Iberia/S
Incanto
Jack Falstaff
Jake's on the Lake/E
Jardinière
Joe DiMaggio's
Junnoon/S
Kan Zaman
Kingfish/S
Kokkari Estiatorio
Lanesplitter/E
Last Supper Club
Lavanda/S
Le Colonial
Left Bank/N/S
Le Petit Robert
Levende
Le Zinc
Lime
Luka's Taproom/E
Luna Park
Lure/S
MacArthur Park/S
Maddalena's/S
Mamacita
Mantra/S
Manzanita/N
MarketBar
Martini House/N
Maverick
Mecca
Medjool
Mendocino Hotel/N
Michael Mina
Modern Tea
MoMo's
Montrio Bistro/S
Moody's Bistro/E
Moose's
Mustards Grill/N
Myth
Nepenthe/S

Nihon
Nizza La Bella/E
NoPa
North Coast Brewing/N
N.V./N
Oliveto/E
One Market
Ora/N
O'Reilly's Holy Grail
Ottimista Enoteca
Ozumo
Palio d'Asti
Pangaea/N
Park Chalet
paul k
Pearl Alley Bistro/S
Pianeta/E
Picaro
Picco/N
P.J. Steak/N
Plouf
Plumed Horse/S
Poleng Lounge
Ponzu
Public
Puerto Alegre
Ramblas
Range
Redd Restaurant/N
Rest. LuLu/Petite
River Ranch Rest./E
Rogue Chefs/S
RoHan Lounge
Rose Pistola
Rose's Cafe
Roy's
Sam's Anchor/N
Sardine Factory/S
Scott Howard
Sea Salt/E
Shanghai 1930
Sino/S
Slow Club
Sol y Lago/E
Sonoma Meritage/N
Soule Domain/E
Spago Palo Alto/S

Sparrow
Sunnyside Resort/E
Suppenküche
Sushi Groove
Tablespoon
Tamarine/S
Terzo
Tokyo Go Go
Tonga Room
Town Hall
Townhouse B&G/E
Trader Vic's/E
Tra Vigne/N
Tres Agaves
2223
Underwood Bar/N
Va de Vi/E
Velvet Cantina
Washington Sq. B & G
Waterfront
Wild Goose Rest./E
Willi's Seafood/N
Wine Spectator/N
Zax Tavern/E
Zibibbo/S
Zin/N
Zuni Café
Zuppa
Zuzu/N

Natural/Organic
Absinthe
Acme Chophouse
Adagia/E
Albion River Inn/N
A.P. Stump's/S
Barndiva/N
Basin/S
Bistro Don Giovanni/N
Blue Plate
Boonville Hotel/N
Boulette's Larder
Breads of India/E
Brigitte's/S
Buckeye Roadhse./N
Cactus Taqueria/E
Cafe Beaujolais/N

Café Gratitude
Café Gratitude/E
Cafe La Haye/N
Caffé Verbena/E
Chez Panisse/E
Coi
Cool Café/S
Della Fattoria/N
Eccolo/E
Erna's Elderberry/E
Farmhouse Inn/N
1550 Hyde Café
Firefly
Fish/N
Flavor/N
Flea St. Café/S
Foreign Cinema
Gayle's Bakery/S
Green Chile Kitchen
Hayes St. Grill
Insalata's/N
Jack Falstaff
John Ash & Co./N
John Bentley's/S
Jojo/E
Julia's Kitchen/N
jZcool/S
Kitchen at 868 Grant/N
Lalime's/E
Lark Creek/E
Lark Creek Inn/N
Las Camelias/N
La Toque/N
L'Auberge Carmel/S
Ledford House/N
Lettus: Cafe Organic
MacCallum House/N
Madrona Manor/N
Manka's Inverness/N
Marché/S
Marché aux Fleurs/N
Marinus/S
Market/N
MarketBar
Martini House/N
Masa's
Medicine Eatstation

Mendo Bistro/N
Millennium
Mixt Greens
Model Bakery/N
Moki's Sushi
Navio/S
Nick's Crispy Tacos
Nicky's Pizzeria Rustica
NoPa
N.V./N
O'Chamé/E
Olema Inn/N
Oliveto/E
One Market
Pangaea/N
Pappo/E
Parcel 104/S
Passionfish/S
Pauline's Pizza
Pearl Alley Bistro/S
Picco/N
Pilar/N
Pine Cone Diner/N
Pizza Antica/E
Pizzaiolo/E
Pizzeria Tra Vigne/N
PJ's Oyster Bed
Quince
Range
Ravens Rest./N
Rest. at Stevenswood/N
Richmond Rest.
Ritz-Carlton Din. Rm.
Rivoli/E
Rogue Chefs/S
Rubicon
Santi/N
Sea Ranch Lodge/N
Seaweed Café/N
Sent Sovi/S
Sharon's By Sea/N
Slanted Door
Soizic/E
St. Orres/N
Syrah/N
Tabla/N
Tablespoon

Tacubaya/E
Tartine Bakery
Town Hall
2223
Underwood Bar/N
Venus/E
Viognier/S
Water St. Bistro/N
Willi's Seafood/N
Willi's Wine Bar/N
Willow Wood Mkt./N
Woodward's Garden
Yankee Pier/S
Yumma's
Zaré/N
Zatar/E
Zax Tavern/E
zazu/N
Zuni Café
Zuzu/N

Noteworthy Newcomers

Ame
Annalien/N
Avenue G
Bar Crudo
Bar Tartine
Bistro 1689
Bong Su
Bovolo/N
Brick
Café Gratitude
Café Gratitude/E
Cafe Grillades
Cav Wine Bar
Coi
Crave
Cuvée/N
de Young Cafe
Dosa
Eguna Basque
farmerbrown
(415) Asian
Joe DiMaggio's
Junnoon/S
La Ciccia
Lettus: Cafe Organic

Lure/S
Mamacita
Mantra/S
Medicine Eatstation
Mixt Greens
Modern Tea
NoPa
N.V./N
O'Reilly's Holy Grail
Ottimista Enoteca
Pappo/E
Range
Redd Restaurant/N
Rest. at Meadowood/N
Rist. Amoroma/E
Rogue Chefs/S
Scott Howard
Sea Salt/E
Sebo
Senses Rest.
Sino/S
Sol y Lago/E
Sparrow
supperclub
Tamarindo Antojeria/E
Terzo
Thea Mediterranean/S
Tres Agaves
T Rex Barbecue/E
Woodhouse Fish Co.

Offbeat
Ace Wasabi's
Albona Rist.
AsiaSF
Avatars/N
Aziza
Bambuddha
Barndiva/N
Basque Cultural Ctr./S
Blowfish Sushi
Buca di Beppo
Buca di Beppo/S
Buckeye Roadhse./N
Café Gratitude
Café Gratitude/E
Caffe Macaroni

Casa Orinda/E
Caspers Hot Dogs/E
Cha Cha Cha
Destino
Duarte's Tavern/S
E&O Trading Co./N
Fish/N
Flying Fish Grill/S
Frjtz Fries
Helmand
House of Chicken/Waffles/E
Jimtown Store/N
Jodie's Rest./E
Joe's Cable Car
Kan Zaman
Katia's Tea Rm.
Khan Toke
Lovejoy's Tea Rm.
Martini House/N
Matterhorn Swiss
Maykadeh
Millennium
Nick's Crispy Tacos
Puerto Alegre
Ravens Rest./N
Red's Java House
RoHan Lounge
Sino/S
Spettro/E
St. Orres/N
supperclub
Thai Buddhist Temple/E
Tonga Room
Trader Vic's/E
Venezia/E
Yoshi's/E
Zante

Outdoor Dining
(G=garden; P=patio;
S=sidewalk; T=terrace;
W=waterside)
Absinthe (S)
À Côté/E (P)
Adagia/E (P)
Alexis Baking Co./N (S)
Angèle/N (P,W)

Anton & Michel/S (G,P,W)
Aperto (S)
Applewood Inn/N (G,T)
A.P. Stump's/S (P)
A Tavola/S (S)
Auberge du Soleil/N (T)
Baker St. Bistro (S)
Bambuddha (P,W)
Barbara Fishtrap/S (P,S,W)
Barndiva/N (G,P)
Barney's (P)
Barney's/E/N (P)
Basin/S (P)
Bay Wolf/E (T)
Beach Chalet (W)
Betelnut Pejiu Wu (S)
B44 (S)
Bistro Aix (P)
Bistro Boudin (P)
Bistro Don Giovanni/N (P,T)
Bistro Elan/S (P)
Bistro Jeanty/N (P)
Bistro Liaison/E (P)
Bistro Vida/S (S)
Blackhawk Grille/E (P,T,W)
Blue Plate (G,P)
Bo's Barbecue/E (T)
Bouchon/N (P)
Boulange (S)
Bridges/E (P)
Brindisi Cucina (S)
Brix/N (P)
Bucci's/E (P)
Buckeye Roadhse./N (P)
Bungalow 44/N (P)
Cactus Taqueria/E (S)
Cafe Bastille (S,T)
Cafe Citti/N (P)
Café Claude (S)
Café Fanny/E (P)
Café Rouge/E (P)
Café Tiramisu (S)
Caffè Museo (S)
Casanova/S (P)
Cascal/S (P)
Catch (P,S)

Celadon/N (P)
César/E (P)
Cha Am Thai/E (P)
Charanga (P)
Chaya Brasserie (P,S)
Cheesecake Factory (P,T)
Chez Maman (S)
Chez Papa Bistrot (S)
Chez Spencer (G,P)
Chez TJ/S (T)
Chloe's Cafe (S)
Chow/Park Chow (P,S,T)
Chow/Park Chow/E (P)
Cindy's Backstreet/N (P)
Citron/E (P)
Club XIX/S (P,W)
Cole's Chop House/N (T,W)
Cool Café/S (P)
Cork/N (P)
Côté Sud (P)
Cucina Paradiso/N (P,W)
Delancey St. (P,S)
Delfina (P)
Della Santina's/N (G,P)
Deuce/N (G,P)
Doña Tomás/E (G,P)
Dopo/E (S)
Dry Creek Kitchen/N (S)
Duck Club/S (P)
Eccolo/E (P)
El Dorado Kitchen/N (P,W)
El Paseo/N (P)
Emporio Rulli (P,S)
Emporio Rulli/N (S)
Enrico's Sidewalk (P)
Étoile/N (P,T,W)
Everett & Jones/E (P,S)
Farmhouse Inn/N (T)
Fenton's Creamery/E (P)
Fish/N (T,W)
Flavor/N (P)
Flea St. Café/S (P)
Dipsea Cafe/Flying Pig/N (G)
Fog City Diner (S)
Fonda Solana/E (S)
Foreign Cinema (P)
Frantoio/N (G,P)

Frjtz Fries (P)
Fumé Bistro/N (P)
Gabriella Café/S (P)
Gayle's Bakery/S (P)
General Café/N (T,W)
girl & the fig/N (P)
Grasing's Coastal/S (P)
Gregoire/Socca Oven/E (S)
Guaymas/N (P,T,W)
Harmony Rest./N (S)
Hog Island Oyster (P,W)
Home (P)
Hurley's/N (P)
Hyde St. Bistro (S)
Iberia/S (P)
Il Davide/N (P)
Il Fornaio (P)
Il Fornaio/E/N/S (P)
Incanto (S)
Isa (P)
Jack Falstaff (P)
Jimmy Bean's/E (S)
Jimtown Store/N (P)
John Ash & Co./N (P)
Kenwood/N (G)
Kingfish (S)
La Note/E (P)
Lark Creek/E (P)
Lark Creek Inn/N (P)
LaSalette/N (P)
La Strada/S (T)
Le Charm Bistro (P)
Le Colonial (P)
Left Bank/E/N/S (P,S)
Le Zinc (G)
Lion & Compass/S (P)
Lucy's/N (P)
MacCallum House/N (T)
Madrona Manor/N (T)
Marché aux Fleurs/N (P)
Maria Manso/N (P)
MarketBar (P)
Martini House/N (P)
Meadowood Grill/N (T)
Medjool (P)
Mezze/E (S)
Mistral/S (P,W)

MoMo's (T)
Monti's Rotisserie/N (P)
Moosse Cafe/N (T)
Mo's (P)
Napa Valley Grille/N (P)
Nepenthe/S (P,W)
Nizza La Bella/E (S)
O'Chamé/E (P)
Olema Inn/N (G)
Oliveto/E (S)
Pangaea/N (T)
Parcel 104/S (P)
Park Chalet (G,W)
Pasta Moon/S (P)
Pazzia (P)
Piatti/E/N/S (P,W)
Piazza D'Angelo/N (P)
Picante Cocina/E (P)
Piperade (P)
Pizza Antica/E/S (P)
Pizzeria Tra Vigne/N (P)
Pizzetta 211 (S)
P.J. Steak/N (P)
Plouf (S)
PlumpJack Cafe/E (P)
Poggio/N (S)
Postino/E (P)
Press/N (P)
Prima/E (P)
Ravenous Cafe/N (P)
Red's Java House (P,W)
Rick & Ann's/E (P)
Ritz-Carlton Terrace (T)
Rose Pistola (S)
Rose's Cafe (S)
Roy's at Pebble Beach/S (P)
Rutherford Grill/N (P)
Santi/N (P)
Savor (G,P)
Scoma's/N (P,W)
Sea Salt/E (P)
Seaweed Café/N (P,S)
71 Saint Peter/S (P)
Sharon's By Sea/N (P,W)
Sierra Mar/S (T,W)
Slow Club (S)
Sociale (P)

Sonoma Meritage/N (G,P)
South Park Cafe (S)
Spago Palo Alto/S (G,P)
St. Michael's/S (S)
Straits Cafe/S (P)
Sushi Ran/N (P)
Tarpy's Roadhouse/S (P)
Tartine Bakery (S)
Taylor's Automatic (P)
Taylor's Automatic/N (G,P)
Ti Couz (S)
Townhouse B&G/E (P)
Town's End (P)
Trader Vic's/S (T)
Tra Vigne/N (G)
Underwood Bar/N (P)
Universal Cafe (P)
Va de Vi/E (S,T)
Wappo Bar/N (P)
Waterfront (P,W)
Water St. Bistro/N (P)
Wente Vineyards/E (P)
Willi's Seafood/N (P)
Willi's Wine Bar/N (P)
Wine Spectator/N (T)
Yankee Pier/N/S (P)
Yumma's (G)
Zaré/N (P)
Zazie (G)
Zibibbo/S (G,P)
Zinsvalley/N (P)
Zucca/S (S)
Zuni Café (S)

People-Watching

Absinthe
Ace Wasabi's
À Côté/E
Ana Mandara
Andrew Jaeger's
Asia de Cuba
AsiaSF
Balboa Cafe
Bambuddha
Barndiva/N
Bar Tartine
Belden Taverna

Betelnut Pejiu Wu
Bing Crosby's/E
Bistro Don Giovanni/N
Bistro Jeanty/N
BIX
Blowfish Sushi
Bong Su
Bouchon/N
Boulevard
Brick
Brigetender's Tavern/E
Bungalow 44/N
Cafe Bastille
Café Claude
Café de la Presse
Cascal/S
Catch
Cav Wine Bar
César/E
Cha Cha Cha
Chaya Brasserie
Chez Panisse Café/E
Circolo
Cottonwood/E
Crave
Dosa
downtown/E
Downtown Bakery/N
Dragonfly/E
E&O Trading Co./N
Enrico's Sidewalk
Evvia/S
Fahrenheit Ultra/S
Flea St. Café/S
Foreign Cinema
Fresh Ketch Rest./E
Frisson
Gar Woods Grill/E
Grasshopper/E
Harmony Rest./N
Jack Falstaff
Jake's on the Lake/E
Jardinière
Julia's Kitchen/N
Junnoon/S
Last Supper Club
Left Bank/N

Levende
Lime
Lure/S
Mamacita
Mario's Bohemian
MarketBar
Martini House/N
Maverick
Mecca
Medjool
Mijita
Moody's Bistro/E
Moose's
Mustards Grill/N
Myth
Nectar Wine
Nihon
NoPa
Ottimista Enoteca
Pasta Pomodoro
Picco/N
P.J. Steak/N
Poggio/N
Postrio
Public
Redd Restaurant/N
Rest. LuLu/Petite
River Ranch Rest./E
Rose Pistola
Rose's Cafe
Sam's Anchor/N
Scala's Bistro
Scott Howard
Sino/S
Spago Palo Alto/S
Sunnyside Resort/E
supperclub
Sushi Groove
Tamarine/S
Tokyo Go Go
Town Hall
Tra Vigne/N
Tres Agaves
Tsunami Sushi
2223
Village Pub/S
Viognier/S

Zibibbo/S
Zuni Café
Zuppa

Power Scenes
Alexander's Steak/S
Ana Mandara
Aqua
Arcadia/S
Asia de Cuba
Auberge du Soleil/N
bacar
Big 4
Blackhawk Grille/E
Bouchon/N
Boulevard
Chaya Brasserie
Chef Chu's/S
downtown/E
Evvia/S
Fifth Floor
Fleur de Lys
Forbes Mill Steak/E/S
Gary Danko
Hawthorne Lane
Il Fornaio/S
Jack Falstaff
Jardinière
Jeanty at Jack's
Kokkari Estiatorio
Le Central Bistro
Le Colonial
Lion & Compass/S
Martini House/N
Masa's
Michael Mina
Mistral/S
Moose's
Myth
One Market
Ottimista Enoteca
Ozumo
Parcel 104/S
Park Grill
Pisces/S
Plumed Horse/S
Postrio

Special Features

Press/N
Redd Restaurant/N
Ritz-Carlton Din. Rm.
Rubicon
Sam's Grill
Sanraku
Silks
Spago Palo Alto/S
Tadich Grill
Tommy Toy's
Town Hall
Village Pub/S
Viognier/S
Zuni Café

Pre-Theater Dining
(Call for prices and times)
Chapeau!
Clémentine
Colibrí Mexican
Hayes St. Grill
Hyde St. Bistro
Indigo
Jardinière
La Scene Café
paul k
Postrio
Rue Saint Jacques
Venus/E

Private Rooms
(Restaurants charge less at
off times; call for capacity)
Absinthe
Acme Chophouse
À Côté/E
Acquerello
Adagia/E
Alegrias
Alexander's Steak/S
Alfred's Steak
Ana Mandara
Andalu
Angèle/N
Anton & Michel/S
A.P. Stump's/S
Arcadia/S

Auberge du Soleil/N
Aziza
bacar
Baraka
Barndiva/N
Basin/S
Bay Wolf/E
Bella Vista/S
Betelnut Pejiu Wu
Big 4
Bing Crosby's/E
Bistro Aix
Bistro Liaison/E
Blackhawk Grille/E
Blue Plate
Boca/N
Boonville Hotel/N
Boulevard
Bridges/E
Brix/N
Buca di Beppo/S
Buckeye Roadhse./N
butterfly embarcadero
CAFÉ KATi
Café Rouge/E
Campton Place
Caprice/N
Carnelian Room
Carneros/N
Casanova/S
Cetrella Bistro/S
Cha Cha Cha
Chantilly/S
Chaya Brasserie
Chef Chu's/S
Chez TJ/S
Cindy's Backstreet/N
Citizen Thai
Citron/E
Cliff House Bistro
Club XIX/S
Cortez
Cosmopolitan
Cyrus/N
downtown/E
Dry Creek Kitchen/N
El Paseo/N

270

Emile's/S

Eos Rest./Wine Bar

Erna's Elderberry/E

Eulipia/S

Fandango/S

Farallon

Fifth Floor

Flea St. Café/S

Fleur de Lys

Florio

Foreign Cinema

Frantoio/N

French Laundry/N

Frisson

Garibaldis/E

Gary Chu's/N

Gary Danko

girl & the fig/N

Grand Cafe

Grasing's Coastal/S

Harris'

Hawthorne Lane

Hurley's/N

Iberia/S

Il Davide/N

Il Fornaio

Il Fornaio/S

Incanto

Indigo

Insalata's/N

Jardinière

Jeanty at Jack's

John Ash & Co./N

John Bentley's/S

Kenwood/N

Khan Toke

Kokkari Estiatorio

Kurt's Carmel Chop House/S

La Folie

La Forêt/S

Lalime's/E

Lark Creek Inn/N

La Strada/S

Last Supper Club

La Toque/N

L'Auberge Carmel/S

Lavanda/S

Le Colonial

Ledford House/N

Left Bank/E/N/S

Le Papillon/S

Lion & Compass/S

Little River Inn/N

MacCallum House/N

Maddalena's/S

Madrona Manor/N

Manresa/S

Manzanita/N

Marché/S

Marinus/S

Martini House/N

Masa's

Maya

Mecca

Millennium

Montrio Bistro/S

Moose's

Morton's Steak

Myth

Navio/S

North Beach Rest.

Olema Inn/N

Oliveto/E

One Market

Ozumo

Pacific's Edge/S

Palio d'Asti

Parcel 104/S

Passionfish/S

Pauline's Pizza

Pesce

Piatti/N/S

Piazza D'Angelo/N

PJ's Oyster Bed

P.J. Steak/N

Plumed Horse/S

PlumpJack Cafe

PlumpJack Cafe/E

Poggio/N

Ponzu

Postino/E

Postrio

Press/N

Prima/E

R & G Lounge
Rest. LuLu/Petite
Rio Grill/S
Rist. Ideale
Ritz-Carlton Din. Rm.
Robert's Whitehouse/S
Rose Pistola
Roy's
Rubicon
Ruth's Chris Steak
Santi/N
Sardine Factory/S
Sauce
Scala's Bistro
Scott's/E
Sea Ranch Lodge/N
Seasons
71 Saint Peter/S
Shadowbrook/S
Shanghai 1930
Silks
Slanted Door
Soi Four/E
Soizic/E
Spago Palo Alto/S
St. Orres/N
Straits Cafe/S
Syrah/N
Tamarine/S
Tarpy's Roadhouse/S
Terra/N
Ti Couz
Tommy Toy's
Town Hall
Townhouse B&G/E
Trader Vic's
Trader Vic's/E/S
Tratt. La Siciliana/E
Tra Vigne/N
2223
231 Ellsworth/S
Underwood Bar/N
Vic Stewart's/E
Village Pub/S
Viognier/S
Wappo Bar/N
Wente Vineyards/E

Wine Spectator/N
Yank Sing
Zarzuela
Zax Tavern/E
Zibibbo/S
Zinsvalley/N
Zuppa

Prix Fixe Menus
(Call for prices and times)
Absinthe
Acquerello
Ajanta/E
Alamo Square
Anjou
Aqua
Asia de Cuba
Auberge du Soleil/N
Aziza
Baker St. Bistro
Bistro Liaison/E
BIX
Boonville Hotel/N
Bouchée/S
Brigitte's/S
Café Marcella/S
Carnelian Room
Casanova/S
Cetrella Bistro/S
Chantilly/S
Chapeau!
Chaya Brasserie
Chez Panisse/E
Chez Panisse Café/E
Chez Spencer
Chez TJ/S
Christophe/N
Citron/E
Côté Sud
Cyrus/N
Dry Creek Kitchen/N
Duck Club/E
Ecco/S
Erna's Elderberry/E
Espetus Churrascaria
Étoile/N
Farallon

Firefly
Fleur de Lys
Florio
Fork/N
Fournou's Ovens
French Laundry/N
Gary Danko
Gaylord India/S
girl & the fig/N
Grand Cafe
Grasing's Coastal/S
Greens
Hana Japanese/N
Helmand
Hurley's/N
Indigo
Jardinière
Juban/S
Julia's Kitchen/N
Kyo-Ya
La Folie
La Forêt/S
Lark Creek Inn/N
La Strada/S
La Toque/N
Le Charm Bistro
Ledford House/N
Left Bank/S
Le Papillon/S
Le Zinc
MacCallum House/N
Madrona Manor/N
Mandarin
Manka's Inverness/N
Manresa/S
Marica/E
Marinus/S
Market/N
Martini House/N
Masa's
Maya
Michael Mina
Millennium
Moose's
Navio/S
Pacific's Edge/S
Pisces/S

Ponzu
Postrio
Ritz-Carlton Din. Rm.
rnm
Robert's Whitehouse/S
Roy's
Sanraku
Santé/N
Seasons
Sent Sovi/S
71 Saint Peter/S
Shanghai 1930
Sierra Mar/S
Silks
Slanted Door
South Park Cafe
St. Orres/N
Syrah/N
Tao Cafe
Tommy Toy's
Ton Kiang
Town's End
Tratt. La Siciliana/E
2223
231 Ellsworth/S
Viognier/S
XYZ

Quiet Conversation
Acquerello
Alexander's Steak/S
Applewood Inn/N
Auberge du Soleil/N
Bay Wolf/E
Bella Vista/S
Cafe Jacqueline
Campton Place
Casanova/S
Chantilly/S
Chez Panisse/E
Chez TJ/S
Cyrus/N
Duck Club/E/N/S
El Paseo/N
Farmhouse Inn/N
Fifth Floor
Fleur de Lys

Forbes Mill Steak/E/S
Fournou's Ovens
Gary Danko
Lalime's/E
La Toque/N
L'Auberge Carmel/S
Lovejoy's Tea Rm.
Madrona Manor/N
Manresa/S
Marché aux Fleurs/N
Masa's
O'Chamé/E
Oswald/S
Pacific's Edge/S
Park Grill
Postino/E
Quince
Rest. at Meadowood/N
Seasons
Silks
Soule Domain/E
Sparrow
St. Orres/N
SUMI
Terzo

Raw Bars
Absinthe
Acme Chophouse
Angèle/N
A.P. Stump's/S
Aqua
bacar
Bar Crudo
Bistro Vida/S
Blowfish Sushi
Blowfish Sushi/S
Bouchon/N
Café Rouge/E
Cetrella Bistro/S
Farallon
Fish/N
Flea St. Café/S
Fog City Diner
Foreign Cinema
(415) Asian
Fresca

Fresh Ketch Rest./E
Godzila Sushi
Hog Island Oyster
Kingfish
Kingfish/S
Left Bank/S
O'Reilly's Holy Grail
Osake/Sake 'O/N
Pearl Oyster Bar/E
Pesce
Rest. LuLu/Petite
Scott Howard
Seasons
Sierra Mar/S
Sonoma Meritage/N
Station House Cafe/N
Sushi Ran/N
Swan Oyster Depot
Ti Couz
Willi's Seafood/N
Woodhouse Fish Co.
Yabbies Coastal
Yankee Pier/N/S
Yuzu
zazu/N
Zibibbo/S
Zucca/S
Zuni Café

Romantic Places
Acquerello
Ahwahnee Din. Rm./E
Albion River Inn/N
Alexander's Steak/S
Ana Mandara
Anton & Michel/S
Applewood Inn/N
Auberge du Soleil/N
Aziza
Barndiva/N
Bella Vista/S
Big 4
Bing Crosby's/E
Bistro Clovis
Bistro Elan/S
Bistro Vida/S
Boulevard

Cafe Beaujolais/N
Cafe Jacqueline
Caprice/N
Carnelian Room
Casanova/S
Cav Wine Bar
Chantilly/S
Chapeau!
Chez Panisse/E
Chez Spencer
Chez TJ/S
Christophe/N
Christy Hill/E
Citron/E
Coi
Cool Café/S
Cyrus/N
Duck Club/E/N/S
El Paseo/N
Emile's/S
Erna's Elderberry/E
Étoile/N
Farmhouse Inn/N
Fifth Floor
Flea St. Café/S
Fleur de Lys
French Laundry/N
Fresh Cream/S
Gabriella Café/S
Garden Court
Gary Danko
Incanto
Indigo
Jardinière
John Ash & Co./N
John Bentley's/S
Katia's Tea Rm.
Khan Toke
La Folie
La Forêt/S
Lalime's/E
L'Amour/le Four
La Note/E
Lark Creek Inn/N
La Toque/N
L'Auberge Carmel/S
Le Papillon/S

Les Amis
Little River Inn/N
MacCallum House/N
Maddalena's/S
Madrona Manor/N
Manka's Inverness/N
Mantra/S
Marché aux Fleurs/N
Marinus/S
Martini House/N
Masa's
Matterhorn Swiss
Medjool
Michael Mina
Moosse Cafe/N
Napa Wine Train/N
O'Chamé/E
Olema Inn/N
Pacific's Edge/S
Picco/N
Quince
Rest. at Meadowood/N
Rest. at Stevenswood/N
Ritz-Carlton Din. Rm.
Ritz-Carlton Terrace
River Ranch Rest./E
Robert's Whitehouse/S
Roy's at Pebble Beach/S
Rue Saint Jacques
Salute E Ristorante/E
Sea Salt/E
Sent Sovi/S
71 Saint Peter/S
Shadowbrook/S
Sierra Mar/S
Silks
Slow Club
Soizic/E
Sol y Lago/E
Soule Domain/E
St. Michael's/S
Stokes/S
St. Orres/N
Sunnyside Resort/E
supperclub
Terra/N
Terzo

Special Features

Venticello
Viognier/S
Wente Vineyards/E
Wild Goose Rest./E
Wolfdale's/E
Woodward's Garden
Zagora
Zarzuela
Zax Tavern/E

Senior Appeal
Acme Chophouse
Acquerello
Alfred's Steak
Alioto's
Anton & Michel/S
Bella Vista/S
Big 4
Bing Crosby's/E
Caprice/N
Chantilly/S
Christophe/N
Christy Hill/E
Cole's Chop House/N
Cook St. Helena/N
Cyrus/N
Duck Club/E/N/S
Emile's/S
Eulipia/S
Fior d'Italia
Fleur de Lys
Forbes Mill Steak/E/S
Fournou's Ovens
Garden Court
Harris'
Hayes St. Grill
House of Prime Rib
Izzy's Steak
Joe DiMaggio's
La Ginestra/N
Lalime's/E
Le Central Bistro
Masa's
Morton's Steak
North Beach Rest.
Plumed Horse/S
Rest. at Meadowood/N

Robert's Whitehouse/S
Rotunda
Sardine Factory/S
Scoma's
Soule Domain/E
Tadich Grill
Vic Stewart's/E

Singles Scenes
Ace Wasabi's
Andalu
Asia de Cuba
Balboa Cafe
Bambuddha
Barndiva/N
Beach Chalet
Betelnut Pejiu Wu
BIX
Blowfish Sushi
Blue Plate
butterfly embarcadero
Cafe Bastille
Café Claude
Cascal/S
Catch
Cha Cha Cha
Circolo
Cosmopolitan
Cottonwood/E
Dragonfly/E
E&O Trading Co.
E&O Trading Co./S
Elite Cafe
Emmy's Spaghetti
Fahrenheit Ultra/S
Firecracker
Foreign Cinema
(415) Asian
Frisson
Frjtz Fries
Gar Woods Grill/E
Guaymas/N
Home
Jack Falstaff
Jake's on the Lake/E
Kan Zaman
Kingfish/S

Kwanjai Thai
Levende
Lime
Luna Park
Mecca
Medjool
MoMo's
Moody's Bistro/E
Nectar Wine
Nihon
Ottimista Enoteca
Ozumo
Pearl Alley Bistro/S
PJ's Oyster Bed
Poleng Lounge
Public
Puerto Alegre
Ramblas
River Ranch Rest./E
rnm
RoHan Lounge
Rose Pistola
Sam's Anchor/N
Seven/S
Sino/S
Slow Club
Sunnyside Resort/E
Sushi Groove
Ti Couz
Tokyo Go Go
Tres Agaves
Tsunami Sushi
2223
Universal Cafe
Velvet Cantina
Zibibbo/S
Zuni Café

Sleepers
(Good to excellent food, but
little known)
Avatars/N
Bar Crudo
Belden Taverna
Brigitte's/S
Chantilly/S
Chapter & Moon/N

Coi
Cook St. Helena/N
Cucina Paradiso/N
Della Fattoria/N
Dragonfly/E
El Metate
Foothill Cafe/N
Giordano Bros.
Jodie's Rest./E
Joe's Cable Car
Kitchen at 868 Grant/N
L'Auberge Carmel/S
La Victoria Taqueria/S
Ledford House/N
Les Amis
Little Star Pizza
Maria Manso/N
Marica/E
Maykadeh
Mendo Bistro/N
955 Ukiah/N
N.V./N
Olema Inn/N
Olivia/E
Osake/Sake 'O/N
Oswald/S
Pangaea/N
Pearl/N
Pizza Azzurro/N
Pizzeria Picco/N
Ravens Rest./N
Rendezvous Inn/N
Restaurant/N
Richmond Rest.
Robert's Whitehouse/S
Saha
Seaweed Café/N
St. Orres/N
Suriya Thai
Tabla/N
Tamarindo Antojeria/E
Uva Trattoria/N
Water St. Bistro/N
Woodward's Garden
YaYa
Yuzu

Tasting Menus

Acquerello
Alexander's Steak/S
A.P. Stump's/S
Aqua
Auberge du Soleil/N
Aziza
Imperial/Berkeley Tea
Imperial/Berkeley Tea/E
Bistro V/N
Bong Su
Bouchée/S
Cafe Gibraltar/S
Campton Place
Chantilly/S
Chapeau!
Chez Spencer
Chez TJ/S
Citron/E
Côté Sud
Cyrus/N
Dry Creek Kitchen/N
Duck Club/E
Ecco/S
El Dorado Kitchen/N
Étoile/N
Fifth Floor
Fior d'Italia
Fork/N
French Laundry/N
Frisson
Gary Danko
Hana Japanese/N
Harmony Rest./N
Jardinière
Julia's Kitchen/N
Kaygetsu/S
Koi Palace/S
Kyo-Ya
La Folie
La Forêt/S
La Toque/N
L'Auberge Carmel/S
Le Papillon/S
MacCallum House/N
Madrona Manor/N
Manresa/S
Marinus/S
Martini House/N
Masa's
Medicine Eatstation
Michael Mina
Millennium
Moody's Bistro/E
Navio/S
Pacific's Edge/S
Pisces/S
Postrio
Redd Restaurant/N
Rest. at Meadowood/N
Ritz-Carlton Din. Rm.
Rubicon
Sanraku
Santé/N
Sea Ranch Lodge/N
Senses Rest.
Sent Sovi/S
71 Saint Peter/S
Shanghai 1930
Sociale
Sonoma Meritage/N
Sparrow
supperclub
Syrah/N
Tommy Toy's
231 Ellsworth/S
XYZ

Teen Appeal

Barney's
Barney's/E/N
Beach Chalet
Buca di Beppo
Buca di Beppo/S
Burger Joint
Cactus Taqueria/E
Cheesecake Factory
Cheesecake Factory/S
FatApple's/E
Fenton's Creamery/E
Fog City Diner
Gar Woods Grill/E
Goat Hill Pizza
Hard Rock Cafe

Jake's on the Lake/E
Joe's Cable Car
Lettus: Cafe Organic
MacArthur Park/S
Max's
Max's/E/N/S
Mel's Drive-In
Mo's
Park Chalet
Pauline's Pizza
Picante Cocina/E
Pizza Antica/E
Pizzeria Picco/N
Rutherford Grill/N
Sardine Factory/S
Shen Hua/E
Sunnyside Resort/E
Taylor's Automatic/N
Tonga Room

Theme Restaurants
Bing Crosby's/E
Buca di Beppo
Buca di Beppo/S
Hard Rock Cafe
Joe DiMaggio's
Max's
Max's/E/N/S
Napa Wine Train/N
supperclub

Trendy
Ace Wasabi's
À Côté/E
Amber Rest./E
Ame
Aqua
Asia de Cuba
A 16
Azie
Balboa Cafe
Bambuddha
Barndiva/N
Bar Tartine
Betelnut Pejiu Wu
Bing Crosby's/E
Bistro Don Giovanni/N

BIX
Blowfish Sushi
Blue Jay Cafe
Blue Plate
Bocadillos
Bong Su
Bouchon/N
Boulevard
Brick
Buckeye Roadhse./N
Bungalow 44/N
Café Fanny/E
Café Rouge/E
Cascal/S
Cav Wine Bar
César/E
Cetrella Bistro/S
Cha Cha Cha
Charanga
Chez Nous
Chez Panisse Café/E
Chez Papa Bistrot
Cindy's Backstreet/N
Circolo
Crave
Deep Sushi
Delfina
Doña Tomás/E
Dosa
downtown/E
Dry Creek Kitchen/N
E&O Trading Co./N
Ebisu
Emmy's Spaghetti
Enrico's Sidewalk
Eos Rest./Wine Bar
Evvia/S
Fahrenheit Ultra/S
Farallon
farmerbrown
Flea St. Café/S
Fonda Solana/E
Foreign Cinema
Fringale
Frisson
Garibaldis/E
girl & the fig/N

Globe
Iluna Basque
Isa
Jack Falstaff
Jake's on the Lake/E
Jardinière
Junnoon/S
Last Supper Club
Levende
Lime
Limón
Luna Park
Mamacita
Martini House/N
Maverick
Mecca
Medjool
Moose's
Mustards Grill/N
Myth
Naked Fish/E
Nihon
NoPa
Osha Thai Noodles
Ottimista Enoteca
Ozumo
Pearl Oyster Bar/E
Piazza D'Angelo/N
Picco/N
Piperade
Pizza Antica/S
Pizzeria Delfina
Pizzeria Picco/N
Plouf
PlumpJack Cafe
Poggio/N
Postino/E
Postrio
Press/N
Public
Rest. LuLu/Petite
rnm
Rose Pistola
Rose's Cafe
Santi/N
Scott Howard
Sebo

Sino/S
Slanted Door
Slow Club
Spago Palo Alto/S
supperclub
Sushi Groove
Tamarine/S
Terzo
Ti Couz
Tokyo Go Go
Town Hall
Trader Vic's/E/S
Tres Agaves
Tsunami Sushi
2223
Universal Cafe
Village Pub/S
Willi's Seafood/N
XYZ
Zibibbo/S
Zuni Café
Zuppa
Zuzu/N

Valet Parking

Abigail's Bakery
Absinthe
Acme Chophouse
Ahwahnee Din. Rm./E
Albona Rist.
Amber Rest./E
Ame
Americano
Ana Mandara
Andalu
Anzu
Aqua
Arcadia/S
Asia de Cuba
Auberge du Soleil/N
Azie
Aziza
bacar
Balboa Cafe
Big 4
Bing Crosby's/E
BIX

Blowfish Sushi/S
Bong Su
Boulette's Larder
Boulevard
Bridges/E
Buckeye Roadhse./N
butterfly embarcadero
Campton Place
Caprice/N
Casa Orinda/E
Cha Am Thai
Chantilly/S
Chaya Brasserie
Cheesecake Factory/S
Citizen Cake
Club XIX/S
Coco 500
Coi
Cole's Chop House/N
Crustacean
Delancey St.
Duck Club/E
Ecco/S
El Raigon
Emile's/S
Enrico's Sidewalk
Evvia/S
Farallon
Fifth Floor
Fior d'Italia
Fleur de Lys
Florio
Foreign Cinema
Fournou's Ovens
Fringale
Frisson
Garibaldis
Garibaldis/E
Gary Danko
Grand Cafe
Harris'
Hawthorne Lane
Hayes St. Grill
Home
House of Prime Rib
Il Fornaio
Il Fornaio/E/S

Insalata's/N
Jack Falstaff
Jardinière
Joe DiMaggio's
Jordan's/E
Kingfish
Kingfish/S
Kokkari Estiatorio
Kuleto's
Kuleto's/S
Kwanjai Thai
Kyo-Ya
La Folie
Lark Creek Inn/N
La Scene Café
L'Auberge Carmel/S
Lavanda/S
Le Colonial
Left Bank/E/N
Le Petit Robert
Lion & Compass/S
Mangarosa
Mantra/S
Marinus/S
Masa's
Matterhorn Swiss
Maykadeh
Mecca
Medjool
Millennium
MoMo's
Moose's
Morton's Steak
Myth
Nob Hill Café
NoPa
North Beach Rest.
N.V./N
One Market
O'Reilly's Holy Grail
Ozumo
Pacific's Edge/S
Parcel 104/S
Piazza D'Angelo/N
Picco/N
Pizzeria Picco/N
Plumed Horse/S

PlumpJack Cafe
Poggio/N
Ponzu
Postino/E
Postrio
Prima/E
Quince
Rest. LuLu/Petite
Rist. Capellini/S
Rist. Milano
Ritz-Carlton Din. Rm.
Ritz-Carlton Terrace
rnm
Rose Pistola
Roy's at Pebble Beach/S
Rubicon
Ruth's Chris Steak
Santé/N
Scoma's
Scott Howard
Scott's/E
Seasons
Shanghai 1930
Sierra Mar/S
Silks
Slanted Door
Spago Palo Alto/S
Suppenküche
supperclub
Terzo
Thanh Long
Tokyo Go Go
Tommy Toy's
Townhouse B&G/E
Trader Vic's
Trader Vic's/E
Tres Agaves
231 Ellsworth/S
Venticello
Waterfront
Wente Vineyards/E
Wine Spectator/N
XYZ
Yankee Pier/N
Zibibbo/S
Zuni Café
Zuppa

Views

Ahwahnee Din. Rm./E
Albion River Inn/N
Alioto's
Americano
Angèle/N
Applewood Inn/N
A. Sabella's
Auberge du Soleil/N
Barbara Fishtrap/S
Barndiva/N
Beach Chalet
Bella Vista/S
Imperial/Berkeley Tea/E
Bistro Boudin
Bistro Don Giovanni/N
Blackhawk Grille/E
Boulette's Larder
Brigetender's Tavern/E
Brix/N
Cafe Beaujolais/N
Cafe Gibraltar/S
Caprice/N
Carnelian Room
Chaya Brasserie
Cheesecake Factory
Chez TJ/S
Christy Hill/E
Cliff House Bistro
Club XIX/S
Cool Café/S
Cucina Paradiso/N
Delancey St.
de Young Cafe
Dragonfly/E
Duck Club/E/N/S
Enrico's Sidewalk
Eos Rest./Wine Bar
Erna's Elderberry/E
Étoile/N
Fish/N
Fresh Cream/S
Gaylord India/N
General Café/N
Greens
Guaymas/N
Hog Island Oyster

Il Fornaio/S
Jake's on the Lake/E
John Ash & Co./N
Jordan's/E
Julia's Kitchen/N
Kenwood/N
La Forêt/S
Lark Creek Inn/N
Ledford House/N
Little River Inn/N
Mandarin
McCormick & Kuleto
Meadowood Grill/N
Mijita
Mistral/S
MoMo's
Moosse Cafe/N
Mo's
Napa Valley Grille/N
Napa Wine Train/N
Navio/S
Nepenthe/S
One Market
Ozumo
Pacific's Edge/S
Park Chalet
Piatti/N/S
Poggio/N
Press/N
Ravens Rest./N
Red's Java House
Rest. at Meadowood/N
Rest. at Stevenswood/N
River Ranch Rest./E
Rivoli/E
Rotunda
Roy's at Pebble Beach/S
Salute E Ristorante/E
Sam's Anchor/N
Scoma's
Scoma's/N
Scott's/E
Sea Ranch Lodge/N
Shadowbrook/S
Sharon's By Sea/N
Sierra Mar/S
Slanted Door

Sol y Lago/E
Sutro's at Cliff Hse.
Trader Vic's/E/S
Waterfront
Wente Vineyards/E
Wine Spectator/N
Zaré/N

Visitors on Expense Account

Acquerello
Alexander's Steak/S
Aqua
Auberge du Soleil/N
Azie
Boulevard
Campton Place
Carnelian Room
Chez Panisse/E
Chez TJ/S
Club XIX/S
Cyrus/N
Dry Creek Kitchen/N
Erna's Elderberry/E
Eulipia/S
Evvia/S
Fifth Floor
Flea St. Café/S
Fleur de Lys
Forbes Mill Steak/S
French Laundry/N
Fresh Cream/S
Gary Danko
Greens
Harris'
Jack Falstaff
Jardinière
John Ash & Co./N
Kaygetsu/S
Kokkari Estiatorio
Kyo-Ya
La Folie
La Forêt/S
Lark Creek Inn/N
La Toque/N
L'Auberge Carmel/S
Mandarin

Manresa/S
Marinus/S
Masa's
McCormick & Kuleto
Michael Mina
Morton's Steak
Napa Wine Train/N
Oliveto/E
Pacific's Edge/S
Park Grill
Plumed Horse/S
Press/N
Rest. at Meadowood/N
Ritz-Carlton Din. Rm.
Ritz-Carlton Terrace
Roy's
Roy's at Pebble Beach/S
Santé/N
Sea Ranch Lodge/N
Seasons
Sent Sovi/S
71 Saint Peter/S
Shanghai 1930
Sierra Mar/S
Silks
Sino/S
Spago Palo Alto/S
Tommy Toy's
Village Pub/S

girl & the fig/N
Harmony Rest./N
Incanto
Kuleto's
La Toque/N
Le Zinc
Liberty Cafe
Martini House/N
Maverick
Millennium
Napa Wine Train/N
Nectar Wine
Ottimista Enoteca
Pearl Alley Bistro/S
Picco/N
Prima/E
Rest. LuLu/Petite
Sabor of Spain/N
Sushi Ran/N
Tartine Bakery
Uva Trattoria/N
Va de Vi/E
Vivande Porta Via
Wente Vineyards/E
Willi's Seafood/N
Willi's Wine Bar/N
Yabbies Coastal
Zibibbo/S
Zin/N

Wine Bars

A 16
bacar
Bar Tartine
Bouchée/S
Bounty Hunter/N
Cav Wine Bar
César/E
Cork/N
Cucina Paradiso/N
Cucina Rest./Wine Bar/N
El Paseo/N
Eos Rest./Wine Bar
1550 Hyde Café
fig cafe & winebar/N
Frascati
General Café/N

Winning Wine Lists

Absinthe
Acme Chophouse
À Côté/E
Acquerello
Albion River Inn/N
Alexander's Steak/S
Alioto's
All Season's Cafe/N
Ame
Angèle/N
Anton & Michel/S
A.P. Stump's/S
Aqua
A 16
Auberge du Soleil/N
Azie

bacar
Bar Tartine
Bay Wolf/E
Bella Vista/S
Bistro Aix
Bistro Clovis
Bistro Don Giovanni/N
Bistro Ralph/N
Blackhawk Grille/E
Bocadillos
Bouchée/S
Bouchon/N
Boulevard
Bridges/E
Brix/N
CAFÉ KATi
Cafe La Haye/N
Campton Place
Carnelian Room
Carneros/N
Casanova/S
Cav Wine Bar
Celadon/N
César/E
Cetrella Bistro/S
Chapeau!
Chez Panisse/E
Chez Panisse Café/E
Chez TJ/S
Citron/E
Club XIX/S
Cole's Chop House/N
Cork/N
Côté Sud
Cuvée/N
Cyrus/N
Deuce/N
downtown/E
Dry Creek Kitchen/N
El Paseo/N
Emile's/S
Eos Rest./Wine Bar
Erna's Elderberry/E
Étoile/N
Fandango/S
Farallon
Farmhouse Inn/N

1550 Hyde Café
Fifth Floor
fig cafe & winebar/N
Flea St. Café/S
Fleur de Lys
Forbes Mill Steak/E/S
Fournou's Ovens
French Laundry/N
Frisson
Gabriella Café/S
Gary Danko
girl & the fig/N
Gordon's/N
Grasing's Coastal/S
Greens
Hawthorne Lane
Incanto
Indigo
Jack Falstaff
Jardinière
Jeanty at Jack's
John Ash & Co./N
Julia's Kitchen/N
Kenwood/N
Kokkari Estiatorio
Kuleto's
Kuleto's/S
Kurt's Carmel Chop House/S
La Folie
La Forêt/S
Lark Creek Inn/N
LaSalette/N
La Toque/N
L'Auberge Carmel/S
Lavanda/S
Ledford House/N
Le Papillon/S
Liberty Cafe
Luella
Madrona Manor/N
Manresa/S
Manzanita/N
Marché/S
Marinus/S
Martini House/N
Masa's
Meadowood Grill/N

Mecca
Mendo Bistro/N
Michael Mina
Millennium
Monti's Rotisserie/N
Montrio Bistro/S
Moose's
Mustards Grill/N
Myth
Napa Valley Grille/N
Napa Wine Train/N
Navio/S
955 Ukiah/N
North Beach Rest.
N.V./N
Oliveto/E
One Market
Oswald/S
Ottimista Enoteca
Pacific's Edge/S
Palio d'Asti
Pangaea/N
Park Grill
Passionfish/S
Pearl Alley Bistro/S
Picco/N
Pilar/N
Piperade
Pisces/S
P.J. Steak/N
Plumed Horse/S
PlumpJack Cafe
PlumpJack Cafe/E
Poggio/N
Postrio
Prima/E
Quince
Redd Restaurant/N
Rest. at Meadowood/N
Rest. LuLu/Petite
Rio Grill/S
Ritz-Carlton Din. Rm.
Rivoli/E
Rose Pistola
Roy's
Roy's at Pebble Beach/S
Rubicon

Sabor of Spain/N
Santé/N
Santi/N
Sardine Factory/S
Scala's Bistro
Sea Ranch Lodge/N
Seasons
Sent Sovi/S
Sierra Mar/S
Silks
Slanted Door
Sol y Lago/E
Spago Palo Alto/S
St. Michael's/S
St. Orres/N
Sushi Groove
Sushi Ran/N
Syrah/N
Terra/N
Terzo
Town Hall
Tra Vigne/N
231 Ellsworth/S
Va de Vi/E
Vic Stewart's/E
Village Pub/S
Viognier/S
Wappo Bar/N
Wente Vineyards/E
Willi's Seafood/N
Wine Spectator/N
Yabbies Coastal
Zibibbo/S
Zin/N
Zinsvalley/N
Zuni Café

Worth a Trip
Albion
   Albion River Inn/N
   Ledford House/N
Berkeley
   César/E
   Chez Panisse/E
   Chez Panisse Café/E
   Lalime's/E
   Rivoli/E
   Zachary's Pizza/E

Big Sur
  Sierra Mar/S
Boonville
  Boonville Hotel/N
Carmel
  Bouchée/S
  L'Auberge Carmel/S
  Marinus/S
  Pacific's Edge/S
El Granada
  Cafe Gibraltar/S
Forestville
  Farmhouse Inn/N
Fort Bragg
  Mendo Bistro/N
  Rendezvous Inn/N
Geyserville
  Santi/N
Graton
  Underwood Bar/N
Gualala
  St. Orres/N
Half Moon Bay
  Cetrella Bistro/S
  Navio/S
Healdsburg
  Cyrus/N
  Dry Creek Kitchen/N
  Madrona Manor/N
  Manzanita/N
  Willi's Seafood/N
Inverness
  Manka's Inverness/N
Kenwood
  Kenwood/N
Larkspur
  Emporio Rulli/N
  Lark Creek Inn/N
  Left Bank/N
Little River
  Little River Inn/N
Livermore
  Wente Vineyards/E
Los Gatos
  Manresa/S
Mendocino
  Cafe Beaujolais/N
  MacCallum House/N

Menlo Park
  Flea St. Café/S
  Kaygetsu/S
  Marché/S
Mill Valley
  Buckeye Roadhse./N
Monterey
  Montrio Bistro/S
  Stokes/S
  Tarpy's Roadhouse/S
Mountain View
  Chez TJ/S
Napa
  Angèle/N
  Celadon/N
  Julia's Kitchen/N
  Mustards Grill/N
  Pilar/N
Oakhurst
  Erna's Elderberry/E
Oakland
  À Côté/E
  Bay Wolf/E
  Oliveto/E
  Zachary's Pizza/E
Pacific Grove
  Fandango/S
Palo Alto
  Cool Café/S
  Evvia/S
  Junnoon/S
  Mantra/S
  Spago Palo Alto/S
  Tamarine/S
  Zibibbo/S
Pebble Beach
  Roy's at Pebble Beach/S
Pescadero
  Duarte's Tavern/S
Rohnert Park
  Hana Japanese/N
Rutherford
  Auberge du Soleil/N
  La Toque/N

San Anselmo
  Insalata's/N
San Jose
  A.P. Stump's/S
  Arcadia/S
  Emile's/S
  La Forêt/S
  Le Papillon/S
San Mateo
  Lure/S
  Viognier/S
San Ramon
  Cafe Esin/E
Santa Rosa
  John Ash & Co./N
  Willi's Wine Bar/N
Saratoga
  Plumed Horse/S
Sausalito
  Sushi Ran/N
Sebastopol
  K&L Bistro/N

Sonoma
  Cafe La Haye/N
  girl & the fig/N
St. Helena
  Cindy's Backstreet/N
  Market/N
  Martini House/N
  Press/N
  Terra/N
  Tra Vigne/N
Woodside
  Bella Vista/S
  John Bentley's/S
  Village Pub/S
Yosemite Nat'l Park
  Ahwahnee Din. Rm./E
Yountville
  Bistro Jeanty/N
  Bouchon/N
  Étoile/N
  French Laundry/N
  Redd Restaurant/N

Alphabetical
Page Index

Places outside of San Francisco are marked as follows:
E=East of SF; N=North; and S=South.

vote at zagat.com   289

Alphabetical Page Index

Alphabetical Page Index

Alphabetical Page Index

Alphabetical Page Index

Alphabetical Page Index

Alphabetical Page Index

Alphabetical Page Index

Wine Vintage Chart

This chart is designed to help you select wine to go with your meal. It is based on the same 0 to 30 scale used throughout this *Survey*. The ratings (prepared by our friend **Howard Stravitz**, a law professor at the University of South Carolina) reflect both the quality of the vintage and the wine's readiness for present consumption. Thus, if a wine is not fully mature or is over the hill, its rating has been reduced. We do not include 1987, 1991–1993 vintages because they are not especially recommended for most areas. A dash indicates that a wine is either past its peak or too young to rate.

	'85	'86	'88	'89	'90	'94	'95	'96	'97	'98	'99	'00	'01	'02	'03	'04
WHITES																
French:																
Alsace	24	–	22	27	27	26	25	25	24	26	23	26	27	25	22	–
Burgundy	26	25	–	24	22	–	28	29	24	23	26	25	24	27	23	24
Loire Valley	–	–	–	–	–	20	23	22	–	24	25	26	27	25	23	–
Champagne	28	25	24	26	29	–	26	27	24	23	24	24	22	26	–	–
Sauternes	21	28	29	25	27	–	21	23	25	23	24	24	28	25	26	–
German	–	–	25	26	27	25	24	27	26	25	25	23	29	27	25	25
California (Napa, Sonoma, Mendocino):																
Chardonnay	–	–	–	–	–	–	–	–	–	24	25	28	27	26	–	
Sauvignon Blanc/Sémillon	–	–	–	–	–	–	–	–	–	–	–	–	27	28	26	–
REDS																
French:																
Bordeaux	24	25	24	26	29	22	26	25	23	25	24	28	26	23	25	23
Burgundy	23	–	21	24	26	–	26	28	25	22	27	22	25	27	24	–
Rhône	–	–	26	29	29	24	25	22	24	28	27	27	26	–	25	–
Beaujolais	–	–	–	–	–	–	–	–	–	–	–	24	–	25	28	25
California (Napa, Sonoma, Mendocino):																
Cab./Merlot	27	26	–	–	28	29	27	25	28	23	26	22	27	25	24	–
Pinot Noir	–	–	–	–	–	–	–	–	24	24	25	24	27	28	26	–
Zinfandel	–	–	–	–	–	–	–	–	–	–	–	–	26	26	28	–
Italian:																
Tuscany	–	–	–	25	22	25	20	29	24	28	24	26	24	–	–	
Piedmont	–	–	24	26	28	–	23	26	27	25	25	28	26	18	–	–
Spanish:																
Rioja	–	–	–	–	–	26	26	24	25	22	25	25	27	20	–	–
Ribera del Duero/Priorat	–	–	–	–	–	26	26	27	25	24	26	26	27	20	–	–

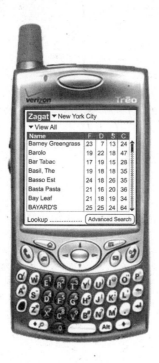

1 640